Blockchain and Climate Action

Blockchain and Climate Action

Enhancing ESG and Carbon Markets through Financial Technology

Edited by
Dominik Skauradszun, Walter Blocher, Florian Möslein,
Carsten Müller, Eric Nowak, Nils Urbach and
Georg von Wangenheim

DE GRUYTER

ISBN 978-3-11-170660-3
e-ISBN (PDF) 978-3-11-170671-9
e-ISBN (EPUB) 978-3-11-170681-8
DOI https://doi.org/10.1515/9783111706719

Library of Congress Control Number: 2025943146

Bibliographic information published by the Deutsche Nationalbibliothek
The Deutsche Nationalbibliothek lists this publication in the Deutsche Nationalbibliografie; detailed bibliographic data are available on the internet at http://dnb.dnb.de.

Cover image: wayra/iStock/Getty Images Plus
Typesetting: Integra Software Services Pvt. Ltd.

www.degruyterbrill.com
Questions about General Product Safety Regulation:
productsafety@degruyterbrill.com

Contents

Foreword — VII

Preface — IX

Carsten Mueller and Leah Kling
1 Tokenising the voluntary carbon credit market: Harnessing opportunities for sustainable development — 1

Masud Sultan, Vincent Schaaf, Nils Urbach, Cara Reuner, and Niklas Soltner
2 The early challenges in voluntary carbon markets: An interview-based analysis of past and present problems — 35

Peter Gruber, Leah Kling, and Eric Nowak
3 Conditions for tokenisation of carbon standard-issued credits as third-party crypto instruments — 47

Georg von Wangenheim and Leon Krug
4 VCCs, Tokenisation and the EU CBAM: Some microeconomics of VCCs — 73

Masud Sultan, Vincent Schaaf, and Nils Urbach
5 Application of blockchain in voluntary carbon markets: A multiple case study on emergent implementations and their challenges — 95

Jonathan Lautenschlager, Marike Reinelt, Vincent Schaaf, Nils Urbach, and Valeriya Arnold
6 From project design to retirement: The role of blockchain along the voluntary carbon credit lifecycle — 133

Dominik Skauradszun and Sebastian Böhning
7 Applicable law in the supply chains of VCC tokens — 151

Leon Krug and Walter Blocher
8 VCC tokenisation: Navigating legal frameworks and designing for regulatory compliance — 179

Florian Möslein and Frieda Mainka
9 Voluntary carbon credits and digital product passports: Similarities and differences — 227

Sebastian Böhning and Dominik Skauradszun
10 VCC tokens' civil law – ownership, transfer and liability under Union and German law — 239

Valeriya Arnold, Vincent Schaaf, Nils Urbach, and Jonathan Lautenschlager
11 Designing a framework for a blockchain-based voluntary carbon credit lifecycle — 261

List of figures — 289

List of tables — 291

Index — 293

Foreword

The idea of using financial markets to control pollution was first proposed by the American economist Thomas Crocker in 1966. In his book *Pollution, Property and Prices*, he suggested introducing a market-based system that would use instruments to limit water pollution caused by industrial waste. At that time, few could have predicted that environmental pollution would go far beyond visible water contamination, affecting entire ecosystems and posing a serious threat to our planet.

Since 1966, much has changed. Today, emissions trading has become a central part of environmental policy. CO_2 certificates and those emission certificates regulated by the European Union are now seen as standard financial products and are increasingly used as investment opportunities. In 2023, South Korea led the world by covering 98.5% of its emissions CO_2-pricing through such a system. Among the top ten countries, eight are in Europe, including Switzerland (Statista). This makes the European Union by far the biggest player in emissions trading, well ahead of other major economies like the United States and China. Germany, the EU's largest economy, is expected to account for €13.34 billion of the €22.49 billion global market value of the Emissions Trading System in 2025—making it one of the top participants (Statista). While this is a positive development, there are still major regional differences, and emissions trading remains relatively small when compared to the overall economic output of many countries. However, as environmental regulations are expected to become much stricter in the coming years and decades, emissions trading is likely to grow significantly in importance.

As is often the case, several developments have come together—and emissions trading is now intersecting with the emerging phenomenon of tokenization. Like any financial product that requires either an analog or digital registry entry, emissions trading instruments can be tokenized using distributed ledger technology, particularly blockchain. A prominent example of this is the emergence of Voluntary Carbon Credits (VCCs). The idea behind VCCs was first introduced in the Kyoto Protocol, further developed in the Paris Agreement, and has now entered the realm of tokenization.

This handbook aims to explore both developments—technological and regulatory—from technological, economic, legal and legal-policy perspectives. It highlights the specific advantages and opportunities that blockchain technology can offer in the trading of VCCs, as well as the challenges it presents. In this respect, the value of this handbook can hardly be overstated. It represents a significant scientific and societal contribution in terms of sustainability and the advancement of tokenization.

The reader is guided through the process of tokenization and its specific conditions in the context of VCCs in a detailed and structured manner. The book includes engaging interviews that shed light on past and present challenges in VCC trading, as well as a major case study analyzing emerging implementations and their practical hurdles.

https://doi.org/10.1515/9783111706719-203

From a civil law perspective, key legal questions regarding the ownership, transferability and liability of VCCs are carefully examined. A particular focus is placed on the crucial step of retirement, which is discussed in depth.

The editors and authors lead the reader on an engaging and intellectually rewarding journey. Their timely and meaningful contribution to this dynamic and increasingly important field deserves the highest recognition.

Dr. Johannes Meier, Marburg University, Germany

Preface

As Minister for Digitalization and Innovation of the State of Hesse, I am committed to supporting and promoting initiatives that advance the responsible use of digital technologies for the common good. We founded the Centre Responsible Digitality (ZEVEDI) to foster interdisciplinary research at the intersection of law, technology and society.

ZEVEDI is an inspiring example of how digital transformation can be shaped through collaborative research and academic excellence. I am particularly pleased with the project group TOSCA – Tokenizing Sustainability: Carbon Credits, Accountability, and ESG in Supply Chains, which showcases the remarkable outcomes of interdisciplinary cooperation guided by an unwavering commitment to responsibility and a resolute vision for sustainability.

This volume, Blockchain and Climate Action – Enhancing ESG and Carbon Markets through Financial Technology, brings together the results of this ambitious research endeavour. The authors confidently present novel applications of blockchain technology in supporting environmental goals, ensuring regulatory compliance, and enhancing transparency in carbon markets.

I congratulate the authors on this valuable contribution and wish them continued success with their important work.

Prof. Dr. Kristina Sinemus
Hessian Minister for Digitization and Innovation

https://doi.org/10.1515/9783111706719-204

Carsten Mueller and Leah Kling

1 Tokenising the voluntary carbon credit market: Harnessing opportunities for sustainable development

Abstract: This research develops and explores the process of tokenising the voluntary carbon credit market and its potential to drive sustainable development. Tokenisation, the process of converting carbon credits into digitally represented tokens on a blockchain, promises to address current issues of transparency, efficiency, and liquidity in the market. Through a concise yet informative exploration of this technology and its role in the voluntary carbon market, we formalise the general process of carbon tokenisation. We present the opportunities for tokenisation through well-supported arguments backed by relevant interdisciplinary research. Furthermore, the study analyses current practices and case studies to underscore the relevance of these opportunities. This assessment aims to demonstrate how tokenisation can contribute to a more robust, accessible, and effective voluntary carbon market, supporting global efforts to mitigate climate change and promoting the broader objective of sustainable development.

Keywords: Blockchain, Carbon Credits, Sustainability, Tokenisation, Voluntary Carbon Market

1 Background —— 2
2 Carbon pricing —— 4
3 Voluntary carbon credits —— 4
4 Challenges in current voluntary carbon markets —— 7
5 Introduction to tokenisation —— 7
6 Process of carbon tokenisation —— 8
7 Current state of carbon tokenisation in practice —— 10
8 Opportunities for carbon tokenisation —— 12
8.1 Market accessibility —— 13
8.2 Transparency and trust —— 14
8.3 Efficiency and scalability —— 19
8.4 Innovation and new markets —— 21
8.5 Diversification benefits —— 25
9 Regulatory considerations —— 26
10 Outlook and potential —— 26
11 Conclusion —— 27

https://doi.org/10.1515/9783111706719-001

1 Background

Climate change has a storied history, a history which is ongoing and will become ever more important in the coming decades. Although we commonly attribute the awareness of climate change to the more recent 21st century, its history and awareness stretch back to the early 19th century to the discovery of the Greenhouse Effect by Joseph Fourier in 1824. Awareness of the impact of fossil fuels on global temperatures was largely disregarded until the 1970s when these issues began to be seriously considered as contributing to climate change by the international community.

The first international discussion on the environment took place in 1972 at the first United Nations (UN) Conference on the Human Environment in Stockholm. This event set the stage for the development of environmental policies at both the national and international levels. Having brought international awareness to the environment, a flood of scientific research during the 1970s and 1980s increasingly linked human activities, including burning fossil fuels and deforestation, to the increase of greenhouse gases in the atmosphere, which was subsequently linked to global warming.[1]

Given the increasing evidence of climate change, along with growing environmental awareness and corresponding actions, such as the creation of environmental organisations like Greenpeace, political and diplomatic efforts began to shift towards supporting climate action. 1988 saw the creation of the Intergovernmental Panel on Climate Change (IPCC) by the UN Environment Programme (UNEP) and the World Meteorological Organization (WMO). The creation of the IPCC marked a significant step towards understanding the drivers of climate change and supporting international policy coordination on climate change.

With this new international focus on the climate, a series of events throughout the 1990s further enhanced global cooperation on combating climate change. Following the first Assessment Report of the IPCC in 1990, the United Nations Framework Convention on Climate Change (UNFCCC) was established in 1992 at the Earth Summit in Rio de Janeiro. The development of the UNFCCC provided a framework aiming to stabilise greenhouse gas concentrations in the atmosphere. Along with the establishment of the UNFCCC, annual Conference of the Parties (COP) meetings were introduced to review and monitor the implementation of the UNFCCC, culminating in the development of the Kyoto Protocol at COP3 in 1997. The Kyoto Protocol was a groundbreaking international agreement that set binding targets for 37 countries to reduce greenhouse gas emissions (GHG). Through this agreement, international emissions trading mechanisms were introduced alongside the Clean Development Mechanism (CDM) and the Joint Implementation (JI). While developments were taking place under the UNFCCC, the UN was also developing the Millennium Development Goals, later converted into the Sustainable Development Goals (SDGs), which were intimately linked to environmental protection and development. These goals framed the challenge of climate change in the broader socio-political landscape, laying out the necessity for tackling not only climate change but its associated precipitators and consequences. The

Kyoto Protocol came into force in 2005 and faced criticism during its tenure regarding environmental integrity, equity and fairness, market functionality, lack of ambition, implementation and compliance, long-term effectiveness, and economic and social impacts. Lessons learned from the Kyoto Protocol played an important role in shaping the aims of the Paris Agreement in 2015, which was adopted at COP21.

The Paris Agreement notably extended participation to achieve global coverage, including countries previously excluded from the Kyoto Protocol, and acknowledged the critical role of developing countries in addressing climate change. Long-term temperature targets were set with the goal of keeping global temperatures well below 2 degrees Celsius above pre-industrial levels, while pursuing efforts to limit the increase to 1.5 degrees Celsius.

Importantly, Art. 6 of the Paris Agreement outlines cooperative approaches that countries may utilise to achieve their nationally determined contributions (NDCs) using market and non-market mechanisms. A key outcome of Art. 6 is the prescription of a market for emission reductions (or credits) between countries aimed at ensuring environmental integrity and preventing double-counting of Internationally Transferred Mitigation Outcomes (ITMOs). Concerns about double-counting were rife under the Kyoto Protocol and a focus on eliminating such issues has driven the establishment of many proposed solutions regarding accounting for carbon offsets and reductions, particularly through blockchain applications. In addition to outlining necessary carbon market mechanisms, the Paris Agreement emphasised unifying global standards and goals for emissions reductions, applicable not only to compliance carbon markets but also voluntary carbon markets (VCMs). Ensuring carbon credits represent real and verifiable reductions has become the focus of many initiatives in VCMs. This chapter will focus on the opportunities in the VCM and how blockchain technology can address them.

More recently, a global stocktake was completed alongside COP28 in Dubai in 2023, providing a comprehensive evaluation of progress towards the goals of the Paris Agreement. The report highlighted continued and urgent need for action to meet the target of 2 degrees Celsius under the Paris Agreement, while noting current global efforts were insufficient to limit global warming to 1.5 degrees Celsius above pre-industrial levels. The conference went on to underscore the growing financial burden of climate change and emphasised the need for a transition away from fossil fuels while increasing the global energy capacity from renewable energy sources.

The historical progression of the climate change discourse has largely focused on laying the foundational framework for international coordination and policy development. Recent efforts have increasingly sought to implement effective carbon pricing mechanisms. This can be seen in the shift from the Kyoto Protocol's foundational market-based approach to the sophisticated, multilayered strategies seen in the Paris Agreement. An examination of trends in carbon-related commitments reveals '[on] the whole, 89 countries, representing 86% of global emissions, had adopted net-zero commitments at the end of 2022, with target dates ranging from 2035 to 2060'.[2]

2 Carbon pricing

Typical means of pricing carbon have been established through the implementation of Emissions Trading Systems (ETS) and carbon taxes. Both carbon taxes and ETS set direct prices on carbon in contrast to indirect carbon prices, such as through energy efficiency standards. A deep exploration into carbon pricing reveals there has been growth in ETS prices in most jurisdictions; however, some countries have postponed price increases. As of 2023, ETS and carbon taxes in operation cover approximately 24% of global GHG emissions, where around 19% and 6% of global GHG emissions are covered by ETS and carbon taxes, respectively.[3] This coverage represents significant growth in the coverage of carbon pricing from only 0.49% of global GHG emissions in 1990.[3] During this same period, from 1990 to 2024, we have seen steady increases in the price level of CO_2 emissions on national levels; despite increasing carbon prices, there still exists vast disparities in the general levels of carbon prices among countries. Carbon prices are typically expressed as the cost per metric tonne of carbon dioxide and its equivalents (1 tCO_2e). As of 1 April 2024, carbon prices ranged from USD 0.61/tCO_2e to USD 167.17/tCO_2e in Indonesia and Uruguay respectively.[3]

In addition to ETS and carbon taxes, we have also seen a more recent proliferation of carbon crediting mechanisms. Carbon credits aim to put a direct price on carbon through issuing tradable credits (representing 1 tCO_2e) that are generated through reductions in emissions. These credits represent reductions through either carbon avoidance or carbon removal activities. As of 2024, there are 35 governmental crediting mechanisms implemented globally with an additional 11 currently under development[3]. In addition to government crediting mechanisms, several independent crediting mechanisms exist, most notably, Gold Standard (GS) and the Verified Carbon Standard (VCS) by Verra. In 2023, a total of 5.7 billion carbon credits were issued: 3.3 billion through international mechanisms such as the CDM, 450 million through governmental mechanisms, and 1.9 billion through independent mechanisms.[3] This highlights the significant role independent mechanisms play in issuing carbon credits. Similar to pricing heterogeneity in the compliance market, voluntary carbon credits (VCCs), verified through independent mechanisms, exhibited a range of carbon prices depending on many factors, including the type of underlying project related to the credit, geography, and crediting mechanism employed, among other factors; on average, buyers paid USD 6.53/tCO_2e on the voluntary market in 2023.[4]

3 Voluntary carbon credits

When discussing carbon credits, it is important to distinguish between VCCs and compliance carbon credits. Compliance carbon credits are issued and regulated by governmental and international bodies, generally as a part of national government emissions targeting schemes. They commonly operate under cap-and-trade systems, whereby a national allowable level of emissions is set, and carbon credits are then either auctioned off or freely allocated. In contrast to compliance carbon markets where participation is mandatory for GHG emitting firms, participation in the VCM is not mandated by law but rather driven by organisations and individuals who wish to proactively offset their emissions; organisations generally participate in this market to fulfil corporate social responsibility (CSR) commitments.

The mechanism underlying the VCM also fundamentally differs from the mechanisms underlying the compliance carbon markets. In compliance markets such as the European Union (EU) Emission Trading System (ETS), national carbon emission targets are set by the EU; then, carbon allowances are issued through auctions or free allocations, which permit a company to emit one tonne of CO_2e per allowance.[5] Rather than requiring emitters to purchase carbon allowances, the VCM issues carbon credits for every tonne of CO_2e reduced, avoided, or removed from the atmosphere. Compliance carbon markets directly incentivise emission reductions through reductions to the emissions cap over time; however, these markets are often criticised for having carbon leakage, where emissions are outsourced to jurisdictions with less stringent, or no, emission regulations. While compliance carbon markets may simply lead to carbon leakage, the VCM provides direct incentives tied to measurable emission reductions. One could argue that VCMs play a growing role in reducing total global GHG emissions, especially as CSR becomes a central concern for companies and individuals alike.[5]

The scope of projects covered by the VCM is generally more varied than those covered under compliance markets. For example, the EU ETS scheme covers primarily CO_2 emissions from electricity and heat generation, energy-intensive industry sectors such as oil refineries and raw materials production, aviation, and maritime transport.[6] Conversely, in VCMs such as under Verra's Voluntary Carbon Standard (VCS), the coverage of projects is broader, including projects related to agriculture, forestry, and other land use projects in addition to energy, industrial, waste, and transport projects.[7] In fact, as of 31 March 2024, 38.3% of all VCCs issued by the four largest issuers were related to forestry and land use and 32.3% were related to renewable energy projects.[8]

The VCM also plays a fundamental role in allocating resources equitably among regions. This role is especially pronounced when examining the geographical distribution of total carbon emissions compared to those covered under a governmental compliance scheme. Figure 1.1 shows the geographical disparity of carbon emissions covered under governmental compliance mechanisms.

The left plot shows the total official cumulative carbon emissions from 1990 through 2022 by geographical region; we see that carbon emissions are relatively distributed among regions. In contrast, the right plot shows that the cumulative carbon emissions during this period actually covered under government compliance mechanisms are disproportionately concentrated primarily in Europe and Central Asia. Broken down by income group,[9] high-income countries represent 25.52% of cumulative

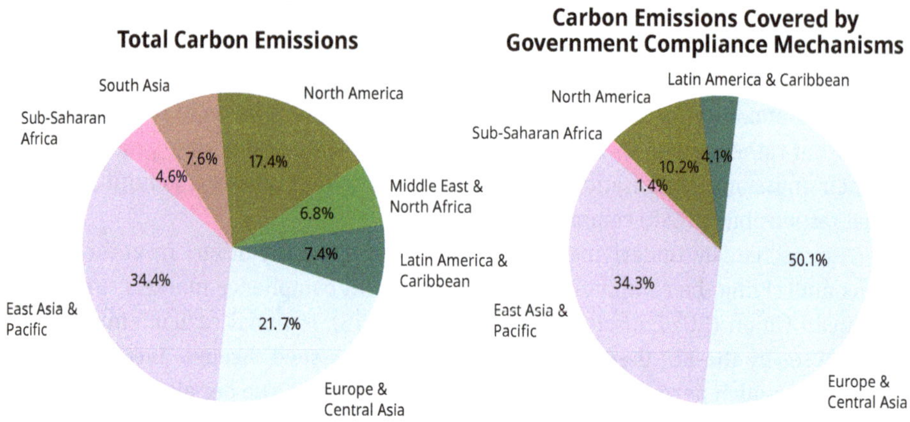

Figure 1.1: Comparison of Total Cumulative Carbon Emissions Versus Carbon Emissions Covered Under a Government Compliance Scheme for 1990–2022.
Source: *Authors' Own, based on data from multiple sources.*[10]

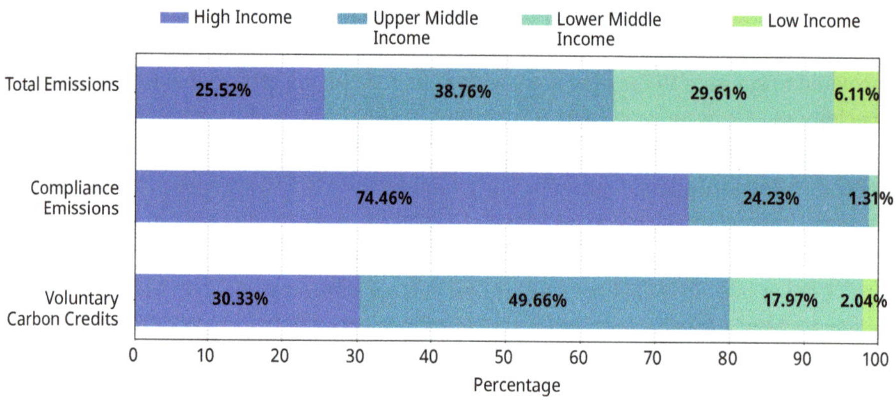

Figure 1.2: Representation of Country Income Groupings by Total Emissions, Emissions Under Government Compliance Mechanisms, and Voluntary Carbon Credits.
Source: *Authors' Own, based on data from multiple sources.*[13]

global carbon emissions from 1990 to 2022,[11] while they represent 74.46% of emissions covered under government compliance schemes during this same period.[12]

This means that lower- and middle-income countries and countries in the global south are underrepresented in compliance carbon markets. This underrepresentation provides a profound opportunity in the VCMs, whereby funds from high-income countries are transferred to projects in low- and middle-income countries. Figure 1.2 shows the relative representation of each country-level income group by its relative total emissions, emissions covered under a government compliance mechanism, and representation in the top four VCM registries. As can be seen, the representation by income level in the VCM is more proportional to the total global emissions by income level, providing significant value to lower- and middle-income countries.

4 Challenges in current voluntary carbon markets

Despite their great potential, VCMs are not without their flaws. Miltenberger, Jospe, and Pittman provide a detailed critique of VCMs.[14] We will highlight a few of the important challenges briefly. The criticism of greenwashing has been longstanding, especially in the early days of VCMs; this is compounded by the fact that many projects lack the necessary transparency to confirm the quality of their carbon credits. This problem may be partially addressed by ensuring sound monitoring, reporting, and verification (MRV); however, the quality of MRV varies greatly among VCC standards bodies.

A central criticism driving new initiatives for carbon accounting under the Paris Agreement is the proliferation of double-counting.[15] Double-counting in the VCM may occur when one project is listed on multiple voluntary carbon registries, allowing for the underlying credits to be claimed more than once. This may also occur due to difficulties establishing ownership of VCCs, allowing multiple entities to claim the offsets.

Greenwashing and double-counting are surface-level problems, largely affected by more fundamental issues in VCMs, especially the fragmentation of the market and standards that have compounding effects. Some independent registries strictly prohibit projects from being cross-listed on multiple registries, for example, Gold Standard[16] and Verra;[17] however, some smaller independent bodies do not explicitly preclude cross-listing. Even with the prohibition of cross-listing, such activity may be difficult to identify due to a lack of standardisation within the industry.

Fragmented standards are especially rife, contributing to issues of greenwashing. Recent work has examined the impact of the role MRV plays in crediting issues. Problems with methodologies have led to the gross overissuance of carbon credits, especially in relation to REDD+ projects.[18] Generally, many of the issues underlying VCCs are attributable to the lack of standardisation in the industry.

5 Introduction to tokenisation

When we discuss carbon tokenisation, it is first important to understand what the technology behind it is so we have a framework for understanding the mechanisms of tokenisation. Tokenisation in terms of blockchain is the act of converting ownership or rights into a digitally represented form recorded on a blockchain. To understand what exactly this means, it is useful to understand the origins of this technology. Distributed Ledger Technology (DLT) is a concept dating back to the 1970s and 1980s when work on distributed databases[19] and efficient and secure verification of data began.[20] This technology aimed to create a decentralised environment, creating trust among network participants. This trust arose out of the ability of this technology to provide transparency and immutability of the data stored in the distributed databases, later DLT.

Since its inception, DLT has grown vastly in its implementations and utilisation. Largely popularised by the application of the technology to the Bitcoin network in 2008,[21] its use in the emergence of other cryptocurrencies has led to a market size of USD 2.47 trillion as of June 2024.[22] The prospect to record transactions on a public, immutable ledger has led to additional applications of the technology to convert real-world rights and assets to a digitally represented form, recorded on blockchains through the process of tokenisation.

6 Process of carbon tokenisation

To understand the role of blockchain technology in carbon tokenisation, it is valuable to first review the lifecycle of a typical VCC project. Figure 1.3 highlights the high-level lifecycle of a VCC project in accordance with using a traditional voluntary carbon registry such as Verra. First, a project idea is initiated, the project design is detailed, and the project leaders apply for validation and registry through a voluntary carbon registry. The carbon registry then confirms the project adheres to its standards and verifies or rejects the project; once verified, the project is then registered on the corresponding registry. Next, the project is implemented and monitored, receiving periodic verification assessed by third-party monitoring services. Upon successful completion of key milestones, carbon credits are then issued; these credits are recorded in the registry database and transferred into the project developer's registry account.

Having been deposited into the developer's account, these credits can then be traded in the VCM. Alternatively, these credits may be tokenised and subsequently traded on a blockchain, if authorised by the registry[23] using varying methodologies depending on the carbon bridge used. The credits may be traded by interested parties in their respective markets; then, once a party wishes to retire the credit and claim a carbon offset, a retirement request is sent to the registry. The credit is subsequently retired, and the registry records the retirement, updating the registry.

While the lifecycle of a carbon credit in traditional markets is relatively well established and straightforward, the tokenisation of carbon credits is fraught with criticisms and challenges, which will be briefly addressed later. Here, we will briefly outline the main ideas underlying the tokenisation process previously employed by major carbon bridges. Figure 1.4 shows the general process of carbon tokenisation used by major carbon bridges such as Toucan, C3, and Moss.

To bridge a carbon credit from traditional registries, the carbon credit in the traditional registry is first transferred into a custodial account in the name of the bridging

Figure 1.3: Lifecycle of a Typical Voluntary Carbon Credit.
Source: *Authors' Own.*

Figure 1.4: Process of Carbon Credit Tokenisation.
Source: *Authors' Own.*

service; this credit is then retired on the traditional registry when the corresponding carbon token is minted on a blockchain as a Non-Fungible Token (NFT) and the underlying project metadata is stored.[24] Commonly, bridging services engage in pooling activities, where a smart contract is executed, locking the NFT into the smart contract and simultaneously minting a fungible token.[25] Once the carbon token is created, as an NFT or fungible token, it is then deposited into the user's digital wallet and tokens are then traded either in peer-to-peer transactions or in the relevant digital marketplaces. When a token holder wishes to claim the underlying carbon offset, the holder requests the bridging service to retire the token, whereby it is sent to a designated wallet and permanently removed from circulation.[26] This process describes a one-way carbon bridge, where once on the blockchain, the carbon token cannot be converted back into a traditional registry credit. Conversely, the development of two-way carbon bridges has been established, allowing the underlying registry credit to remain active and have its retirement triggered by the corresponding token retirement.[27]

7 Current state of carbon tokenisation in practice

The full and current state of carbon tokenisation of the VCC is incredibly difficult to understand and quantify due to the fragmentation of this market. While there are some well-known and large players in the space, there are many more small players and new emerging initiatives. For example, large carbon token projects such as KlimaDAO and Flowcarbon have been reported on by large news platforms such as the *Wall Street Journal,*[28] *Bloomberg,*[29] and the *Financial Times,*[30] raising public awareness about carbon tokenisation. However, there are many smaller carbon token initiatives that go relatively unnoticed by those not intimately familiar with the carbon token space.

Generally, the major carbon token initiatives appear to be concentrated on improving market efficiency and access. This typically takes the form of two distinct activities; first, there are the initiatives that focus primarily in managing the tokenisation process itself. These players deal with the details and methods for getting VCCs on the blockchain in preparation for trading in marketplaces. Second, there are initiatives primarily dedicated to serving as marketplaces for those looking to buy and sell tokenised credits. However, not all initiatives are confined to fulfilling a single activity in the value chain. In fact, many initiatives engage in more than one of these roles with some initiatives even venturing into fulfilling other roles in the voluntary carbon lifecycle. Some focus on native tokenisation whereby they develop their own project standards, monitoring, and verification requirements and no carbon bridging takes place, but rather the project issues a native digital token, for example, Coorest.[31]

To understand the role carbon tokenisation projects play in markets, we can look at trading and marketplace platforms such as KlimaDAO, Air Carbon Exchange, Regen, Senken, and many others. In most of these marketplaces, there is an option to purchase credits directly linked to a specific project, such as in Regen Market. Or, another common approach is to market a fungible token representing carbon offsets in an underlying pool, as in the case of KlimaDAO. Some markets rely on carbon bridging services to provide the supply of tokens; for example, KlimaDAO partners with Toucan, C3, and Moss to bridge all its credits. Since KlimaDAO is the most well-known carbon token project, we can expect that Toucan, C3, and Moss are likely the three largest carbon bridges. Currently, Toucan, which is the largest source of credits for

KlimaDAO, has not tokenised any additional credits from Verra or Gold Standard since May 2022 after both Verra and Gold Standard banned unauthorised tokenisation of their credits, which is still in effect in 2024.[32] As a result of this ban, we have seen a shift towards using credits from other carbon registries for tokenisation, for example, Toucan's tokenisation of Puro.earth credits.[33]

To understand more about the carbon credits being bridged, we will look at activity related to KlimaDAO. As of July 2024, KlimaDAO has made 20,393,479 tokenised carbon credits available in its marketplace, with 88.58% of its credits having been bridged by Toucan, 10.83% by Moss Earth, and 0.59% by C3. KlimaDAO has essentially pooled credits from Toucan, Moss, and C3 and issued a new fungible token representing a claim on the pool. This means Toucan tokens make up the majority of the pool and represent a significant number of credits bridged. We will examine the extent of tokenisation by Toucan as an indication of the tokenisation of Verra credits.

We can quantify the extent of tokenisation of Verra's carbon credits by examining the underlying credits attributed to Toucan in the Verra registry. Toucan has tokenised a total of 22,119,807 credits issued by Verra; this includes credits issued between 2009 and 2022. During this same period, Verra issued a total of 1,093,576,461 carbon credits. This means that Toucan bridged approximately 2% of the carbon credits Verra issued in this period. Previously, we looked at the representation by region and income group for compliance carbon programmes and VCMs. Using the registry data from Verra, we can look at what tokenisation means in terms of the projects that underlie tokenised credits and what types of projects are tokenised.

In Figure 1.5, we show two interesting observations. First, the regional representation in the Verra registry for issuances between 2009 and 2022 tends to represent regions with a higher number of developing economies, a result that contrasts with the representation of total emissions and compliance emissions in Figure 1.1. Second, we

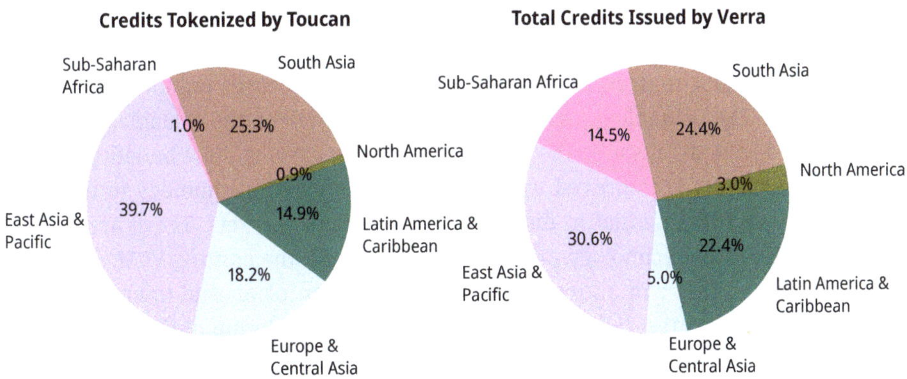

Figure 1.5: Verra Voluntary Carbon Credits Tokenised.
Source: *Authors' Own.*[34]

see that in comparison to the projects in the Verra registry, the credits tokenised by Toucan tend to be more concentrated in Europe and Central Asia and less concentrated in sub-Saharan Africa, suggesting a difference in the underlying carbon credit portfolio of carbon tokens in comparison with the overall market. These differences suggest that the demand and supply for tokenised credits might differ fundamentally from traditional markets.

We can also see in Figure 1.6 that credits in high-income countries represent less of the total tokenised credits when compared with the total credits issued by Verra between 2009 and 2022. While this supports the expectation that tokenisation may improve accessibility to credits from developing countries in general, we see credits from low-income countries are minimally represented in the Toucan portfolio.

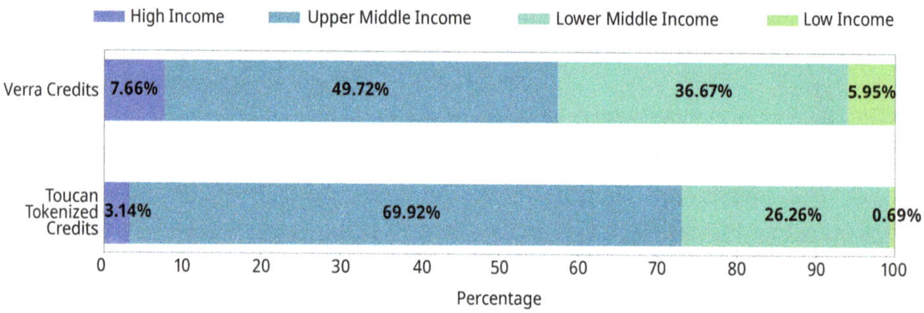

Figure 1.6: Comparison of Verra Credit Portfolio Between Toucan Tokenised Credits and All Verra Issued Credits Between 2009 and 2022.
Source: *Authors' Own.*[35]

8 Opportunities for carbon tokenisation

Blockchain's ability to provide immutable transaction records enhances trust and transparency. The technology has also proven to be efficient and scalable, especially with recent developments over the past few years. Considering these benefits, general market accessibility is improved when applying blockchain technology to the VCM. Blockchain has the potential to disrupt current carbon markets. There are several new innovations the technology presents as solutions for the existing VCM, especially smart contracts, that can allow for the full integration of an end-to-end solution, which is of great interest to the international community. On top of these opportunities, the discussion inevitably expands into what new markets can be reached with blockchain. Previously, we saw that tokenised carbon credits appear to represent different carbon projects in comparison to the traditional VCM (Figures 1.5 and 1.6). Although more research into this area is needed to determine if this is a wider trend or limited to the case study of Toucan. From here on, we discuss the especially relevant cases which would extend the market reach beyond simply corporate demand but also include consumer demand and the potential role of tokenised credits in the compliance market. Finally, we briefly discuss the potential for a tokenised carbon asset class to provide diversification benefits to the broader market of investors, improving overall market liquidity.

8.1 Market accessibility

Since its creation, blockchain has been heralded as a means to improve market accessibility, especially in developing countries.[36] The technology is easy to access since all that is required is a digital device, an Internet connection, and a digital wallet. Part of the allure of the technology is the ability to improve transparency and trust, which results in greater market participation and, as a result, higher market liquidity. Additionally, the efficiency gains and automation from the technology reduce transaction costs as intermediaries are no longer needed. The possibility for fractional ownership of crypto assets also lowers investment thresholds for potential buyers. Overall, these benefits should translate to increased inclusivity by allowing participation from individuals and smaller entities in the network[37] while also providing the same benefits to large participants.

Problems with market structure in the VCM are pervasive and have far-reaching ramifications for all participants. In fact, in a recent survey by NASDAQ, 25% of VCM participants noted that the current market issues prevent them entirely from entering the market with an additional 16% and 40% noting severe and moderate restrictions inflows, respectively.[38] An assortment of foundational issues underlies this core problem, including poor pricing efficiency, poor trading liquidity, fragmented standards and markets, and general inefficiencies. Current VCCs are typically traded in over-the-counter markets and often incur high transaction fees, poor informational transparency, and high search costs. The current leading market is the Carbon TradeXchange.[39] In this market, participation is limited to large enterprises and corporations; credits are sold in large, costly lots; auction mechanisms utilised have lengthy trading and settlement times; and participants face high overall transaction costs, including search and sourcing costs. In addition to markets for VCCs, projects themselves often have difficulties registering for several reasons, mainly due to problems with efficiency.

Blockchain presents a few opportunities to improve market accessibility for both buyers and sellers of VCCs. First, it would lower entry barriers for individuals and small businesses, especially through the ability to purchase individual credits and through fractionalisation. Individuals could better offset their personal emissions, expanding the market. Centralised market platforms that pull data directly from the blockchain allow users to more easily compare carbon credits before purchasing. The fact that many token markets are publicly accessible rather than behind a wall only accessible to corporate buyers not only helps participation rates but also improves general market efficiency and price discoverability. The greatest benefit is how improved market accessibility will enhance liquidity in carbon token markets. Faster, more efficient trading mechanisms foster greater participation. Liquidity would also be enhanced through pooling protocols, which provide the ability to trade fractional ownership of pooled carbon credits. This can allow buyers to reduce investment risk when purchasing credits, negating the need for extensive research into individual carbon credit projects. The ability to purchase pooled credits alone significantly reduces barriers to entry for smaller entities and individuals.

Like buyers, sellers receive much the same benefits. Lower costs and accessible marketplaces can reduce the amount of time it takes sellers to sell their credits. Tokenisation projects with their own standards can also streamline the process for sellers, reducing barriers and facilitating participation. Generally, small projects are more susceptible to the challenges in existing markets, whereas blockchain can allow for their participation in carbon token markets. Small projects facing high costs to entry, which is a common issue,[40] are more likely to become funded in carbon token markets, where funding is more accessible. Additionally, the ability to pool credits means that projects that may otherwise be considered too risky become funded; however, careful market design and possible regulation will be required to ensure pools operate transparently and maintain market integrity.

We have seen that market accessibility is a major problem for existing VCMs, where markets are opaque and mostly exclusive to large institutional investors. With blockchain technology, the market opens to smaller participants, both buyers and sellers looking to engage in the VCM, will be enabled with blockchain technology. Demand for carbon offsets by individuals and small entities is already evident;[41] blockchain will simply provide the means to open this market more to such participants.

8.2 Transparency and trust

The ability to timestamp and trace ownership is of great importance in the digital world, where it can often be difficult to ascribe ownership to digital assets.[42] By nature, blockchain technology lends itself to improved transparency in its related markets through the utilisation of DLT technology. The immutable record, which stores all transactions, is easily audited and publicly available, if it is a public blockchain. Private blockchains may still be audited by permissioned members, still allowing for monitoring. Nonetheless, participants can easily review previous history and confirm the legitimacy of activity on the blockchain. This means that every token or coin on a blockchain can have its full history traced from address to address, which means there is a clear audit trail. Since the ledger is publicly accessible, the data on a blockchain can be verified by any participant, reducing the risk of fraud.

When understanding the role of blockchain in trust and transparency, one must first understand how the relationship between trust and transparency arises. Transparency is the absence of asymmetric information; it occurs in markets where individuals have information on the quality of goods and services. Asymmetric information is linked to inefficient markets, exemplified by the infamous Lemon's Problem.[43] In terms of VCMs, this manifests as buyers not knowing the quality of the carbon offsets they are purchasing. Essentially, there is a risk for buyers of purchasing a poor-quality VCC; transparency is a way to resolve risk and create trust. This ability to resolve risk has been well studied in two relevant strands of literature: governance and supply chain.

First, the relationship between trust and transparency has been well-studied in corporate governance, where organisations that are more transparent in their governance tend to have higher levels of stakeholder trust;[44] this result is also paralleled in the public policy literature. The participation of corporations in the VCM is often used as a tool for CSR. In participating in CSR, especially regarding the corporations' environmental impact, it is important that stakeholders are able to transparently evaluate the corporation's actions. The overuse of environmental claims, especially in regard to actions that are in fact not environmentally friendly, is known as greenwashing. Greenwashing has been directly linked to lower levels of green trust in corporations,[45] a result that can be mitigated by improving traceability of carbon offset purchases using blockchain. Second, there are similar findings linking transparency to trust in product markets, where supply chain transparency leads to increased consumer trust and willingness to purchase products. Yavaprabhas et al. provide a comprehensive literature review on trust, transparency, and the role of blockchain in developing this in supply chains.[46]

Transparency and trust play multiple roles when we consider the lifecycle of carbon credits. In Figure 1.3, we are reminded of the roles in the VCC value chain. Having trust and transparency improves all processes in the value chain and provides significant benefits in role 6, the trading and utilisation of carbon credits. More specifically, they have implications in CSR, VCC quality and traceability, and market participation. We will briefly discuss VCCs as a product that buyers obtain with the goal of using the credits to offset their carbon emissions. Traditional registries have put in good effort to maintain transparency and trust. For instance, the utilisation of public, searchable registries by Verra and Gold Standard ensures transparency and allows credits to be attributed to both their sources and end-users, where the end-user is the user that claims the credit upon retirement. Despite these efforts, issues such as greenwashing and over-issuance have been reported, raising questions about the quality of carbon credits, ultimately putting into question the ability to trust carbon credit impact claims. The existence of fragmented standards does not help matters; the risk of double-counting carbon credits is difficult to estimate, given the extent of fragmentation and lack of full transparency.[47]

The ability for participants to directly participate in maintaining and governing blockchains also increases trust. Increased participation in a blockchain network enhances trust by decentralising the network, making it safer and more secure. Commonly used Proof-of-Stake protocols have embedded mechanisms that incentivise honest behaviour in the nodes, since participant nodes must put up collateral to support their validations. Although there are still challenges with this approach, with a sufficiently decentralised network, this mechanism enhances trust and improves the reliability of the data. Similarly, many blockchains are governed through Decentralised Autonomous Organisations (DAOs), allowing the community to directly participate in decision-making, increasing the probability of resulting in a transparent and fair system.

Although blockchain appears to improve trust in the system, not all proponents agree that blockchain is a trust-enhancing technology but rather a technology used to navigate trustless markets. In the absence of trust, users can rely on the application of smart contracts, using blockchain technology, to facilitate transactions. Smart contracts can automate and enforce agreements in situations where participants do not trust each other; this technology provides additional security and reduces the need for trust. Primarily, smart contracts are used for financial and legal transactions in the digital space.[48] Even the willingness to use a smart contract itself can serve as a signal to a user's authenticity, reducing information asymmetry in transactions.[49]

Blockchain technology's ability to enhance transparency and trust has direct and tangible benefits for tokenised VCCs. First, tokenised carbon credits can be easily traced back to their original projects, but many protocols directly link project metadata to carbon tokens, negating the need to audit the original registry but rather allowing important information to be easily referenced. It is also common for carbon token marketplaces to provide full project information, increasing verifiability, especially for projects that can be electronically monitored. Even in the event of project information being difficult to access, the availability of a public ledger to all participants means that the full history of the credit can be traced back to its origination point. A publicly available ledger also allows regulators to verify data and reduces the risk of double-counting.[50] Double-counting, under the tokenisation method we discussed earlier, is typically prevented by retiring the underlying credits in a custodial account on the underlying registry upon tokenisation and later retiring the tokenised credits in a digital custodial account when the offset is requested by the user. There is also the potential for native tokenisation with their own standards, which has the added benefit of ensuring that carbon credits are exclusively represented by a specific carbon token, avoiding coordination issues with physical registries.

The ease of auditing the public ledger has a few important benefits. First, the balances of carbon credits held by organisations are publicly available on the organisation's related wallet addresses, which stakeholders can easily audit. This is especially true when an organisation has a single wallet where all its carbon credits are held and has publicly verified its wallet address. This is far more efficient to audit in comparison to existing systems, where multiple registries would need to be checked. The ability to view all blocks on a public ledger can also improve price discovery, especially if carbon tokens are purchased with another cryptocurrency. In some types of markets, this transparency can have negative effects due to not being able to hide transactions,[51] however, the general VCM would benefit from this transparency.

How does this all translate to an opportunity for carbon tokenisation? It is well documented in the financial literature that trust increases market participation.[52] We could reasonably expect this observation to apply to carbon token markets, especially as more data becomes available. Increased participation in VCMs would mean increased access to funding for carbon mitigation and sequestration projects. This would materialise in lower interest rates on funding with more projects being funded, ultimately leading to positive environmental and social benefits.

Case study: Toucan protocol

Earlier, we discussed in brief the Toucan Protocol and how it has affected carbon tokenisation. In this section, we expand on how it exemplifies trust and transparency by implementing a blockchain solution in the VCM. This case study will detail the mechanisms of transparency and provide an example of how carbon credits can be traced to their origin.

The Toucan Protocol was founded in 2021 with the aim of providing improved transparency in the VCM. It focuses on partnerships with traditional VCC registries, currently with Puro Registry, to bridge traditional VCCs onto the blockchain, where the credits can then be traded with instant settlements, providing full data transparency on the source of credits and verifying any retirements. Since its inception, it has facilitated the trade of over USD 4 billion of carbon credits, retired nearly 300,000 tonnes of credits, and bridged over 20 million credits.[53] As part of its core business values, Toucan aims to embody the 10 core carbon principles.[54] As of 2024, Toucan has announced collaborations with major organisations such as the World Economic Forum, Gold Standard, and the World Bank, solidifying its importance in the international drive to enhance VCMs. Having previously engaged in tokenising Verra's VCUs, Toucan has shifted to its current focus and partnership with the Puro Registry, tokenising biochar carbon, due to a ban on tokenisation by Verra and Gold Standard for their credits.

Toucan's bridging process is closely aligned with that outlined earlier in Figure 1.4. To begin the bridging process, a user must hold the Puro Earth CORCs (CO_2 Removal Credits) they wish to bridge and hold them in their registered Puro Earth account. The user then requests the initiation of bridging directly from Toucan; at this point, the user provides the serial numbers and project name of the credits from Puro they would like to tokenise. They then specify the wallet address to which they wish to send the tokenised credits. Once the request is received, Toucan locks the corresponding CORCs on the Puro registry through an integrated API, preventing double tokenisation. Next, an NFT is minted, attaching the project's metadata to the token using a smart contract. Then, the NFT is sent to Toucan's Biochar pool, and subsequently, fungible CHAR tokens are minted on the Celo blockchain using ERC-20 standards. These fungible tokens are then deposited into the user's account with one CHAR token for every one CORC bridged. Given its integration with the Puro registry via an API, Toucan has also developed the means for a two-way bridge so the user can convert their digital CHAR tokens back into active Puro CORCs. This API integration also allows for better handling of retirements; for example, when a user wishes to retire a CHAR token, claiming the carbon offset, the carbon token is retired on-chain while a retirement request is simultaneously sent to the Puro registry. The Puro CORC is then retired, and the digital CHAR token is destroyed. Since these processes are digitally integrated, they occur within minutes.[55]

To exemplify the transparency of this process, we examine the traceability of the CORCs underlying Toucan's Biochar pool. On Toucan's website, there is a dashboard dedicated to displaying data on its carbon pools and the underlying projects.[56] In this application, the user can clearly see the current composition of the carbon pool, broken down by blockchain. This shows the total amount of bridged carbon along with retirements and prices. In its explorer section, the user can directly view projects that have been bridged from Puro and deposited into the carbon pool; every project contains the unique project ID from the Puro Registry as well as the full project data, including all metadata and related documents. To confirm the status of the CORCs on the Puro registry, the user can simply look up the project ID and find the full details of CORC issuances related to the project. To distinguish credits bridged by Toucan from other retirements, Toucan makes sure to list 'TOUCAN' followed by the corresponding address into which the tokenised credits were deposited to ensure the user of the Puro registry can identify the credits attributed to Toucan's bridge. One can even audit all bridged credits directly on the Puro registry by searching 'Toucan' in the retirement purpose field; here, the full portfolio of pooled CORCs would be displayed to the user.[57]

The Toucan Protocol is a great example of how blockchain can enhance trust and transparency in VCMs. Although Toucan is providing an innovative and integrated solution with Puro Earth, there are still more opportunities to enhance transparency and trust, such as providing digital project audits directly to token holders from the underlying projects, providing additional evidence of the actual environmental impact underlying the tokenised credits. Going forward, collaboration and integration with Verra and Gold Standard would enhance trust in Toucan's pooled tokens as these organisations have strong reputations built on existing public trust.

8.3 Efficiency and scalability

The decentralised nature of blockchain eliminates the need for intermediaries by automating transactions, thereby reducing transaction time and costs. Often, blockchain transactions are settled through smart contracts, which ensure instant and error-free settlement. In the carbon lifecycle, smart contracts can be employed to automate steps throughout the lifecycle of a carbon credit. In the early days of blockchain technology, there were concerns about long transaction times and scalability. However, these concerns have been almost entirely resolved with the current state of the technology.

Blockchain is especially suited to handle large transaction volumes efficiently, especially with recent innovations. Ethereum, the largest blockchain currently, is frequently used by blockchain initiatives and is often employed in carbon tokenisation solutions. Previously, the Solana blockchain had the highest transaction-per-second capacity, being able to handle up to 65,000 transactions per second.[58] After the recent Dencun update[59] to the Ethereum blockchain, on 13 March 2024, Ethereum's Layer 1 capacity expanded to be able to handle up to 100,000 transactions per second.[60] For perspective, Ethereum is widely used by many tokens and coins. Its highest number of daily transactions to date has been 1.96 million,[61] which corresponds to an average of 22 transactions per second. Even more frequently used blockchains, such as Solana,[62] report average transactions well below the upper bound for both Ethereum and Solana. This means scalability, at least in the current market, should not be an issue with blockchain solutions.

Another concern noted with using blockchain technology is the need for nodes to store the data of the blockchain. Since blockchains record every transaction to have occurred on-chain, the data storage requirements can be quite extensive. For instance, the current size of the Ethereum blockchain is approximately 1.12TB,[63] although recent developments with Dencun have enabled transaction data to be compressed, reducing data storage requirements. A better solution to this problem is the implementation of Layer 2 solutions, which function as secondary chains off the main blockchain (Layer 1) and then periodically align the transaction record back with the main chain.[64] Layer 2 solutions increase transaction speeds, lower transaction costs, support greater scalability, and enhance user experience. The Polygon blockchain is a well-known application of a Layer 2 solution.

The current VCM has experienced significant inefficiencies where existing infrastructure leads to long processing times in every part of the carbon credit lifecycle, largely due to the proliferation of manually managed processes. The average project registration process alone can take several months to years to complete. In fact, the 2023 survey conducted by NASDAQ to survey participants of all parts of the carbon credit lifecycle showed that 25% of respondents rated traditional VCM as inefficient or highly inefficient.[65] These difficulties translate to realised impacts on project developers and carbon credit buyers. Projects face funding challenges, especially cash flow problems when faced with long registration and processing times. Additionally, projects may lack the resources to navigate the administrative burden and engage in MRV processes, especially problematic for smaller projects, often excluding them from the VCM entirely. Secondly, poor market accessibility and transparency lead to higher costs. The MRV burden and high intermediation costs contribute to higher carbon credit prices and transaction costs. Additionally, the difficulty navigating existing carbon marketplaces can be complex, leading to even more participation barriers for buyers. While there are some existing carbon exchanges, such as the Carbon TradeXchange, that purport to offer scalability and efficiency, the reality is that they lack the efficiency and transparency that can be realised by employing blockchain solutions.

Blockchain can be implemented in the current carbon credit lifecycle either fully, providing end-to-end coverage or covering partial roles. Currently, most projects play partial roles in the lifecycle, primarily covering the trading and marketplace process. However, using Web3 technology, an end-to-end solution is possible, where all tasks are automated and built on infrastructure that integrates fully and seamlessly. For example, the utilisation of the Internet of Things (IoT) can provide real-time data collection and monitoring for many projects, such as measuring renewable energy generated by solar power projects. This enhances the accuracy and reliability of carbon credit verification while simultaneously making monitoring cheaper and more efficient. Carbon trading and marketplaces have already been vastly improved by blockchain technology. Blockchain has been shown to minimise transaction costs, allow for 24/7 trading, improve information transparency, and provide automatic execution of trades. In comparison, the largest traditional exchange can settle transactions instantly; however, it largely relies on auction mechanisms to sell large batches of carbon credits, significantly extending the amount of time required to find a suitable buyer.[66]

Here, we have outlined exactly how blockchain technology itself is efficient and scalable. There are many inefficiencies in the existing VCM, inefficiencies that can be fixed through the implementation of blockchain and Web3 solutions. Improvements in efficiency would directly translate into improved accessibility for both project owners and buyers, propelling forward many smaller carbon initiatives and participants. While it is difficult to estimate the future requirements of a blockchain-based carbon credit solution, given the current capabilities of the technology and its rate of improvement, the technology itself is doubtful to restrict the ability of the network to meet demand.

Case study: Coorest

We briefly discussed the implementation of an end-to-end solution as a potential application of blockchain in the carbon space to effectively reduce all existing inefficiencies with the current VCM. Here, we look at a case study that works on doing exactly that. Coorest was founded in 2021 with the aim of improving transparency and efficiency in the existing VCM. They implemented an end-to-end solution utilising several Web3 integrations to achieve a fully digital and decentralised carbon tokenisation solution.[67] They focused exclusively on forestry projects. Here, we detail the implementation of this solution and the realised efficiency gains.

Having developed its own certified standard, the Coorest Carbon Standard allows for the native tokenisation of carbon credits rather than bridging credits from other registries.[68] As administrators of its own standard, Coorest has reduced registration fees for project owners and simplified the registration process. Project owners can register their projects directly with Coorest, although there is still extensive work required to provide appropriate documentation to ensure project eligibility and quality as in traditional registries. However, once the project is registered, the process becomes streamlined. For every tree digitally documented, Coorest issues an NFTree, which represents the real-world asset. Once the NFTree is issued, digital monitoring, reporting, and verification (dMRV) are carried out by Coorest by using a Web3 integration with Chainlink, where API data is requested from Floodlight's biomass satellite data.[69] This allows off-chain data gathered by Floodlight to come on-chain and verify a project's carbon credits. All project data is maintained in the CCS Registry and is regularly updated with yearly monitoring reports generated by the satellite data feed. Having digitally verified the project, each NFTree then mints a CCO2 token for every kilogram of CO_2 absorbed by the tree. NFTrees can be bought and sold in the Venly Marketplace, another Web3 integration. The CCO2 token also currently trades on the Polygon blockchain but has no dedicated marketplace as of 2024. Having obtained CCO2 tokens, the user can decide to retire them and claim the offsets directly through Coorest's decentralised application.[70] The retirements are recorded, and token holders are issued a Proof of Carbon Compensation (PoCC) Certificate, which is an NFT recorded on the Polygon blockchain.

The solution offered by Coorest presents a good example of how Web3 applications can be leveraged in the carbon credit lifecycle to automate processes such as MRV that are otherwise difficult and costly. Issuing blockchain-native credits also removes many inefficiencies and issues in the lifecycle of a carbon token when compared to carbon bridging; both minting tokens and retiring tokens are streamlined and automated.

8.4 Innovation and new markets

8.4.1 Technological innovations

Blockchain technology is constantly changing and evolving, which means that this technology can increasingly support new applications. What started out as a relatively simple cryptocurrency in 2008, has evolved into several more advanced applications. Improvements in technology will inevitably lead to more widespread adoption and applications. In the carbon credit market, tokenisation would not have been possible without the advent of these technologies, so they serve as drivers for sustainability and change.

One of the major innovations in this market that has allowed for the creation of tokenisation has been the development of smart contracts. While a relatively established idea,[71] the technological implementation and widespread use did not occur until the rise of smart contracts alongside the creation of Ethereum in 2015.[72] Smart contracts allow for advanced contract programming that automatically executes based on preprogrammed conditions. These contracts provide opportunities for integration within the VCC verification process, especially with their ability to integrate with other data sources into the blockchain. Additionally, the contracts can be programmed with dynamic pricing mechanisms that can adjust based on underlying conditions. As an example, a possible implementation could be to adjust the carbon credit price on the first sale based on underlying measures of carbon credit quality collected from prespecified data sources. Where this technology really presents an opportunity for market advancement is through its integration with emerging technologies such as the IoT and other digital monitoring technologies, including geographic information systems (GIS) and remote sensing. For example, initial satellite imagery can be used to assess the project zone of a reforestation project. Once trees are planted, soil monitoring sensors can be deployed in the soil to collect real-time data on soil conditions. Meanwhile, growth monitoring can be conducted by regular analysis of satellite imagery. Once appropriate milestones are met based on data from monitoring, smart contracts can ensure the automatic issuance of carbon credits. Together, these technologies can provide real-time project reports and allow for continuous time monitoring, in comparison to the discrete monitoring used in the current VCM, where reports are conducted at certain intervals, commonly only yearly. This technology plays a strong role in enhancing transparency, trust, efficiency, and scalability, which we discussed earlier.

Not only do smart contracts provide opportunities for continuous monitoring, but they are the foundations for Web3 technology[73] that can be implemented to decentralise the entire VCM. The adoption of Web3 represents the shift from centralised to decentralised systems; this hinges on employing smart contracts to automate delivery. A full Web3 solution could cover automated verification and issuance of credits, facilitate trade, automate retirement processes, provide decentralised governance to the network, and integrate into existing systems. With Web3 comes the emergence of DAOs where governance is carried out among participants of the network by leveraging smart contracts;[74] this again has benefits to the earlier discussed topics, especially for transparency and trust. Overall, the innovation of smart contracts is adaptable and can be implemented in creative ways. We have only outlined some of the applications in the basic VCM, but other applications, such as creating new financial instruments can be carried out using this technology.

Smart contracts can allow for the construction of complicated financial instruments without the need for intermediaries. Utilising the technology, advanced contracts can be programmed to execute automatically. When looking at the traditional carbon credit activity, only 61% of activity is carried out in spot markets. Carbon forward markets make up the other 39% of all carbon credit activity.[75] Currently, tokenised credit transactions are almost entirely concentrated in spot markets. The utilisation of smart contracts in developing carbon forward tokens represents a significant opportunity that would likely enhance the flow of funds to projects in developing countries. Allowing projects to obtain funding in advance to support their projects rather than waiting until project maturity to cash in on gains.

8.4.2 New markets

CSR has become an increasing concern for stakeholders and has been a well-documented phenomenon that will continue to grow; 67% of corporate demand for VCCs is driven by stakeholder demand and 33% by demand to meet net-zero commitments.[73] We also see an increasing amount of disclosure of sustainability information by companies, driven by changes in stakeholder expectations as well as developments in regulation and reporting requirements.[76] Carbon tokens can be used to meet these goals of both CSR and net zero commitments by companies while providing traceable impacts for stakeholders to view. The adoption of carbon tokens in supply chains also has the ability to be implemented in supply chain monitoring, which presents an interesting opportunity for companies to further improve the traceability of their net-zero actions.

While the primary demand for VCCs comes from corporations, we are also seeing trends in consumer markets for VCCs. There is increasing demand and interest in carbon credits from consumers; many consumers note issues with the existing VCM as barriers to participation.[77] Most of these barriers, such as transparency and pricing inefficiencies would be at least partially resolved by adopting carbon tokenisation; however, additional efforts to inform consumers about the technology may be required to precipitate adoption. In this market, there are solutions increasingly targeted towards consumers, such as personal carbon footprint calculators and the ability to integrate carbon offsets while making online purchases, but there is still more potential to launch blockchain solutions in this market.

Currently, there are no issued tokenised compliance carbon credits, but this may also present a significant market opportunity. There is an increasing level of interest in implementing a blockchain solution at the international level to serve the requirements of the Paris Agreement and improve country-level carbon accounting.[78] There have been a few initiatives that have aimed to explore this market, such as the World Bank Climate Warehouse, which tested the ability of the technology to fully integrate and fulfil the needs of markets and the UNFCCC.[79] This proposed solution aims to integrate the entire carbon credit ecosystem into an end-to-end solution for carbon markets, and it integrates independent, national, UNFCCC, and D4C registries. Even without tokenisation of the compliance market, there are some country-level compliance schemes that in fact accept VCCs as offsets against carbon taxes; for instance, South Africa accepts some Verra VCUs as offsets.[80] Given these possible integrations, the question of tokenisation in the compliance market becomes more nuanced with a possible goal of fully integrating all carbon markets into a unified system.

While these three markets represent most of the demand for VCCs themselves, there is also the matter of having a ready supply of projects to fill this demand. As we saw in Figure 1.2, developing countries are profoundly underrepresented by compliance schemes; as a result, the VCM plays an important role in providing representation of these countries in carbon markets. The fact is that as a world we aim to meet net-zero commitments, and this requires participation and representation in all countries. We have already developed the idea that blockchain would lower barriers to smaller projects, which more commonly operate in developing countries, allowing for their representation in the VCM. This outcome is critical for sustainable development, especially when we consider the spillover effects of investment in economies, and can be secured by improving VCM solutions, ensuring increased accessibility. Carbon forward tokens could play a significant role in reaching this market as we have so far seen that even though projects in developing countries are more likely to be tokenised, see Figure 1.6, least developed countries are still underrepresented in carbon markets. More research would need to be conducted as to why this is the case, but it is quite likely attributable to the lack of project viability absent additional funding opportunities. Overall, the global supply and demand of VCCs is sure to become increasingly important as the world races to mitigate climate change.

8.4.3 Case study: Senken and Vlinder in the world's first carbon forward token

Here, we look at a specific project and the impact of blockchain technology and financial innovation on funding sustainable development. We established the potential for tokenisation of carbon forward contracts; this solution was realised in 2023, when Vlinder and Senken launched the first carbon forward token.[81] The underlying project is a mangrove restoration project that aims to reforest 1500 ha of degraded mangrove along the Kwale, Kilifi, and Tana River counties in Kenya and remove 727,418 t of CO_2e. The project will not only result in carbon removals but also wider community benefits outlined in the project documents on Verra. For this project to take place, it required an initial investment of USD 537,500. It was expected that after 2–3 years of implementation, the project would issue enough carbon credits to be self-sustaining, by selling the issued credits on the market. However, the initial investment was critical to implement the project, as in many projects in developing countries, where funds are scarce. To serve this need, Vlinder provided the initial investment required while simultaneously issuing carbon forward tokens to cover these project costs.

The carbon forward tokens were initially sold on the Senken marketplace for the 2024–2025 carbon credit vintage. The mechanics of this project saw the issuance of a

FCO2 (a carbon forward token), initially issued and available for purchase on Senken. The idea is that subsequently, after the carbon credits are verified, this FCO2 can be swapped for a spot carbon token, a TCO2, and can then be retired as the holder claims the offset. This first vintage appears to serve as more of a pilot project for issuing carbon forward tokens, details are publicly available on the actual mechanics and details of the forward contract.[82] However, for the vintages from 2026 onwards, Vlinder has partnered with Solid World to sell the FCO2 tokens.[83] Here, there are more details on the mechanics and processes underlying the contracts.[84] Vlinder has guaranteed the delivery of the VCCs against the forward tokens to be delivered no later than 60 days after the credits have been issued by Verra. Solid World retains Forward Clips against every Forward Contract issued and from this creates a Collateralized Basket Token (CBT), which is the pool of Forward Clips. Buyers can then purchase Forward Clips from the pool. At any point, the Forward Clip holder can redeem the contract for the underlying Forward Delivery Commitment (as long as certain conditions are met).[85] This implementation of forward tokens remains to be fully explored and represents a significant opportunity, given that 39% of the traditional VCM is concentrated in forward markets.[86] Although there are some working implementations of forward tokens,[87] many of the contract details and legality are currently unknown.

8.5 Diversification benefits

Carbon credits also offer the potential for investors to invest in a new asset class, translating to portfolio diversification benefits. Some medium-term studies empirically show increased Sharpe ratios from investing in carbon forwards Swinkels and Yang show diversification benefits on the risk-return of portfolios when holding compliance carbon futures; however, this type of portfolio increases liquidity risk due to frictions in current carbon markets.[88] Additionally, they find that there is a poor correlation in prices across regions, suggesting the presence of global diversification benefits. More recently, Behr, Mueller, and Orgen[89] showed diversification benefits from investing in VCC futures in addition to compliance futures, yet there are still market efficiency and liquidity issues. It tends to be more difficult for individual investors to invest in these derivative markets, given the relatively large number of underlying credits and the cost relative to individual investor portfolios. Here, blockchain solutions, by permitting fractional ownership, especially in pooled tokens, can allow individual investors to enter this market and obtain additional diversification benefits for their portfolios.

Another consideration is the diversification benefits of the carbon asset class in managing long-term risks, particularly climate risks, such as physical and transition risks. The literature looking at short-term and cross-sectional effects of ESG diversification tends to find benefits of diversification into carbon-related assets.[90] However, several papers suggest climate risks should be distinctly evaluated in portfolios as distinct risk factors to hedge against. Chepni et al. show that the diversification benefits from investing in ESG assets in general depend on the type of climate risk being hedged against, where there are stronger effects of hedging against physical climate risk in comparison to transition risk.[91] This means that during periods of high physical climate risk, it is beneficial to invest in ESG assets, while this relationship is not so apparent for managing transition risks of portfolios. Both transition risk and physical risk are difficult to quantify, leading to difficulties in portfolio optimisation. However, across many studies, there appears to be evidence that ESG-related investments, and especially direct investments in carbon credits, can help reduce portfolio risk. As transition and physical risk increase, carbon credits as an asset class are increasingly important for investors looking to hedge against these risks.

9 Regulatory considerations

Implementations of carbon tokens must take into consideration the applicable regulatory frameworks that apply to them, which are steadily increasing in number as efforts to regulate crypto assets become more important. In the European Union, the Markets in Crypto-Assets Regulation[92] intends to provide a comprehensive framework for regulating crypto assets. Comparatively, in the United States, there is debate on whether carbon tokens are classified as securities falling under the purview of the Securities and Exchange Commission or the Commodity Futures Trading Commission. The purview depends on whether carbon tokens meet the Howey Test criteria.[93] Regulating the VCM itself is another important consideration since regulation in this market would likely improve trust and transparency, which we have established as being critical to having well-functioning markets. Here, we have questions, such as how to reconcile the fragmentation in the market and ensure the issuance of high-quality carbon credits. This becomes especially important as we consider the increasing number of integrations of VCCs into national compliance mechanisms, as in Colombia[94] and South Africa.[95] Additionally, since 2022, Verra[96] and Gold Standard banned the unauthorised tokenisation of their carbon credits, so not only do national laws need to be considered but the terms and conditions of voluntary carbon registries must be followed. Overall, the existing and emerging regulations applicable to tokenising carbon credits are complex and multi-fold; other chapters in this volume discuss the nuances with existing regulations and how they may apply to tokenised carbon credits.

10 Outlook and potential

Overall, blockchain's ability to support DAOs will likely be instrumental not only for overhauling the current VCM but possibly other financial markets as well. Given the concerns regarding transparency, quality, efficiency, and general market issues in the current VCM, it would seem that blockchain solutions can entirely address the current shortcomings. However, it should be noted that decentralised networks are secure and safe only when they have a high number of independent, distributed participants. As a result, when structuring new blockchain solutions, it is paramount to consider the potential vulnerabilities of the technology to ensure successful implementation.

Carbon forward tokens also provide a significant opportunity in the carbon tokenisation market, especially considering the prevalence of forward tokens in traditional markets. There is a clear demand for forward tokens, which would prove instrumental in directly providing project funding to small projects.

Carbon tokens not only enable individual investors to meet their carbon reduction goals but also increase the flow of funds to developing countries through the VCM, supporting low-carbon and carbon-removal projects. This is vital to the global goal of achieving net-zero emissions since currently developing countries are poorly represented by compliance emissions schemes. Investment in carbon tokens would thus lead to direct effects of reducing CO_2e in the atmosphere and transferring funds to least developed countries, where they are most needed. Overall, using blockchain in the VCM presents an opportunity that is still relatively underdeveloped and has the potential for high impact.

11 Conclusion

We have examined advancements in the climate change discourse and regulations that have led to concerted global efforts in addressing climate change. Although the percentage of carbon emissions covered by compliance schemes has risen over the past decades, there is still low emission coverage by such schemes in developing countries. Tokenisation of carbon credits presents a solution to many of the issues that inhibit the potential of the VCM to have a strong impact on climate change. We established that blockchain technology would greatly improve market efficiency, which would ensure that funds go to projects that can best use them to reduce and capture atmospheric carbon emissions. The VCM plays an important role in remedying the lack of representation of compliance emissions schemes. We have also explored how tokenisation can further remedy this, especially through issuing carbon forward tokens that could provide pre-funding to small projects that would otherwise not be able to take place.

Carbon tokenisation is not one unified process but rather encompasses several different processes implemented by organisations that find unique ways to use blockchain across the carbon credit lifecycle. The development of two-way carbon bridges and end-to-end solutions appears to be the most promising and comprehensive solutions, but the optimal solution is difficult to predict currently. We have focused on outlining the opportunities for carbon tokenisation, drawing upon several sources to support our conclusions, including technical whitepapers, industry reports and surveys, and related academic research. It is clear that solutions in this market will rely on diverse stakeholders coming together to reach an optimal solution, especially considering the complexity of the market. Good solutions require expertise from climate experts, lawyers, governments, economists, corporations, and individuals. By considering blockchain technology as a solution for the VCM, and potentially the overall carbon market, policymakers could optimise the market for higher impact, contributing better to the global goal of mitigating climate change.

Notes

1 National Research Council (US) Ad Hoc Study Group on Carbon Dioxide and Climate, 'Carbon Dioxide and Climate: A Scientific Assessment' (National Academy of Sciences 1979).
2 World Bank, 'The State and Trends of Carbon Pricing 2023' (World Bank 2023).
3 World Bank Group, 'State and Trends of Carbon Pricing Dashboard' https://carbonpricingdashboard.worldbank.org accessed 17 June 2024.
4 Ecosystem Marketplace, 'State of the Voluntary Carbon Market 2024' (Ecosystem Marketplace 2024) https://www.ecosystemmarketplace.com/publications/2024-state-of-the-voluntary-carbon-markets-sovcm/ accessed 3 February 2025.
5 Sun Y Lee and Craig E Carroll, 'The Emergence, Variation, and Evolution of Corporate Social Responsibility in the Public Sphere, 1980–2004: The Exposure of Firms to Public Debate' (2011) 104 Journal of Business Ethics 115–131 https://doi.org/10.1007/s10551-011-0893-y accessed 24 December 2024.; Eva M Sánchez-Teba, Maria D Benítez-Márquez, Guillermo Bermúdez-González, and Maria del Mar Luna-Pereira, 'Mapping the Knowledge of CSR and Sustainability' (2021) 13(18) Sustainability 10106 https://doi.org/10.3390/su131810106 accessed 24 December 2024.; Miglė Jakučionytė-Skodienė, Ričardas Krikštolaitis, and Genovaitė Liobikienė, 'The Contribution of Changes in Climate-Friendly Behaviour, Climate Change Concern and Personal Responsibility to Household Greenhouse Gas Emissions: Heating/Cooling and Transport Activities in the European Union' (2022) 246 Energy 123387 https://doi.org/10.1016/j.energy.2022.123387 accessed 24 December 2024.
6 Directive (EU) 2023/959 of the European Parliament and of the Council of 10 May 2023 amending Directive 2003/87/EC establishing a system for greenhouse gas emission allowance trading within the Union and Decision (EU) 2015/1814 [2023] OJ L 130/134 https://eur-lex.europa.eu/eli/dir/2023/959/oj/eng accessed 19 January 2025.
7 Verra, 'VCS Program Methodologies' (Verra 2024) https://verra.org/methodologies-main/#vcs-program-methodologies accessed 22 June 2024.
8 Barbara K Haya, Aline Abayo, Ivy S So, and Micah Elias, 'Voluntary Registry Offsets Database v11' (Berkeley Carbon Trading Project, University of California, Berkeley, May 2024) https://gspp.berkeley.edu/faculty-and-impact/centers/cepp/projects/berkeley-carbon-trading-project/offsets-database accessed 22 June 2024.
10 Cumulative carbon emissions for 1990–2022 were computed from Monica Crippa, Diego Guizzardi, Federico Pagani, Manjola Banja, Marilena Muntean, Eduard Schaaf, Wouter Becker, Francesca Monforti-Ferrario, Roberto Quadrelli, Ana Risquez Martin, Parisa Taghavi-Moharami, Giacomo Grassi, Simone Rossi, João Brandão de Melo, Diana Oom, Ana Branco, Javier San-Miguel, and Elisabetta Vignati, 'GHG Emissions of All World Countries – JRC/IEA 2023 Report' (Publications Office of the European Union 2023). Cumulative carbon emissions covered under government compliance schemes computed

from World Bank 2023 (n 3). South Asia has zero emissions covered under government compliance schemes from 1990 to 2022.

9 World Bank, 'Country and Lending Groups' (World Bank 2023) https://datahelpdesk.worldbank.org/knowledgebase/articles/906519 accessed 22 June 2024.

11 Monica Crippa, Diego Guizzardi, Federico Pagani, Manjola Banja, Marilena Muntean, Eduard Schaaf, Wouter Becker, Francesca Monforti-Ferrario, Roberto Quadrelli, Ana Risquez Martin, Parisa Taghavi-Moharami, Giacomo Grassi, Simone Rossi, João Brandão de Melo, Diana Oom, Ana Branco, Javier San-Miguel, and Elisabetta Vignati, 'GHG Emissions of All World Countries – JRC/IEA 2023 Report' (Publications Office of the European Union 2023).

12 World Bank Group (n 3).

13 Total carbon emissions and compliance carbon emissions represent the cumulative emissions from 1990 to 2022. Voluntary carbon credits are cumulative for the years 1996–2024. Countries were grouped according to 2024 World Bank Income Groups (n 10). Sources: Voluntary carbon credits are the total issued credits from (n 8). Cumulative emissions for 1990–2022 were computed from (n 11) and compliance emissions were computed from (n 3).

14 Oliver Miltenberger, Caitlin Jospe, and James Pittman, 'The Good Is Never Perfect: Why the Current Flaws of Voluntary Carbon Markets Are Services, Not Barriers to Successful Climate Change Action' (2021) 3 Frontiers in Climate https://www.frontiersin.org/articles/10.3389/fclim.2021.686516/full accessed 22 June 2024.

15 Lambert Schneider, Maosheng Duan, Robert Stavins, Kelley Kizzier, Derik Broekhoff, Frank Jotzo, Harald Winkler, Michael Lazarus, Andrew Howard, and Christina Hood, 'Double Counting and the Paris Agreement Rulebook' (2019) 366 Science 180 https://doi.org/10.1126/science.aay8750 accessed 3 February 2025.

16 Gold Standard, 'Registry App Terms of Use' (Gold Standard for the Global Goals 2022) https://globalgoals.goldstandard.org/t-preview-registry-app-terms-of-use/ accessed 22 June 2024.

17 Verra, 'Verra Registry Terms of Use' (Verra April 2024) https://verra.org/wp-content/uploads/2024/04/Verra-Registry-TOU-April-2024-FINAL.pdf accessed 22 June 2024.

18 Grayson Badgley, Jeremy Freeman, Jacob J. Hamman, Barbara Haya, Anna T. Trugman, William R. L. Anderegg, and Danny Cullenward, 'Systematic Over-Crediting in California's Forest Carbon Offsets Program' (2021) Global Change Biology https://onlinelibrary.wiley.com/doi/epdf/10.1111/gcb.15943 accessed 22 June 2024.

19 Bruce G. Lindsay, Patricia G. Selinger, C. Galtieri, Jim N. Gray, Raymond A. Lorie, T. G. Price, F. Putzolu, Irving L. Traiger, and B. W. Wade, 'Notes on Distributed Databases' (IBM Research Report RJ2571 1979) https://dominoweb.draco.res.ibm.com/a776ec17fc2fce73852579f100578964.html accessed 23 June 2024.

20 Ralph C Merkle, 'A Digital Signature Based on a Conventional Encryption Function' (1987) https://people.eecs.berkeley.edu/~raluca/cs261-f15/readings/merkle.pdf accessed 23 June 2024.

21 Satoshi Nakamoto, 'Bitcoin: A Peer-to-Peer Electronic Cash System' (2008) https://bitcoin.org/bitcoin.pdf accessed 22 June 2024.

22 Forbes, 'Crypto Prices' (Forbes 2024) https://www.forbes.com/digital-assets/crypto-prices/ accessed 22 June 2024.

23 Verra, 'Verra Registry – Terms of Use' (April 2024) https://verra.org/wp-content/uploads/2024/04/Verra-Registry-TOU-April-2024-FINAL.pdf accessed 24 June 2024; Gold Standard, 'Registry App Terms of Use' (20 May 2022) https://globalgoals.goldstandard.org/t-preview-registry-app-terms-of-use/ accessed 24 June 2024.

24 C3, 'Carbon Bridge' https://docs.c3.app/the-basics/carbon-bridge accessed 24 June 2024; Moss, 'MCO2 Token' https://mco2token.moss.earth/ accessed 24 June 2024; Toucan, 'How Bridging Works' https://docs.toucan.earth/toucan/carbon-bridge/puro-carbon-bridge/how-bridging-works accessed 24 June 2024.

25 Toucan, 'What is a Carbon Pool?' https://docs.toucan.earth/toucan/carbon-pools/what-is-a-carbon-pool accessed 24 June 2024; C3, 'Carbon Pools' https://docs.c3.app/the-basics/carbon-pools accessed 24 June 2024.

26 Toucan, 'Carbon Retirements' https://docs.toucan.earth/toucan/retire-credits accessed 24 June 2024.

27 Thallo, 'Thallo Deploys Two-Way Carbon Credit Bridge to Celo' (21 August 2023) https://www.thallo.io/thallo-deploys-two-way-carbon-credit-bridge-to-celo/ accessed 24 June 2024.

28 Gerald Porter Jr and Joe Wallace, 'Cryptocurrency Traders Move Into Carbon Markets' (Wall Street Journal, 9 January 2022) https://www.wsj.com/articles/cryptocurrency-traders-move-into-carbon-markets-11641826402 accessed 4 July 2024.

29 Natalie Wong, 'WeWork Founder Adam Neumann's Flow Draws Crypto Interest' (Bloomberg 8 September 2022) https://www.bloomberg.com/news/articles/2022-09-08/wework-founder-adam-neumann-s-flow-draws-crypto-interest accessed 4 July 2024.

30 Kenza Bryan and Patrick Temple-West, 'The utopian world where carbon and crypto meet' (Financial Times 2022) https://www.ft.com/content/8f1dca1d-6b81-4f13-9ad5-e0058eeba808 accessed 22 June 2024.

31 Coorest, 'Coorest Whitepaper 3.0' (GitBook) https://coorest.gitbook.io/coorest-whitepaper-3.0 accessed 4 July 2024.

32 Verra, 'Verra Statement on Crypto Market Activities' (25 November 2021) https://verra.org/statement-oncrypto accessed 16 July 2024.

33 Toucan, 'Pools' (Toucan) https://app.toucan.earth/pools accessed 4 July 2024.

34 Comparison between total credits bridged by Toucan from Verra between 2021 and 2022. These credits include original issuances dating back to 2009. For comparison, we take all credits issued by Verra between 2009 and 2022 as this represents the credits possibly eligible for tokenisation by Toucan while accounting for the possibility of a cutoff date for credit age. Source: Verra, 'Search VCS' (Verra) https://registry.verra.org/app/search/VCS accessed 4 July 2024.

35 Total carbon credits issued by Verra between 2009 and 2022 were used for this analysis since the credits tokenised by Toucan were issued between 2009 and 2022. We have assumed some internal preference by Toucan for credits issued between 2009 and 2022, so we have used this as the pool of possible credits eligible for tokenisation from Toucan. Source: Verra. 'Verra Registry Database' https://registry.verra.org/app/search/VCS accessed 4 July 2024.

36 World Bank Group, 'Distributed Ledger Technology (DLT) and Blockchain' (2017) https://documents1.worldbank.org/curated/en/177911513714062215/pdf/122140-WP-PUBLIC-Distributed-Ledger-Technology-and-Blockchain-Fintech-Notes.pdf accessed 7 July 2024.

37 Paolo Martino, 'Blockchain Technology and the Banking Industry' in *Blockchain and Banking* (Palgrave Pivot, Cham, 2021) https://doi.org/10.1007/978-3-030-70970-9_3 accessed 7 July 2024.

38 Nasdaq and ValueExchange, 'Scaling Carbon Markets: A New Market Blueprint for 2024' (2024) https://www.nasdaq.com/solutions/marketplace-technology/scaling-carbon-markets-report accessed 7 July 2024.

39 CTX, 'Home' (2024) https://ctxglobal.com/ accessed 7 July 2024.

40 Nasdaq and ValueExchange (n 37).

41 Deloitte, 'Financial Firms Carbon Offset Market' (2023) https://www2.deloitte.com/us/en/insights/industry/financial-services/financial-services-industry-predictions/2023/financial-firms-carbon-offset-market.html accessed 7 July 2024.

42 Stuart Haber and Wakefield Scott Stornetta, 'How to Time-Stamp a Digital Document' (1991) 3 Journal of Cryptology 99 http://www.staroceans.org/e-book/Haber_Stornetta.pdf accessed 23 June 2024.

43 George A. Akerlof, 'The Market for "Lemons": Quality Uncertainty and the Market Mechanism' (1970) 84 Quarterly Journal of Economics 488.

44 Jiyun Kang and Gwendolyn Hustvedt, 'Building Trust Between Consumers and Corporations: The Role of Consumer Perceptions of Transparency and Social Responsibility' (2014) 125 Journal of Business Ethics 253 https://doi.org/10.1007/s10551-013-1916-7.

45 Yu-Shan Chen and Ching-Hsun Chang, 'Greenwash and Green Trust: The Mediation Effects of Green Consumer Confusion and Green Perceived Risk' (2013) 114 Journal of Business Ethics 489 https://doi.org/10.1007/s10551-012-1360-0.
46 Kongmanas Yavaprabhas, Mehrdokht Pournader, and Stefan Seuring, 'Blockchain as the "Trust-Building Machine" for Supply Chain Management' (2023) 327 Annals of Operations Research 49 https://doi.org/10.1007/s10479-022-04868-0.
47 Megan Stubbs, Katie Hoover, Jonathan L. Ramseur, and Genevieve K. Croft, 'Agriculture and Forestry Offsets in Carbon Markets: Background and Selected Issues' (Congressional Research Service Report R46956 3 November 2021) https://crsreports.congress.gov/product/pdf/R/R46956 accessed 23 June 2024.
48 Aggelos Kiayias (ed), *Financial Cryptography and Data Security: 21st International Conference, FC 2017, Sliema, Malta, April 3–7, 2017, Revised Selected Papers* (Lecture Notes in Computer Science, vol 10322, Springer International Publishing 2017) https://doi.org/10.1007/978-3-319-70278-0.
49 Lin William Cong and Zhiguo He, 'Blockchain Disruption and Smart Contracts' (2019) 32 Review of Financial Studies 1754 https://doi.org/10.1093/rfs/hhz007.
50 Grammateia Kotsialou, Karlygash Kuralbayeva, and Timothy Laing, 'Blockchain's Potential in Forest Offsets, the Voluntary Carbon Markets and REDD+' (2022) 49 Environmental Conservation 137 https://doi.org/10.1017/S0376892922000157.
51 David Yermack, 'Corporate Governance and Blockchains' (2017) 21 Review of Finance 7 https://doi.org/10.1093/rof/rfw074.
52 Adnan Balloch, Anamaria Nicolae, and Dennis Philip, 'Stock Market Literacy, Trust, and Participation' (2015) 19 Review of Finance 1925 https://doi.org/10.1093/rof/rfu040; Luigi Guiso, Paola Sapienza, and Luigi Zingales, 'Trusting the Stock Market' (2008) 63 Journal of Finance 2557 https://doi.org/10.1111/j.1540-6261.2008.01408.x.
53 Toucan, 'Home' (2024) https://toucan.earth/home/ accessed 7 July 2024.
54 ICVCM, 'Core Carbon Principles' (2024) https://icvcm.org/core-carbon-principles/ accessed 7 July 2024.
55 Toucan, 'Puro Bridge Explained' (2024) https://blog.toucan.earth/puro-bridge-explained/ accessed 7 July 2024.
56 Toucan, 'App' (2024) https://app.toucan.earth/ accessed 7 July 2024.
57 Puro.earth, 'Carbon Sequestration Retirements' (2024) https://registry.puro.earth/carbon-sequestration/retirements accessed 7 July 2024.
58 Solana, 'Network Performance Report July 2023' (2023) https://solana.com/news/network-performance-report-july-2023 accessed 7 July 2024.
59 Ethereum Foundation, 'Dencun Mainnet Announcement' (2024) https://blog.ethereum.org/2024/02/27/dencun-mainnet-announcement accessed 7 July 2024.
60 Ethereum Foundation, 'Danksharding' (2024) https://ethereum.org/en/roadmap/danksharding/ accessed 7 July 2024.
61 Etherscan, 'Ethereum Network Transactions Chart' (2024) https://etherscan.io/chart/tx accessed 7 July 2024.
62 Solscan, 'Analytics' (2024) https://solscan.io/analytics accessed 7 July 2024.
63 Etherscan, 'Ethereum Chain Data' (2024) https://etherscan.io/chartsync/chaindefault accessed 7 July 2024.
64 Ethereum Foundation, 'Scaling' (2024) https://ethereum.org/en/developers/docs/scaling/ accessed 7 July 2024.
65 Nasdaq and ValueExchange (n 37).
66 CTX, 'Auctions' (2024) https://ctxglobal.com/auctions/ accessed 7 July 2024.
67 Coorest, 'Coorest Whitepaper 3.0' (2024) https://coorest.gitbook.io/coorest-whitepaper-3.0 accessed 7 July 2024.

68 Coorest, 'CCS Registry' (2024) https://coorest.gitbook.io/ccs-registry accessed 7 July 2024.
69 Coorest, 'Coorest Dapp Manual' (2024) https://coorest.gitbook.io/coorest-dapp-manual accessed 7 July 2024.
70 Coorest, 'App' (2024) https://app.coorest.io/ accessed 7 July 2024.
71 Nick Szabo, 'Smart Contracts: Building Blocks for Digital Markets' (1996) Extropy 16 https://www.truevaluemetrics.org/DBpdfs/BlockChain/Nick-Szabo-Smart-Contracts-Building-Blocks-for-Digital-Markets-1996-14591.pdf accessed 7 July 2024.
72 Ethereum Foundation, 'Ethereum Whitepaper' (2024) https://ethereum.org/en/whitepaper/ accessed 7 July 2024.
73 Ethereum Foundation, 'Web3' (2024) https://ethereum.org/en/web3/ accessed 7 July 2024.
74 Ethereum Foundation, 'DAO' (2024) https://ethereum.org/en/dao/ accessed 7 July 2024.
75 Nasdaq and ValueExchange (n 37).
76 OECD, 'Global Corporate Sustainability Report 2024' (2024) https://www.oecd-ilibrary.org/governance/global-corporate-sustainability-report-2024_8416b635-en accessed 7 July 2024.
77 BCG, 'The Next Frontier in Carbon Credits: Consumers' (2023) https://web-assets.bcg.com/bd/db/3eb796c842e6be7a36a6314d4268/bcg-the-next-frontier-in-carbon-credits-consumers-march-2023.pdf accessed 7 July 2024.
78 Marco Schletz, Laura A. Franke, and Søren Salomo, 'Blockchain Application for the Paris Agreement Carbon Market Mechanism—A Decision Framework and Architecture' (2020) 12 Sustainability 5069 https://doi.org/10.3390/su12125069 accessed 7 July 2024.
79 World Bank, 'Climate Warehouse Simulation III: Final Report' (September 2022) https://ik.imagekit.io/mtozw1gojis/world-bank/IDU_09ef226cf0a663041d60869f07078d1af9fd3_1_02812f780c_qwekFtJkY.pdf accessed 7 July 2024.
80 Carbon Tax Act 15 of 2019 (Republic of South Africa) https://cer.org.za/wp-content/uploads/2019/05/Carbon-Tax-Act-Regulations.pdf accessed 7 July 2024; Verra, 'VCS in South Africa' (2024) https://verra.org/vcs-in-south-africa/ accessed 7 July 2024.
81 Senken, 'Senken Has Launched the World's First Public Sale of Carbon Forward Tokens' (2024) https://www.senken.io/blog/senken-has-launched-the-worlds-first-public-sale-of-carbon-forward-tokens accessed 7 July 2024.
82 Senken, 'Papariko – Restoration of Degraded Mangrove Areas in Kenya' (2023) https://app.senken.io/forwards/1?tradeType=forwardContract accessed 4 December 2023.
83 Solid World, 'Vlinder Papariko Project' (2024) https://app.solid.world/projects/4/vlinder-papariko?buy=1 accessed 7 July 2024.
84 Solid World, 'Whitepaper' (2024) https://docs.solid.world/ accessed 7 July 2024.
85 Solid World, 'Terms' (2024) https://app.solid.world/terms accessed 7 July 2024.; Solid World, 'Tokenisation Terms (Version 1.0)' (2024) https://docsend.com/view/f7973uxcmczrcdyu accessed 7 July 2024.
86 Nasdaq and ValueExchange (n 37).
87 Solid World, 'Projects' (2024) https://app.solid.world/projects accessed 7 July 2024.
88 Laurens Swinkels and Jieun Yang, 'Investing in Carbon Credits' (2023) 27(1) Journal of Alternative Investments https://www.pm-research.com/content/iijaltinv/early/2023/08/01/jai20231195 accessed 7 July 2024.
89 Carsten Mueller, Papa Orgen, and Patrick Behr, 'Portfolio Allocation and Optimization with Carbon Offsets: Is it Worth the While?' (2023) 5 Journal of Climate Finance 100019 https://doi.org/10.1016/j.jclimf.2023.100019 accessed 7 July 2024.
90 Robert F. Engle, Stefano Giglio, Bryan Kelly, Heebum Lee, and Johannes Stroebel, 'Hedging Climate Change News' (2020) 33(3) Review of Financial Studies 1184 https://doi.org/10.1093/rfs/hhz072 accessed 7 July 2024; Mats Andersson, Patrick Bolton, and Frédéric Samama, 'Hedging Climate Risk' (2016) 72(3) Financial Analysts Journal 13 https://doi.org/10.2469/faj.v72.n3.4 accessed 7 July 2024.

91 Onur Cepni, Riza Demirer, Long Pham, and Luigi Rognone, 'Climate Uncertainty and Information Transmissions Across the Conventional and ESG Assets' (2023) 83 Journal of International Financial Markets, Institutions and Money 101730 https://doi.org/10.1016/j.intfin.2022.101730 accessed 7 July 2024.
92 Regulation (EU) 2023/1114 of the European Parliament and of the Council of 31 May 2023 on markets in crypto-assets and amending Regulations (EU) No 1093/2010 and (EU) No 1095/2010 and Directives 2013/36/EU and (EU) 2019/1937 [2023] OJ L150/40 https://eur-lex.europa.eu/legal-content/EN/TXT/?uri=CELEX%3A32023R1114&pk_campaign=todays_OJ&pk_source=EURLEX&pk_medium=TW&pk_keyword=Crypto%20assets&pk_content=Regulation&pk_cid=EURLEX_todaysOJ accessed 7 July 2024.
93 SEC, 'Framework for "Investment Contract" Analysis of Digital Assets' (2019) https://www.sec.gov/files/dlt-framework.pdf accessed 7 July 2024.
94 Ley 1819 de 2016 (Republic of Columbia) https://www.minambiente.gov.co/wp-content/uploads/2022/01/10.-Ley-1819-de-2016.pdf accessed 7 July 2024.
95 Carbon Tax Act 15 of 2019 (Republic of South Africa) https://cer.org.za/wp-content/uploads/2019/05/Carbon-Tax-Act-Regulations.pdf accessed 7 July 2024.
96 Verra, 'Statement on Crypto' (2024) https://verra.org/statement-on-crypto/ accessed 7 July 2024.

Masud Sultan, Vincent Schaaf, Nils Urbach, Cara Reuner, and Niklas Soltner

2 The early challenges in voluntary carbon markets: An interview-based analysis of past and present problems

Abstract: This chapter explores the structural challenges in Voluntary Carbon Markets (VCM), which act as a complementary tool to the Compliance Carbon Markets (CCM), forming a part of the global response to mitigate climate change. Understanding and addressing these challenges is crucial to unlocking VCM's potential to channel investments towards sustainable practices and the reduction of greenhouse gas emissions. Through an integrated approach of academic discourse and qualitative thematic analysis based on interviews conducted with founders in the VCM space, this research highlights the key obstacles faced by these markets in terms of market integrity, transparency, regulatory deficiencies, and technological gaps. The findings suggest that improved governance, clearer regulatory frameworks, and adoption of innovative technologies are critical to overcoming these barriers. Strengthening these aspects will enhance the credibility, transparency, and effectiveness of carbon markets, enabling them to function as more reliable mechanisms to combat climate change.

Keywords: blockchain, regenerative finance, VCC, VCM

1 Introduction —— 35
2 Challenges in voluntary carbon markets —— 37
3 Qualitative analysis of the voluntary carbon market —— 38
3.1 Opaque market structure —— 39
3.2 Lack of global governance —— 40
3.3 Lack of supply —— 41
3.4 Restricted accessibility —— 43
4 Conclusion —— 43

1 Introduction

Climate change is one of the most critical global challenges and the emission of carbon-based greenhouse gases (GHGs) has caused global warming already exceeding 1°C.[1] The consequences are increased intensity and severity of droughts, water scarcity, wildfires, rising sea levels, flooding, melting polar ice, catastrophic storms, and declining biodiversity. In 1992, the first globally adopted climate treaty, the United Nations Framework Convention on Climate Change, was adopted by 166 countries, en-

https://doi.org/10.1515/9783111706719-002

tered into force in 1994, and as of November 2024 encompasses 198 parties.[2] In the subsequent Kyoto Protocol in 1998, industrialised countries and economies committed to reduce GHG emissions in accordance with agreed individual targets.[3] Over time, it became apparent that the agreement had several limitations. Remarkably, developing countries such as China and India were not subject to emission reduction targets. Additionally, some significant emitters either did not ratify the agreement (e.g., the United States) or withdrew from it later (e.g., Canada). This led to the Paris Agreement, the most significant international climate agreement to date, signed in 2015. The primary objective of the Paris Agreement is to hold the increase in the global average temperature to well below 2°C above pre-industrial levels and to pursue efforts to limit the temperature increase to 1.5°C above pre-industrial levels.[4]

Carbon markets represent an economic and market-based approach to address climate change by facilitating the purchase and trading of carbon credits. These markets can be divided into two types. Compliance Carbon Markets (CCM) operate under mandatory legal frameworks by national or supranational authorities. Participants, such as large corporations operating in regulated jurisdictions, must acquire carbon allowances corresponding to their emissions, typically on an annual basis. These allowances are either allocated by regulatory bodies or sold directly, and companies that emit less than their allowance can sell surplus credits.

Voluntary Carbon Markets (VCM), in contrast, issue carbon credits to projects that achieve verified emission reductions or carbon capture. These credits can be acquired by companies or individuals as proof of their contribution to emission reductions. Although these credits cannot be used in most compliance markets, companies often purchase and retire them to claim carbon neutrality beyond regulatory requirements, while individuals use them to offset personal emissions, such as those from air travel.

Carbon markets play a critical role in reducing GHG emissions by mobilising investment in sustainable practices and incentivising lower emissions.[5] However, their effectiveness is limited by persistent structural challenges. Decentralised information systems such as blockchain, particularly its tokenisation capabilities, are frequently proposed as solutions to these challenges. This chapter aims to analyse and understand these challenges in both the VCM and CCM, drawing insights from academic literature and qualitative thematic analysis of interviews with founders in the VCM space. Moreover, it indicates how blockchain technology could be used as a novel approach to solve these challenges, with a more comprehensive review of the application of blockchain to be discussed in later chapters of this anthology.

The remainder of this chapter is structured as follows. First, it analyses the intricacies of the VCM, highlighting the significant potential they hold for climate action. However, through issues such as market integrity, the varying quality of carbon credits, and regulatory framework deficiencies, this potential is hindered. These challenges contribute to a fragmented market, further complicated by fraudulent activities and the pervasive issues of double-counting and double-issuance of credits. Furthermore, the lack of transparency and poor price discovery pose significant barriers to market scalability and participation. Second, we present a thematic qualitative analysis based on interviews of industry players specifically working on blockchain solutions to solve the inherent challenges of the VCM conducted in 2022. This analysis offers insights from a participant's perspective on the VCM and reveals the depth of market fragmentation, governance challenges, financing gaps, restricted market accessibility, and the operational hurdles in monitoring, reporting, and verification (MRV) processes.

By examining voluntary markets and integrating insights from qualitative research, this chapter contributes to a more nuanced understanding of the current state and the interdependent challenges. It emphasises the need for enhanced governance, regulatory clarity, and innovative solutions to ensure that carbon markets can effectively contribute to the global fight against climate change.

2 Challenges in voluntary carbon markets

The VCM embodies significant potential to facilitate climate action; however, its current state is fraught with severe challenges that compromise its function and scalability. A cursory review of the literature reveals that issues of market integrity, ranging from the quality of carbon credits to regulatory frameworks, take centre stage in the collective academic and industry critique.[6]

Market integrity is severely hampered by a lack of precise and universal definitions and benchmarks for what constitutes 'high-quality' carbon credits. Criteria such as additionality, prevention of double-counting, carbon leakage avoidance, and permanence are variably applied, leading to diverse, and often non-comparable, credit types.[7] Contrasting the tightly regulated ETS under MiFID in the EU, VCM carbon credits suffer from the absence of a unified regulatory status, resulting in a largely ungoverned market characterised by varying qualities and types of carbon credits.[8] Added to this, the VCM was also impacted by fraudulent activities, including the sale of counterfeit or non-existent credits and the manipulation of project metrics to falsely inflate credit counts.[9] Perhaps the most prominent integrity issues are double-counting and double-issuance of credits, as articulated by Interpol (2013).[10] Double-counting occurs within and across borders, with reductions in GHG emissions claimed multiple times by both host nations of reduction projects and purchasers of carbon credits, confounding actual climate mitigation progress.[11] Meanwhile, double-issuance refers to projects registered through multiple standards bodies, further complicating the market landscape.

Transparency, an essential pillar for a robust VCM, remains deficient. Post-issuance traceability of credits is impaired, obscuring the transaction history of emissions avoided or reduced.[12] Variance in project quality creates a heterogeneous market and a trust deficit for investors and end users. Additionally, with many low-quality credits remaining unsold, the market faces an oversupply, leading to low prices and unclear returns on investment for climate change mitigation endeavours. While some investors are willing to pay premiums to support such initiatives, the market's opacity and inefficiencies deter wider participation.[13]

Crucial to advancing the VCM are concerted efforts for enhanced governance and regulatory clarity paralleled with ardent calls for standardisation. Such actions, for example, the Core Carbon Principles (CCPs) from the Integrity Council for the Voluntary Carbon Market (ICVCM), aim at achieving transparent, universally recognised quality benchmarks for credits, simplifying pricing, and invigorating market participation.[14] In this light, the adoption of Article 6 mechanisms within the Paris Agreement is seen as a promising step towards offering nations cost-effective mitigation options, provided there is a clear understanding and implementation of additionality. This concept is fundamental in determining if emission reductions are genuine, requiring a rigorous examination of whether such reductions surpass business-as-usual scenarios.[15] To circumvent the inflation of emission credits, experts suggest an algorithmic approach to assess activities against NDC stipulations, ensuring mitigation actions are verifiable and quantifiable.[16] Lastly, to achieve integration with compliance markets, careful policy analysis is imperative. A credible and transparent VCM may emerge as an impactful tool against climate change, provided stakeholders, including regulators, project developers, and technologists, can navigate and break down the market complexities delineated herein.

In addressing these mentioned multifaceted challenges, blockchain technology is often posited as a transformative solution. Distributed ledger technology (DLT), with its inherent transparency and record immutability, could theoretically mitigate some of the aspects of fraud and double-counting risks. Still, these approaches encounter complex challenges, and a lack of comprehensive and systematic reviews of blockchain initiatives limits understanding of their potential impact on the VCM.[17]

3 Qualitative analysis of the voluntary carbon market

This section delivers the findings from the qualitative thematic analysis. Having explored the broad challenges and briefly how blockchain could help in the VCM, it becomes apparent that these markets are complex and multi-faceted. To deepen our understanding of these challenges, especially within the VCM, we conducted eleven semi-structured interviews in 2022 with experts that all had a C-level position and at least five years of experience in the VCC market. The interviews were recorded and transcribed and analysed through thematic qualitative analysis. The goal is to identify the challenges within the legacy system of the VCM from a market participant perspective. The qualitative thematic analysis of the interview data included repeated analysis cycles from which we derived four main challenges identified in the VCM. First, the differences between standard providers in the market and the lack of transparency have resulted in opaque market structures. Second, the lack of global governance results in substantial fluctuations in project quality, requiring investors to conduct extensive research and leverage expertise, which in turn hinders broader adoption. Third, the financing gap refers to the challenge where nature-based solutions (NBS) projects require upfront investment but generate returns only after successful implementation. Finally, the dominance of over-the-counter (OTC) trading in the VCM restricts accessibility to carbon credits, limiting participation from a broader range of stakeholders.

3.1 Opaque market structure

A key challenge in the VCM, as identified through the qualitative thematic analysis, is its opaque market structure in legacy systems, which leads to many adverse chain effects across the VCM. Interviewees repeatedly pointed to the historical fragmentation of standards as a major issue, along with the presence of numerous intermediaries, such as brokers, which has contributed to market opacity. Many interviewees highlighted that this lack of transparency leads to inefficiencies and fraud. The trading history of one carbon credit is intransparent due to the market's OTC trading venues. One co-founder reported from his experience:

> Carbon credits were partially purchased for USD 3/tCO_2 in South Africa, which traded in Germany on the market for USD 15/tCO_2. Legacy systems take much value out of the market, and in that way, the VCM will not scale. (Co-Founder, personal communication, 2022)

Traditional standards such as Verra or Gold Standard dominate the market, with approximately 80% of projects passing through Verra for verification and registry documentation. These entities act as sole registry operators but do not facilitate direct trading. In most cases, the current owner of a carbon credit is not publicly disclosed. As a result, interviewees emphasised the difficulty potential buyers face in identifying credit owners for transactions. Additionally, low transparency leads to higher risks for brokers, compelling them to charge higher margins and intensifying market inefficiencies.

The opaque market structure and fragmentation through different standard bodies in the legacy system have further adverse effects on market participants on the supply and demand side. First, opacity in the OTC market and fragmentation hamper transparent price signals, which leads to inefficient pricing of carbon credits. Consequently, new project development is impeded due to the lack of price signals. One co-founder stresses that this problem becomes especially evident for potential project developers geographically separated from critical buyers primarily situated in the northern hemisphere.

> The lack of transparency means there are no price signals for African landowners, that need to base decisions on project development opportunities via transparent price signals. (Co-Founder, personal communication, 2022)

The thematic analysis finds that the lack of transparency in the market leads to a lack of price signals and high price premiums through intermediation. As a result, opaque markets do not only have adverse effects on the supply side but also on the demand side. Purchasing is complex as there is no widely adopted pricing benchmark for comparable carbon credits. Many interviewees confirm the vast differences in project quality, intensifying the problem of the absence of price signals. Buyers lack confidence in the market due to the difficulty of assessing project quality and determining whether the price they pay reflects the project's actual value. Additionally, buyers must rely on intermediaries to facilitate transactions. Thus, the core challenge of maintaining and verifying the integrity of the VCM and individual VCCs can also, partially, be attributed to the lack of transparency. This problem includes questions such as the performance, that is, the fulfilment of set goals, or the existence of projects associated with the credits. When buying carbon credits for a project, it is not easy to understand the project's level of permanence or the associated co-benefits. Depending on the project type, co-benefits are defined as the additional benefits on communities, society, or biodiversity. The thematic analysis finds that there could often be negative co-benefits. The lack of transparency at the project level and in the market makes it difficult for investors to understand what a fair price for a given carbon credit is. Even if the trading of carbon credits was transparent, it is still challenging to understand a reasonable price for a given carbon credit when there is no underlying transparency on the quality and the nature of the projects. The thematic analysis adds further evidence to challenges in carbon markets as it identifies that the opaqueness of the market, in addition to fragmentation of standards, imposes complexities and effort on potential buyers and impedes efficient pricing.

3.2 Lack of global governance

Another major challenge in the market identified by the qualitative thematic analysis is the lack of global governance and oversight over key participants in the VCM. This also includes the issue of incomplete or unclear regulations and a lack of standardisation of contracts, decreasing the level of comparability. In addition, there is a limited amount of contract standardisation. The interviews have confirmed that the issue is not only evident in legacy systems but also increasingly caused by evolving blockchain initiatives addressing the VCM. One interview showed how creating new financial instruments referred to as 'ex-ante credits' by some blockchain initiatives like Flowcarbon adds a new layer of complexity (Head of Business Development, personal communication, 2022). Ex-ante credits are generally recognised as forward contracts for carbon credits, that is, the purchase of a promise for the delivery of a carbon credit in the future, aiming to accelerate the upfront financing for projects. Looking to the future, with forward carbon credits evolving as a trending financial instrument endorsed by some market participants, there is still no regulation. One interviewee exemplified this with the following excerpt:

> There is much uncertainty about what is actually in the contracts. That is one of the most significant challenges on the demand side. Customers need to know what they are purchasing, and regulations around the standardisation of contracts can create more customer confidence. (Business representative, personal communication, 2022)

At the level of international carbon markets, considerable ambiguity exists around the use of carbon credits generated in the VCM towards the Nationally Determined Contributions (NDCs) in the Paris Agreement. According to a business representative (personal communication, 2022), there are the first countries that count carbon credits produced in their country to reach the NDC goals of the individual countries and thus cannot be used for compensation purposes in the VCM. A business representative remarks on the following ambiguity around NDCs as follows:

> We do not know which countries will take this step, which will not, and what exactly it will look like. (Business representative, personal communication, 2022)

These findings add further relevant insights into the challenges of carbon markets. Many interviewees draw a critical consequence that the lack of global governance in coordinating international political matters and contract standardisation leads to less market liquidity, which is a central obstacle to growing the VCM. The thematic analysis has shown that carbon blockchain initiatives add a new layer of complexity in setting contract standardisation. While global initiatives such as the Taskforce on Scaling Voluntary Carbon Markets (TSVCM) can add to the standardisation component, they do not provide policy guidance on matters presently associated with international negotiations, such as the regulations underlining Article 6 of the Paris Agreement. Once the negotiations are finalised, the VCM needs to comply with these guiding principles, which could provide beneficial regulatory guidance but could also potentially harm maturing business models within the VCM.

3.3 Lack of supply

Another challenge in the VCM identified by the qualitative thematic analysis of the interviews is the lack of project supply. The problem can also be related to the previously highlighted challenges but is further increased by a substantial financing gap in NBS, especially for small-sized projects. One co-founder particularly points out the geographic gap between project issuance and buyers as an obstacle to scaling NBS:

> Project financing in the global south is a significant problem, involving all financial requirements up to the sale of carbon credits. While projects in the northern hemisphere are relatively easy to finance, the global south is affected by a large financing gap. (Co-founder, personal communication, 2022)

The thematic analysis reveals that there is primarily a financing gap prevailing in the pre-financing stage of NBS and is associated mainly with the inefficiencies of legacy systems. Ultimately, land and human capital are available but financing is the biggest challenge. Funding is primarily required for project development itself as well as the verification of standards. As MRV processes cannot be fully automated (yet), verifiers of traditional standards like Verra or Gold Standard demand huge costs for on-site visits unbearable for smaller projects:

> The projects involve several verification steps, while the pre-financing at the first stage alone costs about EUR 100,000. (Co-founder, personal communication, 2022)

Interview partners also highlight that often pre-financiers such as banks only step in too late. Generally, this issue hampers the verification of smaller projects, but ultimately many NBS start as small-scale projects that could lead to high carbon sequestering potential when scaled. One co-founder highlights the presence of this challenge for smaller projects even in the northern hemisphere. The choice of applied standards depends mainly on the MRV costs and the associated plot size of the afforestation project. A co-founder from a German start-up demonstrates the issue with the following example of afforestation projects in Germany:

> External verification such as the Gold Standard or Verra would not be worthwhile when starting with pilot projects because of the small size. In Germany, many forest owners may own plots scattered around regions. (Co-founder, personal communication, 2022)

The thematic analysis revealed costly MRV processes, high verification costs, especially in relative comparison to small projects, and a lack of financing for NBS in the pre-financing stage, hindering project development and thus, VCC supply. Furthermore, the challenges stem from costly processes to verify and issue carbon credits. The processes encompass submitting project descriptions at the beginning of the life cycle, validation by third-party auditors, and the verification of the actual emission reports. The registries and standard bodies often operate in analogue and manual processes, resulting in high costs. Some projects can cost up to USD 60,000 for verification by a third-party auditor. In addition, the thematic analysis revealed that validation and verification work is not always of sufficient quality, creating an increasing delay in the verification of projects because the information is incomplete for the methodology used for carbon credit issuance.

3.4 Restricted accessibility

Another challenge in the market identified by the qualitative thematic analysis is the limited access to carbon credits, including barriers to market entry. One co-founder stresses that gatekeepers still dominate carbon markets. Licenses or registrations are often required to trade carbon credits. In addition, another co-founder remarks on the lack of accessibility to advanced financial instruments, such as forward contracts for carbon credits, and argues that the market continues to face weak demand. He suggests that the issue can be resolved by creating more accessible purchase mechanisms, especially for retail buyers, and enhancing market appeal through innovative financial instruments:

> A big problem that some disagree with is the demand problem, which is increasingly solved because companies commit themselves to become CO_2 neutral. The concept has not arrived with the accessibility and penetration needed at the retail level. (Co-founder, personal communication, 2022)

Interview findings indicate that persistent barriers to accessing carbon credits remain a key challenge in legacy VCM markets. However, accessibility is just one of several challenges the market faces. Interviewees also point out that the concept of offsetting has yet to reach the necessary scale at the retail level. While demand for carbon credits is projected to increase over the following decades, both individual and institutional investors still have a limited understanding of offsetting, preventing broader market adoption. One co-founder (personal communication, 2022) claims that awareness of the business-to-customer (B2C) sector will be built only through better accessibility and attractive financial use cases.

4 Conclusion

VCM play a critical role in mitigating climate change. However, this study highlights several challenges they face. Our analysis highlights significant barriers to their effectiveness, including issues of market integrity, transparency, and regulatory deficiencies. The fragmentation of standards and lack of unified regulatory frameworks hinder the scalability and credibility of carbon markets. Furthermore, the absence of global governance and standardisation complicates the seamless integration needed for these markets to function optimally.

Addressing these multifaceted challenges requires concerted efforts towards improved governance and the establishment of clearer regulatory frameworks.

By enhancing regulatory clarity and embracing technological innovations, the potential for carbon markets to become robust tools for combating climate change can be realised. Furthermore, collaboration between research and practice is required to gain a deeper understanding of the complexities of carbon markets and offer insights on how to enhance their credibility, transparency, and overall effectiveness in advancing sustainable development.

Notes

1 Rebecca Lindsey and Luann Dahlman, 'Climate Change: Global Temperature' (Climate.gov 2024) http://www.climate.gov/news-features/understanding-climate/climate-change-global-temperature accessed 5 January 2025.
2 UNFCCC (United Nations Framework Convention on Climate Change), Status of Ratification of the Convention https://unfccc.int/process-and-meetings/the-convention/status-of-ratification-of-the-convention accessed 5 January 2025.
3 United Nations, Kyoto Protocol to the United Nations Framework Convention on Climate Change (1998) https://unfccc.int/resource/docs/convkp/kpeng.pdf accessed 10 January 2025.
4 UNFCCC (United Nations Framework Convention on Climate Change), Key Aspects of the Paris Agreement https://unfccc.int/most-requested/key-aspects-of-the-paris-agreement accessed 5 January 2025.
5 Harry Fearnehough and others, 'Future Role for Voluntary Carbon Markets in the Paris Era: Final Report' (Umweltbundesamt (German Environment Agency) 2020) https://www.umweltbundesamt.de/sites/default/files/medien/5750/publikationen/2020_11_19_cc_44_2020_carbon_markets_paris_era_0.pdf accessed 5 January 2025.
6 Tim Adams, Bill Winters and Annette Nazareth, 'Taskforce on Scaling Voluntary Carbon Markets – Phase II Report Summary' (Institute of International Finance 2021) https://www.iif.com/Portals/1/Files/TSVCM_Phase_2_Report_Summary.pdf accessed 5 January 2025; Christopher Blaufelder and others, 'A Blueprint for Scaling Voluntary Carbon Markets to Meet the Climate Challenge' (McKinsey & Company 2021) https://www.mckinsey.com/~/media/mckinsey/business%20functions/sustainability/our%20insights/a%20blueprint%20for%20scaling%20voluntary%20carbon%20markets%20to%20meet%20the%20climate%20challenge/a-blueprint-for-scaling-voluntary-carbon-markets-to-meet-the-climate-challenge.pdf accessed 5 January 2025; International Criminal Police Organisation (INTERPOL), 'Guide to Carbon Trading Crime' (2013) https://www.interpol.int/content/download/5172/file/Guide%20to%20Carbon%20Trading%20Crime.pdf accessed 5 January 2025.
7 Blaufelder and others (n 6).
8 Malwina Burzec and Kasia Kaczynska Lewis, 'Voluntary Carbon Market' (EY (Ernst & Young) 2021) https://www.ey.com/en_pl/law/voluntary-carbon-market accessed 5 January 2025.
9 INTERPOL 'Guide to Carbon Trading Crime' (n 6).
10 INTERPOL 'Guide to Carbon Trading Crime' (n 6).
11 Lambert Schneider and others, 'Double Counting and the Paris Agreement Rulebook' (2019) 366 Science 180; Fearnehough and others (n 5).
12 Blaufelder and others (n 6).
13 Rupert Edwards, 'Harnessing Private Investor "Willingness-to-Pay" for Climate Change Mitigation: A Mechanism to Co-Fund Public Commitments to Achieve the Goals of the Paris Agreement' (Forest Trends 2019) https://www.forest-trends.org/wp-content/uploads/2019/05/doc_5752.pdf; Adam Sipthorpe and others, 'Blockchain Solutions for Carbon Markets Are Nearing Maturity' (2022) 5 One Earth 779.
14 Integrity Council for the Voluntary Carbon Market (ICVCM), The Core Carbon Principles (CCPs) https://icvcm.org/core-carbon-principles/ accessed 5 January 2025.
15 Axel Michaelowa and others, 'Additionality Revisited: Guarding the Integrity of Market Mechanisms under the Paris Agreement' (2019) 19 Climate Policy 1211.

16 Axel Michaelowa and Sonja Butzengeiger, 'Ensuring Additionality under Art. 6 of the Paris Agreement: Suggestions for Modalities and Procedures for Crediting of Mitigation under Art. 6.2 and 6.4 and Public Climate Finance Provision under Art. 6.8' [2017] Discussion paper https://perspectives.cc/wp-content/uploads/2023/10/Ensuring_additionality_under_Art._6_of_the_Paris_agreement_Michaelowa_Axel__Butzengeiger_Sonja_2017.pdf accessed 5 January 2025; Michaelowa and others (n 16).
17 Edward Dodge, 'Chapter 16 – Carbon Deposits—Using Soil and Blockchains to Achieve Net-Zero Emissions' in Alastair Marke (ed), *Transforming Climate Finance and Green Investment with Blockchains* (Academic Press 2018) https://www.sciencedirect.com/science/article/pii/B9780128144473000161 accessed 5 January 2025.

Peter Gruber, Leah Kling, and Eric Nowak

3 Conditions for tokenisation of carbon standard-issued credits as third-party crypto instruments

Abstract: This chapter reviews tokenisation of voluntary carbon credits (VCCs). While tokenisation as a concept promises several advantages, current initiatives are plagued by issues revolving around time and cost, fragmentation and infrastructure, and trust and integrity. Based on a first principal analysis of the workings and promises of blockchain technology, we provide a set of conditions for successful blockchain solutions in the voluntary carbon market. We explicitly recommend native tokenisation managed by well-established carbon registries. Finally, we present specific recommendations for a blockchain-based VCC ecosystem that offers opportunities for third parties to drive innovation and market growth.

Keywords: Blockchain, Carbon Credits, Sustainability, Tokenisation, Voluntary Carbon Market

1 Introduction — **48**
2 Literature review — **49**
  2.1 Carbon markets — **49**
  2.2 Issues with the current VCM — **50**
  2.3 Blockchain — **53**
3 Tokenisation of Verra's VCUs and the subsequent ban — **56**
  3.1 Method of tokenisation by Toucan, Moss and C3 — **56**
  3.2 The Ban on tokenisation by Verra and Gold Standard — **59**
4 Three options for the VCM — **60**
  4.1 No tokenisation by existing registries — **61**
  4.2 Tokenising traditional credits — **61**
  4.3 Native tokenisation — **63**
  4.4 What tokenisation cannot solve — **64**
5 Our solution — **65**
  5.1 Choosing a blockchain and token type — **65**
  5.2 Creating the smart contract — **66**
  5.3 Market design — **66**
  5.4 What registries should avoid — **68**
6 Conclusion — **68**

https://doi.org/10.1515/9783111706719-003

1 Introduction

In recent years, the global fight against climate change has accelerated initiatives to address rising global temperatures and other environmental challenges. The Paris Agreement of 2015 has been pivotal in aligning global efforts to limit the increase in global temperatures to 2°C above pre-industrial levels with an emphasis on limiting temperature increases to the more ambitious target of 1.5°C above pre-industrial levels.[1] As part of these efforts, the Paris Agreement emphasises the need to achieve a balance between human-caused greenhouse gas emissions and removals by carbon sinks.[2] Regulatory schemes to limit carbon emissions have been in place since 1990 but have only seen significant growth in scope over the past decade to the point where they currently cover 24% of global greenhouse gas (GHG) emissions.[3] In comparison, a voluntary carbon market (VCM) aimed at carbon removals and additional mitigation arose in the early 2000s with the American Carbon Registry issuing the first voluntary carbon credit (VCC) in 2002.[4] Since then, numerous independent carbon registries have been created, and the market has rapidly expanded. Currently, an estimated 2 billion VCCs have been issued by large independent registries, representing projects across various sectors, geographies, and vintage years.[5] Verra and Gold Standard are the two largest VCC registries, having issued an estimated 63.0% and 15.8% of all credits, respectively.

Tokenisation is the creation of digital representations of assets – including physical, financial, and intangible assets – on a blockchain. Carbon tokenisation – more precisely, tokenisation of carbon credits or carbon emission rights – is a relatively new concept that has been employed to create digital representations of VCCs on the blockchain. The first instance of carbon credit tokenisation dates to around 2017.[6] In the following years, initiatives aimed at creating carbon tokens proliferated. In 2021, Toucan, the largest carbon tokenisation project, was officially launched.[7] They tokenised just over 22 million of Verra's Verified Carbon Units (VCUs), representing approximately 2% of all Verra credits issued by 2021. Other smaller players were also tokenising Verra VCUs and Gold Standard's (GS) Verified Emissions Reductions (VERs) at this time, but their tokenised volumes were significantly lower than that of Toucan. Amid growing concerns from Verra and Gold Standard about the impact of tokenisation on the integrity of the VCM and their business models, they both updated their terms of service in May 2022 to, in effect, ban unauthorised tokenisation of their carbon credits.[8] This ban was justified as necessary to evaluate the impact of tokenisation on their business models and to address investor concerns about its implications. Following this, Verra and Gold Standard began public consultations to determine the best approach to addressing these concerns.[9] This chapter expands on the responses provided by Peter Gruber and Eric Nowak to Verra and Gold Standard's public consultations on carbon tokenisation, which were not publicly released.

The goal of any technological innovation in the VCM should be to provide funding for projects. The current VCM faces challenges on both the supply and demand sides of the market. The challenges are so pervasive that 25% of market participants find them prohibitive, completely preventing their participation in the market.[10] Improving market efficiency not only directs funds towards projects in need – providing investors with financial returns in the form of carbon credits – but also facilitates CO_2 capture and mitigation. In this chapter, we examine the structure of the current VCM, existing tokenisation initiatives, and the fundamentals of blockchain as first principles. This foundation allows us to articulate our proposed native tokenisation solution for the market. Native tokenisation is the process where VCCs are issued directly on-chain, with all registry data stored on the blockchain, rather than being recorded in traditional registries first. We explain how this approach addresses a number of existing challenges in the VCM and propose specific requirements and roles for traditional registries within our proposed solution.

The chapter will proceed as follows: first, we establish the foundational knowledge through a literature review. We begin with a primer on the importance and functioning of carbon markets, followed by a detailed explanation of blockchain technology—covering different types of databases (centralised, decentralised, and distributed ledger technology), innovations that have addressed early blockchain limitations (e.g., Layer 2 solutions), and the energy consumption and carbon footprint of blockchain. From this, we build the understanding of blockchain's relevance to carbon markets, particularly its potential for implementation under Article 6.2 of the Paris Agreement, the only formal literature currently available on the subject.

We then provide a detailed account of the events surrounding VCM tokenisation, focusing on key facts and clearly outlining the tokenisation system design that operated on a large scale between 2020 and 2022. Having developed the necessary background, we present the three primary strategies for addressing tokenisation by traditional registries, relating these to existing challenges observed in the market. From this analysis, we clarify which problems tokenisation can and cannot solve and recommend the solution of native tokenisation. Finally, we offer a specific list of recommendations for implementing this solution and explicitly outline what traditional registries should avoid doing.

2 Literature review

2.1 Carbon markets

In a 2013 study, evaluating 11,944 scientific articles examining global warming, it was found that there is a general consensus among scientists that global warming is a scientifically observed fact and is primarily driven by human activities.[11] Studies spanning decades collectively agree on the impact of CO_2 and its equivalents (CO_2e) on global warming.[12] Estimates of per capita global GHG emissions in 2019 ranged from 2.6 to 19 metric tonnes of CO_2e (tCO_2e), underscoring the need for urgent action to mitigate emissions.[13]

To curb rising global CO_2e levels, policymakers have implemented regulatory mechanisms that impose financial costs on emissions and incentivise reductions. These schemes are implemented by regional, national, and international governments and bodies, often in the form of a carbon tax or the issuance of emission allowances. Carbon taxes price all emissions produced by an entity, determining a cost based on the level of pollution, to be paid to the government. Complementarily, emission allowances are issued to companies through emission trading systems (ETSs), where they can bid for allowances that permit them to produce a predetermined level of emissions. The objective of this market is to impose a financial cost directly linked to emissions.

While regulatory schemes play an important role in reducing GHG emissions, they currently only cover 24% of total annual recorded emissions.[14] Many countries face significant barriers to implementing these systems, including political resistance, economic constraints, and governance challenges. VCMs offer a distinct value proposition compared to regulatory schemes. Instead of charging for emissions, the VCM incentivises carbon mitigation and capture by issuing credits based on the amount of CO_2e a project has captured or avoided relative to business-as-usual baselines. These credits can then be sold, providing additional revenue streams for projects aimed at reducing emissions. In effect, this creates a positive financial incentive, contrasting with the approach of regulatory schemes. The VCM plays a crucial role in facilitating funding for projects directly aimed at combating climate change.

The general structure of the VCM is discussed in Chapter 1; here, we focus on its importance in combating climate change. This market provides an important supplement to regulatory efforts aimed at limiting emissions, especially in developing countries that often lack the governance required to implement effective regulatory schemes.[15] The funds channelled through the VCM are used to fund diverse projects, importantly, forestry and land-use projects which are key to reducing atmospheric carbon.[16] However, despite the potential of the VCM, it captures only a fraction of global GHG emissions. In 2023, an estimated 5.7 billion VCCs were issued, with 1.9 billion originating from independent mechanisms such as Verra and Gold Standard.[17] Comparatively, the 1.9 Gt CO_2e offset by the voluntary market is still dwarfed by the massive 53.0 Gt CO_2e released into the atmosphere in 2023.[18] For this market to scale, both experts and participants have noted a number of core issues that must be addressed before it can expand.[19]

2.2 Issues with the current VCM

The VCM faces far-reaching issues affecting every level of its functioning, ranging from criticisms and debates over methodologies to difficulties accessing markets for buying and selling credits.[20] The challenges can be categorised into two primary categories: scientific and economic. We will focus on addressing proposed solutions to the economic challenges while leaving the scientific basis and application of standards to experts well-versed in scientific methodologies for measuring carbon emissions and removals. Numerous international news sources have published critiques concerning the scientific foundation and computational methodologies of carbon credits, with a particular emphasis on forestry credits.[21] We would be remiss not to address these concerns at all but will simply state that this is an area of significant debate within the carbon markets. Much of this criticism arises from the lack of incorporation of updated scientific findings and rigorous methodologies into some of the standards and methodologies applied in the market. Regarding economic challenges, numerous issues have been cited by both academic sources and widely available general publications. Primarily, these issues centre on the fundamental challenges for high-functioning markets, including high search costs, low transparency, barriers to participation, poor standardisation, and information asymmetry, among others.

Although many issues regarding the VCM have been discussed in numerous sources, to the best of our knowledge, only one publicly available source attempts to survey market participants to assess the actual scale of these issues. A 2023 survey conducted by Nasdaq of VCM participants indicated that multiple market issues are significantly inhibiting the flow of funds and limiting participation in the VCM.[22] These issues are pervasive across all types of participants, including project owners, financiers, intermediaries, market operators, investors, and, most notably, corporate end-users. In the survey, 56% of corporate end-users indicated that they were constrained by 51–100% in their ability to participate in the VCM. To better understand the types of issues faced across market stages, we present a chart that illustrates the extent of each issue by grouping the underlying survey data into broader categories and averaging the percentage of participants affected by each specific issue across market functions. In Figure 3.1, we see that cost and time-related challenges are pervasive among the activities of project listing, settlements, and verification. This is especially important regarding the settlement process, since this is the process that facilitates the trade of VCCs and the ability for investors to access this market. The challenges related to cost and time largely stem from the fact that 94% of participants rely on phone calls and emails to manage their current activities.[23] These difficulties are further exacerbated by market fragmentation. Consistent with broader discussions, fragmentation, and infrastructure issues pose significant challenges for participants, particularly in relation to transaction settlements, reinforcing concerns about market inefficiencies.

As of October 2023, an estimated 48 different standards schemes were in place, with recent years witnessing a significant increase in the emergence of new standards bodies.[24] Fragmentation is a major issue in the traditional VCM, where 52% of project financiers must navigate at least four registries.[25] Investors' lack of confidence in carbon credit quality and pricing leads to poor risk management and re-

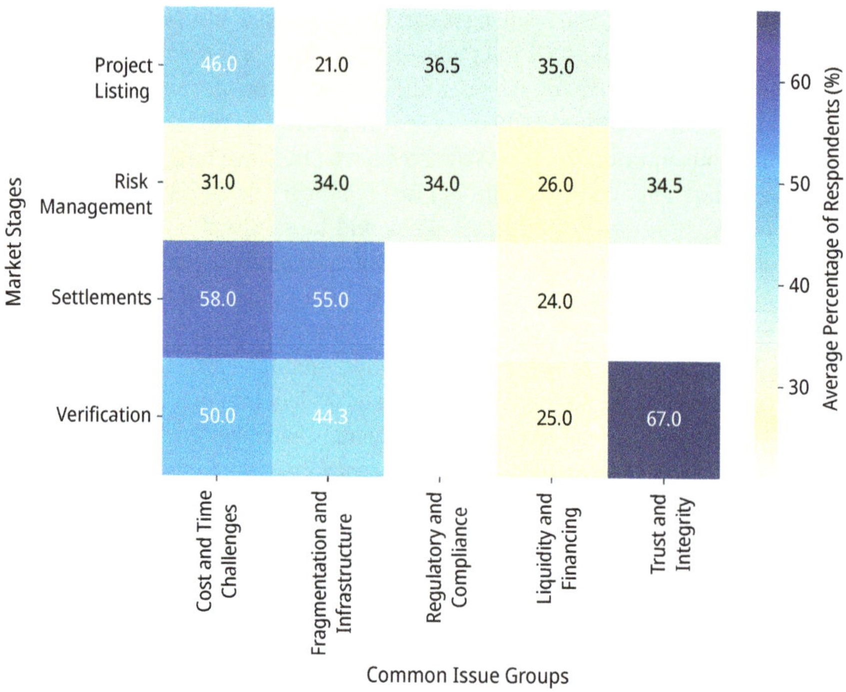

Figure 3.1: Heatmap of Averaged Percentage of Respondents Affected by Grouped Challenges Across Market Stages in the Voluntary Carbon Market.
Source: *Authors' Own, based on data from Nasdaq and The ValueExchange (n 8).*[26]

duces financiers' willingness to fund new projects. More specifically, significant challenges arise in utilising existing systems, not only due to their extensive requirements but also their reliance on outdated technology, which hinders market scalability. Considering the VCM system more broadly, many of its core challenges stem from low transparency and trust, with 30% of participants lacking confidence in pricing and 25% identifying efficiency issues.[27] Addressing this problem and evaluating potential solutions have led to the consideration of blockchain technology to mitigate some of these challenges.

Compounding these operational inefficiencies is a general lack of trust and integrity, particularly in project verification. Due to the market's fragmentation—with numerous standards and registries—participants struggle to maintain consistent verification criteria, further eroding confidence. These interconnected issues naturally prompt an examination of blockchain technology, which offers the potential for shared, transparent records and standardised processes to help address these fundamental challenges.

The VCM, as a subset of carbon markets, has been identified as a key area for the effective application of blockchain technology. However, this market currently faces substantial challenges that are far-reaching and hinder its proper functioning. Some of these challenges are well-suited for blockchain solutions, which could not only enhance market efficiency but also facilitate much-needed funding for carbon projects—despite the recognised potential of blockchain in the VCM, its application remains underexplored in academic research. Additionally, the market is largely influenced by relatively inexperienced players, whose experimental approaches have introduced both challenges and opportunities. While imperfect, these early efforts offer valuable lessons and insights for developing a robust and scalable blockchain-based solution tailored to the unique needs of the VCM. We will address the core issues in more detail in the background section, where we also address the current realities of this market.

2.3 Blockchain

2.3.1 Ledger databases

Digital, centralised databases have been in place for over 50 years.[28] They offer efficient management of data, enabling ease of maintenance and implementation due to their single-point architecture. These types of databases are beneficial for data used primarily by a few actors who trust each other. As computers spread, so did databases resulting in instances in which a single database was stored on multiple computers, presenting new challenges for maintaining data consistency. These types of distributed systems are greatly beneficial if there is a major risk of failure to a centralised source or if the centralised source cannot be trusted. However, decentralised systems present unique challenges since many copies of the database must be updated, maintained, and synchronised. This means higher hardware and computational costs associated with maintaining many copies of the database. In a system devoid of trust issues, the trade-off between centralised and decentralised databases is one between the security and maintenance costs of centralised systems versus hardware and energy costs in decentralised systems. Trust is not a problem that is automatically addressed by moving to a decentralised system; the decentralised system must be constructed in a way that makes data tampering very difficult and costly.

In a partial solution, ledger databases can help combat tampering by creating a database that is only additive and not reductive. This means the database is an immutable source of truth that is critical in auditing and tracing transactions. This means that past errors in the database cannot be corrected but rather require a corrective entry. This is inefficient for databases that are frequently updated, especially those with frequent changes such as tracking financial transactions, since funds can be spent before the correction is implemented causing issues. One benefit of ledger databases is their potential transparency. All transactions are recorded and thus auditable; however, this can be undesirable in cases where account holders wish to maintain privacy. This privacy issue can be addressed in two ways: first, account identifiers could be anonymous, such as providing an account number with no additional information. Second, private or semi-private ledgers could be utilised. Although as you increase the level of privacy by creating private ledgers, you make the system more centralised, exposing it to the problems of a centralised database. But, still in this system, you have the possibility of tampering with the ledger.

The blockchain is a distributed ledger of transactions that is cryptographically secured to render it tamper-proof. Concretely, any blockchain must solve two problems: to ensure that only legitimate transactions are added to the ledger and to prevent tampering with already recorded transactions. To do so, blockchains use two cryptographic functions, as well as one important mathematical concept. The blockchain, being public and distributed, allows everybody to submit transactions – including potentially fraudulent ones. Any blockchain must therefore first and foremost block unauthorised transactions (which could be used to steal cryptocurrency) or the impersonation of participants. The authenticity of transactions is ensured by adding a cryptographic signature to each transaction. This signature is unique to each account. The signature algorithm is designed to be easy to verify but hard to forge.

Everybody can verify the authenticity of a transaction – including miners (or validators), who collectively decide whether or not a transaction is authentic and should be added to the blockchain. This decision mechanism is called consensus. The details differ slightly between blockchains, but any consensus includes some form of incentives for miners to reject fraudulent transactions.

Once a transaction has been added to the blockchain, it must be ensured that it is not tampered with retrospectively. This is achieved by chaining transactions using a hash. The hash is a cryptographic function that summarises potentially very large input data into a single number, usually of length 256 bits. The hashing algorithm is designed to be easy to verify but hard to forge. To increase efficiency, several transactions are collected into a so-called block. Once a block is complete, the miners calculate the hash of the block data, which is added as the first entry to the next block. This chaining ensures that it is impossible to change one entry without having to change (and recalculate) every subsequent entry. While this technology was first devised in the 1990s in the context of digital timestamping, it was famously popularised by Satoshi Nakamoto, who created Bitcoin, the first cryptocurrency.[29]

2.3.2 Blockchain innovations

Blockchain technology has exploded in popularity, leading to many new applications of the technology. Notable was the development of smart contracts, digital contracts programmed to execute algorithmically, on the Ethereum blockchain.[30] The introduction of Ethereum was aimed at creating a more flexible blockchain with the ability to programme and facilitate fully decentralised applications on the blockchain. This type of contract effectively executes independently of any actors after two parties decide to enter the contract.[31] These smart contracts effectively pre-programme all the permissions of participant nodes and dictate who can carry out what function.[32]

Smart contracts are used for tokenisation, that is, to create a blockchain representation of real-world or digital assets. Such tokens can contain a limited amount of additional information, for example, the hash of a description of the asset. This ensures the integrity and immutability of any description of what a token represents. Tokens can be fungible or non-fungible, with the former being standardised like currency units or shares in a company, and the latter representing unique objects, such as art or real estate. Initial applications of fungible tokens were cryptocurrencies, while early non-fungible tokens (NFTs) were used to represent digital art.

This distinction is relevant in the context of the VCM. Projects are unique and not standardised and must, therefore, be represented by NFTs. A tonne of carbon emissions saved, on the other hand, is standardised and interchangeable; hence, VCCs must be represented by fungible tokens.

On many chains, smart contracts can be written to regulate how tokens can be created ("minted"), used, traded, and retired ("burned"). In a more complex form, smart contracts can execute transaction logic automatically if called upon. This makes it possible to create complex assets, including derivatives, on the blockchain. If smart contracts require real-world data, they can refer to Oracles.[33] Smart contracts can also be used to create, in effect, a distributed and secure database, such as a land registry.[34]

Programming smart contracts requires, beyond a certain level of technical expertise, a complete template that anticipates any contingency.[35] Recent developments have mitigated these challenges. Modern blockchains such as Solana or Algorand provide digital assets as native objects, obviating the need for smart contracts for the creation of basic assets. Generative AI and new languages such as PyTEAL or Rust easily facilitate the writing of more complex contracts. Smart contracts can also be written in such a way that they can be amended if all parties (or a predefined majority) agree. Independent auditors verify smart contracts, providing an opinion on their logic and security measures.[36]

While blockchain technology provides significant promise in reducing transaction costs, improving transparency, and facilitating transactions between parties who do not trust each other, there are still barriers to implementation. One major barrier is the negative public perception of blockchain due to its association with large-scale frauds and hacks, especially in the early days of Bitcoin.[37] Blockchains are also perceived to have a negative environmental impact – a particularly important concern for the VCM. However, this argument has always been flawed, as many relevant blockchains are either carbon-neutral (such as Algorand) or have a minimal carbon impact (such as Solana). With the transition to Ethereum 2, all relevant blockchains that could enable VCC solutions have a minimal carbon impact. It remains true that the Bitcoin chain requires an enormous amount of energy, but this chain is not suited for smart contracts anyway.

Lack of regulation and difficulties in tracing fraud have also been issues in this market but are slowly being addressed by the implementation of new rules and regulations, such as the Markets in Crypto-Assets Regulation in the European Union.[38] These developments are critical, especially as blockchain may be able to play a role in trustless systems and facilitate transactions and contracts that could not take place otherwise. One such application is in the VCM, where issues with trust and transparency have led to significant market frictions, prohibiting the scaling of this very important market.

2.3.3 Blockchain and carbon markets

Blockchain has been proposed as a solution for several markets that aim to support the net-zero transition, including energy grids, supply chains, ETS, and the VCM.[39] We are interested in the specific application to carbon markets, especially the VCM where the technology is proposed as a solution to address the core challenge of trust.[40] In related literature, tokenisation has been heralded as a possible solution to meet the goals outlined in Article 6.2 of the Paris Agreement.[41] The main concern it aims to address is that of double-counting in the mechanism while also maintaining transparency. Franke, Schletz, and Salomo outline a decision-making framework for whether to implement a blockchain solution in this market after advocating for its implementation in a related paper arguing that blockchain will help to integrate the numerous national-level emission accounting systems that are proving difficult for a fully functioning accounting mechanism.[42] Taking into account the recommendation of blockchain as a solution for the VCM, especially the mechanism outlined under the Paris Agreement, we focus on how blockchain may actually be implemented in carbon markets.

3 Tokenisation of Verra's VCUs and the subsequent ban

3.1 Method of tokenisation by Toucan, Moss and C3

Large-scale tokenisation of Verra credits began in 2021, with Toucan tokenising tens of millions of Verra VCUs (see Figure 3.2) by employing a smart contract to bridge the credits on-chain. 'Bridging' refers to the transfer of assets on or off the blockchain. Alongside Toucan, two other initiatives, Moss and C3, also bridged Verra's VCUs. Collectively, they bridged 25,352,895 Verra VCUs before ceasing these efforts and shifting to other activities. However, this activity ignited debate and raised concerns about the impact of tokenisation on the existing VCM.

Given concerns over the impact of tokenisation on the VCM, both Gold Standard and Verra implemented a ban on unauthorised tokenisation of their carbon credits in May 2022. We now outline the specific mechanisms through which Verra's VCUs were being tokenised and the rationale behind the ban. This analysis will help contextualise current market challenges within the broader VCM and its tokenisation while also providing background to support our proposed solution of native tokenisation.

Figure 3.3 illustrates the process used by Toucan, Moss, and C3 to bridge Verra's VCUs onto the blockchain. The process begins with the issuance of VCUs to project developers (step 1), which are then traded in over-the-counter (OTC) markets (step 2). At this stage, the tokeniser acquires ownership of the credits (step 3), and this ownership is updated within Verra's registry accounts. However, this information is not publicly accessible unless the account holder has opted to use a public sub-account to demonstrate ownership of the credits.

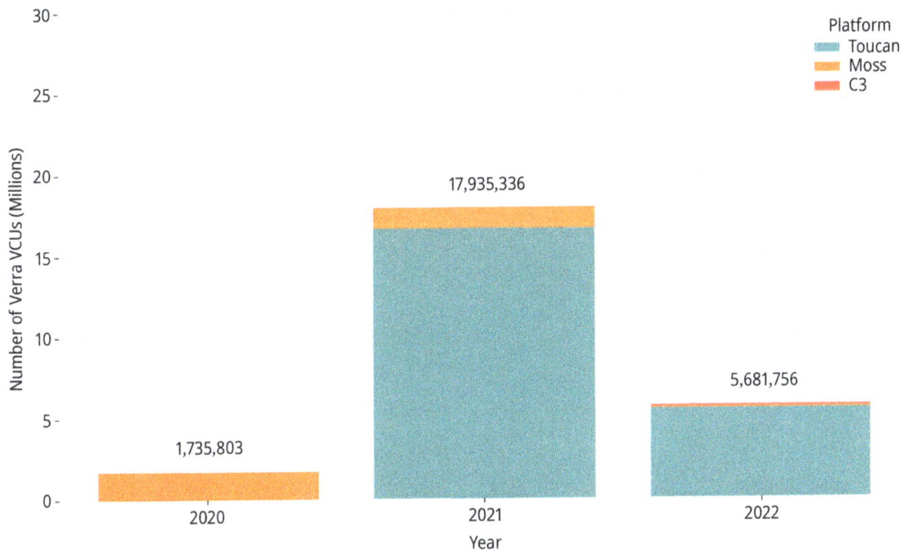

Figure 3.2: Verra VCUs Tokenised by the Three Major Carbon Bridges.
Source: *Authors' Own, based on data from Verra's VCU Registry.*[43]

The next step involves retiring the credits in Verra's VCU Registry (step 4). Tokenisation is then initiated via a predefined smart contract operating on the chosen blockchain (step 5). During this process, the serial numbers of the VCUs are embedded into the metadata of the minting transaction, attributing the newly minted token to its underlying VCU (step 6). Simultaneously, the wallet addresses receiving the tokens are recorded in Verra's registry under the retirement beneficiary. This dual recording on both the blockchain and Verra's registry completes the bridging process, with the token entering circulation on the blockchain as a fungible asset (step 7).

These tokenised credits are issued as fungible tokens, where one token corresponds to one carbon credit from the underlying pool of bridged credits. However, this method introduced potential risks, as low-quality credits could be bridged, degrading the overall pool quality. When a wallet address holding a token initiated a

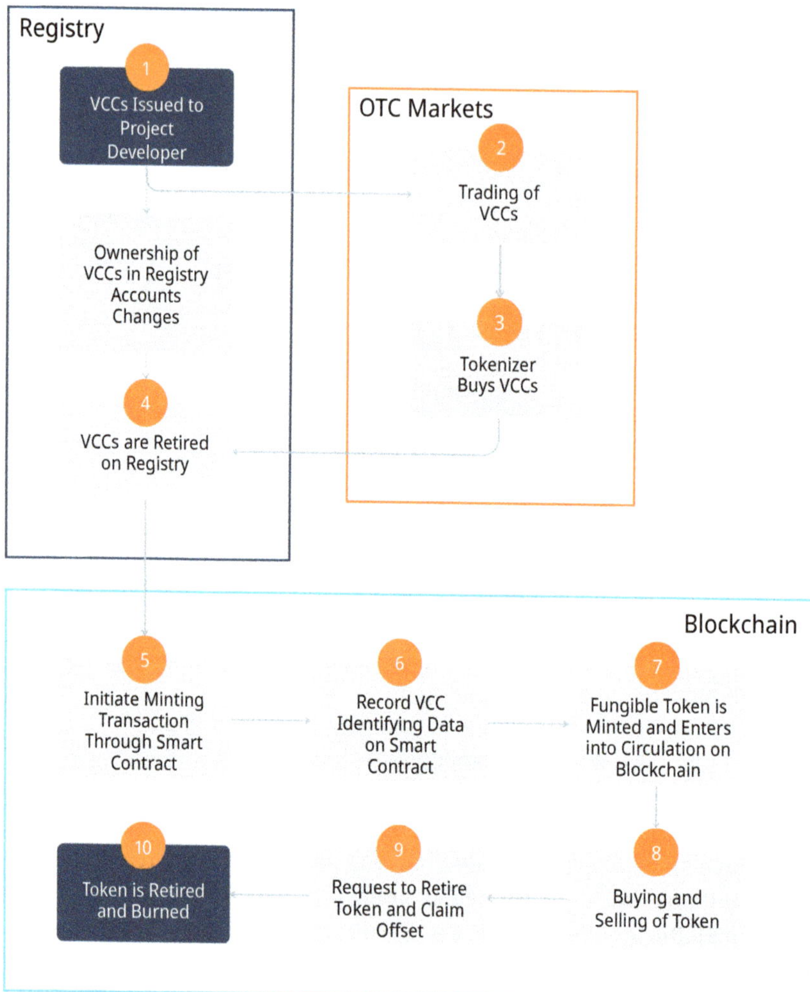

Figure 3.3: Process of Tokenising Verra's VCUs Used by Toucan, Moss, and C3.
Source: *Authors' Own.*

request to retire the token and claim the carbon offset (step 9), the token would then be retired and burned (step 10).

A key issue with this approach lies in the fact that Verra's terms and conditions state that the right to claim a carbon credit is extinguished upon its retirement in the registry. Despite this, the retired credits were traded on the blockchain under the assumption that they continued to represent valid claims on Verra's VCUs. This system required significant coordination between the traditional registry and the blockchain, as the actual claim to the carbon credit was only extinguished after a specific retirement request. This added complexity highlights the challenges of integrating blockchain technology with traditional registry systems.

3.2 The Ban on tokenisation by Verra and Gold Standard

Tokenisation of Verra's credits began in 2020, and by November 2021, Verra issued a statement regarding crypto market activities, specifically noting they were not responsible for tokenised credits and that, once credits are retired, the legal and beneficial interest in the credit is extinguished.[44] Despite this statement, tokenisation activities continued. Amidst growing concern over the practice, the International Emissions Trading Association (IETA) issued a document outlining initial guiding principles for carbon tokenisation.[45] Key recommendations included ensuring credit quality, synchronising tokens with underlying registries, avoiding the minting of tokens for retired credits, applying know-your-customer (KYC) checks in the crypto market, and solidifying investor safeguards, particularly for retail customers.

Despite these guidelines, operations tokenising VCCs proceeded unchanged, prompting Verra to raise specific concerns.[46] These included risks of fraud in the crypto market, lack of environmental integrity, reputational harm, regulatory uncertainty, and legal ambiguity. A pivotal issue leading to the eventual ban on unauthorised tokenisation was how the process was conducted. By retiring credits in the Verra registry prior to tokenisation, the practice created confusion for investors, as it was unclear who the beneficiary of the retired credits was. The intention of retiring a credit, according to Verra, is to signify that the retiring entity is claiming the carbon offset. This issue was explicitly addressed in Verra's Registry Terms of Use, which, in 2021,[47] stated:

> *The User acknowledges and agrees that, if the User wishes Verra to cancel or retire Instruments, upon such cancellation or retirement:*
> (a) *all legal and beneficial title and interests in such Instruments will be extinguished; and*
> (b) *neither Verra, the User, nor any other person with Legal or Beneficial Ownership Rights will have any further rights to take the benefit of such Instruments nor the underlying Environmental Benefits corresponding to such Instruments.*

It is evident that the act of retirement is intended to signal to investors that the claim on the credit has been extinguished. This is inconsistent with the subsequent advertising and sale of tokenised credits as claims on carbon credits. In this context, the tokenisation project acts as the user holding an account with Verra, through which they retired the offsets. However, these retired offsets were effectively securitised as digital assets, further complicating the interpretation of their status and use.

The practice of retiring credits on traditional registries and subsequently trading them in crypto markets had the potential to confuse investors and jeopardise the reputation of Verra, as well as Gold Standard, although the latter experienced minimal tokenisation of its credits. Consequently, in May 2022, both Verra and Gold Standard updated their Terms of Use and issued statements explicitly banning the unauthorised tokenisation of their credits.[48] To explore the potential for tokenisation of carbon credits and the integration of blockchain technology in the VCM, Verra and Gold Standard launched public consultations, engaging a range of experts to evaluate the conditions under which tokenisation could be permitted.[49]

The initial public consultations on the issue were concluded in January and February 2023.[50] The general consensus aligned closely with the initial guidelines of the IETA in 2021, suggesting that a viable solution involves creating custodial accounts where KYC checks are applied to entities participating in the tokenisation of credits.[51] This approach could potentially mitigate certain reputational risks.

However, maintaining such a dual system—combining both on- and off-chain registries—would introduce additional requirements. These include the capability to bridge credits back off-chain via a two-way bridge and the need for frequent synchronisation between centralised registry databases and the blockchain. Even with these measures, fundamental concerns, such as transparency, would remain unresolved within this framework.

For these reasons, we advocate for native tokenisation of the registries themselves. By adopting native tokenisation, traditional registries like Verra and Gold Standard can directly address critical market issues, including the pervasive lack of transparency and trust. The remainder of this chapter will clarify the problems that tokenisation can and cannot solve, followed by a detailed set of specific requirements necessary for implementing an effective native tokenisation solution.

4 Three options for the VCM

Currently, there are three approaches to addressing carbon tokenisation in the VCM. The first is to resist all forms of tokenisation. However, this is nearly unfeasible given the widespread existing implementation of tokenisation and the growing competition from native tokenisation projects. Nonetheless, we will discuss the scenario of no tokenisation to contrast it with tokenisation solutions and illustrate the limitations of tokenisation in addressing VCM challenges.

The second approach is to permit the tokenisation of traditional VCCs, such as those issued by Gold Standard and Verra, which we examined in Section 3. While this approach has the potential to address some issues, such as improving transparency with respect to on-chain ownership, other challenges persist. This remains the case regardless of whether a two-way bridge—a possible solution for the VCM to allow credits to be bridged back off-chain—is implemented or not.

The third approach involves native tokenisation, a fully integrated blockchain solution where all aspects of the system operate on-chain from credit issuance to credit retirement. While this approach resolves the most significant challenges, it is still unable to address certain issues in the VCM, such as some types of fraud.

4.1 No tokenisation by existing registries

For the sake of comparability between systems and comprehensive analysis, we will examine a scenario in which no tokenisation occurs. This scenario should be understood as one in which all the previously discussed challenges from Section 2.2 persist within the traditional system, while native tokenisation projects continue to develop alongside the traditional system that solves some of the challenges but not others.

In this scenario, by taking no action, traditional registries cannot prevent new market entrants from implementing blockchain-based solutions. These blockchain solutions could pose a competitive threat to the business models of traditional registries and, in some cases, potentially displace them. While legacy systems may attempt to counteract this new competition, they would need to evolve significantly to address the same challenges that blockchain solutions aim to resolve—an endeavour that is inherently difficult within centralised frameworks.

The primary advantage of legacy systems is their established presence and the trust they have built among existing participants. However, trust alone is probably insufficient to address the fundamental transparency issues that continue to undermine market efficiency. Without enhanced transparency, risks such as double-counting and inefficient market functioning remain unmitigated.

4.2 Tokenising traditional credits

The second approach involves the tokenisation of traditional carbon credits—a solution previously implemented by Toucan and others, which became a source of controversy in the VCM. While this implementation presented certain challenges, it also introduced valuable mechanisms for addressing some of the existing inefficiencies in the market, especially those related to settlement. Blockchain enables fast and easy transactions, especially in contrast with the OTC structure of the current market. This would significantly reduce the cost and time associated with trading VCCs.

By tokenising traditional credits and creating on-chain representations, more transparency in ownership can be introduced. However, this transparency applies only to on-chain credits, while the ownership of paper-based credits remains obscured by traditional registry systems. As a result, it may remain unclear who holds the original traditional credits that were tokenised. One proposed solution to this issue is the use of immobilisation accounts, where credits are held for the entire period they are tokenised until retirement. While this approach could mitigate ownership ambiguities, it would require registries to modify their existing systems.

Beyond ownership transparency, tokenising traditional credits offers additional benefits. Blockchain technology, as a flexible and programmable infrastructure, allows for greater interoperability and efficiency in the carbon markets, particularly using smart contracts. It enables credit divisibility, facilitating broader market participation and supporting the development of new financial products, for example, fungible tokens that represent claims to a token pool, reducing risk. Furthermore, tokenisation enhances integration with other markets. Further integration with other stages of the VCM could be developed in the future, such as futures contracts. By reducing reliance on intermediaries, blockchain-based systems create a more streamlined and efficient trading environment, ultimately enhancing trust and market functionality.

While tokenising traditional credits addresses some challenges, primarily those related to trading, it fails to resolve others, such as data integrity, fragmentation, and double-counting. As illustrated in Figure 3.3, this system does not address issues arising from the processes that support the issuance of VCCs. This is particularly significant given that many project developers encounter substantial challenges in securing funding, listing projects, and meeting MRV requirements. Furthermore, concerns about the integrity of project-related information persist, as the potential for data tampering remains in the absence of secure, timestamped record-keeping that is publicly auditable.

Another major challenge is market fragmentation, which exacerbates issues related to time, cost, liquidity, and financing. Fragmentation arises from the increasing number of registries, methodologies, and standards—an issue that persists regardless of blockchain implementation. As dissatisfaction with existing solutions grows, alternative approaches will inevitably emerge unless traditional registries take proactive steps to improve their systems. Given blockchain's distinct value proposition for the VCM, new registries leveraging blockchain-based market solutions have already begun to reshape the market landscape.

Additionally, the tokenisation of traditional credits introduces an added layer of complexity, as it requires tokens to be issued on top of existing registry credits, necessitating coordination across multiple systems. This complexity amplifies the risk of double-counting, as there is no effective mechanism to control how many times a credit is tokenised or to track its use once tokenised. Without adequate safeguards, such a system risks undermining the very integrity and transparency that tokenisation aims to enhance.

Several problematic scenarios arise concerning the accurate counting of credits. First, a traditional credit can be retired and subsequently tokenised multiple times, as there is no robust mechanism to prevent this occurrence. In such cases, market efficiency is critical, as the system must be able to detect and address double-counting effectively. Second, a traditional credit could be tokenised without first being retired, creating multiple representations of the same credit, further increasing the risk of double-counting.

Additionally, concerns related to market reputation persist, particularly with the tokenisation of existing credits. This approach has already been perceived as confusing to investors (see Section 3.2), especially when tokenised representations of already retired credits are sold, a concern discussed earlier.

In summary, while tokenising traditional credits enhances transparency for on-chain transactions, introduces credit divisibility, and facilitates integration with other markets, it fails to fully address the core challenge of preventing double-counting. Additionally, the reputational risks associated with tokenising retired credits remain unresolved, unless significant innovations are introduced into existing systems. However, the extensive changes required to implement the necessary fixes and ensure the functionality of this system would demand considerable effort, outweighing the perceived benefits.

Given these limitations, we advocate for a native tokenisation solution. This approach not only addresses the challenges outlined here but also offers a more straightforward implementation while resolving inefficiencies that arose earlier in the VCC issuance process. The following section will explore the advantages of native tokenisation and why it represents the most effective approach for the market.

4.3 Native tokenisation

We believe that native tokenisation offers the most effective solution for the VCM by leveraging blockchain's unique attributes to enhance transparency and trust. By migrating entire registries onto a single blockchain, transparency is maximised, eliminating the need for synchronisation between multiple systems.

As previously discussed, tokenisation of traditional credits only provides partial transparency, as it applies solely to on-chain assets. In contrast, moving entire registries on-chain ensures full-system transparency, preventing opacity in any part of the market. A fully on-chain registry offers a publicly accessible audit trail, enabling participants to track ownership and transactions in real time.

Beyond transparency, native tokenisation facilitates the development of Web3 applications that can query, summarise, and present blockchain data in user-friendly formats. These applications can provide interfaces similar to traditional web platforms, making blockchain interaction more intuitive for market participants. Unlike fragmented systems where users must verify whether a credit exists on-chain and in a traditional registry, a fully on-chain registry eliminates these discrepancies, ensuring consistency across the entire system. This framework prevents overselling by making ownership records instantly and publicly verifiable.

Beyond improving market functioning, native tokenisation also enhances key processes such as project registration, MRV, and carbon credit data management. Integrating blockchain into MRV processes offers significant advantages in streamlining VCC issuance, particularly through the use of digital MRV (dMRV) systems, such as Oracles, which automate data verification. By reducing reliance on manual processes, native tokenisation can substantially improve efficiency, accuracy, and trust in credit issuance. Native tokenisation could also facilitate the creation of an on-chain governance system, allowing all stakeholders to participate in the management of carbon credits.

4.4 What tokenisation cannot solve

Native tokenisation resolves many of the key challenges in the current VCM. We have outlined the feasibility of the three primary solutions and their effectiveness in addressing existing inefficiencies. However, it is important to recognise that some challenges within the VCM cannot be solved by tokenisation alone.

The first is fragmentation across registries, standards, and methodologies. Market fragmentation occurs independently of tokenisation, as new players will continue to enter whenever inefficiencies persist and barriers to entry remain low. However, blockchain itself does not inherently drive fragmentation; rather, it is a tool that new entrants have leveraged to introduce solutions.

Another critical limitation is that tokenisation cannot prevent fraud at the project level. While tokenisation eliminates the double-selling of credits within a single registry, it does not prevent a project from registering with multiple registries and selling credits across different systems. Similarly, double-counting at the country and project levels remains an unresolved issue, as these systems are not integrated with blockchain-based registries.

Additionally, tokenisation is largely ineffective in preventing fraud in project documentation and monitoring. The creation of project documents and monitoring reports typically occurs before credits are issued, involving project developers and third-party verifiers. Since blockchain solutions are applied at the registry level, they cannot address fraud in the underlying project data. However, certain aspects of verification could be improved by integrating Internet of Things (IoT) devices and Oracles, which enable blockchain-based validation of project data and monitoring reports in select cases.

Having established the capabilities and limitations of tokenisation—particularly native tokenisation—in addressing VCM challenges, we now turn to specific design recommendations for implementing an effective native tokenisation system.

5 Our solution

We advocate for native tokenisation as the path forward for the VCM. Only through a native tokenisation system can core issues of transparency and trust be effectively addressed. While the advantages of blockchain technology have been discussed in previous sections, this section outlines the key requirements for designing an effective native tokenisation solution.

5.1 Choosing a blockchain and token type

When selecting a blockchain for tokenisation, its environmental impact—particularly its energy consumption and associated carbon emissions—must be carefully considered. This is especially relevant given that the VCM itself is designed to incentivise emissions reductions and removals. At a minimum, the blockchain chosen for tokenisation should utilise a proof-of-stake consensus mechanism. Ideally, a fully carbon-neutral blockchain should be used, such as Algorand, which is highly energy efficient and achieves carbon neutrality by offsetting emissions with carbon credits.

Once a blockchain is selected, an appropriate token standard must be determined. In this case, the registry should issue NFTs to represent carbon credits. Each NFT would serve as a unique digital representation of a specific carbon credit issued to a project for a particular vintage year, mirroring how traditional registries currently operate. It is essential to use NFTs rather than fungible tokens, as fungible tokens function more like pooled financial instruments and introduce additional risk management complexities. Instead, fungible tokens could be issued by other entities that develop structured systems for pooling NFTs and managing the associated risks.

Additionally, the implementation of NFTs should align with standard commodity contracts to facilitate market adoption and trading. This alignment must be explicitly considered during the design phase. Furthermore, NFTs should be designed to allow for fractionalisation, as this is crucial for expanding market participation. Fractionalisation enables smaller investors to enter the market and offset their personal carbon footprints, thereby increasing accessibility and liquidity within the VCM.

5.2 Creating the smart contract

When designing a blockchain solution for the VCM, care must be given to writing the smart contract that underlies the registry in a sound and secure manner. Third-party audits of the smart contract should be conducted to ensure the code is free of bugs and to increase trust among participants using the tokens generated and managed by the contract. A key aspect of smart contract design is the clear definition of minting and burning roles to ensure that only the appropriate parties can mint (issue) and burn (retire) tokens. Minting permissions should be granted exclusively to the registry itself, ensuring that only verified projects registered with the registry body can generate new tokens. This process could be further reinforced by integrating Validation and Verification Bodies (VVBs) into the smart contract, assigning them a validator role, which would be required to authorise the issuance of new credits. There are many design choices that must be considered when defining the smart contract roles to ensure that fraud risks are minimised. For instance, minting permissions should be strictly reserved for registries, as they are the designated issuers of credits, while burning permissions could be structured in a more flexible way. During design, it is also important to determine which project-related information should be recorded on-chain. The smart contract should define the metadata attached to tokens, ensuring that each token contains unique project identifiers such as vintage year and serial number. However, a key consideration is balancing transparency with computational efficiency—incorporating more information increases visibility but also demands greater computing power. The contract must be structured to maximise transparency without imposing excessive technical burdens, ensuring a practical and scalable implementation.

5.3 Market design

Aside from technical considerations, key market characteristics must be addressed to ensure the successful adoption of a native tokenisation solution. Market functioning considerations should focus on developing and administering the necessary financial products that are crucial for a well-functioning market. In implementing native tokenisation, registries should focus solely on issuing credits and leave the construction of more complex financial instruments to other entities, as registries are not specialised in administering such instruments. Allowing market participants to develop these financial products fosters competition, leading to more efficient and innovative market solutions.

Two key financial products should be developed to facilitate adoption and a fully integrated market. The first is the creation of fungible tokens that function as investment pools of carbon credits. Fungible tokens provide an opportunity for diversification, reducing the risks associated with participation in carbon markets. These pools would enhance price stability and increase liquidity for investors. Effective administration of these pools is crucial to prevent the inclusion of low-quality credits. Drawing lessons from the mismanagement of mortgage-backed securities during the 2007–2009 financial crisis, pool administration should align incentives and exhibit transparency to ensure trust in the system. Various models can be employed for managing token pools. One potential approach is to use a Decentralised Autonomous Organisation (DAO), where pool participants vote on which credits to include, mitigating the incentive to introduce low-quality credits. Other solutions could be designed to address this challenge, but the fundamental principle remains that registries should not engage in managing or creating these pools. The second key financial product is the creation of a futures market for carbon credits. If the entire registry is on-chain, this market can be efficiently structured using smart contracts. Smart contracts enable the automatic execution of agreements, reducing counterparty risk and enhancing market efficiency. By leveraging blockchain infrastructure, a futures market can ensure transparent, reliable, and automated contract execution.

Next is the need for standardisation. Standardising not only the structure of NFTs but also fungible tokens, futures, and other financial products is essential for increasing adoption and ensuring seamless integration across market participants. The establishment of standardised marketplaces supports liquidity, price discovery, and overall market efficiency.

Creating accessible marketplaces requires making them intuitive and easy for investors to engage with. This can be achieved by developing traditional web-based interfaces that abstract away the blockchain layer. While transparency remains a key feature, blockchain technology should not be presented as the primary focus for investors. Instead, emphasis should be placed on the practical benefits it provides, such as the ability to view summary information on circulating credits and to transparently audit retired credits.

To interact with the system, stakeholders will require a blockchain wallet in some capacity. However, efforts should be made to simplify this requirement through user-friendly integrations that minimise friction and facilitate seamless participation in the carbon market.

Requiring all participants to independently obtain a wallet service could deter adoption, making it a crucial consideration when designing the registry and marketplace infrastructure. Custodial wallets, while offering ease of use, come with legal and regulatory obligations that may complicate their integration into a platform. Non-custodial wallets provide an alternative, but participants must fully understand the risks associated with different wallet types to mitigate challenges that have historically plagued cryptocurrency markets, such as the loss of private keys, rendering wallets inaccessible. One possible solution is to engage a third-party service provider to offer custodial wallets that function as user accounts. Alternatively, participants could be given the choice to manage their own non-custodial wallets, depending on their level of familiarity with blockchain technology. Large institutional participants, such as corporations, would likely have the infrastructure to securely manage wallet keys using distributed databases and encryption technologies. Since blockchain wallets are anonymous by default, an option should be provided for organisations to verify and publicly claim their wallet addresses. This is essential for creating a transparent and auditable record of the carbon offsets retired by each entity and should be regarded as an industry standard. Having outlined the key considerations for registries implementing blockchain solutions and the market factors that must be addressed, it is now important to define the boundaries of registry responsibilities.

5.4 What registries should avoid

While moving registries on-chain can enhance transparency and trust, there are limits to the roles registries should assume. Registries should not function as decentralised exchanges (DEXs) where individuals deposit funds into accounts for purchasing credits. Administering a DEX requires specialised expertise that falls outside the scope of registries and involves complex legal and regulatory requirements. Similarly, registries should not be responsible for creating or managing complex financial instruments, as these activities should be left to market participants with the necessary expertise.

In summary, registries should remain focused on their core function—maintaining records of carbon credits. The primary recommendation is for registries to transition fully on-chain to leverage the benefits of blockchain technology.

6 Conclusion

Blockchain technology has the potential to fundamentally reshape the VCM by addressing key challenges related to transparency, trust, and efficiency. Through native tokenisation, where registries fully migrate their operations onto the blockchain, many of the existing inefficiencies in the VCM can be mitigated. Native tokenisation provides an immutable, publicly auditable ledger that enhances market accessibility and ensures greater accountability in credit issuance and trading. However, the benefits of tokenisation must be considered alongside its limitations. While it improves transparency and transaction efficiency, it does not address project-level fraud or guarantee the environmental integrity of underlying credits. Tokenisation alone cannot resolve issues stemming from inconsistencies in the application of methodologies and standards. To fully realise the potential of blockchain in the VCM, its implementation must be guided by strong principles and complemented by the adoption of environmentally sustainable technologies. As the market continues to evolve, solutions that integrate tokenisation with enhanced project verification and harmonised standards will be necessary. By addressing these challenges holistically, the VCM can strengthen its role in climate finance and contribute more effectively to global carbon reduction efforts. A well-implemented tokenisation framework will not only enhance trust and efficiency but also drive innovation and expand the impact of the VCM in advancing global sustainability objectives.

Notes

1 Paris Agreement (adopted 12 December 2015, opened for signature 22 April 2016, entered into force 4 November 2016) UNTS vol 3156 I-54113, art 2(1)(a).

2 Paris Agreement (adopted 12 December 2015, opened for signature 22 April 2016, entered into force 4 November 2016) UNTS vol 3156 I-54113, art 4(1).

3 World Bank Group, 'GHG Emissions Coverage | Carbon Pricing Dashboard' (World Bank 2024) https://carbonpricingdashboard.worldbank.org/compliance/coverage accessed 17 July 2024.

4 Barbara K Haya, Aline Abayo, Ivy S So, and Micah Elias, 'Voluntary Registry Offsets Database v11' (Berkeley Carbon Trading Project, University of California, Berkeley, May 2024) https://gspp.berkeley.edu/faculty-and-impact/centres/cepp/projects/berkeley-carbon-trading-project/offsets-database accessed 22 June 2024.

5 Barbara K Haya, Aline Abayo, Ivy S So, and Micah Elias (n4).

6 Veridium Labs, 'Veridium Labs Launches Token Sale, Creating Global Marketplace for Carbon Credits & Natural Capital' (The Blockchain 30 August 2017) https://www.the-blockchain.com/2017/08/30/veridium-labs-launches-token-sale-creating-global-marketplace-carbon-credits-natural-capital/ accessed 5 February 2025.

7 Toucan, 'About Toucan' (Toucan, 2024) https://toucan.earth/about-toucan/ accessed 5 February 2025.

8 Verra, 'Verra Addresses Crypto Instruments and Tokens' (Verra 2024) https://verra.org/verra-addresses-crypto-instruments-and-tokens/ accessed 5 February 2025; Gold Standard, 'Conditions for Consenting to Tokenisation of Gold Standard-Issued Credits' (Gold Standard 2025) https://www.goldstandard.org/consultations/conditions-for-consenting-to-tokenisation-of-gold-standard-issued-credits accessed 5 February 2025.

9 Verra, 'Public Consultation: Verra's Approach to Third-Party Crypto Instruments and Tokens' (Verra 3 August 2022) https://verra.org/public-consultation-verras-approach-to-third-party-crypto-instruments-and-tokens accessed 5 February 2025; Gold Standard, 'Gold Standard Announces Proposals to Allow Creation of Digital Tokens for Carbon Credits' (Gold Standard 14 September 2022) https://www.goldstandard.org/news/gold-standard-announces-proposals-allow-creation-digital-tokens-carbon-credits accessed 5 February 2025.

10 Nasdaq and The ValueExchange, 'Scaling Carbon Markets: A New Market Blueprint for 2024' (2024) https://www.nasdaq.com/solutions/marketplace-technology/scaling-carbon-markets-report accessed 26 November 2024.

11 John Cook, Dana Nuccitelli, Sarah A Green, Mark Richardson, Bärbel Winkler, Rob Painting, Robert Way, Peter Jacobs, and Andrew Skuce, 'Quantifying the Consensus on Anthropogenic Global Warming in the Scientific Literature' (2013) 8(2) *Environmental Research Letters* 024024.

12 Jule G Charney and others, *Carbon Dioxide and Climate: A Scientific Assessment* (National Academy of Sciences 1979); Gunnar Myhre, E J Highwood, K P Shine, and Frode Stordal, 'New Estimates of Radiative Forcing Due to Well-Mixed Greenhouse Gases' (1998) 25(14) *Geophysical Research Letters* 2715–2718.

13 IPCC, Climate Change 2023: Synthesis Report. Contribution of Working Groups I, II and III to the Sixth Assessment Report of the Intergovernmental Panel on Climate Change [Core Writing Team, Hoesung Lee, and José Romero (eds)] (IPCC 2023 Geneva) 184 https://www.ipcc.ch/report/ar6/syr/downloads/report/IPCC_AR6_SYR_FullVolume.pdf accessed 5 February 2025.

14 World Bank Group (n 3).

15 Vittoria Battocletti, Luca Enriques, and Alessandro Romano, 'The Voluntary Carbon Market: Market Failures and Policy Implications' (2024) 95(3) *University of Colorado Law Review* https://lawreview.colorado.edu/print/volume-95/the-voluntary-carbon-market-market-failures-and-policy-implications/ accessed 5 February 2025.

16 Yude Pan and others, 'A Large and Persistent Carbon Sink in the World's Forests' (2011) 333 *Science* 988–993; Josep G Canadell and Michael R Raupach, 'Managing Forests for Climate Change Mitigation' (2008) 320 *Science* 1456–1457; Stibniati S Atmadja and others, 'How Do REDD Projects Contribute to the Goals of the Paris Agreement?' (2022) 17 *Environmental Research Letters*.

17 World Bank Group, 'Carbon Pricing Dashboard' (World Bank 2024) https://carbonpricingdashboard.worldbank.org/compliance/coverage accessed 17 July 2024.

18 Monica Crippa, Diego Guizzardi, Federico Pagani, Manjola Banja, Marilena Muntean, Eduard Schaaf, Wouter Becker, Francesca Monforti-Ferrario, Roberto Quadrelli, Ana Risquez Martin, Parisa Taghavi-Moharami, Giacomo Grassi, Simone Rossi, João Brandão de Melo, Diana Oom, Ana Branco, Javier San-Miguel and Elisabetta Vignati, 'GHG Emissions of All World Countries – JRC/IEA 2023 Report' (Publications Office of the European Union 2023).

19 Nasdaq and The ValueExchange (n 8).

20 Edward Mitchard and others, 'Serious Errors Impair an Assessment of Forest Carbon Projects: A Rebuttal of West et al. (2023)' (12 December 2023) SSRN https://ssrn.com/abstract=4661873 accessed 5 February 2025; Timothy A West and others, 'Action Needed to Make Carbon Offsets from Forest Conservation Work for Climate Change Mitigation' (2023) *Science*; Evan Coleman and others, 'Carbon Credits and Credibility: A Collaborative Endeavor' (2024) *MIT Climate & Sustainability Consortium* https://climate.mit.edu/credibility-of-carbon-credits accessed 26 December 2024; Nasdaq and The ValueExchange (n 8).

21 Patrick Greenfield, 'Revealed: Forest Carbon Offsets Biggest Provider Verra Is Worthless' (*The Guardian* 18 January 2023) https://www.theguardian.com/environment/2023/jan/18/revealed-forest-carbon-offsets-biggest-provider-worthless-verra-aoe accessed 5 February 2025.

22 Nasdaq and The ValueExchange (n 8).

23 Nasdaq and The ValueExchange (n 8).

24 Hamerkop Climate Impacts, 'The Ever-Expanding World of Carbon Certification Standards' (*Hamerkop Blog* 26 November 2024) https://www.hamerkop.co/blog/the-ever-expanding-world-of-carbon-certification-standards accessed 5 February 2025.

25 Nasdaq and The ValueExchange (n 8).

26 Data for this figure is sourced from a survey by Nasdaq and The ValueExchange (n 8) of participants in the VCM where respondents indicated whether they were affected by specific challenges. These challenges were grouped into five broad categories: Cost and Time Challenges, Fragmentation and Infrastructure, Regulatory and Compliance Issues, Liquidity and Financing Barriers, and Trust and Integrity Concerns. Each challenge was analysed across four key market stages: Project Listing, Verification, Settlements, and Risk Management. The heatmap displays the average percentage of respondents who reported being affected by a given challenge at each stage. Darker shades indicate a higher percentage of affected respondents, while lighter shades indicate a lower impact. Empty cells represent missing data, meaning insufficient responses were available for that challenge-market stage combination. This visualisation helps identify key bottlenecks and areas requiring intervention to improve market efficiency.

27 Nasdaq and The ValueExchange (n 8).

28 Edgar F Codd, 'A Relational Model of Data for Large Shared Data Banks' (1970) 13(6) *Communications of the ACM* 377–387 https://doi.org/10.1145/362384.362685 accessed 5 February 2025.

29 Satoshi Nakamoto, 'Bitcoin: A Peer-to-Peer Electronic Cash System' (31 October 2008) https://bitcoin.org/bitcoin.pdf accessed 5 February 2025; Stuart Haber and W Scott Stornetta, 'How to Time-Stamp a Digital Document' (1991) 3 *Journal of Cryptology* 99–111 https://doi.org/10.1007/BF00196791 accessed 5 February 2025.
30 Nick Szabo, 'Smart Contracts: Formalizing and Securing Relationships on Public Networks' (1997) 2(9) *First Monday* https://firstmonday.org/ojs/index.php/fm/article/download/548/469 accessed 5 February 2025; Vitalik Buterin, 'Ethereum: A Next Generation Smart Contract and Decentralised Application Platform' (2013) https://github.com/ethereum/wiki/wiki/White-Paper accessed 5 February 2025.
31 Konstantinos Christidis and Michael Devetsikiotis, 'Blockchains and Smart Contracts for the Internet of Things' (2016) 4 *IEEE Access* 2292–2303 https://doi.org/10.1109/ACCESS.2016.2566339 accessed 5 February 2025.
32 Solidity, *Solidity Documentation v0.8.28* (2024) https://docs.soliditylang.org/en/v0.8.28/ accessed 24 December 2024.
33 Konstantinos Christidis and Michael Devetsikiotis (n 31).
34 Chromaway, A Blockchain-Based Property Registry (2015) https://web.archive.org/web/20160304150308/http://chromaway.com/papers/A-blockchain-based-property-registry.pdf accessed 5 February 2025.
35 Loi Luu, Duc-Hiep Chu, Hrishi Olickel, Prateek Saxena, and Aquinas Hobor, 'Making Smart Contracts Smarter' in Proceedings of the 2016 ACM SIGSAC Conference on Computer and Communications Security (CCS '16) (Association for Computing Machinery 2016) 254–269 https://doi.org/10.1145/2976749.2978309 accessed 5 February 2025.
36 Ivan Popchev, Irina Radeva, and Veneta Velichkova, 'Auditing Blockchain Smart Contracts' in Proceedings of the 2022 International Conference Automatics and Informatics (ICAI) (2022) 276–281 https://doi.org/10.1109/ICAI55857.2022.9960058 accessed 5 February 2025.
37 Solidus Labs, Rug Pull Report (2022) https://www.soliduslabs.com/reports/rug-pull-report accessed 5 February 2025; Rachel Abrams, 'Apparent Theft at Mt. Gox Shakes Bitcoin World' (The New York Times, New York, 24 February 2014) https://www.nytimes.com/2014/02/25/business/apparent-theft-at-mt-gox-shakes-bitcoin-world.html accessed 5 February 2025.
38 Regulation (EU) 2023/1114 of the European Parliament and of the Council of 31 May 2023 on markets in crypto-assets, and amending Regulations (EU) No 1093/2010 and (EU) No 1095/2010 and Directives 2013/36/EU and (EU) 2019/1937 [2023] OJ L 150, p. 40–205.
39 Arsenii Vilkov and Gang Tian, 'Blockchain's Scope and Purpose in Carbon Markets: A Systematic Literature Review' (2023) 15(11) *Sustainability* 8495 https://doi.org/10.3390/su15118495 accessed 6 February 2025.
40 Grammateia Kotsialou, Karlygash Kuralbayeva, and Timothy Laing, 'Blockchain's Potential in Forest Offsets, the Voluntary Carbon Markets and REDD+' (2022) 49(3) *Environmental Conservation* 137–145 https://doi.org/10.1017/S0376892922000157 accessed 6 February 2025.
41 Laura A. Franke, Marco Schletz, and Søren Salomo, 'Blockchain Application for the Paris Agreement Carbon Market Mechanism—A Decision Framework and Architecture' (2020) 12(12) *Sustainability* 5069 https://doi.org/10.3390/su12125069 accessed 6 February 2025.
42 Laura A. Franke, Marco Schletz, and Søren Salomo, 'Designing a Blockchain Model for the Paris Agreement's Carbon Market Mechanism' (2020) 12(3) *Sustainability* 1068 https://doi.org/10.3390/su12031068 accessed 6 February 2025.
43 Computations for this graph are based on the identified VCUs in the Verra registry which were retired and included wallet addresses corresponding to Toucan, Moss, or C3 in the retirement details. Verra, *Verra Registry – Verified Carbon Units (VCUs) Search* (2025) https://registry.verra.org/app/search/VCS/VCUs accessed 6 February 2025.
44 Verra, 'Verra Statement on Crypto Market Activities' (25 November 2021) https://verra.org/statement-oncrypto accessed 16 July 2024.

45 International Emissions Trading Association (IETA), 'IETA Council Task Group on Digital Climate Markets: Key Findings and Recommendations' (28 March 2022) https://www.ieta.org/ieta-council-task-group-on-digitalclimate-markets-key-findings-and-recommendations accessed 16 July 2024.
46 Verra, 'Verra Addresses Crypto Instruments and Tokens' (25 May 2022)) https://verra.org/verra-addressescrypto-instruments-and-tokens accessed 16 July 2024.
47 Verra, *Verra Registry Terms of Use* (September 2021) https://vcmintegrity.org/wp-content/uploads/2023/09/Verra-Registry-TOU-September-2021_FINAL-1.pdf accessed 24 December 2024.
48 Verra, 'Verra Addresses Crypto Instruments and Tokens' (25 May 2022)) https://verra.org/verra-addressescrypto-instruments-and-tokens accessed 16 July 2024.
49 Verra, 'Public Consultation: Verra's Approach to Third-Party Crypto Instruments and Tokens' (3 August 2022) https://verra.org/public-consultation-verras-approach-to-third-party-crypto-instruments-andtokens accessed 16 July 2024.; Gold Standard, 'Gold Standard Announces Proposals to Allow Creation of Digital Tokens for Carbon Credits' (14 September 2022) https://www.goldstandard.org/news/gold-standardannounces-proposals-allow-creation-digital-tokens-carbon-credits accessed 16 July 2024.
50 Verra, 'Verra Concludes Consultation on Third-Party Crypto Instruments and Tokens' (17 January 2023) https://verra.org/verra-concludes-consultation-on-third-party-crypto-instruments-and-tokens accessed 16 July 2024; Gold Standard, 'Tokenisation Consultation Feedback and Next Steps' (21 June 2024) https://www.goldstandard.org/news/tokenisation-consultation-feedback-and-next-steps accessed 16 July 2024.
51 Verra, 'Public Consultation on Crypto Instruments and Tokens' (August 2022) https://verra.org/wpcontent/uploads/2022/08/Verra-Public-Consultation-on-Crypto-Instruments-and-Tokens.pdf accessed 16 July 2024.; Gold Standard, 'Consultation on Tokenisation: September 2022' (September 2022) https://goldstandard.cdn.prismic.io/goldstandard/0cd3dd77-850a-4578-be26-dbbb7cc8f3a2_consultationtokenisation_september2022_0.pdf accessed 16 July 2024.

Georg von Wangenheim and Leon Krug

4 VCCs, Tokenisation and the EU CBAM: Some microeconomics of VCCs

Abstract: In light of the menaces of global climate change, governments, firms, and consumers aim at reducing greenhouse gases. They can change their own behaviour or buy Voluntary Carbon Credits (VCCs). Thus, they claim credits for someone else's reduction of emissions or removal of greenhouse gases from the atmosphere. In this chapter, we describe the microeconomic background of the market for VCCs and reasons for its potential failure: information asymmetries and high costs of searching for contract partners on a worldwide level. We discuss possible remedies for overcoming these reasons for failure. In particular, two recent developments might contribute to the market's functioning: tokenisation of VCCs on blockchains and the EU Carbon Border Adjustment Mechanism (CBAM), in which VCCs could be included as alternatives to governmental carbon prices in third countries. Our conclusions on the success of tokenisation are ambiguous, while we are more optimistic about the effect of including VCCs in the CBAM—although the CBAM regulation currently still excludes VCCs.

Keywords: Microeconomics of voluntary carbon markets, market failure, information asymmetries, VCC, VCM

1 Introduction —— 73
2 Standard structure of VCC markets —— 74
3 VCC markets and asymmetric information —— 79
4 Economic effects of tokenising VCCs —— 83
4.1 Reducing information asymmetries —— 83
4.2 Increasing tradability of carbon credits —— 85
5 CBAM and VCCs —— 88
6 Conclusions —— 90

1 Introduction

In light of the menaces of global climate change, governments, firms, and consumers aim at reducing greenhouse gas (henceforth simply: "carbon") emissions or even removing them from the atmosphere. The individual goals of doing so may range from intrinsic motivation to contribute to climate protection over mere green marketing to

https://doi.org/10.1515/9783111706719-004

simple compliance with legal requirements, but whatever the goals are, scarcity of resources implies that climate protection can best be achieved if all agents choose efficient means for their carbon reduction or removal.

In particular in industrialised countries, the most efficient way for firms or consumers to reduce or remove carbon from the atmosphere is not to do so on their own but to pay others (very often, but not always in the global South) to reduce carbon emissions or remove carbon from the atmosphere. The efficiency of this division of labour follows directly from the fact that the marginal costs of climate action vary dramatically across the world.[1]

However, this process of offsetting one's own carbon emissions by emission reductions or carbon removals of others also requires a sufficiently reliable way of purchasing the credits for someone else's emission reduction or carbon removal—in other words, it requires a well-functioning carbon market. In fact, such a market for Voluntary Carbon Credits (VCCs)[2] has evolved, in which VCCs are credits based on some form of carbon emission reduction or removal certified by a private agency. As allowances in emission trading systems (ETSs) refer to one metric tonne that may be emitted, one VCC usually refers to one metric tonne of reduced or removed CO_2.

Obviously, such privately certified carbon emission reductions or removals are susceptible to a bagful of information asymmetry problems. This chapter aims at describing these problems in detail and thereby explaining the economics of VCCs. In particular, we want to elucidate the conditions under which VCCs may become credible evidence of effective offsets of one's emissions and may thus become marketable goods. This endeavour first requires describing the basic structure of VCC markets[3] (Section 2) and studying its problems of, and solutions for, asymmetric information (Section 3). Using this framework, we will then study two major changes to the ecosystem of VCCs. In line with the main topics of this book, we will first study how tokenising VCCs may improve the VCC market, mainly by overcoming information asymmetries and by fostering the tradability of VCCs (Section 4). Second, we will study the effects of the inclusion of VCCs into the European Carbon Border Adjustment Mechanism (CBAM), which would treat expenses for VCCs as deductible from the CBAM certificate price like carbon prices charged outside the European Union (Section 5). Section 6 will summarise and conclude the chapter.

2 Standard structure of VCC markets

For the remainder of this chapter, we define VCCs as the material or immaterial representation of a right to be credited—upon "retirement" of the VCC—for the reduction of carbon emissions or the removal of carbon from the atmosphere by one metric tonne of CO_2 or its equivalents. This right is granted by the issuer of the VCC. It obliges the issuer to confirm to third parties that it is the owner of the VCC and nobody else who is to be credited for the reduction or removal of the carbon emissions when the VCC is retired. The issuer will or at least may hinder others from claiming the same reduction or removal of greenhouse gas emissions by notice of cease and desist or a corresponding court action. The careful reader will have observed that according to this definition, the right represented by VCCs is a right *in personam* but not a right *in rem*.

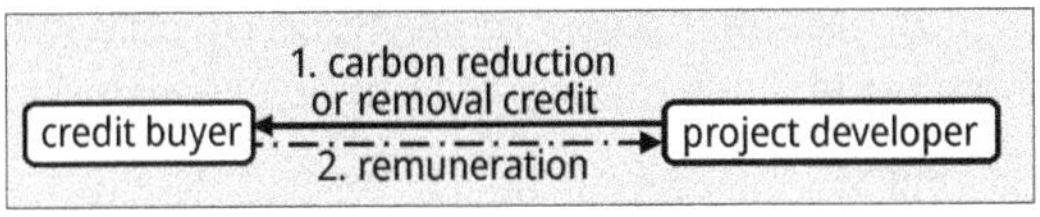

Figure 4.1: Idealised market for VCC when information is assumed to be complete and symmetric.

To best understand their structure and the way VCC markets function, it is helpful to first consider an idealised market of only project developers and VCC buyers in which all information is complete (Figure 4.1). In this market, the project developers reduce or remove carbon, issue corresponding VCCs, and sell them to buyers (arrow 1 in Figure 4.1). Buyers pay a remuneration (arrow 2) and may eventually retire their VCCs in order to claim the carbon reduction or removal in a convincing way. They do so to prove their climate-friendly behaviour or production to their contract partners, to fulfil some legal or moral obligations to reduce or remove carbon emissions or simply to soothe their bad conscience after some climate-damaging behaviour. Due to our assumption of complete information, VCCs are valuable only inasmuch as the project developers do not benefit from this activity other than from receiving the remuneration from the buyer. In particular, the value of the VCCs to the buyers declines by any subsidy or tax reduction that the developers receive from their government for their carbon reduction or removal activity. Similarly, the value of VCCs to the buyers declines by the value of the project developers' compliance with obligations achieved by their reduction or removal of carbon emissions underlying the specific VCCs. The requirement that owners of VCCs are credited for the reduction or removal of carbon emissions only upon the retirement of the VCCs avoids loss of value of VCCs due to double-use.

Several instances of asymmetric information and non-verifiability preclude the existence of such an idealised market in reality. The buyers typically can neither verify that the project developer has actually reduced emissions or removed carbon from the atmosphere (this is often referred to as the *additionality problem*) and stored it safely for a long period of time (referred to as *reversal risk*) nor that the developer did not benefit from the carbon reduction/removal in other ways than by the remuneration paid for by the credit buyer (once more an expression of the *additionality problem*). Further, they cannot be sure that the project developer does not sell VCCs for the same carbon reduction or removal more than once (referred to as the *double-*

use problem). The fact that the buyers can neither verify these actions nor their absence creates incentives for sellers to grossly overstate their emission reductions or removals—and obscure other benefits from their climate-friendly activity—for the monetary benefit associated with selling the credits. The asymmetric-information and the non-verifiability problem may be exacerbated by the buyer clearly preferring large quantities of carbon credits to high-quality ones (*warm-glow problem* for consumers and *greenwashing problem* for undertakings).[4] As discussed already by George Akerlof for used cars and insurances in his seminal paper on asymmetric information,[5] these circumstances preclude a market for high-quality VCCs unless remedies to overcome the problems evolve and are viable.

The first two remedies that come to a lawyer-economist's mind when discussing asymmetric information on the quality of goods—and that were already briefly mentioned by Akerlof—are guarantees and reputation. However, a guarantee by the project developer tends to be futile since the buyer will not automatically trust the developer's ability and willingness to fulfil the guarantee, possibly after decades. Reputation will also not work because the project developer often tends to be too small and new to build up a reputation on a worldwide market since reputation requires a history of a similar length as the future for which quality has to be upheld.[6]

Certification is the third standard remedy to market failures due to asymmetric information that can develop spontaneously in the market.[7] This remedy can be expected to be partially successful based on theoretical considerations and in fact is by far the most relevant remedy that has evolved. Certification improves the buyer's information on the quality of the emission reduction or removal project in two different ways. First and obviously, the certifier provides additional information on the quality of the project to the buyer. Second, the project developer sends a trustworthy signal of quality to the buyer: only project developers with high quality are willing to bear the risk of paying for the certification process in vain, because their risk of not getting the certification is substantially lower than the corresponding risk for a low-quality developer.[8]

For certification to be successful in these two ways, it needs the stipulation of general criteria and their application to the specific case. In the economic theory of certification, both stipulation and application of criteria are usually performed by one unitary *certification agency*.[9] However, it is helpful for understanding the market for VCCs to separate the *standard setter*, who formulates the general criteria and eventually grants the certification, from the *validation and verification body* (VVB), which applies the criteria to the specific project. These criteria cover several dimensions: (1) the effectiveness of the specific project with respect to the amount of carbon reduced or removed; (2) the longevity of this reduction or removal; (3) the absence of double-uses of the carbon reduction or removal; and (4) further characteristics of the project developer or the project that may be relevant to the credit buyer.

In addition to the lemons problem, due to asymmetric information, the market suffers from a second market imperfection: project developers and the credit buyers, often located on different continents, have major difficulties finding each other. A trading platform is therefore needed to bring the two together—and to facilitate further trades in case the buyer wants to resell his credits. In fact, many such intermediaries have taken up business and offer their services to solve these problems. If credits may be transferred from the initial buyer to further buyers, a registry of credit ownership is also needed. Otherwise, additional information asymmetries that come with those transactions would endanger the existence of such a resale market. Often, the trading platform and the ownership registry work hand-in-hand and sometimes they even coincide.

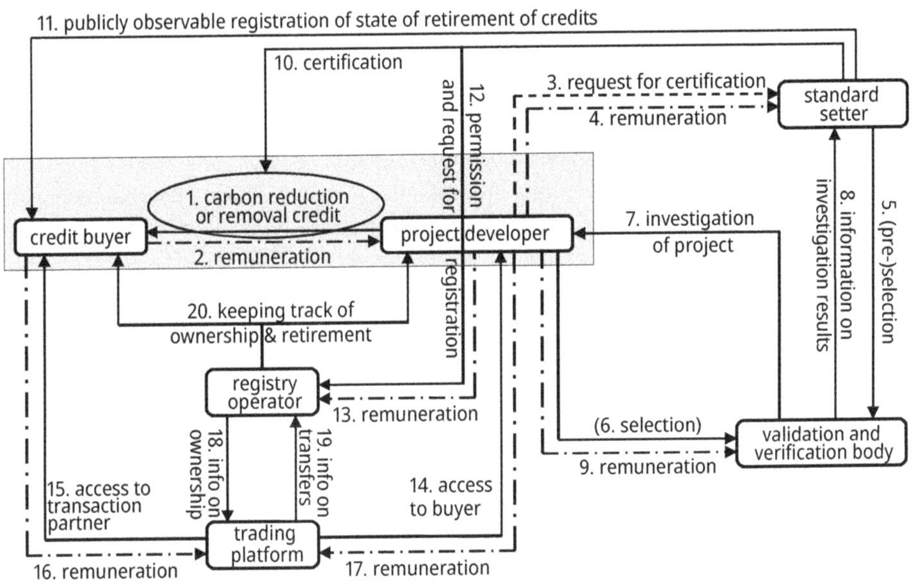

Figure 4.2: Structure of market for VCCs acknowledging information asymmetries and their remedies.

To fully comprehend the VCC market, one thus must consider four more agents in addition to the project developer and the credit buyer: the standard setter, the VVB, the operator of the trading platform, and the operator of the registry of ownership (which may also register the state of retirement). There are various degrees of integration of the four additional agents, but describing the market is easier by addressing them individually. In the following paragraphs, we will describe the enlarged market with all six agents to lay the grounds for a subsequent and more detailed discussion of possible remedies to the market imperfections.

The core of the enlarged market model is the idealised market that we described before. We complement this core in two directions: the process of certifying compliance with the standards (arrows 3 to 13 in Figure 4.2) and the trade of VCCs, which is registered in a registry and eased by trading platforms (arrows 14 to 20). The certification process starts with the project developer asking the standard setter to certify that the project complies with his standards (arrow 3) and paying for the certification (arrow 4). The standard setter then either selects a VVB or pre-selects a set of qualified VVBs (arrow 5) from which the project developer may select one (arrow 6). The selected VVB investigates the project, validates the amount of its carbon reduction or removal, and verifies that this reduction or removal actually takes or has taken place and is not used for other purposes by the developer (arrow 7). The investigation may also refer to other characteristics of the project or its developer that could be relevant for the credit buyer and thus for the standard. The VVB informs the standard setter about the results of its investigation (arrow 8). Typically, the VVB is remunerated by the project developer (arrow 9), or rarely by the standard setter. The standard setter then certifies that and to what amount the project reduces carbon emissions or removes carbon (arrow 10), which gives the credit buyers more reliable information on the quality of credits they buy. Some standard setters operate their own registry of the state of retirement of the credits and make this state publicly observable (arrow 11). Finally, the standard setter permits, or even requires, the project developer to register the VCCs with one specific, any, or a selected set of registries (arrow 12) and the project developer pays for the registration (13). Some standard setters register directly without any action from the project developer.

This creation of certified credits, which takes place before the credits are transferred to the buyer, is often called the *primary market* for carbon credits, because the standard setters "sell" the credits they created through the certification to the project developer. The first sale of certified credits from the project developer to the credit buyer would then take place on the *secondary market*. However, this first sale by the project developer is comparable to the initial offering of securities in general. In line with the standard terminology of financial economics, we therefore will say that the sale of the VCC from the project developer to the first buyer takes place on the primary market. The term "secondary market" will only refer to trades to which the project developer does not need to be one of the contract partners.

Arrows 14 to 20 in Figure 4.2 describe all sales of VCCs, be they on the primary market (after certification!) or on the secondary market. The relevant agents here are the operators of registries and the operators of trading platforms for VCCs. The services of the trading platform operator are more or less standard as in any other two-sided market: The operator provides project developers with easy access to credit buyers (arrow 14) and credit buyers with easy access to project developers or other credit buyers in case the buyer wants to resell his credits (arrow 15). In exchange, the platform operator charges either the project developer or the credit buyer or both for his services (arrows 16 and 17), depending on the relative price elasticities of their demand for the platform services.[10] The trading platforms receive their information on the ownership of VCCs from the registry (arrow 18) and inform the registry about the transfer of the VCCs, when trading partners have concluded their deed to transfer

VCCs (arrow 19). Finally, the registry operator operates records of who owns the credits and, unless standard setters operate their own registry of the state of retirement (arrow 11), whether they have already been retired or not to avoid double-counting of credits (arrows 20), which is particularly relevant if a secondary market for VCCs exists.

In reality, the four additional agents described in Figure 4.2 rarely are all separate individuals. Sometimes, standard setters operate their own registry (Verra[11] or Puro.earth[12]) or platform and registry operators coincide (Gold Standard[13] and Gold Standard Marketplace[14]). When independent platform operators restrict the VCCs supplied on their market to those produced by standard setters that comply with certain minimum standards, they also take the quality-ensuring functions of the certifiers of certifiers.

Sometimes, in particular, when the standard setter also operates the platform, the platform operators' services may even go further: they buy the certified VCCs from the project developer and sell them to the credit buyer on their own accounts and may even buy VCCs back and resell them. We refrain from including all these variations in Figure 4.2 to avoid confusion for the reader.

In this section, we have described what we perceive to be the typical structure of VCC markets. However, standard setters implicitly or explicitly define the structure of the market for carbon credits certified under their standards. This implies that the Voluntary Carbon Market (VCM) is to some degree fragmented and there are different market structures more or less for all standard setters and platform operators. Still, we think that the description given above is a reliable starting point for understanding VCC markets, even if one or more practical elements deviate from this description. We hold the view that such variations at most partly solve the problems that are to be discussed in Section 3—if they do at all.

3 VCC markets and asymmetric information

The complex market structure of the enlarged market model that we developed in the previous section is rooted in an attempt to reduce information asymmetries between credit buyers and project developers and to alleviate search-market problems. However, enlarging the market by the four additional agents (standard setter, VVB, trading platform operator, and registry operator) fails to fully eliminate the information asymmetries; a non-negligible amount of them is merely shifted to other transactions within the complex market structure: Standard setters and VVBs are intermediaries who themselves are subject to severe information-asymmetry problems as well. As is standard with any certification of the quality of experience and credence goods,[15] the certification of VCCs in itself is an experience or credence good. The integrity of standard setters, VVBs, and registry operators must not simply be assumed, but requires sufficiently strong incentive mechanisms to deter standard setters and VVBs from false certification and registry operators from corrupt registration. In this section, we study these mechanisms and the conditions under which they make the market viable and not fall victim to Akerlof's lemons problem. We start by identifying the elements of the market that deviate from the ideal of a perfect market.

To better judge the effectiveness of remedies for asymmetric-information problems, we distinguish between four features on which the credit buyer is less informed than the project developer:

(1) Most obvious is the information on the amount, the effectiveness, and the permanence of carbon emissions reductions or removals. While this feature obviously could be further differentiated, we treat it as one unitary aspect labelled "*quality*" of carbon reductions or removals since the remedies for this information asymmetry are the same for all its aspects.
(2) The information on whether these carbon reductions or removals have been used only once to create carbon credits—the absence of double-issuance.
(3) The information on whether the project developer has sold the credits only once (and not used them in any other way)—the absence of double-spending.
(4) Last is the information on whether the credit has not yet been retired—the absence of double-use.

In the secondary market, these features of asymmetric information may be weaker due to less information of the respective seller, but they still hinder the market from developing. At least information on the absence of double-use may also be a more severe problem in the secondary market.

When looking for remedies for these information asymmetries, we should note that the first two are in the realm of the standard setter and the VVB. The third is mainly in the realm of the registry operators. However, for excluding registration of the same credits in other registries, they may depend on the cooperation of the standard setter. Finally, reliable information on the retirement of credits can only come from the registry operator or the standard setter, depending on who records the state of retirement.

As for the idealised market, we consider the usual remedies that are standard in any law-and-economics discussion of asymmetric information in contracts on goods or services. We again start with guarantees as a signal for high quality. For the standard setter, guarantees for their certification deserve a much broader discussion than for the project developer. One could imagine standard setters promising to replace any credits for which the underlying projects turn out to be of lower quality than certified, either in kind by credits from another, high-quality project or by reimbursing the price paid for the credits or even the price to be paid for replacing the credits. In fact, some standard setters offer such guarantees for their certification, though with limitations like the Gold Standard's buffer pool for removal certificates,[16] which is limited to a certain percentage of the total credits. Two reasons hinder unlimited and thus more informative guarantees. On the one hand, the value of guaranteed VCCs would be substantially larger than the revenue the standard setters collect from their certification. Granting such guarantees would thus severely endanger the solvency of the standard setter. On the other hand, the guarantee is not only a signal of good quality but also an insurance against bad luck. It is far from obvious that the standard setter is less risk averse than the credit buyer with respect to the credit's failure risk. Thus, there may be good reasons for leaving the risk with the credit buyer.

The second standard remedy for pre-contractual asymmetric information on the quality of a good or a service is reputation. However, it is hardly possible for project developers to build up a reputation for developing only good projects given the young age of the market and the time span for which the carbon reduction or removal must be effective to yield any reputational merit. In addition, reputation can only function as a remedy for experience goods if the reputable firm is sufficiently large to fear losses from the destruction of its reputation that are larger than its potential gain from selling poor quality credits. Hence, only very large project developers or consortia of developers who are perceived as one unit can use their reputation as a signal for the good quality of their projects: Only for them, the gains from saving expenses on the quality of a single project are not worth the lost future profits that depend on their good reputation.

Reputation is, however, more likely to be a remedy for the information asymmetry when we look at standard setters in their role as certifiers. For them, the single project, from which they may earn higher profits from reneging on their own standards, is too small relative to the reputation they could lose.[17] Still, their past lifetime is also too small relative to the required duration of carbon reductions and removals to make reputation a perfect remedy to this information asymmetry.

The remaining alternative remedies for the asymmetric-information problem are governmental or private quality control, both for the projects' quality and for the quality of the certification process. We shall discuss the matter of governmental quality control in the later section on the CBAM (Section 5). As we have already integrated project certification into our model of the market, only private certification of the certification process deserves some consideration at this point. At first glance, it may seem as though one might run into an infinite regress in the matter. However, every stage of certification may add at least a little to the credibility of quality promises at previous stages. In fact, we do observe such second-layer certification: all major standard setters strive for, or proudly publish, approval of their methodologies by the *Integrity Council for the Voluntary Carbon Market.*[18] While comparing the certification of VCCs to other private certification systems, we expect further organisations to evolve that evaluate and certify certifiers of carbon credits.

So far, we have discussed certification as a possible remedy for asymmetric information, only for the first two aspects of VCCs that suffer from information asymmetries, namely the quality of the underlying carbon reduction or removal and the absence of double-issuance. We still need to take a closer look at the third and fourth information asymmetries, referring to the absence of double-spending and double-use of VCCs. Both may endanger the success of registries and thus of the entire VCC market. If registry operators cannot convince the credit buyer that both problems will not occur and thus devalue the buyer's credits, the market for registries will end up as a market for lemons and probably disappear.

The problems of guarantees for the absence of double-spending and double-use of VCCs are similar to those of guarantees for the quality of the underlying carbon reduction or removal and the absence of double-issuance. Again, the value of the VCCs registered is much larger than the remuneration paid for the services of the registry. Hence, the expected costs of complying with the guarantee will be too large relative to the registry's share value, even when the probability of double-spending or double-use of VCCs is small.

Reputation for a reliable platform and registry organisation may emerge, although—given the decades for which registration must persist—they face similar problems of an extremely long time horizon as the standard setters and VVBs. However, unlike standard setters and VVBs, trading platform and registry operators can reduce their temptation to exploit their reputation by stretching their remuneration over the entire period of registration of a VCC. Then, at no time is it worthwhile for them to take the price they already received for their services and forgo the reputation-based future profits from newly contracted registration services. Their promise to keep up their reputation is thus credible.[19]

A positive effect could also be had through the transfer of an existing positive reputation in other markets to the carbon credit's secondary markets. Thus, we expect that operators of platforms for other markets will enter the market for carbon credits within the coming years. Such a development could possibly be blocked by standard setters who operate their own platforms by prohibiting project developers from cross-listing. However, we so far do not observe much activity by large standard setters in this direction, except for bans on trading tokenised VCCs. In the case of platform operators from different markets entering the market for carbon credit platforms, we also expect them to carry over the certification systems that have prevailed for their existing market platforms (e.g., Trusted Shops). In theory, we could apply the argument of transferring reputation from other markets to VCCs also to the operators of registries. However, we are not aware of other markets, in which privately organised registries are relevant.

In this and the foregoing section, we have argued that information asymmetries render the idealised market with complete information impossible and that complementing the market for VCCs by certification by standard setters and VVBs mitigates the problem but fails to solve it completely. The reason for the latter pessimism is that in the case of VCCs, neither guarantees nor reputation mechanisms can remedy the information asymmetries inherent to certification. Even for the registration of the ownership and the retirement status of VCCs, information asymmetries that hamper the evolution of a well-functioning market prevail. Next, we turn to two new developments which might affect this ecosystem by increasing the reliability of information or by changing incentives to accept low-quality credits: the emergence of possibilities to tokenise carbon credits on distributed ledgers, such as blockchains, and the European CBAM.

4 Economic effects of tokenising VCCs

4.1 Reducing information asymmetries

Over the last decade and a half, blockchains[20] have proven to be very reliable means of storage for all types of data,[21] including smart contracts.[22] The most prominent example of a well-functioning blockchain application is the Bitcoin blockchain on which ownership and transfers of Bitcoins are registered in such a reliable way that the system warrants enough trust for the market value of one Bitcoin to grow from less than 0.10 USD/BTC before 2010 to more than 100,000 USD/BTC in early 2025.[23]

While the Bitcoin blockchain is focused on running and protecting the Bitcoin ledger —which is mainly a dynamic registry of present and past ownership of Bitcoins—other blockchains are more flexible and can easily host other registries. Ethereum is the flagship of this other class of blockchains. With a market capitalisation of about a quarter of that of Bitcoin, Ethereum is the second largest blockchain, more than twice as large as the next blockchains, Tether and Ripple, the value of which has dramatically risen in late 2024.[24] A large number of proposals to run VCC registries and certification systems on derivatives of, or alternatives to, Ethereum have been suggested.[25] Many of them have failed.[26] Others still exist and strive to become a permanent and prevailing phenomenon in the VCC market.[27] Even most authors of this book are generally positive for the perception of tokenisation being a mechanism to solve many of the information problems of the VCC market.[28] The first part of this section aims at carefully investigating which of the information asymmetries previously discussed in this chapter may be (further) reduced by tokenisation of VCCs.

To avoid ambiguities: When we talk about *tokenisation* or *tokenising* VCCs, we refer to digital representations of the VCCs or digital versions of the VCCs on a blockchain. In the former case, a transfer of the token will require the parties to also transfer the VCC and thus the right *in personam* against the VCC issuer as described at the beginning of Section 2. In the latter case, the right *in personam* against the VCC issuer is transferred by the transfer of the token. At least in the latter case, the blockchain takes over the role of the registry of ownership and possibly also of the registry of the retirement state. In any case, reliability and trustworthiness of the registry are of utmost importance. Blockchains have properties that seem to meet this requirement.

Any information stored in a blockchain is often said to be immutable.[29] However, in reality, this crucially depends on the specifics of the ledger. For example, it is often argued that information on the Bitcoin blockchain, whose consensus mechanism is proof-of-work, can only be amended and not changed retrospectively. However, the ledger will only remain immutable as long as the difficulty to write the next valid block is sufficiently high. Then, rewriting previous blocks is simply too expensive because it requires too much computation power. But should a large proportion of the miners of the Bitcoin blockchain decide to reallocate their computational power (or, equivalently, the underlying financial resources to buy the next generation computational power) to other uses, the immutability of the Bitcoin blockchain would vanish. Anyone with more computing power than the remaining miners combined could alter all blocks that were mined after the blockchain's loss of computing power.[30] Similarly, should miners in the Ethereum blockchain, for which the consensus mechanism is proof-of-stake, for any reason stop staking substantial amounts of their wealth in Ethers, fraudulent miners could stake enough resources in mining to be able to change the information stored on the blockchain.[31] Both hypotheticals are extremely unlikely, not the least because such actions run against the interests of all miners in nearly all circumstances, but the examples do illustrate that no blockchain or distributed ledger is immutable per se, but only due to resources spent on protecting the blockchain against ex-post mutations. Hence, the immutability, particularly of small blockchains that are independent of, that is, not anchored in[32] or building on, one of the large blockchains, does not exist in practice.[33]

Similarly, other properties often associated with blockchains, such as transparency, traceability of records, and resilience, also depend on the specifics of the blockchain used.[34] As a general rule, small blockchains, that is, blockchains running on a small number of nodes and running independently of one of the large blockchains in the sense mentioned before, will not reliably exhibit these properties. Tokenisation of VCCs may be based on large blockchains and thus may have these acclaimed properties of blockchains. However, even if one takes this for granted, one has to carefully study which information is protected by the blockchain and which information remains outside the blockchain and thus fails to benefit from its advantageous properties.

Simply using tokenisation of VCCs to improve the registry of ownership and of the state of retirement may protect the registry from fraud. However, tokenisation itself will not directly improve the validation and verification processes. The reason is simple: this process is not threatened by changing information that has already been entered into a registry but by producing wrong information from the very beginning. There may be a small indirect effect, though: all information that enters the blockchain remains there forever. Hence, VVBs cannot claim that they did not enter the data into the registry that can be found on the blockchain. It is therefore more likely that VVBs will be held responsible for what information they provided in the past. This may improve incentives to only provide correct information. Similar arguments hold for the certifier and even for the project developer. Still, this indirect effect is small and thus employing a blockchain to run the registry fails to substantially improve the certification process.

Although tokenisation of VCCs on single blockchain registries fails to overcome most asymmetric-information problems in the primary market, it may solve most problems in the secondary market besides the double-use of VCCs by cross-listing them on several independent registries—be they blockchain-based or not. The use of tokenisation may be at its prime on the secondary market, as here, double-use is less of a problem and traceability of ownership is the most relevant function of the registry.

4.2 Increasing tradability of carbon credits

On the secondary market, tokenisation may have an additional advantage besides reducing information asymmetries. Tokenisation could reduce transaction costs, mainly costs of controlling the accuracy of the registry, and thus increase tradability of VCCs on the secondary market. While tradability is not an advantage *per se*, we claim that tradability is desirable both to society as a whole and to individual buyers or sellers of VCCs for three distinct reasons.

The first of these reasons is the possibility of intertemporal financing of carbon projects. The secondary market allows investors and speculators to invest in carbon reduction or removal projects even if they do not have any interest in carbon credits. Accordingly, credit buyers who actually want to retire carbon credits and project developers do not need to enter the market at the same time. Project developers may set up their carbon reduction or removal project long before there is demand for retiring credits.

The second reason is insurance against buying too many VCCs. This could happen, for example, if producers regularly buy VCC to offset the emissions from their production but then happen to produce substantially less than planned. Or a flight passenger bought VCCs with the ticket and then has to cancel his journey. With a well-functioning secondary market, on which an owner of carbon credits can resell them, the risk of buying too many credits becomes small. More people will dare to buy an amount of VCC that might be beyond their emissions.

The third reason is that intermediate ownership of carbon credits by experts may increase their trustworthiness and thus their value to future buyers. This possibility is based on the reputation of the intermediate expert owners, which may be a self-supporting equilibrium. Consider a secondary market in which the quality and thus the value of carbon credits is unclear in the sense that it has a probability distribution on a given, non-degenerate support. By collecting information on the underlying projects, experts may reduce the variance of the distribution and perhaps also its support. If they so do, they can simply publish the information or sell the information to traders or engage in trade themselves.

We do not consider the first alternative any further as it does not result in any revenues to pay for the expert's labour. Engaging in trade themselves may be worthwhile in one equilibrium (one of several!). If they buy (and sell) only high-quality credits, they may build up a reputation for doing so. If they do, later buyers become willing to pay a higher price for credits that were owned—and thus in a sense endorsed—by a reputable expert in the past. If this increased willingness to pay is large enough relative to the expert's costs of collecting information on credit qualities, then the profits from buying and selling credits after gathering and using information on their quality will be a sufficient incentive for the expert to engage in this activity and keep up his reputation rather than exploiting and destroying it. One should be aware, though, that this equilibrium, if it exists at all, is not unique. Like in any market with asymmetric information, there is always a second equilibrium in which no one trusts intermediate expert owners and thus no expert has an incentive to buy and resell high-quality carbon credits. Which of the equilibria is reached depends to a large degree on the history of the system itself. Building up a reputation from scratch is difficult, in particular, if the reputation refers to long-lasting qualities of a product—as is the case for VCCs. It is therefore more likely that this reputation-by-endorsement mechanism works, if the intermediate buyers can rely on reputation previously earned in other markets.

Since these equilibria with intermediate expert owners, who signal the high quality of the credits by their mere intermediate ownership, may exist or not, we take a closer look at the effect of tokenisation of VCC on these equilibria. We claim that tokenisation of VCCs tends to increase the likelihood that these equilibria exist, that they are stable, and that the market reaches these equilibria. The reason for this is that tokenisation on a publicly observable blockchain makes previous ownership by an expert observable and verifiable, if the previous owners want to reveal their identity, which obviously is part of the equilibrium strategy of expert owners.

Obviously, selling the expert's information to some other trader who then takes the role of the expert trader as just described, would work or fail equally well. There is thus no need to discuss this alternative use of the expert's information in detail.

As mentioned before, double-use of projects or credits cannot be hindered by tokenisation if it takes place on multiple competing platforms, because then project developers can still double-use their project by certifying with more than one certifier and after certification, they could still sell the same carbon credit on several trading platforms if they have separate registries. Several authors therefore suggest centralising registration of certification, ownership, and (non-)retirement to a single all-encompassing registry.[35] Three ways of such a monopolisation of the registry seem to be possible. First, the hitherto independent operators of registries could collaborate to integrate their registries in a joint registry. Second, one of the existing registries or a completely new registry could benefit from direct and indirect network effects to take over all competing registries, whether blockchain-based or not. Third, one or more governments could step in and set up a central registry as governments have already done in the past for registration of land ownership and certain intellectual property rights.[36]

Given the extreme geographic mobility of carbon credits, governmental registration would be less comparable to land registration and more to registration of intellectual property rights. For the former, the competent jurisdiction is easily defined by the geographic location of the real estate. Hence, having as many registries as countries (or counties if we look at some states of the USA) is not a problem. For the latter, however, the multiplicity of patent offices and similar registries with different legal rules does pose problems for international use of intellectual property. Similar Problems would become even worse for VCC if all governments created their own registries. But still, given the experience of intellectual property, we would not expect that any country could succeed in centralising all governmental registries in this country's registry. National interests would be too heterogeneous. We will thus not delve deeper into the possibility of centralisation of the registries on the governmental level.[37]

If one of the large registries gained a self-sustaining monopoly due to direct and indirect network effects, more or less all competition laws would require regulation of this monopoly. Again, we would face the problems of interjurisdictional competition. Even though only larger jurisdictions would be effectively competing, whereas smaller jurisdictions would not be able to enforce limits on this monopoly, we still expect severe differences in the goals and rules of the monopoly regulation by large countries. As a consequence, the rules of the registry that are legally acceptable would differ across countries. Effectively, this would most likely prevent one monopoly from being sustainable in all countries, so that we would again end up with several registries with different rules. Hence, the risk of double-registration could be reduced but never prevented completely.

In our opinion, the most realistic way to overcome the double-use and double-registration problems would be a collaboration of many separate registries forming a joint master registry. Setting up this second-order registry on a jointly formed blockchain, perhaps with proof of authority (of all collaborators) as consensus mechanism, seems to be the most straightforward way of collaboration. Still, such a collaboration would likely be judged to be a cartel in many jurisdictions, resulting in similar, though probably not so severe, problems as we have already discussed for the case of one large registry operator becoming a monopolist. At least in some jurisdictions, the potential welfare gain will not be sufficient as a defence against the prohibition to form cartels.

In addition to these legal obstacles towards establishing one overarching registry for the entire world, we would also face practical challenges in forming such a master registry based on the collaboration of the operators of existing registries. In particular, the ideas about desirable qualities of such a master registry are prone to substantial variation across the various operators. As a consequence, operators of large existing registries are unlikely to give up their autonomy to further develop their registry in a way that further increases their market share, but without such restrictions, small registries will not surrender to the joint registry. We thus do not dare to speculate on whether such a collaboration is or will be possible.

5 CBAM and VCCs

Besides tokenisation, the enforcement of the EU CBAM is the second major change that may have a disruptive effect on the VCM.

The central idea of a CBAM is to reinstall a level playing field for carbon-emitting producers in countries with carbon pricing, such as the European Union with its ETS, and producers in countries without any carbon pricing mechanisms. Theoretically, the CBAM concept refers to both imports and exports: The carbon-pricing country levies a duty on imports to offset the cost advantage of foreign producers who are not subject to a carbon price difference. Conversely, the carbon-pricing country subsidises exports to offset the carbon-price disadvantage of the domestic producers on the world market. In practice, the European CBAM only levies costs on importers, because exporter rebates would likely be a violation of World Trade Organization rules.[38] For now, the EU CBAM is restricted to highly carbon-intensive industries to slowly fade out grandfathered free allowances, which served to level the playing field in the past.

Importers to the European Union have to buy and surrender so-called CBAM certificates at the price of EU ETS allowances per tonne of carbon emissions embedded in the product. The embedded emissions comprise all emissions of the production of the imported goods, including all upstream production of the supply chain and all transportation of the goods. The procedure of collecting the information required to determine the amount of certificates needed is complex and is left to others to explore, as the focus of this book is on VCCs rather than on CBAM.[39] In order to avoid a double-burden on imports from countries with an existing carbon pricing system, the number of CBAM certificates to be bought and surrendered is reduced by the carbon price effectively paid abroad in the form of taxes, levies, or fees for carbon emissions or the price for emission allowances purchased in accordance with comparable ETSs.[40] To convert the carbon price effectively paid into a deductible number of CBAM certificates, it has, of course, to be divided by the price of the CBAM certificates. Thus, the deduction does not depend on the amount of carbon emissions, which have been subject to carbon pricing in the country of production, but only on the price paid for these emissions.[41]

Various effects of this system have been discussed in the literature such as the incentive for other countries to implement a carbon price in their home markets in order to redirect the expenses paid for EU CBAM certificates to their own accounts or the incentive for producers to keep production inside the EU, avoiding carbon leakage (one of the main goals of the EU CBAM).[42] In this chapter, we concentrate on the question of whether expenses for VCCs should also be included in the deduction from the CBAM price to be paid by the importer. For the time being, the EU CBAM regulation does not allow this: only prices charged by a government are eligible for deduction.

Suppose that VCCs were eligible for deductions from the CBAM price to be paid by the importer. Then importers and their suppliers from other countries, that is, the foreign producers, have the choice between buying CBAM certificates, paying governmental carbon prices in their home country (if such a carbon price exists), and buying (and retiring) VCCs. It is important to note that their expenses will always be the same as the deduction from the number of required CBAM certificates depends on the amount of carbon reduced or removed in the creation of the VCCs as little as it depends on the amount of emissions for which carbon prices are paid. Only the total carbon price paid and only the total expenses for VCCs—converted via the division by the price of CBAM certificates—determine the deduction from the number of CBAM certificates that have to be surrendered. Thus, there is no inherent incentive to buy cheap VCCs or to prefer VCCs to carbon prices in the production country or to CBAM certificates.

As buying and retiring VCCs do not cost more or less than paying the carbon price of the production country or purchasing and surrendering CBAM certificates, producers and importers can and will rely on other arguments when selecting VCCs for purchase—or opting for the governmental carbon price or the CBAM certificates. As long as they have a preference for climate protection or seek to appear climate conscious to customers, other contracting partners, or even the government of their home country, they are incentivised to achieve the highest possible carbon reduction. They will therefore prefer to select high-quality VCCs that demonstrate effective carbon reduction or removal.

There may, however, be further incentives to deviate from this criterion. For example, the government of the production country might restrict the set of alternatives they can choose from. Alternatively, there might be ways to—fraudulently—recover some of the expenses for VCCs by way of kickback payments. The producer might even be tempted to invest in low-quality project developers, buy and retire their VCCs to deduct these expenses from the EU CBAM bill, and then participate in the profits that the project developer receives from these VCCs.

Because of the latter peril, the EU should not allow VCCs for deduction from CBAM duties unless they meet specific standards or criteria. In particular, the EU should install some minimum requirements that must be met by the VCCs and the underlying projects. Effectively, with a clear definition of these requirements, this is tantamount to indirectly regulating standard setters because if their standards are not at least as strict as the EU standards, their certification will be devaluated dramatically. In this way, accepting VCCs for deduction from CBAM duties would allow the EU to unilaterally determine certification standards as if it could regulate them without international agreement.

Accepting VCCs for CBAM deductions would support carbon reduction and removal, particularly in those countries that oppose implementing governmental carbon prices. We conclude that the EU should allow importers to deduct expenses for VCCs in the same manner as it allows governmental carbon prices to be deducted, if the standard setters who certify VCCs comply with some minimum requirements for their standards. Specifically, the requirements should ensure enforcement and effectiveness in ensuring return payments to the credit buyer from the project developer do not occur.

6 Conclusions

In this chapter, we have explored the microeconomic foundations of VCCs that we think to be most relevant for scaling the VCC market. We first described the market structure of VCC markets, including their certification mechanisms, and then studied in some detail the problems of asymmetric information that the certification and registration system fails to overcome or even contributes to. We used these insights to better understand the effects of two recent developments that may change the market and the effectiveness of VCCs. The first development is the technical innovation of blockchains, which may reduce some information asymmetries. We have shown that tokenisation may have positive effects on the VCC market, but by far cannot address all asymmetric-information problems. The second development is the legal innovation of the EU CBAM, which may substantially increase incentives to buy VCCs if the EU would admit the deduction of expenses for VCCs from the CBAM duty. If the EU would do so and clearly regulate the requirements that VCCs and their underlying projects have to satisfy for deductibility, it could virtually regulate standard setters without the need for international agreement.

We hope that our microeconomics-based description of the structure of the VCC market and its inherent information asymmetries will contribute to the foundations of future research on the market's development. Legal, structural, and technological changes discussed in this book may serve as further illustrations of our approach.

Notes

1 Even when looking at prominent cap-and-trade system for greenhouse gas emissions, we observe that prices and thus marginal avoidance costs differ dramatically: While one EU allowance costs around 60 to 80 EUR per metric ton (European Energy Exchange AG, 'EUA Primary Market Auction Report 2025' (2025), https://public.eex-group.com/eex/eua-auction-report/emission-spot-primary-market-auction-report-2025-data.xlsx accessed 27 February 2025), in California the price is about half as high (California Air Resources Board, 'California Cap-and-Trade Program, Summary of California-Quebec Joint Auction Settlement Prices and Results, Last updated February 2025' https://ww2.arb.ca.gov/sites/default/files/2020-08/results_summary.pdf accessed 27 February 2025). Marginal costs outside these systems tend to be substantially smaller.

2 Some authors and institutions (e.g., UNIDROIT, 'Verified Carbon Credits: Study LXXXVI – Legal Nature of Verified Carbon Credits' (2021), https://www.unidroit.org/work-in-progress/verified-carbon-credits/ accessed 27 February 2025) use the abbreviation for 'Verified Carbon Credits' which describes the same phenomenon that we label 'Voluntary Carbon Credits'.

3 We deviate from the often-used label "voluntary carbon market (VCM)", because that concept may also comprise VCMs that are not based on certificates.

4 For a detailed discussion of this problem, see Vittoria Battocletti, Luca Enriques and Alessandro Romano, 'The voluntary carbon market: Market failures and policy implications' (2024) 95 Colorado Law Review 519; Heidi Crumpler and Philip Grossman, 'An experimental test of warm glow giving' (2008) 92 Journal of Public Economics 1011 show empirically that consumers only care for the amount of money they donate and not the share of this money that really reaches the needy; an early example of greenwashing being discussed in detail is Magali Delmas and Vanessa Burbano, 'The Drivers of Greenwashing' (2011) 54 California Management Review 64; for a recent review of the literature on, and the effects of, greenwashing see Emanuele Teti, Leonardo Etro and Lorenzo Pausini, 'Does greenwashing affect Company's stock Price? Evidence from Europe' (2024) 93 International Review of Financial Analysis 103195.

5 George Akerlof, 'The Market for "Lemons": Quality Uncertainty and the Market Mechanism' (1970) 84 Quarterly Journal of Economics 488.

6 This argument is based on Scott Masten and Renáta Kosová, 'Post-sale service and the limits of Reputation' (2013) 22 Industrial and Corporate Change, 1663—to the best of our knowledge, the only publication dealing explicitly with reputation for the quality of durables that require additional expenses by the producer for a long time after the contract. The authors show that the temptation to exploit any existing reputation grows (and may eventually become destructively large) as long as the stock of past sales that still require expenses to uphold their quality grows. For the case of projects to reduce or remove emissions, the stock of such past projects typically grows at least until the first projects are completed and entail no further expenses.

7 We neglect licensing, the third remedy suggested by Akerlof, because by definition it requires government activity, which runs counter to the very idea of *voluntary* carbon credits.

8 See Michael Spence, 'Job Market Signaling' (1973) 88 Quarterly Journal of Economics 355 for signalling as a solution to information asymmetries in general.

9 For an overview on the economic theory of certification, see Georg von Wangenheim, 'Certification as Solution to the Asymmetric Information Problem?' in Peter Rott (ed) *Certification – Trust, Accountability, Liability* (1st edn, Springer 2019) 12.

10 For the theory of two-sided markets, see Jean-Charles Rochet and Jean Tirole, 'Platform competition in two-sided markets' (2003) 1 Journal of the European Economic Association 990; Marc Rysman, 'The Economics of Two-Sided Markets' (2009) 23 Journal of Economic Perspectives 125.

11 Verra, https://verra.org/ accessed 27 February 2025.

12 Puro.earth, https://puro.earth/ accessed 27 February 2025.

13 Gold Standard, https://www.goldstandard.org/ accessed 27 February 2025.

14 Gold Standard Marketplace, https://marketplace.goldstandard.org/ accessed 27 February 2025.

15 Phillip Nelson, 'Information and Consumer Behavior' (1970) 78 Journal of Political Economy 311, Michael Darby and Edi Karni 'Free Competition and the Optimal Amount of Fraud' (1973) 16 Journal of Law and Economics 67; an often-cited formalisation and extension of the argument is Winand Emons 'Credence Goods and Fraudulent Experts' (1997) 28 RAND Journal of Economics 107; for the certification as a remedy for the resulting problems see Georg von Wangenheim, 'Certification as Solution to the Asymmetric Information Problem?' in Peter Rott (ed) *Certification – Trust, Accountability, Liability* (1st edn, Springer 2019) 12.

16 Gold Standard, 'Gold standard for the global goals – terms and conditions' (2024) https://globalgoals.goldstandard.org/terms-conditions/ accessed 27 February 2025.

17 Vittoria Battocletti, Luca Enriques and Alessandro Romano, 'The voluntary carbon market: Market failures and policy implications' (2024) 95 Colorado Law Review 519, 542–544.

18 Integrity Council for the Voluntary Carbon Market, 'Carbon Core Principles' (2024) https://icvcm.org/core-carbon-principles/ accessed 27 February 2025; see Integrity Council for the Voluntary Carbon Market, 'Assessment Status' (2025) https://icvcm.org/assessment-status/ for approved programs and methodologies.

19 Again, see Masten and Kosová (n. 4) for a formal argument on reputation for long-term durables or services.

20 Strictly speaking, blockchains are only a special case of distributed ledger technologies that have similar desirable properties. For simplicity, we will restrain our argument to blockchains.

21 Krause and others, 'Distributed Ledger Technology (DLT) and blockchain' (*World Bank Group* 2017) https://documents.worldbank.org/en/publication/documents-reports/documentdetail/177911513714062215/distributed-ledger-technology-dlt-and-blockchain accessed 27 February 2025.

22 Smart contracts are more or less complex directions to change stored data after certain, again: more or less complex, triggers. For a quick overview, see Valentina Gatteschi, Fabrizio Lamberti and Claudio Demartini, 'Technology of Smart Contracts' in Larry DiMatteo, Michel Cannarsa and Cristina Poncibò (eds) *The Cambridge Handbook of Smart Contracts, Blockchain Technology and Digital Platforms* (1st edn, Cambridge University Press 2019).

23 E.g., Investing.com, 'Bitcoin Historical Data' https://www.investing.com/crypto/bitcoin/historical-data accessed 27 February 2025.

24 See CoinMarketCap https://coinmarketcap.com/ accessed 27 February 2025.

25 Gary Marchant, Zachary Cooper, and Philip Gough-Stone, 'Bringing technological transparency to tenebrous markets' (2022) 62 Natural Resources Journal 159 optimistically describe four promising examples; other examples would be Toucan https://toucan.earth/ accessed 27 February 2025, Crypto Carbon Company (C3) https://www.c3.app/ accessed 27 February 2025, and Coorest https://coorest.io/ accessed 27 February 2025.

26 Two of the examples listed by Marchant and others (n 25), Nori and Universal Protocol Alliance universalprotocol.io accessed 27 February 2025 have disappeared after publication of the paper.

27 Toucan https://toucan.earth/ accessed 27 February 2025; Crypto Carbon Company (C3) https://www.c3.app/ accessed 27 February 2025; Coorest https://coorest.io/ accessed 27 February 2025.

28 See, e.g., Carsten Mueller and Leah Kling, 'Tokenising the Voluntary Carbon Credit Market: Harnessing Opportunities for Sustainable Development' (2025) in this book and Valeriya Arnold, Vincent Schaaf, Nils Urbach and Jonathan Lautenschlager, 'Designing a Framework for a Blockchain-Based Voluntary Carbon Credit Lifecycle' (2025) in this book.

29 The paper by Marchant and others (n 25) is an example of a really optimistic perspective; other examples are: Justin Macinante 'A Conceptual Model for Networking of Carbon Markets on Distributed Ledger Technology Architecture' (2017) 11 Carbon & Climate Law Review 243; Nicholas Espenan, 'Improving Voluntary Carbon Markets Through Standardization and Blockchain Technology' (2023) 23 Wyoming Law Review 142.

30 Saurabh Singh, Sanwar Hosen and Byungun Yoon, 'Blockchain Security Attacks, Challenges, and Solutions for the Future Distributed IoT Network' (2021) 9 IEEE Access 13938.

31 Marco Di Maggio, 'Blockchain, Crypto and Defi: Bridging Finance and Technology' (1st edn, Wiley 2024) 68–73.

32 Anchoring one blockchain in another occurs when from time to time the hash value (or something similar) of a block of the anchored blockchain is saved in the anchoring blockchain, e.g., the Bitcoin blockchain.

33 Based on the lack of economies of scale in protecting permissionless blockchains against ever larger incentives to attack them, Eric Budish, 'Trust at Scale: The Economic Limits of Cryptocurrencies and Blockchains' (2025) 140 Quarterly Journal of Economics 1 argues that even large blockchains like Bitcoin and Ethereum become far more susceptible to (super)majority attacks than traditional forms of trust with substantial economies of scale (reputation, long-term relationships, collateral, rule of law) if the value of a successful attack becomes large.

34 Again, Marchant and others (n 25) may serve as an example.

35 E.g., Espenan (n 29); Nicole Franki, 'Regulation of the Voluntary Carbon Offset Market: Shifting the Burden of Climate Change Mitigation from Individual to Collective Action' (2022) 48 Columbia Journal of Environmental Law 178.

36 It is noteworthy that during the COP28 in Dubai and at the COP29 in Baku in 2024, there were fierce discussions about whether a registry for International Tradeable Mitigation Offsets should be decentralised (main proponent: USA) or centralised (main proponent: EU); Carbon Market Watch,

'FAQ: Fixing Article 6 carbon markets at COP29' (2024) https://carbonmarketwatch.org/2024/11/06/faq-fixing-article-6-carbon-markets-at-cop29/ accessed 27 February 2025; Roy Manuell and Rebecca Gualandi, 'COP29: Trouble in paradise – After strong start, old conflicts on Article 6 come to the fore' (*Carbon Pulse*, 2024) https://carbon-pulse.com/342379/ accessed 27 February 2025.

37 It is forbidden to link copyright protection to formalities (like registry entries), Art. 5(2) Berne Convention for the Protection of Literary and Artistic Works; for the evolution of copyright law, see Päivi Hutukka, 'Copyright Law in the European Union, the United States and China' (2023) 54 International Review of Intellectual Property and Competition Law 1044.

38 cf Giulia Leonelli, 'Export rebates and the EU Carbon Border Adjustment Mechanism: WTO law and environmental objections' (2022) 56 Journal of World Trade 963.

39 For more information on CBAM, see Christoph Böhringer and others, 'Potential impacts and challenges of border carbon adjustments' (2022) 12 Nature Climate Change 22; Timothé Beaufils and others, 'Assessing different European Carbon Border Adjustment Mechanism implementations and their impact on trade partners' (2023) 4 Nature Communications Earth & Environment 131.

40 Art. 3 (29) Regulation (EU) of the European Parliament and of the Council of 10 May 2023 establishing a carbon border adjustment mechanism (CBAM Regulation).

41 Art. 9 CBAM Regulation.

42 Sigit Perdana and Marc Vielle, 'Making the EU Carbon Border Adjustment Mechanism acceptable and climate friendly for least developed countries' (2022), 170 Energy Policy 113245; Alice Pirlot, 'Carbon Border Adjustment Measures: A Straightforward Multi-Purpose Climate Change Instrument?' (2022) 34 Journal of Environmental Law 25; Ivan Ozai, 'Designing an Equitable Border Carbon Adjustment Mechanism' (2022) 70 Canadian Tax Journal 1.

Masud Sultan, Vincent Schaaf, and Nils Urbach

5 Application of blockchain in voluntary carbon markets: A multiple case study on emergent implementations and their challenges

Abstract: This chapter examines the application of blockchain technology in the voluntary carbon market (VCM), emphasising both the opportunities and challenges encountered by startups in this sector. The effectiveness of carbon markets is currently undermined by operational inefficiencies, legislative uncertainties, and accessibility issues, which impede their potential to mitigate climate change. Through the analysis of five comprehensive case studies—Toucan, Regen Network, Senken, Kumo, and Moss—this chapter illustrates how blockchain can provide innovative solutions, such as tokenisation and blockchain-native registries, to enhance market transparency, efficiency, and participation. However, the study also critically addresses the significant challenges these businesses face, including scalability, compliance with diverse legal frameworks, and integration within existing market structures. The insights gained from this analysis lead to general requirements for the successful implementation of blockchain solutions in carbon markets, highlighting the need for collaborative efforts among stakeholders to overcome these hurdles and drive effective climate action.

Keywords: Blockchain, Regenerative Finance, Tokenisation, VCC, VCM

1 Introduction —— **96**
2 Operational approach —— **97**
3 Case study: Toucan —— **97**
  3.1 Application of blockchain technology —— **98**
  3.2 Challenges and limitations —— **99**
  3.3 Conclusion —— **102**
4 Case study: Regen network development —— **102**
  4.1 Application of blockchain technology —— **103**
  4.2 Challenges and limitations —— **107**
  4.3 Conclusion —— **108**
5 Case study: Senken —— **108**
  5.1 Adoption of blockchain technology —— **109**
  5.2 Challenges and limitations —— **110**
  5.3 Conclusion —— **111**
6 Case study: Kumo —— **112**
  6.1 Application of blockchain technology —— **112**
  6.2 Challenges and limitations —— **113**
  6.3 Conclusion —— **114**

https://doi.org/10.1515/9783111706719-005

7 Case study: Moss — 114
7.1 Application of blockchain technology — 115
7.2 Challenges and limitations — 116
7.3 Conclusion — 117
8 Discussion — 117
8.1 Regulatory and standardisation needs — 119
8.2 Technical infrastructure requirements — 122
8.3 Operational and market dynamics — 125
9 Conclusion — 126

1 Introduction

Climate change represents one of the most pressing challenges of our time, necessitating innovative solutions to reduce greenhouse gas emissions and enhance sustainability.[1] Voluntary Carbon Markets (VCMs) have emerged as a critical mechanism for addressing these issues, allowing organisations and individuals to offset their carbon footprints by investing in projects that reduce or sequester carbon emissions.[2] By providing a market for the trading of carbon credits, VCMs facilitate financial flows towards environmental initiatives, thereby supporting global climate goals.

However, VCMs face significant challenges that hinder their effectiveness.[3] Issues such as market fragmentation, varying credit quality, regulatory inadequacies, and the risk of double-counting all contribute to a lack of trust and transparency within the market. Additionally, the absence of standardised methodologies leads to inconsistencies in credit verification and varying prices, further complicating market dynamics. Against this backdrop, blockchain technology has gained prominence in VCMs.[4] By offering a decentralised, transparent, and immutable ledger, proponents advocate blockchain as a means to enhance the integrity, traceability, and efficiency of carbon credit transactions. However, challenges such as technical interoperability, compliance with diverse legal frameworks, and the quality of tokenised credits pose substantial barriers to its successful implementation. Additionally, the volatility of blockchain-based assets and the potential for regulatory misalignment further complicate the adoption of blockchain solutions in this domain.[5]

This chapter seeks to investigate the practical application patterns of blockchain in VCMs, focusing on the associated challenges and limitations. Thereby, we seek to answer the following research question:

What are the practical application patterns of blockchain in the VCM, and what challenges and limitations do they face?

To answer our research question, we study five real-world cases of blockchain applications in the VCM. The structure of the chapter is organised as follows: the first case study focuses on *Toucan*, one of the earliest projects with the largest amount of tokenised, traditional VCCs, which serves as a foundation for understanding the subsequent case descriptions, as many projects showcase similar challenges or seek to address those faced by Toucan. Following is a second case, *Regen Network*, a platform that integrates ecological restoration with blockchain technology, offering decentralised governance and a comprehensive platform for trading ecosystem service credits. Third, we investigate *Senken*—initially a blockchain-based marketplace for carbon credits that pivoted away from its original model to address challenges related to credit quality and market fragmentation. Subsequently, we showcase *Kumo*, a decentralised finance initiative that aims at transforming carbon credits into legally recognised collateral for debt financing, aiming to bridge the climate finance gap. Last is *Moss*, a climate technology company focused on enhancing accessibility and security in the carbon credit market through the MCO2 token and conservation initiatives in the Amazon rainforest.

Through these case studies, the chapter will explore the multifaceted role of blockchain in VCMs, highlighting both its transformative potential and the hurdles that must be overcome for broader adoption.

2 Operational approach

This study employs a multiple case study methodology, focusing on five selected blockchain-based voluntary carbon credit (VCC) projects. These cases were chosen based on their relative seniority and the availability of information. Each case is examined in detail, beginning with an overview of its fundamental operations and the role of blockchain technology within the VCC framework. Subsequently, the analysis highlights the challenges and limitations faced by each project, providing a comprehensive understanding of the operational landscape in which these blockchain applications operate.

Data collection involved a thorough review of existing literature and project documentation. The analysis framework is designed to facilitate comparative insights across the cases, allowing for the identification of common themes and unique challenges. This structured approach aims to elucidate the potential of blockchain technology in enhancing transparency, efficiency, and participation in VCMs while critically assessing the barriers to its broader adoption.

3 Case study: Toucan

Founded in 2021, Toucan is dedicated to improving global climate action by leveraging blockchain technology to create a more accessible, transparent, and efficient system for VCMs. Positioned in the post-issuance phase of the carbon credit lifecycle, that is, trading and retirement of VCCs, Toucan's initial core function was to tokenise existing carbon credits from traditional registries to the blockchain, enabling their trading and retirement within a decentralised system. Since its launch, Toucan has facilitated the tokenisation of over *USD 100 million worth of carbon credits*, driving a total transaction volume of *USD 4 billion in carbon credit trading volume.*[6] Recently, Toucan has expanded its role beyond tokenisation by launching a marketplace for biochar credit.[7] This case study examines Toucan's blockchain infrastructure and technical innovations, as well as the evolving challenges and limitations in its approach.

3.1 Application of blockchain technology

Toucan's Carbon Bridge is the central infrastructure to integrate carbon credits from traditional off-chain registries, such as Puro.earth,[8] into decentralised blockchain networks.[9] Thus, it facilitates the tokenisation of carbon credits, by acquiring them from traditional providers and representing them with TCO2 tokens. These tokens are embedded with metadata (credit serial number) from which information about the credit's origin, vintage, and certification standard can be deduced. By creating a representation of carbon credits on the blockchain, the Carbon Bridge creates a digital, verifiable claim to an asset that can be traded and retired across decentralised platforms.[10] Furthermore, Toucan supports cross-chain interoperability through a two-way bridge that connects its infrastructure on the Polygon and Celo with the Regen Network's eco registry in the Cosmos ecosystem. When bridging a TCO2 token, for example, from Polygon to Regen Network, the credits are burned on the original chain and minted anew on the target chain to prevent double-counting.[11] The tokens' metadata is retained, including details about the credits' origin, vintage, and project type.[12]

The embedded metadata within each token ensures that the provenance of each credit can be tracked from tokenisation onwards. These characteristics support blockchain's ability to address long-standing issues in the carbon market, such as *traceability and transparency*, at least in the post-issuance phase. The public, append-only nature of blockchain, where each transaction is recorded on a decentralised ledger,[13] ensures full traceability of carbon credits once they are tokenised through the Carbon Bridge. Moreover, by making the transaction history publicly accessible and immutable, the blockchain ensures that after tokenisation each credit can only be claimed once, thus reducing the likelihood of double-counting or using the same credit to offset emissions multiple times.

Another key benefit of the Carbon Bridge is its potential to address *market fragmentation*—a systemic issue in the VCMs, where carbon credits are often separated in disparate registries and platforms, making seamless trading difficult. By enabling credits from traditional registries to move onto blockchain networks, the Carbon Bridge creates a unified environment where credits can be traded and retired freely. This solution could reduce barriers to trading and enhance market accessibility.[14] However, it has to be noted that Toucan's system adds another layer on top of traditional registries, also introducing another aspect of fragmentation and complexity, as further detailed in the following subsection. Besides potentially tackling market fragmentation, Toucan's Carbon pools also aim at improving *liquidity*. By pooling tokenised carbon credits, for example, with similar vintage or project type, Toucan can issue pool tokens such as BCT or NCT, which are standardised and tradable. This pooling mechanism enhances liquidity by simplifying the trading process and allowing credits to be traded in bulk.[15]

Finally, to ensure the environmental impact is permanently accounted for, TCO2 tokens can also be *retired*, ensuring that once a token has been claimed for offset purposes, it is permanently removed from circulation. This involves 'burning' the token, a process in which the token is sent to a null address that is inaccessible and cannot be used by anyone, effectively taking it out of circulation.[16]

3.2 Challenges and limitations

Toucan's approach to integrating blockchain technology within the VCM represents an advancement in potentially addressing some of the industry's issues, such as transparency, liquidity, and market fragmentation. However, several challenges and limitations continue to affect the viability and scalability of blockchain-based solutions in the VCM. This section examines these challenges, providing a comprehensive view of the obstacles Toucan has faced, both historically and in its current operations. It also highlights ongoing limitations that pose risks to the platform's effectiveness and suggests areas for further investigation and improvement.

3.2.1 Evolution of Toucan's tokenisation approach

Toucan's efforts to integrate blockchain technology into the VCM have evolved significantly, shaped by various challenges that the company has encountered over time. The initial approach relied on a one-way bridging process, known as Carbon Bridge v1, in which carbon credits were retired in Verra's registry before being tokenised as TCO2 tokens on-chain. Moreover, there was no way to 'de-tokenise' the carbon credits. Although this allowed for the blockchain-based representation of carbon credits and created a new market for trading tokenised credits, it also introduced complications. In traditional carbon markets, retirement signifies the final use of a credit for offsetting purposes, making it unavailable for further trade. However, Toucan's method of retiring credits during tokenisation but continuing to allow their trade on-chain led to confusion about whether the environmental benefit had already been claimed or was still available for use.[17]

Verra responded to these concerns by banning the tokenisation of retired credits. Instead, Verra has stated that they would be exploring an immobilisation approach, where credits would be immobilised for on-chain use without being permanently retired.[18] Against this backdrop, Toucan adapted by developing a two-way bridge model. For example, the solution implemented with Puro.earth allows tokenised credits to be transferred back to their original registry, addressing some of the transparency and oversight issues associated with the original one-way bridging model. This bi-directional approach ensures that credits can be de-tokenised and restored to their original status in the traditional registry, enhancing traceability and reducing the risk of double issuance.[19] However, while this represents an improvement, it still does not resolve all the complexities related to maintaining consistency across different blockchain networks and traditional registries. This includes challenges such as aligning data formats between registries, reconciling different regulatory requirements across jurisdictions, and ensuring that the credit's status is accurately represented on all platforms. We will elaborate further on these points in the next sections.

3.2.2 Integrity at tokenisation

While tokenisation has the potential to improve transparency and traceability in the VCM, it cannot solve the underlying issues if the quality of the data being tokenised is flawed. Tokenising poor-quality carbon credits risks embedding these problems permanently into the blockchain, rather than addressing them. Therefore, ensuring the integrity of carbon credits at their source remains a significant challenge.

One major cause of this challenge is the fragmented nature of the market, where different standard-setting bodies apply varying criteria for credit issuance, validation, and accounting.[20] While some markets accept older credits, others impose restrictions on their use due to doubts about their additionality and relevance. This lack of consistency also leads to issues in the applied methodologies. For example, avoided deforestation credits, which are commonly used in projects aimed at preventing deforestation in the Amazon, have often been criticised for overestimating emissions reductions due to methodological flaws in baseline calculations.[21]

In the case of Toucan, approximately 28% of the carbon credits tokenised via their platform came from projects largely inactive in traditional markets, and nearly 99% of these credits would not meet the eligibility requirements of the Paris Agreement's Article 6 or the CORSIA offsetting standard.[22] The migration of low-quality credits from these dormant projects into the blockchain system presents a significant risk to the environmental integrity of both the system and the broader carbon market.

What is required, therefore, is a coordinated effort between standard-setting bodies and tokenisation platforms like Toucan to establish unified, high-quality criteria for carbon credits. However, the broader challenge lies in balancing inclusiveness with maintaining environmental integrity, which makes achieving universally accepted standards difficult.[23] Without this alignment, the fragmented market will continue to create challenges for ensuring the integrity of tokenised credits.

3.2.3 Technical, interoperability, and volatility challenges of blockchain-based financial systems

In addition to standardisation issues, technical hurdles also limit the full potential of blockchain solutions in the VCM. Although Toucan has developed a bridge to the Regen Network, which enables interoperability between different blockchain ecosystems, such solutions must be scaled across the entire market. Interoperability at scale is essential for seamless credit transfer, traceability, and market accessibility. To achieve this, unified technical standards across platforms are crucial, ensuring the smooth trading of tokenised credits.

Moreover, ensuring interoperability extends beyond just blockchain-to-blockchain connections. It must also encompass traditional registries, so that credits can move between off-chain and on-chain systems without the risk of double-counting or discrepancies in data integrity. This will require widespread adoption of technical standards and collaboration between all market participants.

Further complicating these efforts is the high volatility in current blockchain-based financial markets. While tokenisation is intended to increase liquidity, the integration into decentralised finance (DeFi) makes them prone to the high volatility of these markets compared to traditional over-the-counter (OTC) markets, as they are often paired against volatile crypto assets on DeFi trading platforms.[24]

3.2.4 Global regulatory frameworks and compliance concerns

Ultimately, the challenges of ensuring credit quality, creating uniform standards, overcoming technical hurdles like interoperability, and addressing market volatility can only be resolved through the establishment of comprehensive, global regulatory frameworks. These frameworks must standardise practices across jurisdictions, ensuring that tokenised credits are uniformly recognised and compliant with high environmental standards.

Regulatory frameworks must also address the evolving nature of the carbon market, taking into account new methodologies for additionality, baseline setting, and monitoring, as well as the integration of tokenised credits into both voluntary and compliance markets like CORSIA or Article 6 of the Paris Agreement. Without these comprehensive regulations, the full potential of blockchain in the VCM will remain constrained by the very issues it seeks to solve.

Blockchain-based platforms like Toucan operate in a complex regulatory environment. Ensuring compliance with varying regional regulations on carbon credits, data privacy, and blockchain transactions is a continuous challenge. Although blockchain can offer greater transparency, this does not automatically align with existing regulatory frameworks, which may not be equipped to handle decentralised systems. The lack of consistent global standards for carbon credits further complicates matters, potentially leading to legal ambiguities that could deter adoption.[25]

3.3 Conclusion

The Toucan case study highlights both the potential and challenges of blockchain-based tokenisation in VCMs. While tokenisation can enhance transparency and liquidity, addressing the challenges of ensuring credit quality, solving technical interoperability, and mitigating volatility are crucial for its overall success. Toucan's evolving strategy—from its initial focus on one-way tokenisation to the development of a two-way bridge—reflects the recognition that a holistic approach is necessary. By addressing both supply and demand, Toucan aims to create a more integrated market solution, but significant challenges remain.

The next case studies will explore additional stages in the carbon credit lifecycle, further contextualising these challenges and the role that blockchain can play in overcoming them.

4 Case study: Regen network development

Regen Network Development, founded in 2017, aims to build a financial ecosystem that rewards ecological restoration by addressing the challenges of unreliable ecological data and inadequate incentives in current environmental systems. By leveraging blockchain technology, it offers a decentralised and transparent platform that supports the entire VCM lifecycle—from the creation and verification to trading and retirement. The platform facilitates ecosystem service credits, which are tradable units that represent measurable ecological outcomes, such as carbon sequestration, biodiversity improvements, and improvements in water quality.[26]

A key aspect that sets Regen Network apart is its decentralised governance model, which allows for the co-development of open methodologies in collaboration with stakeholders, fostering a more flexible and adaptive framework for verifying ecological outcomes. This contrasts with other platforms in the VCM, such as Toucan, where the reliance on existing carbon credit standards has been a challenge. To support the development of this decentralised infrastructure, Regen Network raised USD 12.5 million in its initial funding, which was directed towards building the domain-specific ledger.[27] As of October 2024, over 2 million credits have been issued via the registry, approximately 588,000 credits have been retired, and more than 15 million hectares of land are registered on the platform.[28]

In this case study, we will explore how Regen's end-to-end approach aims to solve challenges observed in the VCM, such as integrity issues, and analyse the potential challenges that emerge from its decentralised structure and technological solutions.

4.1 Application of blockchain technology

Regen Network's blockchain infrastructure provides the foundation for recording and verifying ecological data, as well as trading of ecosystem service credits. At the core of this infrastructure is the *Regen Ledger*, a Proof-of-Stake (PoS) blockchain built on the Cosmos SDK.[29] The ledger enables various stakeholders including land stewards, scientists, and validators to contribute and verify ecological data across a transparent and distributed network.[30] The immutability of a blockchain-based ledger addresses transparency and traceability challenges in the VCM, as discussed in the Toucan case study, though Regen differs by integrating new credit issuance capabilities instead of tokenising existing credits alone eliminating some of the double-counting risks mentioned in the Toucan case.

4.1.1 Ecological state protocols

Ecological State Protocols (ESPs) are the foundational frameworks within the Regen Network, specifying the algorithms, criteria, and benchmarks needed to assess and verify changes in ecological states. Each ESP defines the methods and standards that must be met to produce reliable data on various environmental metrics. For example, an ESP might quantify the amount of carbon sequestered in soil or verify improvements in habitat suitability for specific species. These protocols act as decentralised, digital certifiers with a similar purpose to standard setters such as Verra or Gold Standard.

To ensure that the assessments are accurate and verifiable, the ESPs guide the Monitoring, Reporting, and Verification (MRV) process. Traditional MRV methods can be costly and labour intensive, creating barriers for smaller projects. Regen Network addresses this by integrating technologies such as satellite and drone imagery, IoT sensors, and data from public GIS datasets into the MRV process. By defining what data is needed and how it should be collected, ESPs ensure that the MRV systems gather accurate and reliable information, which is then used to verify ecological claims.

This integration between ESPs and MRV systems allows Regen Network to automate parts of the verification process, aiming at reducing the need for intermediaries and enhancing the efficiency of certification. The use of data collection from multiple sources, including user-submitted inputs and publicly available data, further strengthens the reliability of ecological assessments. By ensuring that all data collected from diverse sources meets the standards set out in the ESPs, Regen Network aims to enhance transparency, traceability, and data integrity, addressing key challenges in the VCM.[31]

4.1.2 Ecological contracts

Complementing ESPs, *Ecological Contracts (ECs)* are smart contract-based mechanisms that facilitate agreements between stakeholders. ECs enable a flexible, milestone-based incentive system, offering incremental rewards as ecological milestones are achieved. ECs aim to improve the issuance models of traditional carbon credits, which typically require long and rigid verification periods, by streamlining the process through a phased structure where each step in the contract must be completed before moving to the next. This allows for faster, more direct incentives, particularly benefiting smaller stakeholders like farmers and community projects who may struggle to navigate traditional carbon market frameworks.[32]

For example, an EC might set up a contract that rewards a farmer for achieving specific carbon sequestration targets in a defined area, with each milestone verified by the ESPs. By directly linking rewards to specific ecological outcomes, ECs aim to reduce the reliance on intermediaries, improving transparency and efficiency across the process. This mechanism ensures that rewards are distributed equitably, encouraging active contributions to environmental goals.[33]

4.1.3 Supply Protocols

Regen Network also uses *Supply Protocols (SPs)*, which integrate verified ecological data directly into supply chains, thereby further enhancing transparency and traceability of CO2 reductions. SPs connect environmental status information with market mechanisms, enabling the seamless tracking of ecological data throughout the supply chain. For example, a reduction of one ton of CO2 is tokenised and can be tracked through its lifecycle, ensuring all relevant information is transparently recorded on the blockchain.[34] This integration facilitates a direct pathway for users to access carbon credits and the associated information on the Regen Marketplace, eliminating inefficiencies associated with traditional intermediaries and making carbon credits more accessible globally.

The adaptability and modular structure of ESPs, ECs, and SPs make them well-suited for diverse ecological contexts. By decentralising and automating parts of the verification process, Regen Network lowers costs and broadens accessibility, particularly for smaller projects. This inclusive approach helps overcome entry barriers often faced by smallholder farmers, Indigenous communities, and other stakeholders, democratising access to regenerative practices.

4.1.4 Decentralised governance (DAO Structure)

While Regen Network's protocol framework provides the foundation, using the right methodologies is essential for ensuring integrity. Regen Network aims to achieve this through its governance model, structured as a *decentralised autonomous organisation (DAO)*. Through this model, diverse stakeholders, including land stewards, scientists, and other contributors, can propose and vote on ecological protocols and methodologies, fostering a bottom-up approach. With this, Regen Network democratises the development of environmental standards and enables communities to design methodologies that suit specific ecosystems and project sizes, contrasting with generalised top-down models that often overlook local nuances. This decentralised approach promotes adaptability and inclusiveness, allowing the standards to evolve based on a broad range of inputs, thus reflecting the ecological and socio-economic diversity of the real world.[35]

However, Regen's governance is not entirely decentralised. It combines decentralised decision-making with a degree of centralised oversight, where 35% of the network's tokens are held by the Regen Consortium, the network's foundation. This strategic allocation introduces stability, aiming to mitigate risks associated with fully decentralised systems, such as vulnerability to network manipulation. By maintaining a qualified minority, the consortium can help stabilise the platform against potential disruptions, ensuring that key governance decisions are not dominated by a small number of actors. This setup strives to balance security with decentralisation, although its long-term effectiveness in maintaining platform integrity and governance adaptability remains an area for further evaluation.[36] Currently, Regen Network is progressing on over 40 methodologies, with three already published and two credit classes prepared for practical use.[37]

4.1.5 Role and utility of the regen token ($REGEN)

The *$REGEN token* is a multi-functional component of the Regen Network ecosystem, designed to support governance, incentivise participation, and aid in network security. As a governance token, $REGEN allows holders to participate directly in Regen Network's DAO. Token holders can vote on ecosystem decisions, including adjustments to ESPs, standards for verification, and overall network parameters.

Beyond governance, $REGEN also serves as an incentive for diverse stakeholder participation. By distributing rewards in $REGEN tokens, Regen Network aims to encourage data contributions and maintain high-quality ecological data inputs. Through its role as a reward mechanism, $REGEN encourages active involvement from a broad spectrum of participants, promoting a more inclusive and representative data ecosystem. Through its staking mechanism, $REGEN also contributes to network security. Validators are required to lock $REGEN tokens as collateral to secure the network and earn rewards for verifying ecological data. This ensures that participants have a vested interest in maintaining network integrity, as their tokens are at risk if they act maliciously or negligently.[38]

4.1.6 Regen registry and marketplace

The *Regen Registry* is a core component of Regen Network's ecosystem, designed to establish and uphold community standards for developing, verifying, and trading ecological credits. Built on the Regen Ledger, the registry offers a decentralised and transparent platform that manages the lifecycle of ecosystem service credits—from project registration and credit issuance to ownership transfer and retirement. This ensures that all credits are fully traceable, immutable, and backed by verifiable data, addressing issues like double-counting, data integrity, and transparency in the VCM.[39] What distinguishes the Regen Registry is its modular design, which allows for the integration of new methodologies and the creation of diverse credit classes. Once the credits are issued, they can be traded or sold on the Regen Marketplace, which can help provide further financial incentives for sustainable practices and ecological restoration.

Building on the foundation established by the Regen Registry, the *Regen Marketplace* was launched in 2022 to enable users to trade, transfer, and retire ecosystem service credits. By providing a seamless pathway from credit issuance to trading, the marketplace tries to address the lack of investment in the VCM. Partnerships with projects like Toucan and Moss expand the reach of the platform and allow credits to be traded across networks.[40] The *Polygon-Nature Carbon Ton (NCT) bridge*, for example, facilitates the seamless movement of credits across ecosystems, enhancing liquidity and enabling decentralised trading.[41] Additionally, the marketplace manages on-chain ecocredit lifecycles, from issuance and trading to permanent retirement, once credits are claimed for offset purposes.[42] This functionality fosters transparency and traceability, strengthening accountability, which is particularly valuable for high-profile buyers.

In 2023, Regen Network introduced a *concierge sales service* to assist corporate buyers with navigating the complexities of purchasing high-integrity carbon credits. By providing tailored guidance, this service aims to ensure that corporate buyers meet high ecological standards in their offset purchases while enhancing trust and accessibility in the VCM.[43] Microsoft, for example, has used the Regen Marketplace to purchase credits like CarbonPlus Grasslands to meet corporate sustainability goals.[44]

4.2 Challenges and limitations

Despite the innovative potential of Regen Network's blockchain-based framework, several challenges and limitations need to be acknowledged. These issues encompass technical, market, governance, and data-related concerns that can impact the overall effectiveness and adoption of the platform. The following only lists challenges that are of specific relevance in the case of Regen Network, neglecting generic challenges of blockchain-based VCCs that were already highlighted in the Toucan case.

4.2.1 Equitable participation and governance imbalances

Regen Network's decentralised governance model, which relies on a DAO, aims to democratise the development of ecological standards. However, achieving true inclusivity remains a significant challenge. Smallholder farmers, indigenous communities, and local stakeholders may face barriers to participation due to limited access to necessary technologies, digital literacy, or expertise in complex governance processes. This can lead to a risk where larger, better-resourced entities dominate decision-making, potentially skewing the development of ecological standards to favour specific interests. Such imbalances threaten the inclusivity that the platform seeks to promote, raising concerns about the fairness and integrity of the system.[45]

Furthermore, Regen Network's governance model, which allows the Regen Consortium to retain a strategic minority of tokens, was designed to mitigate the risks of fully decentralised systems. While this introduces stability, it also creates a paradox. By centralising some decision-making power, the system may inadvertently reproduce power imbalances that the decentralised governance is supposed to address.[46] It is important to monitor how this governance structure evolves, as prolonged centralisation may erode stakeholder trust.

4.2.2 Data integrity and verification challenges

A core feature of Regen Network is its commitment to transparency, particularly through the immutable nature of its blockchain ledger. However, blockchain's transparency does not inherently resolve the issue of data quality. As highlighted by Howson et al. (2019),[47] the value of blockchain lies in the accuracy of the data recorded. Similar to the integrity challenge highlighted in the Toucan case, if flawed or manipulated data is entered, the transparency of the blockchain merely ensures that this poor-quality data is perpetuated across the system. In contrast to Toucan, where the integrity challenge already starts at the VCCs that are onboarded to the blockchain, Regen Network only faces this challenge with respect to the underlying data as tokenisation as the VCCs are issued directly on the blockchain.

Therefore, the effectiveness of the platform hinges on the robustness of its MRV protocols. While Regen has made strides in developing MRV solutions that incorporate data from multiple sources and AI models, these technologies are not infallible. Data collection via remote sensing can be imprecise, and algorithmic models may still face issues of bias and calibration, necessitating continuous refinement to ensure reliability.[48]

4.2.3 Token valuation and economic security risks

A rapid decline in the value of the $REGEN token in 2021 has raised significant concerns for Regen Network's governance model, which relies on staking for network security.[49] With the token's devaluation, economic incentives for validators and participants are weakened, leading to a reduced ability to secure the network and attract new stakeholders. This instability in the token price diminishes its effectiveness as a mechanism for governance, creating risks around reduced engagement and the possibility of opportunistic behavior from those still holding tokens. Thus, utilising a network native token further increases the risks of missing liquidity and high volatility in the cryptocurrency markets, as already highlighted in the Toucan case. The introduction of a new financial asset also introduces further regulatory uncertainties regarding the classification of such a network-native token and the implications, for example, in the context of prospectus or liability obligations.

4.3 Conclusion

Regen Network's approach to creating a decentralised, transparent, and inclusive system for trading ecosystem service credits presents significant opportunities but is not without its challenges. Ensuring equitable participation, maintaining data integrity, overcoming liquidity and volatility risks regarding the native token, and navigating complex regulatory environments are key issues that need to be addressed. While the platform's design seeks to mitigate some of these concerns through innovations in blockchain and governance, their long-term effectiveness will depend on continuous refinement, stakeholder engagement, and adaptability to evolving market and regulatory landscapes.

5 Case study: Senken

Founded in 2021, Senken was initially developed as a blockchain-based marketplace for carbon credits, aiming to address inefficiencies within the VCM, including limited accessibility, market fragmentation, and issues with transparency and liquidity. Targeting the demand side of the VCM, Senken initially sought to streamline trading by aggregating blockchain-native registries alongside tokenised credits through collaborations with projects like Toucan, Thallo, and FlowCarbon, among others. At its peak, Senken has offered over 20 million carbon credits, positioning itself as one of the largest platforms for tokenised credits.[50]

This case study explores the evolution of Senken, its initial adoption of blockchain technology, and the challenges that led to a strategic pivot away from this approach. By analysing the obstacles encountered, it provides insights into why blockchain solutions may not always achieve long-term viability in VCMs and reflects on how Senken's journey illustrates broader trends within the VCC market.

5.1 Adoption of blockchain technology

The previous case studies on Toucan and Regen Network highlight a critical issue in the VCM: Each additional blockchain project, with its distinct technologies, methodologies, and processes, contributes to an increasingly fragmented ecosystem, compounding existing challenges like liquidity and coordination. Senken recognised this existing fragmentation and sought to create a solution that would unify diverse carbon credit sources in one marketplace by bringing together the on-chain and off-chain carbon markets, simplifying user access and trading in the VCM.[51]

Senken's initial platform was designed as a blockchain-based marketplace where users could seamlessly buy, trade, and retire tokenised carbon credits. Built on partnerships with multiple blockchain projects, it aggregated tokenised carbon credits from multiple on-chain registries.[52] Through this, Senken addressed the complex landscape users faced, in which varying standards across platforms hindered straightforward trading and market participation. This consolidation offered the potential for improved liquidity, as a unified marketplace could reduce the inefficiencies and illiquidity typically observed in decentralised carbon credit trading.[53] To further enhance accessibility, Senken implemented a user-friendly, web 2.0-style interface that abstracted the technical complexities typically associated with blockchain. This design allowed users unfamiliar with blockchain to engage with the marketplace as they would with any traditional platform, while still benefiting from blockchain's transparency and traceability.[54]

The process for engaging with Senken's platform was structured as follows:[55]

1. *Automated Wallet Creation* – Upon signing in, users had a Web 3.0 wallet generated automatically in the background, enabling them to hold and transact blockchain-based assets without the need for prior wallet management experience.
2. *Integrated On-Ramp Provider* – Senken partnered with an on-ramp provider, enabling users to fund their accounts in fiat currency, which was then converted into digital assets and transferred to the wallet. This integration allowed for a

seamless transition between traditional and blockchain finance without requiring specialised knowledge from users.

3. *KYC Verification* – To meet regulatory requirements, Senken incorporated a traditional KYC process, ensuring compliance with financial regulations and industry standards.
4. *Transaction Processing and Purchase* – Users could place and confirm their orders within the platform, providing a familiar purchasing experience similar to commonly known digital marketplaces.
5. *Portfolio Management and Tracking* – After purchase, users could access their portfolio in their wallet, viewing detailed information on each credit, including its origin, project type, and environmental impact. This added layer of transparency and traceability facilitated informed decision-making and allowed users to efficiently track the impact of their VCCs.

Senken's interface also incorporated independent carbon ratings and analytical tools,[56] providing users with essential information on various price factors such as registry type, project characteristics, location, and vintage. This level of detail enabled users to make more informed purchasing decisions, with a full record of retired credits accessible in their individual profiles. This approach allowed users, whether corporate or individual, to present verifiable and organised records of their carbon offset actions to stakeholders, enhancing transparency and credibility in a manner previously unavailable in traditional systems. Additionally, by consolidating credits across registries and platforms, Senken enhanced interoperability in carbon trading, with the aim of creating a more integrated and efficient VCM. This approach promised improved price discovery, as the unified marketplace provided clearer visibility into supply and demand trends. In theory, such transparency could support more accurate price signals, potentially mitigating demand and supply imbalances that have historically affected VCMs and laying a foundation for greater market stability and predictability.[57]

5.2 Challenges and limitations

Despite its innovative approach, Senken encountered several challenges that ultimately led to a shift in its business model. Key issues included inconsistencies in project quality and standards, and employed methodologies that limited reliability and trust across the marketplace. The high volatility of the VCM posed additional challenges, contrasting with the stability sought by institutional investors.[58] These challenges align with broader industry observations we discussed in detail in prior case studies, where similar hurdles in earlier stages of the VCM lifecycle amplify issues downstream, ultimately undermining the marketplace credibility in this case.

Additionally, customer feedback emphasised a preference for simplicity over technological complexity in the user interface and experience, particularly among corporate clients, whose primary focus was on accessible, high-quality credits rather than navigating blockchain infrastructure. While Senken's initial blockchain framework showed promise, establishing and maintaining reliability and efficiency across the entire carbon credit lifecycle proved challenging, given the various demands of verification, registry creation, standards consistency, and the complexities of trading and retirement. Recognising that addressing such complex issues exceeded the capacity of a small startup, Senken pivoted away from its blockchain-native marketplace approach. They recognised that simply serving as a transaction layer would be insufficient to uphold credibility and chose to implement their own due diligence assessments to safeguard marketplace integrity.[59] The immediate goal is a trustworthy carbon marketplace that is simple, reliable, and meets corporate standards by reducing barriers and implementing quality assurance, such as Senken's guarantee program and scorecards for project evaluation.

As a result, Senken shifted towards a selective, rigorously structured approach, employing a proprietary due diligence framework to evaluate carbon credits with an emphasis on integrity and environmental impact. This multi-tiered process applies stringent criteria to evaluate projects across various dimensions, with the aim of listing only those that demonstrate a high standard of quality and environmental impact. The five-stage framework includes initial assessments of core project details, evaluation of CO2 impact, examination of non-CO2 benefits (such as biodiversity and social contributions), thorough analysis of data reporting methods, and a final compliance and reputation check. Supported by AI-driven models and validation from climate scientists, this comprehensive due diligence process incorporates over 60 specific criteria across these phases, aiming to minimise risk and bolster marketplace credibility. Notably, compliance with standards like the Integrity Council for the Voluntary Carbon Market's (ICVCM's) Core Carbon Principles (CCPs)[60] and alignment with future regulatory frameworks, such as Nationally Determined Contributions (NDCs)[61] and the European Corporate Sustainability Reporting Directive (CSRD),[62] reflect Senken's commitment to evolving best practices in the VCM. Senken claims that only around 5% of applicants pass this rigorous evaluation, ensuring that listed projects are both high-impact and low-risk.[63]

5.3 Conclusion

The pivot away from a blockchain-native model highlights a fundamental insight for startups in emerging fields: while technology offers transformative potential, it is not a panacea. Ensuring sustainable growth and scalability often requires a mix of innovation and conventional business practices, as well as a realistic assessment of what each approach can accomplish.[64] In Senken's case, the pivot towards a curated, due diligence-based model reflects an understanding that building a robust and credible foundation may require adapting or, in some cases, stepping back from new technological solutions, instead embracing more controlled and quality-assured processes, and aligning closely with evolving regulatory frameworks.

6 Case study: Kumo

Kumo launched in 2022 as a decentralised finance (DeFi) initiative with the objective of creating a nature-backed stablecoin, KumoUSD (KUSD), collateralised by tokenised carbon credits and pegged to the U.S. Dollar. This initial approach aimed to incorporate environmental accountability into financial transactions by directly linking currency to carbon sequestration projects. The protocol allowed users to borrow KUSD at zero interest by locking tokenised carbon credits as collateral. KumoDAO designed the stablecoin to maintain price stability through arbitrage mechanisms, with decisions on acceptable collateral delegated to the DAO. In summary, Kumo adopted the concept of overcollateralised stablecoins pioneered by MakerDAO (now Sky) but limited the selection of assets that could be used as collateral to VCC tokens.[65] Through this model, Kumo sought to transform carbon credits into assets utilisable as collateral, thereby embedding climate accountability into everyday financial activity without altering conventional financial priorities.[66]

6.1 Application of blockchain technology

Kumo, operating at the intersection of climate finance and technology, now primarily focuses on facilitating institutional debt financing for carbon removal projects. Central to its approach is the application of blockchain technology, specifically through tokenisation, to transform *carbon credits* into recognised *collateral* suitable for loans. The primary purpose of tokenisation in Kumo's platform, in this case, is not necessarily to increase transparency or verifiability of the tokens or the underlying VCCs but to establish a legally robust and standardised framework for managing carbon credits as financial assets. Developed in collaboration with legal experts, this process creates a 'legal wrapper' around carbon credits that aims at ensuring compliance with the regulatory and financial standards required by institutional investors.[67]

Project developers often struggle to secure timely funding due to the lengthy and costly process of verifying, registering, and issuing carbon credits.[68] Complex verification procedures and high transaction costs hinder the accessibility of financing, while inconsistent regulatory standards across markets increase uncertainty for investors.[69] By transforming carbon credits into collateralisable assets, Kumo addresses this funding barrier, making carbon credits suitable as reliable assets for debt financing and bridging the gap between financial risk and climate impact.

Kumo's approach caters to two main groups within the VCM: capital providers and project developers. For capital providers, Kumo offers an opportunity to unlock new revenue streams through carbon-backed lending. By structuring carbon credits as legally recognised collateral, Kumo's platform reduces investment risks, making it feasible for traditional lenders to participate in carbon-backed financing. For project developers, Kumo enables the use of debt financing as a non-dilutive funding option, allowing them to leverage carbon credits or off-take agreements to secure loans. This financing structure offers developers a feasible alternative to equity funding, which can be costly and lead to ownership dilution.[70]

Beyond collateralisation, Kumo's platform incorporates automated data aggregation, project assessment, and ongoing monitoring—capabilities anchored by Kumo's proprietary *Carbon-Debt Financeability Framework*. By standardising data and enabling pre-deal assessments, the framework facilitates rigorous and consistent project evaluation, streamlining due diligence for institutional lenders. While Kumo's platform may lack the full transparency associated with public blockchains, it provides a controlled, secure environment that manages the operational and data management demands of carbon-backed financing. This setup aims to reduce operational burdens and streamline data management, thereby enhancing the overall scalability of debt financing in the carbon market.[71]

6.2 Challenges and limitations

While tokenising carbon credits as collateral offers new financing opportunities for climate projects, it presents several potential challenges that need close examination. Many of these challenges, such as regulatory ambiguity, market liquidity, asset quality, and interoperability, have been explained in prior case studies like Toucan and apply broadly across the VCM landscape. For Kumo's approach, these challenges could introduce specific complexities that may influence the viability of tokenised carbon credits as a stable form of collateral, which is essential for the vitality of the collateralisation mechanism.

Factors such as regulatory changes, market sentiment, and project credibility contribute to fluctuations in the value and stability of carbon credits, creating risks similar to those in other markets that leverage complex or illiquid assets. For example, non-standardised or intangible assets, like patents or renewable energy credits, show similar volatility and valuation challenges, leading to issues in their use as secure collateral.[72]

Another risk is the dependency of carbon credits on environmental outcomes and verification standards, which can vary significantly. Without a unified regulatory framework, these assets can be difficult to standardise and reliably assess, increasing the risk for lenders and capital providers.[73] In the case of collateralised carbon credits, this lack of consistency creates uncertainty around credit quality and market valuation, particularly in a fragmented regulatory environment.[74]

Furthermore, securitising carbon credits could introduce systemic risks in the VCM if widespread collateralisation leads to over-reliance on a niche market. This is similar to risks seen in financial markets that have structured products around unstable asset classes, where market shifts can lead to cascading effects.[75] Should carbon credit prices or demand fluctuate, a lack of liquidity and regulatory oversight could impact the VCM's stability and the broader financial market, given the asset class's unique reliance on environmental outcomes and non-traditional valuation metrics.[76]

6.3 Conclusion

This case study of Kumo illustrates how utilisation of carbon credits as collateral can unlock new paths to utilise this asset class, potentially providing a solution to the financing gap and enhancing the VCM's capacity to scale. However, this approach also faces and potentially even amplifies the challenges highlighted in prior cases. Especially asset stability, regulatory alignment, and market reliance are essential to ensure the vitality of the collateralisation mechanism and thus, the viability of the whole platform.

7 Case study: Moss

Moss, founded in March 2020, is a Brazilian climate technology company that leverages blockchain to enhance accessibility and security in the VCC market. Moss' primary mission is to combat climate change and support Amazon rainforest conservation by providing a straightforward digital platform for purchasing and retiring carbon credits. To achieve this, Moss has introduced the MCO2 Token,[77] a blockchain-based digital asset equivalent to one carbon credit, and the Moss Amazon NFT,[78] an asset enabling individuals to contribute to Amazon conservation efforts. The company sources carbon credits from environmental projects in the Amazon that adhere to the REDD+ (Reducing Emissions from Deforestation and Forest Degradation) frameworks, focusing on preventing deforestation and capturing CO2 emissions.[79] Since March 2020, Moss reports on having directed approximately USD 30 million to conservation projects in the Amazon, resulting in the preservation of over 301 million trees and the avoidance of an estimated 1.33 million tons of carbon emissions.[80]

This case study intends to demonstrate that blockchain applications in VCMs need to focus not only on liquidity and decentralisation to maximise the added value. Instead, Moss's model shows that by emphasising security, accessibility, and conservation impact, blockchain can also appeal to stakeholders who prioritise transaction security and efficiency, ease of use, and transparency over speculative investment. By analysing Moss's approach alongside the challenges, this study expands our understanding of blockchain's versatility in VCMs, revealing a model focused on practical environmental impact rather than purely market dynamics.

The following description of Moss's blockchain application draws on the company's 2020 whitepaper and other sources, which were written prior to Verra's ban on blockchain-based tokenisation (see Toucan case study).

7.1 Application of blockchain technology

Moss's blockchain-based tokenisation approach centred around issuing the *MCO2 Token*, an ERC-20 token on the Ethereum blockchain, with each token representing one metric ton of CO_2 equivalent from high-quality carbon credits.[81] The MCO2 Tokens could be purchased through Moss's platform as well as on cryptocurrency exchanges like Coinbase. This approach aimed at addressing inefficiencies in the VCC market by providing a secure and accessible platform for purchasing, tracking, and retiring credits, where existing exchanges and traditional registries often fall short. Therefore, Moss actively curated and purchased carbon credits rather than acting solely as a marketplace. The projects it sourced were certified under the Verified Carbon Standard (VCS) by Verra, with purchase contracts stored in both Moss's internal database and Verra's registry. For each newly acquired carbon credit, Moss minted a corresponding MCO2 Token.[82]

Moss's customer base comprised two main segments: retail customers and institutional clients. For retail customers, Moss retired the carbon credits immediately upon purchase, while institutional clients had access to a customised retirement option, allowing greater flexibility in offset timing.[83] To manage these credits transparently, Moss maintained distinct sub-accounts within the Verra registry for active and retired credits. On the blockchain, Moss used a carbon credit inventory contract to track the total supply of active and retired MCO2 Tokens, aligning this with Verra's sub-accounts. Since the MCO2 Token was fungible, individual tokens were not linked to specific projects. Thus, buyers could not select a specific project for offsetting; each token instead represented a general claim on a carbon credit managed by Moss. The platform also allowed MCO2 holders to burn their tokens, removing them from circulation and receiving a certificate for the retirement of a carbon credit equal to one ton of CO2 emissions.[84]

A defining element of Moss's approach was its custodial role, as it retained custody of both the off-chain credits and associated purchase contracts. This positioning removes the need for additional intermediaries, which might otherwise increase transaction costs and complexity. To secure the buyers' ownership rights, Moss employed a standardised contract known as the *Verified Emission Reduction Purchase Agreement (VERPA)*, which both expedited and secured the legal transfer of carbon credit ownership. Moss also implemented a 'bankruptcy-remote' framework to keep tokenised assets separate from the company's corporate assets, ensuring that in cases of insolvency, token holders' assets would remain legally protected.[85]

Moss's primary motivation for adopting blockchain was to improve transaction security and transparency, while reducing the complexity and costs associated with traditional carbon credit transactions. While transparency and traceability—covered in the Toucan case study—are often cited benefits of tokenisation, Moss emphasises tokenisation primarily as a way to enhance security in carbon offset transactions without introducing new financial assets through a native token.[86] The MCO2 Token facilitates efficient, low-cost transfer of carbon credits between parties, bypassing delays and high fees typical of traditional carbon markets. This blockchain-based system establishes a public, secure, and immutable record, enhancing credibility and reducing transaction hurdles of carbon credits by ensuring that they can be efficiently transferred and retired.

Expanding its blockchain applications, Moss introduced the *Moss Amazon NFT*, an initiative allowing individuals to contribute directly to Amazon rainforest conservation.[87] To secure land for this initiative, Moss or its subsidiary, Terra Vista Gestora de Recursos LTDA, has acquired parcels like 'Fazenda Rio Azul,' ensuring direct custodial oversight of conserved areas. The NFT-based system provides a digital certificate of ownership containing detailed information and data on the title of ownership.[88] Moss has also established a 30-year conservation fund to ensure the ongoing protection of these lands. The fund allocates a portion of NFT proceeds to patrolling and monitoring efforts, supported by geospatial intelligence to prevent deforestation.

7.2 Challenges and limitations

Moss faces many of the general challenges discussed in the Toucan case study, including issues of credit quality, regulatory constraints, and market volatility. Like Toucan, Moss was directly affected by Verra's suspension of blockchain-based tokenisation of retired carbon credits, limiting its access to Verra-certified projects and underscoring the broader uncertainty surrounding tokenised carbon assets. Among the shared challenges, Moss's reliance on the quality of its carbon credits is particularly impactful. Concerns have been raised over the integrity of certain credits, with reports indicating that Moss may have included credits of questionable environmental value. This reliance on subprime credits poses a risk to both Moss's reputation and the broader trust in tokenised carbon credits, especially when transparency around credit quality is limited.[89] Reports also suggest that Moss may have sold the included carbon credits at a significant premium.[90] While profit-making strategies are essential for scaling and sustaining operations, transparency around both pricing and credit quality is crucial for maintaining trust in tokenised carbon credits, especially given the environmental mission Moss promotes.

Although Moss designed the MCO2 Token as a utility token and claimed that it should not have any speculative purpose, listing it on public exchanges exposed it to market fluctuations typical for the cryptocurrency sector. Since reaching an all-time high of USD 21.68 in December 2021, the token's price has dropped significantly, now trading around USD 0.45 as of November 2024.[91] This sharp decline may reflect several factors: general decline in the interest from investors in carbon tokens, Verra's suspension of tokenisation, critiques of the underlying credits' quality, and the inherent volatility of cryptocurrency markets.

7.3 Conclusion

While Moss's use of blockchain technology enhances access to carbon credits for both retail and institutional buyers, it also makes it easier to verify purchases on a public blockchain. However, as with other projects, challenges such as reliance on carbon credit quality, regulatory uncertainties, and market volatility add complexity to this model and raise issues for large-scale adoption of the VCM.

8 Discussion

This discussion interprets and synthesises findings from an analysis of five case studies—Toucan, Regen Network, Senken, Kumo, and Moss—each representing distinct approaches to integrating blockchain technology in the VCM. By analysing these start-ups' strategies, challenges, and opportunities, this section proposes recommendations to support the broader adoption of blockchain solutions in VCMs. While each case study highlights specific aspects of these issues, this section integrates their findings to provide a cohesive understanding of the key obstacles and their potential mitigations.

To achieve this, the discussion is organised into thematic areas:

1. *Regulatory and Standardisation Needs* – Examining the role of unified regulatory frameworks, standardised tokenisation practices, and harmonised methodologies in overcoming fragmentation and establishing trust and transparency.
2. *Technical Infrastructure Requirements* – Highlighting the importance of interoperability, data integrity, and advanced MRV systems for creating a seamless and trustworthy ecosystem.
3. *Operational and Market Dynamics* – Evaluating the potential of blockchain to enhance market liquidity, operational efficiency, and transparency while addressing barriers to equitable participation.

In the following, the key insights on these areas from the five cases will be presented, including avenues for future practical and academic contributions within these areas, as highlighted in Table 5.1. Through this structure, the discussion aims to connect the challenges observed in individual case studies with the overall requirements for maximising blockchain's impact in the VCM. By addressing these interconnected issues, this section not only contextualises the current state of blockchain in the VCM but also lays the groundwork for practical, system-wide recommendations.

Table 5.1: Overview of key insight areas, sub-aspects, and the future academic and practical avenues within.

Area	Sub-aspects	Possibilities for Future Contribution
Regulatory and Standardisation Needs	Unified Regulatory Framework	– Establish a globally harmonised regulatory framework aligned with international agreements, such as Article 6 of the Paris Agreement, to address market fragmentation and establish trust and transparency. – Create cohesive governance structures to support cross-border compatibility and prevent double-counting. – Foster trust by mandating transparency in governance, market operations, and credit verification practices.
	Standardised Tokenisation Methodologies	– Implement universal standards for tokenisation aligned with the Core Carbon Principles and other industry guidelines, including metadata requirements, to enhance comparability and traceability. – Restrict pooling mechanisms that aggregate low-quality credits and incentivise high-integrity projects.
	Harmonised Market Standards for Methodologies	– Align existing methodologies (e.g., Verra, Gold Standard, Puro) to create consistent quality benchmarks and evaluation criteria. – Actively engage smaller stakeholders, indigenous communities, and project developers in methodology creation for inclusivity.
Technical Infrastructure Requirements	Interoperability Across Systems	– Scale cross-chain interoperability solutions to unify fragmented blockchain ecosystems. – Develop metadata layers, such as those proposed by Climate Warehouse, to link on-chain and off-chain registries. – Prevent double-counting through robust cross-registry communication protocols.
	Accurate Measurement Systems for Data Integrity	– Integrate IoT devices and analytical algorithms for real-time monitoring, anomaly detection, and secure data validation. – Develop or extend decentralised sensor networks to expand access to reliable monitoring. – Ensure tamper-proof storage of MRV data on blockchains for auditability and transparency.

Table 5.1 (continued)

Area	Sub-aspects	Possibilities for Future Contribution
	Technical Requirements for Accessibility and Adoptions	– Build user-centric platforms that abstract blockchain complexities for non-technical users, enabling broader participation. – Integrate privacy-preserving technologies (e.g., Zero-Knowledge Proofs) to ensure compliance with data protection regulations while maintaining accountability. – Simplify on- and off-ramping solutions to align blockchain systems with traditional financial processes.
Operational and Market Dynamics	Operational and Transaction Efficiency	– Streamline processes for credit issuance, trading, and retirement by automating workflows and reducing intermediaries. – Standardise contracts and transaction mechanisms to simplify participation and improve scalability.
	Market Dynamics and Financial Stability	– Develop secure financial instruments (e.g., carbon-backed loans, forward contracts) to stabilise funding and mitigate market volatility. – Create liquid secondary markets by fostering investor confidence through transparent pricing and standardised assets. – Align blockchain-based financial solutions with regulatory frameworks to promote institutional adoption.

8.1 Regulatory and standardisation needs

8.1.1 Unified regulatory framework

A unified regulatory framework is the essential foundation for addressing the challenges of integrating blockchain into VCMs. Without a harmonised set of global regulations, the inherent fragmentation of VCMs—spanning diverse jurisdictions, methodologies, and stakeholders—becomes a fundamental barrier to scalability. Blockchain-based solutions, while promising, risk deepening this fragmentation when applied inconsistently, creating isolated systems that fail to interoperate.

The challenges were formalised when Verra suspended the tokenisation of off-chain carbon credits (Verra, 2022). This decision disrupted blockchain-based platforms like Toucan, KlimaDAO, and Moss, which tokenised Verra's credits. The suspension highlighted the dependence of blockchain projects on traditional, centralised standard-setters.

A unified framework establishes the necessary baseline for coordination, ensuring that methodologies, governance practices, and data standards align across platforms. Carbon markets operate within a global context, where cross-border collaboration is critical for addressing climate change. Aligning blockchain solutions with international agreements like the Paris Agreement is not just desirable but essential for their comparability. Article 6 of the Paris Agreement, with its robust accounting rules designed to prevent double-counting, provides a potential foundation for such a framework.[92] Blockchain technology aligns with the bottom-up and decentralised governance ethos attributed to Article 6 of the Paris Agreement, offering benefits such as transparency, traceability, and automation while addressing legacy system challenges like information asymmetry and incompatible data structures.[93] Embedding these principles into regulatory frameworks ensures that tokenised carbon credits can be made universally recognised, traceable, and comparable. This is particularly vital for engaging institutional investors, whose participation hinges on confidence in the legitimacy and reliability of the underlying credits.

Moreover, a unified regulatory framework is not merely about compliance; it can foster trust by enhancing market transparency, efficiency, and consistency. Regulatory clarity, such as the establishment of national or international emissions trading systems, has been shown to improve market activity and efficiency, as evidenced in China's carbon markets following the announcement of the National ETS.[94] By reducing uncertainties and ensuring accountability, such frameworks build the foundational trust needed for stakeholders—from project developers to institutional investors—to confidently engage in carbon markets. This trust arises from the elimination of information asymmetries, the provision of predictable rules for market operations, and the verification of claims. In the context of blockchain applications, regulatory clarity also amplifies the technology's strengths, such as enhancing traceability and automating compliance, within a stable governance environment. Without such clarity, even the most innovative blockchain solutions risk being sidelined and unable to gain traction beyond niche use cases.

This framework is not meant to replace the technical or operational solutions required to address specific challenges, such as interoperability or stakeholder inclusivity. Rather, it creates a structured environment in which such solutions can thrive. It underpins the development of robust secondary markets, facilitates the integration of decentralised and traditional systems, and ensures that stakeholder engagement processes are equitable and transparent.

8.1.2 Standardised tokenisation methodologies

Inconsistent tokenisation methodologies across blockchain-based VCM initiatives present significant challenges to market integrity and scalability. The case studies explored in this chapter reveal the consequences of such inconsistencies, including fragmented approaches to tokenisation, insufficient quality control, and the lack of standardised metadata.

For instance, Toucan's early tokenisation of retired carbon credits led to Verra banning such practices in 2022.[95] Similarly, the tokenisation of low-quality credits revealed the dangers of inadequate criteria. Notably, hydropower credits from a dam in China—dormant for over a decade—were tokenised in large volumes, artificially creating demand for offsets previously excluded from the market.[96] Practices such as KlimaDAO's pooling mechanisms, which focused on 'sweeping the floor' to gather low-cost credits, exacerbated these issues.[97] Such practices raise significant doubts about the environmental integrity of tokenised credits, undermining trust and confidence in the system.

Beyond quality concerns, the lack of uniformity in token formats complicates comparability and traceability. Moss employs fungible tokens (MCO2), Toucan uses a mix of fungible and semi-fungible tokens (BCT, NCT), and some platforms tokenise credits natively while others tokenise existing off-chain credits.[98] Metadata requirements also vary widely, leaving buyers with inconsistent information, hampering transparency and comparability. For example, Moss's MCO2 token does not allow project-specific selection,[99] while Toucan's tokens embed more detailed metadata, such as vintage and project type.[100] The question of whether tokenised credits should be fractionalised further intensifies these issues, as fractionalisation complicates the retirement process, accountability, and traceability.[101]

Efforts like BioCarbon Standard's Tokenisation Guidelines provide a promising foundation for addressing these challenges. These guidelines propose strict criteria for tokenisation, including prohibitions on pooling, clear metadata requirements, and robust monitoring and reporting standards.[102] However, such initiatives remain localised and lack the market-wide harmonisation needed.

By harmonising tokenisation methodologies, the industry can foster comparability, enhance transparency, and build the institutional trust needed for large-scale adoption. This requires clear rules on acceptable tokenisation practices, standardised metadata fields, and alignment with international frameworks such as Article 6 of the Paris Agreement. Without such standardisation, the risk of fragmentation, missing trust and transparency, and inefficiency will persist, limiting the potential of blockchain technology to transform VCMs.

8.1.3 Harmonised market standards for methodologies

The lack of harmonised market standards for methodologies in the VCM complicates efforts in ensuring credit comparability, quality, and integrity. Verra, Gold Standard, and Puro collectively maintain over 90 methodologies, each tailored to specific project types and geographies.[103] While these frameworks provide a solid foundation for credit verification, their divergence complicates the evaluation of credit equivalence and quality, creating inefficiencies and hindering market scalability. As seen in the Toucan and Moss case studies, inconsistencies in credit verification and harmonised methodologies can lead to the tokenisation of credits with unknown environmental value.

Efforts to improve credit quality and comparability are evident in initiatives like the *CCPs* developed by the ICVCM.[104] These principles aim to establish minimum quality thresholds for credits, thereby addressing foundational gaps in ensuring consistency and reliability. However, these initiatives must align and collaborate to achieve cohesive market standards that balance granularity with broader applicability.

Stakeholder engagement is also critical to creating methodologies that are both robust and inclusive. Actively involving smaller entities, indigenous communities, and local stakeholders in methodology development fosters co-benefits such as biodiversity preservation, economic opportunities, and social equity. Regen Network exemplifies this hybrid approach by incorporating decentralised governance to co-develop methodologies with local stakeholders. This process allows for the creation of context-specific protocols that account for ecological variability and local needs.[105] Such models demonstrate how community insights can complement overarching frameworks to produce methodologies that are both practical and comprehensive.

While existing frameworks provide a foundation, gaps remain in harmonising practices, engaging all necessary stakeholders, and addressing project-specific nuances. A collaborative approach that combines top-down guidance with bottom-up innovation offers a path forward. By fostering alignment and promoting cooperation across initiatives, the VCM can develop methodologies that meet market needs while maintaining the highest standards of environmental integrity.

8.2 Technical infrastructure requirements

8.2.1 Interoperability across systems

Interoperability is critical for addressing the fragmentation of blockchain ecosystems and registries in VCMs. Platforms like Toucan, operating on Polygon and Celo, Regen, with its custom ledger built on Cosmos, and Moss, which utilises Ethereum exemplify the diversity of blockchain networks used by startups. While these networks independently offer innovative solutions, their lack of interoperability creates silos that hinder liquidity, limit accessibility, and increase operational inefficiencies. Toucan's cross-chain bridge with Regen Network demonstrates progress towards connecting different networks, allowing credits to move seamlessly between ecosystems. However, this is only an isolated example. Expanding these solutions at scale is essential for creating a cohesive infrastructure that avoids the inefficiencies of isolated ecosystems.

Interoperability also plays a vital role in ensuring the integrity of carbon markets by preventing double-counting. Without reliable communication between systems, the same carbon credit could potentially be tokenised or retired multiple times across separate registries. Cross-registry communication must extend beyond blockchain ecosystems to also encompass traditional registries, ensuring alignment and synchronisation.

The Climate Warehouse initiative exemplifies the potential of metadata layers in bridging these fragmented systems. The metadata layer acts as a bridge, connecting different registries and blockchain networks, creating a comprehensive ecosystem that enhances transparency and accountability.[106] Its prototype testing, involving 30 organisations across national governments, multilateral organisations, and private stakeholders, demonstrated the feasibility of detecting and mitigating risks such as double-counting through the Climate Warehouse's metadata-driven approach.[107]

Scaling these interoperability solutions could improve market liquidity by reducing transaction costs and enabling cross-platform trading.[108] Seamlessly transferring credits across platforms and registries would eliminate barriers to entry, allowing a broader range of stakeholders to participate. Accessibility would also increase, particularly for smaller developers and investors who often face challenges navigating fragmented systems.

8.2.2 Accurate measurement systems for data integrity

The credibility of tokenised credits depends on robust MRV systems. Insights from the case studies reveal that many blockchain-based projects in the VCM have been adversely affected by the low integrity of the underlying carbon credits. In this context, other technical solutions could enhance the immutability ensured by blockchain usage. Internet-of-Things (IoT) devices with secure hardware enable real-time data collection from carbon projects, such as reforestation initiatives or renewable energy installations, providing granular and continuous monitoring of key metrics.[109] Furthermore, fraud detection algorithms could analyse this data to identify inconsistencies, detect anomalies, and enhance the reliability of recorded measurements.

For example, Regen Network has demonstrated how blockchain can integrate with remote sensing technologies and machine learning to securely anchor environmental data in real time. Its CarbonPlus Grasslands methodology uses IoT and satellite data to estimate ecological impacts such as carbon sequestration and biodiversity improvements. By storing this data immutably on a blockchain, Regen enhances trust and transparency in MRV processes, providing a clear link between project activities and environmental outcomes.[110]

Another emerging concept with potential implications for MRV processes in the VCM is Decentralised Physical Infrastructure Networks (DePIN). DePIN applications utilise tokenised incentives to foster the deployment and active participation in distributed physical and digital resource networks.[111] While not yet applied to MRV processes in the VCM, these frameworks have demonstrated value in other sectors, such as decentralised wireless networks, weather monitoring, and mapping systems.[112] DePIN applications utilise blockchain technology to validate data collected by sensors, potentially reducing the centralisation risks that are often associated with traditional environmental monitoring systems. By adopting shared ownership models and automating verification processes, DePIN has the potential to lower infrastructure costs and expand access to reliable monitoring solutions—key barriers in the VCM.

8.2.3 Technical requirements for accessibility and adoptions

For blockchain solutions to gain traction in the VCM, they need to address the distinct needs of both institutional buyers and smaller project developers. Institutions, as the primary drivers of demand, require secure and user-centric platforms that integrate seamlessly into their existing workflows while adhering to regulatory mandates. Smaller stakeholders, particularly project developers in developing regions, face resource and technical constraints that make navigating blockchain systems challenging. Both groups demand solutions that simplify blockchain's complexity without compromising functionality or trust.

Large organisations demand industrial-grade infrastructure to protect sensitive data, secure private keys, and ensure compliance with regulations such as the General Data Protection Regulation (GDPR) and Know Your Customer (KYC) requirements. Blockchain's transparency, while advantageous for accountability, presents challenges for institutions that need to safeguard confidential operations. Privacy-preserving technologies such as Zero-Knowledge Proofs (ZKPs) address these concerns by enabling verifiable transactions without exposing sensitive information.[113] Secure key management systems, multi-signature wallets, and rigorous audits of smart contracts further ensure resilience against breaches, establishing the trust required for institutional engagement. Additionally, on- and off-ramp solutions for fiat transactions simplify integration with traditional financial systems, removing a significant barrier to adoption.

Smaller stakeholders, such as project developers and community organisations, often lack the resources to manage blockchain's technical complexities, including wallet management, fiat conversion, and decentralised exchange operations. Platforms that abstract these complexities through user-centric design enable broader participation. Senken exemplifies this approach by integrating Web2-like interfaces, KYC tools, and fiat on-ramping, creating an accessible platform for non-technical users. Similarly, Kumo addressed institutional needs by introducing a legal wrapper for carbon credits, transforming them into collateral suitable for financial transactions without requiring deep engagement with blockchain systems. Moss's custodial model further streamlined processes by managing the tokenisation and retirement of carbon credits directly on behalf of users.

Accessible systems also have the potential to reduce reliance on intermediaries, lowering transaction costs and directing more value to project developers. Blockchain-based solutions have demonstrated the potential to reduce intermediary roles and associated costs, as seen in cross-border trade applications where agency and operational expenses were significantly lowered.[114] Additionally, user-centric platforms, such as blockchain-based wallets designed for local communities, for example, have demonstrated success in addressing cultural and technical adoption barriers by simplifying interfaces and customising tools for non-technical users.[115] By prioritising usability, blockchain platforms can enable underrepresented groups, such as smallholder farmers and Indigenous communities, to access carbon markets effectively. These adaptations not only broaden participation but also enhance equity within the VCM by creating a more inclusive ecosystem.

8.3 Operational and market dynamics

8.3.1 Operational and transactional efficiency

Blockchain's automated workflows reduce the administrative burden of credit issuance and trading. Traditional systems rely on manual processes, extensive reconciliations, and multiple intermediaries, all of which increase administrative burdens and reduce the efficiency of credit issuance, trading, and retirement. Blockchain technology, as illustrated in the case studies, offers an approach to streamlining these operations. For example, Toucan's or Moss's platform demonstrates how tokenised carbon credits could facilitate faster trading, exchanging ownership, and retiring by eliminating reliance on intermediaries.

However, these efficiency gains are irrelevant if the integrity of tokenised credits is not given, as discussed earlier. When supported by robust standards, governance, and safeguards, blockchain can significantly enhance market efficiency, as demonstrated in the case studies.

8.3.2 Market dynamics and financial stability

Robust financial mechanisms are crucial for scaling the VCM, addressing persistent challenges such as underfunding, low participation, and inefficient pricing structures.[116] As explored in the case studies, blockchain-based solutions offer pathways to address these systemic inefficiencies, fostering price transparency and developing liquid markets, but they also currently still face market-based inefficiencies and high volatility.

Advanced financial instruments, such as forward contracts and carbon-backed loans, provide stable funding to project developers by mitigating market volatility and addressing unpredictable funding cycles. Kumo's carbon-backed loan model aligns carbon credits with traditional financial systems, offering predictable cash flows that stabilise funding for project developers.[117] Such instruments also support transparent pricing models, enabling stakeholders to evaluate the cost-effectiveness of carbon reduction strategies with greater accuracy. Thus, forward market liquidity is seen as an important tool that can help scale the VCM.[118] Moreover, Blockchain's traceable and immutable records, in general, foster investor confidence by ensuring transparent pricing.

However, as discussed earlier, broader adoption of these mechanisms depends on regulatory clarity and standardised practices. By addressing these interconnected issues, blockchain solutions have the potential to drive both financial stability and market expansion, enabling the VCM to meet its climate impact goals more effectively.

9 Conclusion

This chapter has explored the implementation of blockchain technology in the VCM through five case studies: Toucan, Regen Network, Senken, Kumo, and Moss. Each case illustrates the unique opportunities and challenges that arise when integrating blockchain solutions into carbon credit systems. While blockchain holds significant potential to enhance transparency, traceability, and efficiency in carbon transactions, the findings underscore that it is not a panacea for the existing issues plaguing the VCM.

The challenges identified include regulatory fragmentation, varying credit quality, technical interoperability, and market volatility. These obstacles must be addressed comprehensively to ensure that blockchain can effectively support the carbon credit lifecycle, from project design and verification to trading and retirement. A unified global regulatory framework, alongside standardised tokenisation methodologies and robust technical infrastructure, is essential for fostering trust and adoption in the VCM. Moreover, the case studies reveal that while blockchain can streamline processes and enhance market dynamics, the success of these technologies ultimately depends on the collaborative efforts of stakeholders across the entire ecosystem. By engaging diverse actors, including project developers, regulatory bodies, and market participants, the VCM can evolve to meet its climate objectives more effectively.

The challenges need to be addressed by both researchers and practitioners to enable blockchain-based VCC solutions that can successfully tackle the challenges faced in current blockchain and non-blockchain-based VCMs. In particular, policymakers and industry stakeholders must work together to create a tangible but generalisable framework that establishes consistency and regulatory certainty among the plethora of blockchain-based VCC solutions. Furthermore, future research and practitioners should focus on the scalability and interoperability of blockchain solutions, exploring how growing blockchain-based VCMs can be operated on a larger scale. Lastly, all stakeholders must work together to create an inclusive and innovative environment that leverages blockchain's capabilities to drive meaningful climate action, addressing the interconnected challenges that currently impede progress in the VCMs.

Notes

1 Rebecca Lindsey and Luann Dahlman, 'Climate Change: Global Temperature' (*Climate.gov*, 18 January 2024) http://www.climate.gov/news-features/understanding-climate/climate-change-global-temperature accessed 5 January 2025.
2 Harry Fearnehough and others, 'Future Role for Voluntary Carbon Markets in the Paris Era: Final Report' (Umweltbundesamt (German Environment Agency) 2020) https://www.umweltbundesamt.de/sites/default/files/medien/5750/publikationen/2020_11_19_cc_44_2020_carbon_markets_paris_era_0.pdf accessed 5 January 2025.
3 Tim Adams, Bill Winters and Annette Nazareth, 'Taskforce on Scaling Voluntary Carbon Markets – Phase II Report Summary' (Institute of International Finance 2021) https://www.iif.com/Portals/1/Files/TSVCM_Phase_2_Report_Summary.pdf accessed 5 January 2025; Christopher Blaufelder and others, 'A Blueprint for Scaling Voluntary Carbon Markets to Meet the Climate Challenge' (McKinsey & Company 2021) https://www.mckinsey.com/~/media/mckinsey/business%20functions/sustainability/our%20insights/a%20blueprint%20for%20scaling%20voluntary%20carbon%20markets%20to%20meet%20the%20climate%20challenge/a-blueprint-for-scaling-voluntary-carbon-markets-to-meet-the-climate-challenge.pdf accessed 5 January 2025.
4 Adam Sipthorpe and others, 'Blockchain Solutions for Carbon Markets Are Nearing Maturity' (2022) 5 One Earth 779.
5 Peter Howson and others, 'Cryptocarbon: The Promises and Pitfalls of Forest Protection on a Blockchain' (2019) 100 Geoforum 1.
6 'Toucan Documentation' (*Toucan Protocol*, 7 August 2024) https://docs.toucan.earth accessed 2 January 2025.
7 'CHAR | Liquid Market for Biochar Credits' (*Toucan Protocol*, 22 March 2024) https://blog.toucan.earth/onchain-climate-action-char/ accessed 2 January 2025.
8 'Puro.Earth – Carbon Removal Standard and Registry' (*Puro.earth*) https://puro.earth/ accessed 3 January 2025.
9 'Toucan Documentation' (n 6).
10 'Toucan Documentation' (n 6).
11 'Toucan and Regen Network: Expanding Liquidity for Tokenized Carbon Credits' (*Toucan Protocol*, 10 April 2023) https://blog.toucan.earth/toucan-regen-network-bridging-carbon-credits/ accessed 2 January 2025.
12 'Regen Network Launches Bridge to Polygon With Toucan Protocol' (*Polygon Labs*, 4 October 2023) https://polygon.technology/blog/regen-network-launches-bridge-to-polygon-with-toucan-protocol accessed 2 January 2025.
13 Satoshi Nakamoto, 'Bitcoin: A Peer-to-Peer Electronic Cash System' (*Bitcoin Whitepaper*) https://bitcoin.org/bitcoin.pdf accessed 2 January 2025.
14 'Toucan Documentation' (n 6).
15 'Toucan Documentation' (n 6).
16 'Toucan Documentation' (n 6).
17 'Verra Addresses Crypto Instruments and Tokens' (*Verra*, 25 May 2022) https://verra.org/verra-addresses-crypto-instruments-and-tokens/ accessed 2 January 2025; 'Response to Verra's May 25th An-

nouncement' (*Toucan Protocol*, 25 May 2022) https://blog.toucan.earth/response-to-verras-announcement/ accessed 2 January 2025.

18 'Verra Addresses Crypto Instruments and Tokens' (n 17).

19 'Puro Carbon Bridge | Toucan Documentation' (*Toucan Protocol*, 7 August 2024) https://docs.toucan.earth/toucan/carbon-bridge/puro-carbon-bridge accessed 3 January 2025.

20 Hanna-Mari Ahonen and others, 'Governance of Fragmented Compliance and Voluntary Carbon Markets Under the Paris Agreement' (2022) 10 Politics and Governance 235.

21 Thales AP West and others, 'Overstated Carbon Emission Reductions from Voluntary REDD+ Projects in the Brazilian Amazon' (2020) 117 Proceedings of the National Academy of Sciences 24188.

22 Grayson Badgley and Danny Cullenward, 'Zombies on the Blockchain – CarbonPlan' (26 May 2024) https://carbonplan.org/research/toucan-crypto-offsets accessed 26 May 2024.

23 Andrew R Chow, 'The Crypto Industry Was On Its Way to Changing the Carbon-Credit Market, Until It Hit a Major Roadblock' *TIME* (26 May 2022) https://time.com/6181907/crypto-carbon-credits/ accessed 3 January 2025; 'Verra Addresses Crypto Instruments and Tokens' (n 17).

24 Vincent Gramlich and others, 'A Multivocal Literature Review of Decentralized Finance: Current Knowledge and Future Research Avenues' (2023) 33 Electronic Markets 11.

25 Howson and others (n 5); G Booman and others, 'Regen Network Whitepaper' (Regen Network 2021) https://regen-network.gitlab.io/whitepaper/WhitePaper.pdf accessed 3 January 2025.

26 'Credit Protocols' https://www.registry.regen.network/crediting-protocols accessed 6 January 2025.

27 'The Evolution of Regen Network' (*Regen Network*, 31 August 2023) https://medium.com/regen-network/the-evolution-of-regen-network-ae74febe1edf accessed 3 January 2025; 'Ecological State Protocols' (*Regen Network*, 14 January 2019) https://medium.com/regen-network/ecological-state-protocols-1c7e97dadeae accessed 3 January 2025.

28 'Regen Network Website' (*Regen Network*) https://www.regen.network/ accessed 3 January 2025.

29 'Cosmos SDK Documentation' (*Cosmos*) https://docs.cosmos.network/ accessed 3 January 2025.

30 'How to Participate in Governance: Deposits and Voting' (*Regen Network*, 10 June 2021) https://medium.com/regen-network/how-to-participate-in-governance-deposits-and-voting-5068ec20d019 accessed 3 January 2025.

31 Booman and others (n 25); 'Ecological Monitoring Scientific Research Round-Up' (*Regen Network*, 3 May 2022) https://medium.com/regen-network/ecological-monitoring-scientific-research-round-up-e0423859c7eb accessed 3 January 2025.

32 Booman and others (n 25).

33 Booman and others (n 25); 'Ecological Monitoring Scientific Research Round-Up' (n 31).

34 Booman and others (n 25).

35 'Regen Network & Ixo Token Swap' (*Regen Network*, 24 June 2021) https://medium.com/regen-network/regen-network-ixo-token-swap-94138e5a21b0 accessed 3 January 2025.

36 Booman and others (n 25).

37 'The Evolution of Regen Network' (n 27).

38 'How to Participate in Governance: Deposits and Voting' (n 30).

39 'Confidently Invest in High-Integrity Carbon Credits' (*Regen Network*, 3 May 2023) https://medium.com/regen-network/regen-networks-concierge-sales-service-812e1e59ac4f accessed 3 January 2025.

40 'The Evolution of Regen Network' (n 27).

41 'Bringing Digital Carbon to Cosmos with NCT' (*Regen Network*, 16 April 2023) https://medium.com/regen-network/bringing-the-digital-carbon-market-to-cosmos-with-nct-6430ecfb6ccc accessed 3 January 2025.

42 'Bringing Full Ecocredit Lifecycles On-Chain with Regen Ledger v4.0' (*Regen Network*, 31 August 2022) https://medium.com/regen-network/bringing-the-full-eco-credit-lifecycle-on-chain-with-regen-ledger-v4-0-183ca96ea7c7 accessed 3 January 2025.

43 'Confidently Invest in High-Integrity Carbon Credits' (n 39).

44 'The Evolution of Regen Network' (n 27).
45 Yuhan Zhou and others, '"Shadow-Centralization" in Decentralized Autonomous Organizations' (2024) 44 Proceedings of the Internation Conference on Information Systems 2024 https://aisel.aisnet.org/icis2024/blockchain/blockchain/1/; Eleunthia Ellinger and others, 'Skin in the Game: The Transformational Potential of Decentralized Autonomous Organizations' (2024) 48 Management Information Systems Quarterly 245.
46 Booman and others (n 25).
47 Howson and others (n 5).
48 'Ecological Monitoring Scientific Research Round-Up' (n 31).
49 'Regen Network Price Today, REGEN to USD Live Price, Marketcap and Chart' (*CoinMarketCap*) https://coinmarketcap.com/currencies/regen-network/ accessed 6 January 2025.
50 'Senken Democratizes the Market for Carbon Credits, Bringing the Global Climate Economy on-Chain' (*markets.businessinsider.com*) https://markets.businessinsider.com/news/stocks/senken-democratizes-the-market-for-carbon-credits-bringing-the-global-climate-economy-on-chain-1031745897 accessed 5 January 2025; 'Climate Financing | Adrian Wons | Senken' (*Toucan Protocol*, 5 December 2022) https://blog.toucan.earth/senken/ accessed 5 January 2025.
51 'Toucan and Senken Partnership' (*Toucan Protocol Blog*, 22 June 2022) https://blog.toucan.earth/toucan-senken/ accessed 5 January 2025; Podcast with Senken Founder Adrian Wons – Building Trust In Carbon Markets (Directed by ReFi DAO, 2024) https://www.youtube.com/watch?v=_2omSVxW0AU accessed 5 January 2025.
52 'Senken Is Launching on Polygon' (*Senken*, 13 December 2022) https://senken.medium.com/senken-is-launching-on-polygon-91c4ee30cd32 accessed 5 January 2025; 'Toucan and Senken Partnership' (n 51).
53 Darrell Duffie, 'Market Making Under the Proposed Volcker Rule' https://papers.ssrn.com/abstract=1990472 accessed 5 January 2025.
54 'Senken Is Launching the World's First Public Sale of Carbon Forward Tokens' (*Senken*, 31 January 2023) https://senken.medium.com/senken-is-launching-the-worlds-first-public-sale-of-carbon-forward-tokens-d48e8ea7005a accessed 5 January 2025.
55 'Senken Is Launching the World's First Public Sale of Carbon Forward Tokens' (n 54).
56 Dimana Doneva, 'BeZero Carbon And Senken Partner To Host Ratings On The Carbon Credit Marketplace' *Carbon Herald* (29 September 2022) https://carbonherald.com/bezero-carbon-and-senken-partner-to-host-ratings-on-the-carbon-credit-marketplace/ accessed 5 January 2025.
57 Ananth Madhavan, 'Market Microstructure: A Survey' (2000) 3 Journal of Financial Markets 205.
58 Podcast with Senken Founder Adrian Wons – Building Trust In Carbon Markets (n 51).
59 Podcast with Senken Founder Adrian Wons – Building Trust In Carbon Markets (n 51).
60 Integrity Council for the Voluntary Carbon Market (ICVCM), 'The Core Carbon Principles (CCPs)' https://icvcm.org/core-carbon-principles/ accessed 5 January 2025.
61 United Nations Framework Convention on Climate Change (UNFCCC), 'Nationally Determined Contributions (NDCs)' https://unfccc.int/process-and-meetings/the-paris-agreement/nationally-determined-contributions-ndcs accessed 5 January 2025.
62 European Commission, 'Corporate Sustainability Reporting' https://finance.ec.europa.eu/capital-markets-union-and-financial-markets/company-reporting-and-auditing/company-reporting/corporate-sustainability-reporting_en accessed 5 January 2025.
63 'A Guide to Senken's Due Diligence Framework for Carbon Credits' (*Senken*) https://www.senken.io/carbon-credits-due-diligence accessed 5 January 2025.
64 Henry Chesbrough, 'Business Model Innovation: Opportunities and Barriers' (2010) 43 Long Range Planning 354.
65 MakerDao, 'The Maker Protocol White Paper' (2020) https://makerdao.com/en/whitepaper/ accessed 5 January 2025.

66 'Integrate Climate Action in Every Transaction' (*KumoDAO*, 30 January 2022) https://kumodao.medium.com/kumodao-introduction-e6a22a8d3284 accessed 5 January 2025; 'The Essence of KumoDAO — USD StableCoin Backed by Carbon Offsets' (*KumoDAO*, 9 February 2022) https://kumodao.medium.com/kumodao-tl-dr-6754abd5b576 accessed 5 January 2025; 'Carbon Credits Are Beautiful' (*KumoDAO*, 15 June 2022) https://kumodao.medium.com/carbon-credits-are-beatiful-97675f34d42e accessed 5 January 2025.
67 'Kumo · Carbon Secured Lending' (*Kumo.Earth*) https://kumo.earth/ accessed 5 January 2025.
68 Pierre Guigon, 'Voluntary Carbon Markets: How Can They Serve Climate Policies?' [2010] OECD Environment Working Papers https://ideas.repec.org//p/oec/envaaa/19-en.html accessed 5 January 2025; Kate Ervine, 'Diminishing Returns: Carbon Market Crisis and the Future of Market-Dependent Climate Change Finance' (2014) 19 New Political Economy 723.
69 Adams, Winters and Nazareth (n 3).
70 'Kumo · Carbon Secured Lending' (n 67).
71 'Kumo · Carbon Secured Lending' (n 67).
72 Howard E Aldrich and C Marlene Fiol, 'Fools Rush in? The Institutional Context of Industry Creation' (1994) 19 The Academy of Management Review 645; William Mann, 'Creditor Rights and Innovation: Evidence from Patent Collateral' https://papers.ssrn.com/abstract=2356015 accessed 5 January 2025.
73 Kenneth R Richards and Grant Eric Huebner, 'Evaluating Protocols and Standards for Forest Carbon-Offset Programs, Part A: Additionality, Baselines and Permanence' (2012) 3 Carbon Management 393.
74 Thorsten Beck, Asli Demirgüç-Kunt and Ross Levine, 'Finance, Inequality and the Poor' (2007) 12 Journal of Economic Growth 27.
75 Gary Gorton and Andrew Metrick, 'Getting Up to Speed on the Financial Crisis: A One-Weekend-Reader's Guide' (2012) 50 Journal of Economic Literature 128.
76 Malcolm Campbell-Verduyn, 'Bitcoin, Crypto-Coins, and Global Anti-Money Laundering Governance' (2018) 69 Crime, Law and Social Change 283.
77 Moss.Earth, 'Moss Whitepaper' (MossEarth 2020) https://moss.earth accessed 5 April 2024.
78 'Moss NFT Innovation to Save the Amazon Sold out in One Hour' (*Moss*, 9 February 2022) https://medium.com/@moss.earth/moss-nft-innovation-to-save-the-amazon-sold-out-in-one-hour-7281ee356def accessed 5 January 2025.
79 Moss.Earth (n 77); 'Coinbase Lists MCO2 Token' (*Moss*, 7 December 2021) https://medium.com/@moss.earth/coinbase-lists-mco2-token-dfcc38f8587f accessed 5 January 2025.
80 Jennifer Marston, 'Moss.Earth Is Using NFTs, Crypto Carbon Credits to Fight Climate Change' *AgFunderNews* (18 February 2022) https://agfundernews.com/nfts-crypto-carbon-credits-moss-earth-is-using-to-fight-climate-change accessed 5 January 2025.
81 Moss.Earth (n 77).
82 ArmaninoLLP, 'Agreed Upon Procedures Report Prepared for Moss' (2021) https://de.scribd.com/document/699882692/Moss-Earth-AUP-Report-2021-Final-External accessed 10 October 2024; Moss.Earth (n 77).
83 ArmaninoLLP, 'Agreed Upon Procedures Report Prepared for Moss' (2021) https://de.scribd.com/document/699882692/Moss-Earth-AUP-Report-2021-Final-External accessed 10 October 2024; Moss.Earth (n 77).
84 ArmaninoLLP (n 83).
85 Moss.Earth (n 77).
86 Moss.Earth (n 77).
87 'Moss NFT Innovation to Save the Amazon Sold out in One Hour' (n 78).
88 Moss.Earth, 'Moss Amazon Forest NFT – White Paper and FAQ' (2022) https://moss-earth.gitbook.io/moss-amazon-forest-nft-faq accessed 5 January 2025; 'Moss NFT Innovation to Save the Amazon Sold out in One Hour' (n 78).

89 Fabio Teixeira and Avi Asher-Schapiro Foundation Thomson Reuters, 'Fears of "subprime" Carbon Assets Stall Crypto Mission to Save Rainforest' *Reuters* (13 September 2022) https://www.reuters.com/article/idUSL8N2ZM7XE/ accessed 27 May 2024.
90 Teixeira and Foundation (n89).
91 'Moss Carbon Credit Price Today, MCO2 to USD Live Price, Marketcap and Chart' (*CoinMarketCap*) https://coinmarketcap.com/currencies/moss-carbon-credit/ accessed 5 January 2025.
92 World Bank, 'What You Need to Know About Article 6 of the Paris Agreement' (*World Bank*, 17 May 2022) https://www.worldbank.org/en/news/feature/2022/05/17/what-you-need-to-know-about-article-6-of-the-paris-agreement accessed 11 March 2024.
93 Marco Schletz, Laura A Franke and Søren Salomo, 'Blockchain Application for the Paris Agreement Carbon Market Mechanism—A Decision Framework and Architecture' (2020) 12 Sustainability 5069.
94 Teng Ma and others, 'How the Thermal Power Sector Affects Carbon Trading: An Empirical Study on China's Carbon Markets' (2023) 55 Applied Economics 6739.
95 'Verra Addresses Crypto Instruments and Tokens' (n 17).
96 Chris Lang, 'Toucan's Crypto Layer on Top of Carbon Offsets Is Expanding the Market for Toxic Hot Air' (*REDD-Monitor*, 11 April 2022) https://reddmonitor.substack.com/p/toucans-crypto-layer-on-top-of-carbon accessed 24 November 2024.
97 Chow (n 23).
98 'Toucan Documentation' (n 6); Moss.Earth (n 77).
99 ArmaninoLLP (n 83).
100 'Toucan Documentation' (n 6).
101 BioCarbon Cert, 'BioCarbon Guidelines – Tokenization Guidelines for Transparent Practices Connecting Digital Markets' (2024).
102 BioCarbon Cert (n 104).
103 Verra, 'Methodologies' (*Verra Methodologies*, 24 November 2024) https://verra.org/methodologies-main/ accessed 24 November 2024; Gold Standard, 'Methodology – Gold Standard for the Global Goals' (24 November 2024) https://globalgoals.goldstandard.org/documents/methodology/ accessed 24 November 2024; Puro.earth Oy, 'Carbon Removal Methods' (*Puro.earth Oy*, 24 November 2024) https://puro.earth/carbon-removal-methods accessed 24 November 2024.
104 Integrity Council for the Voluntary Carbon Market (ICVCM) (n 60).
105 Booman and others (n 25).
106 Climate Warehouse, 'Climate Warehouse | Climate Action Data Trust' https://www.theclimatewarehouse.org/work/climate-warehouse accessed 5 January 2025.
107 World Bank, 'Climate Warehouse Simulation III – Final Report' (*World Bank*, September 2022) https://documents.worldbank.org/en/publication/documents-reports/documentdetail/099605009212233328/IDU09ef226cf0a663041d60869f07078d1af9fd3 accessed 24 November 2024.
108 Derek Sorensen, 'Tokenized Carbon Credits' (2023) 8 Ledger http://ledger.pitt.edu/ojs/ledger/article/view/294 accessed 6 January 2024; Schletz, Franke and Salomo (n 96).
109 M Babel and others, 'Trust through Digital Identification: On SSI's Contribution to the Integration of Decentralized Oracles in Information Systems' (2023) 60 HMD Praxis Der Wirtschaftsinformatik 478.
110 Regen Network, 'CarbonPlus Grasslands Methodology' (*Regen Marketplace*) https://app.regen.network/methodologies/carbonplus-grasslands accessed 5 January 2025.
111 Zhibin Lin and others, 'Decentralized Physical Infrastructure Network (DePIN): Challenges and Opportunities' http://arxiv.org/abs/2406.02239 accessed 24 November 2024.
112 Lin and others (n 114).
113 Xiaoqiang Sun and others, 'A Survey on Zero-Knowledge Proof in Blockchain' (2021) 35 IEEE Network 198.
114 Xin Tian and others, 'Improving Operational Efficiency through Blockchain: Evidence from a Field Experiment in Cross-Border Trade' (2024) 35 Production Planning & Control 1009.

115 Cristina Viano and others, 'Blockchain Tools for Socio-Economic Interactions in Local Communities' (*Oxford Academic*, 3 January 2022) https://academic.oup.com/policyandsociety/article/41/3/373/6540164 accessed 24 November 2024; Stefano Balbo and others, 'CommonsHood: A Blockchain-Based Wallet App for Local Communities', *2020 IEEE International Conference on Decentralized Applications and Infrastructures (DAPPS)* (2020) https://ieeexplore.ieee.org/document/9126008 accessed 24 November 2024.
116 Gregor Spilker and Nick Nugent, 'Voluntary Carbon Market Derivatives: Growth, Innovation & Usage' (2022) 22 Borsa Istanbul Review S109.
117 'Kumo for Project Developers' (*Kumo.Earth*) https://kumo.earth/project-developers accessed 5 January 2025.
118 Nicolas Kreibich and Lukas Hermwille, 'Caught in between: Credibility and Feasibility of the Voluntary Carbon Market Post-2020' (2021) 21 Climate Policy 939.

Jonathan Lautenschlager, Marike Reinelt, Vincent Schaaf, Nils Urbach, and Valeriya Arnold

6 From project design to retirement: The role of blockchain along the voluntary carbon credit lifecycle

Abstract: The emerging topic of Voluntary Carbon Credits (VCCs) showcases the rapid evolution of a broad spectrum of practical and theoretical concepts. However, this environment entails practical projects with short lifespans as well as the absence of clear and established standards and best practices for the technical concepts and foundations of VCCs. Against this backdrop, we survey and discuss blockchain-based theoretical concepts and technical implementations for VCCs as well as the potentials and challenges of existing approaches based on academic literature and practical use cases. Thereby, we aim to identify best practices as well as pitfalls of existing practical implementations and theoretical concepts and lay the foundation for a standardised technical VCC implementation that can successfully foster a broader adoption and practical diffusion.

Keywords: Voluntary Carbon Credit (VCC) lifecycle, Voluntary Carbon Market (VCM), tokenisation, blockchain, value proposition

1 Introduction —— **133**
2 Background —— **135**
2.1 Blockchain and tokenisation —— **135**
2.2 Voluntary carbon credit lifecycle —— **136**
3 Operational approach —— **137**
4 Results —— **138**
4.1 Blockchain application possibilities —— **139**
4.2 Value proposition of blockchain for VCCs lifecycle steps —— **142**
4.3 Additional requirements —— **143**
5 Discussion and conclusion —— **145**

1 Introduction

The pressing global challenges posed by climate change and environmental degradation have propelled the need for effective solutions, as evidenced by the Paris Agreement and the United Nations' Sustainable Development Goals (SDGs).[1] This collective commitment emphasises the critical importance of environmental sustainability in shaping a viable future for all. In this context, the development of alternative solutions that contribute to solving the climate challenges outlined in the Paris Agreement is essential. For instance, Voluntary Carbon Credits (VCCs) are frequently highlighted as a prominent

https://doi.org/10.1515/9783111706719-006

solution for reducing carbon emissions globally.[2] However, VCC providers and their solutions are facing several challenges when striving to adopt their solution into practice broadly. Current challenges that need to be overcome with VCC solutions on the market include a lack of standardisation, complexity, and opacity in processes related to their creation, transfer, and verification. This lack of standardisation leads to inconsistencies and uncertainties regarding the structure and functionality of VCCs, complicating participation for businesses and investors as well as undermining trust in the market.[3]

Furthermore, verification of the actual climate mitigation efforts represented by VCCs can be challenging and may require time-consuming and costly procedures, affecting market efficiency. Additionally, limited integration and interoperability with existing climate mitigation initiatives or markets can diminish the effectiveness and acceptance of VCCs among various stakeholders. Market volatility caused by supply and demand dynamics, as well as external factors like political decisions and economic trends, contribute to the unpredictability and instability of the VCC market.[4] Moreover, there is a risk of misuse and misconduct, such as greenwashing, where companies make misleading or inaccurate claims about their environmental performance to enhance their image. For instance, this has recently occurred in China, where many already existing facilities in China were submitted as supposedly newly constructed Upstream Emission Reductions (UER) projects in Germany, some without the knowledge and approval of the Chinese owners.[5]

Addressing these challenges requires a careful examination of existing VCC solutions and the implementation of measures to enhance transparency, verifiability, integration, and governance in the market. Blockchain technology, particularly through tokenisation, holds the potential to mitigate these challenges. By leveraging blockchain's decentralised and immutable nature, tokenisation can enhance transparency, traceability, and auditability in VCC transactions, thereby reducing the risk of fraud and enhancing trust among market participants. Furthermore, blockchain-based tokenisation can facilitate seamless integration and interoperability between VCC platforms and existing climate initiatives or markets, fostering greater efficiency and effectiveness in climate mitigation efforts.[6]

In the landscape of sustainability research using blockchain technology, research studies primarily focus on the design and implementation of blockchain solutions for various environmental applications. However, there exists a conspicuous absence of research examining the broader value propositions that blockchain technology offers specifically for VCCs throughout their lifecycle stages. While individual studies may provide insights into specific aspects of VCC design or blockchain implementation, a holistic understanding of the overall value propositions of blockchain technology in this context remains elusive.[7] This research gap highlights the need for a systematic and particularly technical analysis of the potential benefits and challenges that blockchain technology presents across the entire lifecycle of VCCs, from issuance to retirement of VCCs.

Therefore, the objective of this book chapter is to investigate the value propositions that blockchain technology provides for addressing technical requirements in the design of VCC solutions, considering the various stages of the VCC lifecycle. By examining the unique features and capabilities of blockchain technology in facilitating transparent, secure, and efficient VCC transactions, this study aims to investigate how blockchain can contribute to the advancement of sustainable practices in carbon credit markets. Concretely, this book chapter strives to answer the following research question:

RQ: What value propositions does blockchain technology provide for addressing technical requirements when designing voluntary carbon credit solutions considering the VCC lifecycle stages?

Through a comprehensive analysis of existing literature, practical case studies, and theoretical frameworks, this research seeks to provide valuable insights for policymakers, practitioners, and researchers alike, ultimately contributing to the development of more effective and sustainable solutions for addressing climate change by reducing carbon emissions.

The remainder of this chapter is structured as follows. Section 2 outlines the theoretical background of blockchain technology and tokenisation, as well as a detailed description of the VCC lifecycle. Section 3 presents the methodology used, while section 4 highlights the results, emphasising blockchain's value propositions at various stages of the VCC lifecycle. Lastly, Section 5 engages in a discussion of these findings, addressing their implications for the market and technology adoption, and concludes with recommendations for policymakers and practitioners.

2 Background

2.1 Blockchain and tokenisation

In recent years, blockchain technology has emerged as a transformative force reshaping various industries. Functioning as a distributed ledger technology (DLT), blockchain operates within a peer-to-peer network, replicating and synchronising data across multiple nodes to ensure fault tolerance and decentralisation.[8] Its operation relies on public key cryptography to facilitate secure and transparent transactions, executed through a consensus protocol operated by specific nodes.[9] At its core, blockchain utilises an append-only structure in which transactions are grouped into blocks and linked together using hash pointers to form a tamper-proof chain.[10] Each block contains the hash of its predecessor, ensuring the ledger's integrity and immutability, thereby eliminating the need for a central authority, and mitigating the risk of a single point of failure, fostering trust among participants.[11] For instance, this can be illustrated with examples from the cryptocurrency domain, where blockchain technology underpins systems such as Bitcoin and Ethereum, ensuring secure and transparent transactions. Furthermore, tokenisation can be implemented using various technologies, with blockchain providing an effective solution for enhancing transparency and efficiency.

Tokenisation, a prominent application of blockchain, entails representing real-world assets as digital tokens on the blockchain. These tokens democratise access to assets, enable fractional ownership, and facilitate faster and more efficient transactions.[12] Using smart contracts, programmable agreements encoded on the blockchain, tokenisation automates processes such as dividend payments and compliance management, thereby enhancing efficiency and transparency.[13] The convergence of blockchain and tokenisation heralds a new era of innovation and disruption, redefining traditional paradigms of ownership and finance. As these technologies continue to evolve, their impact on finance, commerce, and society is expected to be profound, promoting decentralisation, efficiency, and inclusivity. An illustrative example of this is the tokenisation of company shares through the creation of digital tokens on a blockchain, each representing a fractional ownership in the company. These tokens can subsequently be sold to investors via a Security Token Offering (STO). Trading these tokens on blockchain-based exchanges offers several advantages, such as increasing market accessibility, enhancing liquidity by enabling 24/7 trading, providing additional transparency and security due to the immutability of the blockchain, and reducing costs by eliminating intermediaries such as brokers and clearinghouses. With the described potential and the rising importance of carbon neutrality in combating climate change, tokenisation presents a powerful tool for scaling the use of VCCs. In summary, by creating digital representations of carbon credits on a blockchain, tokenisation can streamline trading, improve traceability, and unlock new market opportunities, driving greater efficiency and accessibility in the growing carbon credit market.

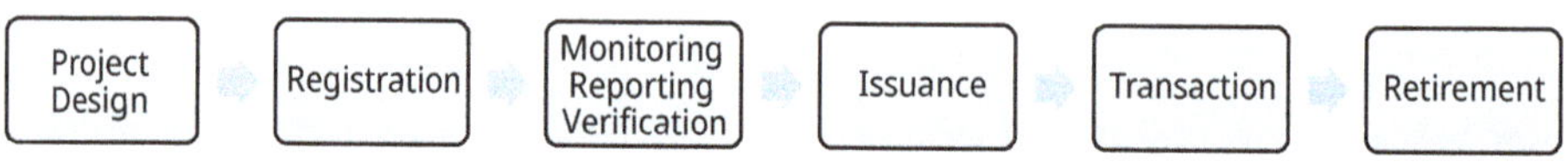

Figure 6.1: VCC Lifecycle Stages.

2.2 Voluntary carbon credit lifecycle

The life of a VCC can be divided into six stages[14] as illustrated in Figure 6.1. The first stage is the *project design*. Initially, the project developers have to conduct a feasibility study and select an accredited standard for quantifying emissions.[15] A feasibility study in this context involves evaluating the technical, economic, and environmental viability of the project, ensuring that it can effectively reduce carbon emissions as intended. It includes assessing the potential environmental impact, costs, benefits, and overall practicality of the project.

Since project designers must submit their design for *registration* under a selected standard in the next step, they typically align their design with the standard's requirements to facilitate approval. The standard in the VCC context refers to a recognised framework or protocol that sets the criteria and methods for measuring, reporting, and verifying the emissions reductions achieved by the project. These standards aim to ensure that the carbon credits generated are credible, consistent, and can be trusted by buyers and regulators. Examples of such standards include Verra, the Gold Standard, Climate Action Reserve, and the American Carbon Registry. To ensure the robustness and reliability of these standards, independent experts conduct comprehensive assessments and verifications.

The project registration is finalised upon approval by the standard setter, which provides project developers with frameworks and guidelines to quantify and certify emission reductions during the subsequent *monitoring, reporting, and verification (MRV)* processes, ensuring verifiable carbon emission compensation.[16] Since project developers are responsible for monitoring emission reductions themselves, the reliability of the project depends on the accuracy of the reported data. Consequently, during this stage, project developers must contact third-party auditors to ensure the accuracy of their claims.[17]

After the MRV processes have successfully finished, the next step is the *issuance* of the corresponding credit by the standard to the project developers. When issuing the credit, it is important to represent the VCC and its ownership digitally and rightfully, which means accurately reflecting ownership and ensuring compliance with established standards and protocols in the issuance and transfer process.[18]

Following issuance, the VCC can be sold on the market, initiating the *transaction* phase. Usually, this will be either done through offtake agreements (contractual arrangements between a producer of goods or services and a buyer), through brokers or other intermediaries that resell the credits, or through exchanges that offer buyers a platform to access potential credits.[19]

The final stage is the *retirement* of the VCC. This generally happens through the final buyer claiming the environmental benefits. During this stage, the credit is permanently removed from the market and is no longer available for transaction, thereby eliminating the risk of double-spending, which refers to the fraudulent use or claiming of the same credit by multiple parties.[20]

3 Operational approach

To answer our research question, we first aimed at conducting a structured literature review.[21] After an initial, explorative search and testing of different keywords, we derived our final search string ('blockchain' OR 'DLT' OR 'distributed ledger' OR 'tokenisation') AND ('carbon' AND ('credits' OR 'markets' OR 'offsets')) and applied it to a broad palette of academic databases, namely Science Direct, IEEE Explorer, AIS eLibrary, ACM Digital Library, and Web of Science. However, from backward and forward searches, we realised the importance of grey literature, that is, non–peer-reviewed literature, in this research stream. Thus, we also incorporated grey literature that we encountered through forward and backward search applied on our white literature and a Google Scholar search.[22] However, even with grey literature, our dataset remained insufficient and incomplete. Thus, we decided to only focus on a detailed investigation of the seminal works collected in our review supplemented with an examination of real-world examples. Furthermore, we draw upon literature from other blockchain applications that present application patterns and knowledge that are transferable to the application of VCC tokenisation.

4 Results

To understand the value propositions that blockchain can offer in the VCC context, we first outline the various ways blockchain can be applied to the overall process or specific steps. These applications are gathered from real-world examples, current VCC literature, or transferred from other BC applications. Subsequently, we abstract the underlying value propositions of blockchain technology for these specific application possibilities and VCCs in general. Finally, we identify additional, more specific requirements for the design of the blockchain system that must be met to fully leverage the value propositions of blockchain for VCCs. An overview of these value propositions is illustrated in Table 6.1.

Table 6.1: BLC Value propositions in the VCC context.

	Step 1 Project Design	**Step 2 Registration**	**Step 3 Monitoring, Reporting, Verification**	**Step 4 Issuance**	**Step 5 Transaction**	**Step 6 Retirement**
Blockchain application possibilities	Committing on a certain project design (including governance and registration) through storing respective data on the blockchain		Committing on reported data	Digital representation of the VCC and its ownership Transfer of ownership		Retirement on the blockchain
			Incorporating trusted oracles with signed data		Transparent markets	

Table 6.1 (continued)

	Step 1 Project Design	**Step 2 Registration**	**Step 3 Monitoring, Reporting, Verification**	**Step 4 Issuance**	**Step 5 Transaction**	**Step 6 Retirement**
			Automatable Verification according to transparent rules			
	Setting up a DAO that governs the respective processes					
Value proposition of BC for VCCs lifecycle step	Immutability/tamper proof					
	Accessibility in public blockchains/transparency					
	Decentralisation/independency from verified third party					
Additional requirements	Verifiability of data origin			Identifiability of owners		
	Selective information sharing			User/owner privacy		
				Ensuring liquid markets		

4.1 Blockchain application possibilities

The life of a carbon credit initially begins with selecting a specific *project design* and registering it under an *accredited standard* and afterwards, *monitoring, reporting, and verifying* the data, enabling the creation of VCCs.[23] All three tasks involve providing reliable information and commitments that must be maintained to ensure the validity of the later-minted credits. By posting this information on a blockchain, it becomes publicly visible and immutable, allowing others to hold the project designer accountable for the information provided. Alternatively, instead of posting all the information, one might post only a hash of the data on the blockchain and provide the remaining information off-chain. This approach still ensures the immutability and verifiability of the data while reducing the load on the blockchain and associated costs. If fully disclosing information might compromise data sensitivity, one might just post the hash of the information on the blockchain but refrain from providing the information itself off-chain upfront. While this would not provide public visibility and verifiability of the information, its immutability would still be secured, e.g., as in the case of a dispute where a project designer is forced to reveal project information, it could be checked whether this information matches the hash that was published on the blockchain. This approach is also used by the Regen Network to ensure the trustworthiness of the collected data.[24]

Another possibility of applying blockchain technology, specifically during *monitoring and reporting* of the VCC lifecycle, is to incorporate trusted oracles responsible for monitoring and reporting the data that can use cryptographic keys to sign the data and ensure its authenticity and traceability. This approach is, for example, already being proposed when it comes to tracing carbon emissions in the electricity sector.[25] Here, similar to VCCs, a core challenge lies in ensuring the validity and integrity of the primary data, such as the amount of carbon emitted during electricity production, or the amount of carbon actually captured during project design. To address this, the integrity of metering devices is periodically verified and then attested to the metering devices through a digital certificate issued by a trusted agent, either directly from a regulatory body or a company certified by such a body. This allows the data reported to the blockchain to be signed with a cryptographic key by the metering devices and appended with the certificate, ensuring that the data was reported by a certified device and has not been altered. Additionally, using hardware security modules (HSM) can further ensure the binding of the certificate to the metering device. The electricity sector benefits from an already established network of sensors, such as smart meter gateways, which can report this data. This task is more complex for VCCs. However, even if only some of the relevant information would be reported like this, for example, using satellite data, signed by the respective satellite to ensure data authenticity, it would already be progress compared to fully untraceable reporting. This approach is, for example, already being used by CarbonStack by creating more transparency for its projects using satellite observation and blockchain technology.[26]

Due to its transparent rules and the possibility offered by smart contracts, blockchain technology could also facilitate automated *verification*. Carbon standard providers could implement some of their verification criteria on the blockchain in the form of smart contracts. This would offer two main benefits: Firstly, the data reported by the project, which was posted on the blockchain in the previous step, could be processed automatically. Secondly, the rules underlying the verification and their enforcement would be conducted transparently, reducing the level of trust required in the standard providers. Certainly, this approach would be highly specific to the concrete use case and would require the implementation of complex verification rules, thereby complicating the integration of all necessary information into smart contracts. However, even if it is not feasible to encode every detail on the blockchain, establishing a fundamental set of rules could significantly enhance the transparency of the process. Until now, carbon credits (VCCs) have not been efficiently translated into smart contracts, even though there is a significant potential for enhancing transactability and standardisation.[27]

Although stages one to three present multiple opportunities for blockchain to enhance transparency, verifiability, and data immutability, in the current VCC market, trusted third-party verifiers are predominantly employed and relied on to ensure the integrity of the information provided, monitored, and reported, and the verification processes that form the first three steps of the VCC lifecycle.[28] When it comes to stages four to six, which will be discussed next, however, blockchain technology already finds application in various ways in today's VCC practice.

Before a VCC can be purchased, it must be *issued* by the standardisation organisation by adding a respective entry in their VCC register. Blockchain can either be incorporated in this step by transferring the VCC register of the standard provider natively on the blockchain or leaving the existing register unchanged and just representing the ownership to specific entries in this register through tokens on the blockchain. Both of these options offer the advantage of immutable records for token transactions and ownership.[29] Additionally, the publicly visible documentation could also counteract the problem of double-counting measurements that are legally required, that is, issuing VCCs for actions that are already obligatory. Only if it is ensured that projects financed through credits do not ultimately displace governmental climate protection measures can one truly speak of 'compensation'.[30] In the first approach, the entire VCC register maintained by the standard provider is migrated to a blockchain-based system. Each issuance of a VCC and subsequent transactions are recorded directly on the blockchain ledger. This method leverages blockchain's inherent properties, such as immutability, transparency, and decentralised consensus mechanisms, to establish a tamper-proof record of VCC ownership and transaction history. By decentralising the VCC register, this approach reduces the risk of data manipulation or unauthorised access, ensuring that stakeholders can verify the authenticity and ownership of VCCs reliably through transparent blockchain records. Alternatively, blockchain technology can tokenise specific entries within the existing VCC register maintained by the standard provider. Instead of migrating the entire register, ownership of VCCs is represented by digital tokens on the blockchain. Each token corresponds to a specific entry in the traditional VCC register, indicating ownership and enabling transparent tracking of ownership transfers on the blockchain platform. This approach is more widespread today as it does not require the direct change of the register infrastructure by the standardisation organisation itself. However, as a result, it introduces a possible vulnerability in the form of another oracle problem instance. It must be ensured that the ownership of the token properly represents ownership of the underlying VCC, that is, that the token represents a righteous VCC and that the ownership of the VCC cannot be transferred independently from the token. An illustrative instance can be observed in the initial implementation of the Toucan Protocol, where VCCs were retired before the process of tokenisation. Consequently, the tokens created within this framework represented VCCs that had already been retired.[31]

After the VCC is represented on a blockchain, the blockchain can also be used to facilitate *transaction* of the VCC. This process, along with the publicly visible record, enables robust accounting practices that prevent ambiguity over ownership and double-counting of emissions reductions.[32] The use of blockchain technology also enhances the transparency of trading and, consequently, the markets.[33] This can facilitate open access to trading platforms, making markets more accessible to the general public. However, while technically feasible, the transfer of tokens between different blockchains that is necessary to maximise this openness still presents a hurdle that often introduces intermediaries responsible for operating the respective bridges between the blockchains. One example is the Toucan Protocol, which acts as a central intermediary with the aim to facilitate the onboarding to and bridging between many different blockchains.[34]

The final step of the VCC lifecycle is its *retirement*, which occurs when the environmental benefit has been claimed by the final buyer. During this phase, the credit is permanently removed from the market and is no longer available for transactions.[35] This is achieved by deactivating the credit on the blockchain, rendering it unusable. Retiring the VCC on the blockchain offers the same advantages mentioned previously: It ensures there is no double-counting and that environmental benefits cannot be claimed multiple times. The Moss MCO2 Token, for instance, employs a Verra registry to provide proof of retirement.

One more possible blockchain application that is not focused on a specific step but can instead be applied to the *whole VCC lifecycle* is establishing a Decentralised Autonomous Organisation (DAO) to govern the respective processes. Doing that could help to automate processes and make them more transparent, as they are guided by a fixed set of rules set by the DAO, for example, in the form of smart contracts. However, as evidenced by the case of Klima DAO, DAOs may encounter limitations when interacting with stakeholders outside the crypto world. This challenge compounds the significant barriers posed by the adoption of novel technology (blockchain), which may not seamlessly integrate with numerous processes external to the crypto sphere.[36]

4.2 Value proposition of blockchain for VCCs lifecycle steps

In the previous section, specific blockchain applications for the VCC lifecycle were presented. These applications leverage a set of fundamental value propositions of blockchain technology that will be highlighted in the following section.

One of the main perks of using blockchain technology is that the data on the blockchain is immutable and therefore tamper-proof. This is especially important when *committing to data*, as it ensures that the data cannot be tampered with afterwards and can be trusted for its validity. Its unchangeable nature and publicly visible record also enable robust accounting practices that prevent ambiguity over ownership and double-counting of emissions reductions.[37] This provides the advantage of bringing transparency to the history of an asset, such as an In-Transit Money Order.[38] Once the token is created, the *ownership* of the credit will also be thoroughly documented, preventing double-spending and reducing the risk of credit theft. Additionally, it ensures that the credit cannot be reactivated after *retirement*.

In addition to recording its history, blockchain technology generally enhances data transparency. Tokenising VCCs strengthens transaction security and traceability while improving their composability by embedding these digital assets more deeply into the blockchain ecosystem.[39] Although VCCs are digital certificates verifying that one ton of CO_2 emissions was avoided by a company or environmental project, the credibility and verifiability of these claims on current exchanges fall short of the transparency that public visibility on a blockchain can provide.[40] Blockchain can effectively address the challenge of limited transparency in the verification process, thereby supporting a transparent and high-quality voluntary carbon market.[41] Importantly, the integration of contracts into the blockchain establishes intrinsic self-regulation, such as IT governance, transparency, security, and self-custody, which significantly enhances the credibility and quality of the global carbon credit system.[42] Specifically, this enables the integration of smart contracts into the VCC system. For instance, data can be verified through technologies such as satellite imagery, making it transparent to all participants. Additionally, the market price of VCCs can be monitored, ensuring the fairness of the system by preventing the sale of VCCs to different individuals at varying prices.

Finally, blockchain offers the possibility of decentralised data storage and a decentralised consensus on future transactions, thus eliminating the dependency on and control over the system of individual third parties. This ensures the availability and the integrity of the data. By storing the data on multiple nodes, no single entity has to trust the other regarding the validity of the information. This mitigates the issue of needing a universally trusted party, which is particularly challenging on a global scale. This advantage is present at each stage of the VCC lifecycle, but the integrity is particularly crucial during steps four to six as the information related to the purchase and retirement history of the VCC is stored.

4.3 Additional requirements

After presenting possible uses of blockchain and highlighting the underlying value propositions, there are still additional requirements and aspects that must be considered to enable a holistic implementation.

Although data becomes completely transparent and immutable once it is placed on the blockchain, there is a challenge in validating the data before it is uploaded. This can be addressed, as proposed above, by using smart contracts to help autonomously monitor the data which, however, needs to be reported by an oracle. Thus, while the verification through the smart contract is trustless and autonomous, there is a challenge in measuring the data used, depending on the carbon-saving project, which still requires trust in the onsite data collection and verification. Then, a trusted third party (such as a verification office) is needed to validate the data before it is uploaded to the blockchain. One could argue that the necessity of a trusted third party at this step could undermine one of the main advantages of using blockchain for VCCs in general: the elimination of the need to trust a specific authority, thereby enabling global trading. This can be problematic if the data uploaded to the blockchain is already faulty. In such cases, while the blockchain will ensure that the data is transparent and immutable, it does not guarantee the validity of the data simply by virtue of being on the blockchain.

Even though transparency is particularly advantageous in the context of VCCs and is considered a means to address existing problems, it can also be detrimental or excessive, posing the question of whether it is necessary to share all information publicly. Maintaining private communication among internal contributors helps safeguard proprietary information and strategic discussions within the blockchain framework.[43] If the fully transparent storage on the blockchain makes sensitive data accessible to everyone, it would be unavoidable to consider implementing a mechanism for selective disclosure. This would involve a more precise selection of the data that is transparently stored on the blockchain and the data for which only a hash or similar representation is stored. The tension between transparency and data privacy in blockchains arises from the need to balance the public accessibility of transaction data, which enhances traceability and verifiability, with the protection of user privacy, which can be compromised by the deanonymisation of pseudonymous transactions through various forensic analyses.[44] This duality poses a challenge as it necessitates the development of identity systems that can provide the benefits of traceability and verifiability enabled through transparency without compromising on data privacy and user security.[45] The trade-off between transparency and traceability of information and data protection is also relevant regarding the identifiability of owners. The issue of privacy must be addressed, as it often contradicts the identifiability of the owner and the transparency of the transaction. For many parties, it is important – or even legally required due to regulations such as Know Your Customer (KYC), Anti-Money Laundering (AML), Countering the Financing of Terrorism (CFT), or the Supply Chain Act – that they know with whom they are interacting. Blockchains, by default, are pseudonymous. Participants only know the addresses involved in transactions, not the actual identities behind those addresses. Therefore, it is necessary to have a mechanism to identify these parties, either directly on the blockchain or off-chain and then only allow addresses that have been verified.

In steps four to six, the ownership and trading of tokens would effectively take place on the blockchain and thus be openly visible. However, this transparency can be problematic for various reasons: Users may not want their transactions to be public, companies may fear for the confidentiality of their business secrets, particularly concerning their balance sheets, and there may even be legal issues such as compliance with the General Data Protection Regulation (GDPR). Therefore, it is essential to ensure that interactions and transactions comply with relevant legal and regulatory requirements while maintaining the advantages of blockchain technology. Balancing transparency with privacy is crucial because it ensures that sensitive personal information remains secure while allowing essential transaction details to be transparently communicated through multiple channels.[46] Therefore, an important challenge is to determine how to implement steps four to six on the blockchain without violating privacy.

The primary idea behind implementing the transaction of the VCCs on the blockchain is to ensure inclusivity in the system. By leveraging the openness of the blockchain, all individuals can participate in token trading. Accessibility is vital because it promotes fairness and inclusivity, allowing a broader range of participants, including smaller entities and individual investors, to engage in trading activities. Blockchain technology can enhance market accessibility by eliminating barriers such as geographical restrictions, reducing reliance on intermediaries, and enabling direct peer-to-peer transactions. Additionally, fractionalisation allows even those with smaller sums to engage in the market, while disintermediation can reduce transaction costs.[47] This democratisation of access can also foster innovation, competition, and efficiency within the market ecosystem. However, these theoretical advantages are rendered ineffective if the market lacks sufficient liquidity, as this results in inefficiency and deters participation. To fully realise the potential benefits, it is crucial to create incentives or establish collaborations that enhance market liquidity, particularly during the bootstrapping phase when the market is just being established and activity is minimal.

5 Discussion and conclusion

The affordances of blockchain technology exhibit a strong fit to the contemporary challenges faced by VCCs, particularly regarding transparency, verifiability, and the removal of intermediaries and central authorities necessitating trust. Its application spans a wide array of use cases across the entire VCC lifecycle. This includes recording the initial project design on the blockchain, reporting data through the blockchain, tokenising and trading VCCs, and ultimately retiring the tokens along with the associated VCCs. However, despite the evident strong alignment between blockchain capabilities and the challenges faced by VCCs, blockchain alone is insufficient to address all VCC challenges comprehensively. While blockchains can guarantee verifiability and integrity for data that is natively stored on them,[48] they fall short in fully ensuring the verifiability and integrity of off-chain data, that is, information that first needs to be onboarded to the blockchain by oracles.[49] However, in the context of VCCs, the integrity and reliability of this off-chain data such as VCC monitoring data plays a crucial role in the overall system integrity and functionality. Consequently, as this data needs to be introduced by oracles, the issue of trust cannot be entirely resolved by blockchain in the context of verifying VCC data and ensuring its accuracy.

Furthermore, although blockchain's disintermediation and instant settlement can enable efficient market infrastructure, and its openness and technological capabilities, such as token fractionalisation, can promote broader market participation, blockchain usage does not directly guarantee achieving market efficiency. Market efficiency is primarily driven by liquidity, which depends on market activity and interest – factors that blockchain technology alone cannot directly address.

Besides the challenges of VCCs that blockchain cannot fully address, the use of blockchain for VCC tokenisation also introduces new challenges. If tokenisation is not implemented natively and the VCC registry is merely mapped onto the blockchain without full integration, a new potential point of failure is created. Ensuring that ownership and control of the token correspond to ownership and control of the VCC is essential to prevent the same VCC from being tokenised multiple times or transferred or retired independently of the token.[50] Additionally, managing data transparency, identifiability, and privacy on blockchains can present risks. While blockchain's openness and transparency can address some data privacy issues, pseudonymity can lead to inferences about actors and their identities, which is insufficient for regulatory compliance.[51] Actors requiring regulatory adherence, such as financial institutions, need additional measures to identify other actors to comply with regulations like KYC, AML, and CFT.

To date, mass adoption of tokenised VCCs, or VCCs in general, remains limited, and the overall market has significantly declined despite sustainability continuing to be a top priority for politics, society, and the economy.[52] This missing adoption is also reflected by the scarcity of academic literature on the topic of VCC tokenisation and long-lasting real-world cases, which could serve as an exhaustive case study. Effectively addressing these challenges and combining blockchain's capabilities with other solutions that can tackle the challenges blockchain alone cannot address is crucial for the successful implementation and widespread adoption of VCCs and might even uncover new blockchain use cases in the context of VCCs, not present in the current literature or practice. In this context, research requires interdisciplinary collaboration to investigate how technical, economic, and legal measures can be combined to tackle VCC challenges in an all-encompassing manner. On the technical side, researchers should especially focus on combining blockchain with other technological primitives such as Zero-Knowledge Proofs, for example, for integrating off-chain data into blockchain systems in a secure and verifiable manner.[53] Practitioners in the field then need to collaborate closely with technologists to implement and test these integrated solutions in real-world settings. This involves piloting projects that utilise blockchain for VCC management, ensuring that tokenisation processes are secure and accurately reflect VCC ownership and control. Practitioners should also develop best practices for maintaining data transparency, identifiability, and privacy on blockchain platforms while obeying regulatory requirements. Regulatory authorities play a critical role in creating a conducive environment for the adoption of blockchain-integrated VCC systems. They should establish clear guidelines and standards for blockchain use in the VCC market, addressing issues such as compliance with KYC, AML, and CFT regulations. Regulatory bodies might also facilitate collaboration between stakeholders by supporting pilot projects and offering regulatory sandboxes for testing innovative solutions.

By addressing these challenges through a collaborative and interdisciplinary approach, stakeholders can ensure the successful implementation and widespread adoption of VCCs. This collective effort could also lead to the discovery of further blockchain applications and solutions that can more effectively address the complexities of the VCC market, ultimately contributing to global sustainability goals.

Notes

1 Nora Wissner and Lambert Schneider, 'Ensuring safeguards and assessing sustainable development impacts in the voluntary carbon market' [2022] White paper, Oeko-Institut eV Panel A: Coverage of Carbon Taxes, Allowance Markets, and Voluntary Offsets 10–12.
2 Dong-Ho Lee, Dong-hwan Kim and Seong-il Kim, 'Characteristics of forest carbon credit transactions in the voluntary carbon market' (2018) 18(2) Climate Policy 235 236–237; Christopher Blaufelder and others, 'A blueprint for scaling voluntary carbon markets to meet the climate challenge' [2021] McKinsey & Company Sustainability and Risk Practices 1 2–3; Eric Nowak, 'Voluntary Carbon Markets' (A SIX White Paper 2022) 7–8.
3 Thibaut Santier, 'The next priorities of the Voluntary Carbon Market for mass adoption: The need for new technologies, carbon policy frameworks, and a meta registry' (Université Paris – Saclay 23 November 2023) 35–40.
4 Nowak (n 2) 5–6.
5 Hans Koberstein, Marta Orosz and Nathan Niedermeier, 'Klimaschutz in China: Milliardenbetrug in der Ölbranche?' (ZDFheute 2024) 28624–28625 https://www.zdf.de/nachrichten/wirtschaft/unternehmen/oelkonzerne-klimaschutz-projekte-china-verdacht-betrug-100.html accessed 3 February 2025.
6 Matthias Babel and others, 'Enabling end-to-end digital carbon emission tracing with shielded NFTs' (2022) 5(S1) Energy Inform 1 5; Laura Franke, Marco Schletz and Søren Salomo, 'Designing a Blockchain Model for the Paris Agreement's Carbon Market Mechanism' (2020) 12(3) Sustainability 1068, 2–5.
7 Franke, Schletz and Salomo (n 6) 15–16; Nicholas P Espenan, 'Improving Voluntary Carbon Markets Through Standardization and Blockchain Technology' (2023) 23(1) Wyoming Law Review 141, 177.
8 Vincent Schlatt and others, 'Blockchain: Grundlagen, Anwendungen und Potenziale' (Fraunhofer Institute for Applied Information Technology FIT 2016) 7–13.
9 Karl Wust and Arthur Gervais, 'Do you Need a Blockchain?' [2018] Crypto Valley Conference on Blockchain Technology (CVCBT) 45, 46–47.
10 Roman Beck and others, 'Blockchain Technology in Business and Information Systems Research' (2017) 59(6) Business & Information Systems Engineering 381.
11 Bert-Jan Butijn, Damian A Tamburri and Willem-Jan van den Heuvel, 'Blockchains: A Systematic Multivocal Literature Review' (2021) 53(3) ACM Computing Surveys 1, 4–5.
12 Butijn, Tamburri and van den Heuvel (n 11) 4.
13 Vincent Gramlich and others, 'A multivocal literature review of decentralized finance: Current knowledge and future research avenues' (2023) 33(1) Electron Markets 1.
14 Raymond Song, Ainjing Li and Caroline Ott, 'How to Build a Trusted Voluntary Carbon Market' (2022) https://rmi.org/how-to-build-a-trusted-voluntary-carbon-market/ accessed 3 February 2025.
15 Song, Li and Ott (n 14); Michal Jirásek, 'Klima DAO: a crypto answer to carbon markets' (2023) 12(4) Journal of Organization Design 271 273.
16 Song, Li and Ott (n 14).
17 Jirásek (n 15) 272–273.

18 Adam Sipthorpe and others, 'Blockchain solutions for carbon markets are nearing maturity' (2022) 5(7) One Earth 779, 783–786.
19 Jirásek (n 15) 273–274.
20 Song, Li and Ott (n 14).
21 Jane Webster and Richard Watson, 'Analyzing the Past to Prepare for the Future: Writing a Literature Review' (2002) 26(2) MIS Quarterly xiii.
22 Vahid Garousi, Michael Felderer and Mika V Mäntylä, 'Guidelines for including grey literature and conducting multivocal literature reviews in software engineering' (2019) 106 Information and Software Technology 101, 102.
23 Song, Li and Ott (n 14).
24 Giesel Booman and others, 'Regen Network Whitepaper' (2021) 12 https://regen-network.gitlab.io/whitepaper/WhitePaper.pdf accessed 3 February 2025.
25 Babel and others (n 6) 6; Matthias Babel and others, 'Vertrauen durch digitale Identifizierung: Über den Beitrag von SSI zur Integration von dezentralen Oracles in Informationssysteme' (2023) 60(2) HMD 478 482.
26 CarbonStack, 'CarbonStack: Offsetting CO2 emissions with high resolution satellite imagery' (2024) https://up42.com/case-study/carbonstack-offsets-co2-emissions-satellite-imagery accessed 3 February 2025.
27 Moss, 'Moss Carbon Credit MCO2 Token White Paper' (2024) 11–12 https://v.fastcdn.co/u/f3b4407f/54475626-0-Moss-white-paper-eng.pdf accessed 3 February 2025.
28 Jirásek (n 15) 283–284.
29 Jirásek (n 15) 283–284.
30 Sebastian Steuer, '"Klimaneutrale" Produkte im Lauterkeitsrecht' [2022] GRUR Gewerblicher Rechtsschutz und Urheberrecht 1408.
31 CarbonCredits, 'Verra Bans Tokenizing Retired Carbon Credits, Proposes Immobilizing Credits' (CarbonCreditsCom 2022) https://carboncredits.com/verra-suspension-carbon-credits-proposes-immobilizing-credits/ accessed 3 February 2025.
32 Sipthorpe and others (n 18) 783–785.
33 Jirásek (n 15) 273–274.
34 Toucan, 'Carbon bridge | Toucan Documentation' (2024) https://docs.toucan.earth/toucan/carbon-bridge accessed 3 February 2025.
35 Song, Li and Ott (n 14).
36 Jirásek (n 15) 280–281.
37 Sipthorpe and others (n 18) 783–785.
38 Franke, Schletz and Salomo (n 6) 3.
39 Moss (n 27) 4.
40 Moss (n 27) 29–32.
41 Song, Li and Ott (n 14).
42 Moss (n 27) 63–65.
43 Jirásek (n 15) 283–284.
44 Vincent Gramlich and others, 'In Decentralized Finance Nobody Knows You Are a Dog' [2024] Proceedings of the 57th Hawaii International Conference on System Sciences (HICSS) 6–7.
45 Gramlich and others (n 44) 6–7.
46 Jirásek (n 15) 283–284.
47 Franke, Schletz and Salomo (n 6) 5–6.
48 Sipthorpe and others (n 18) 780.
49 Song, Li and Ott (n 14).
50 Jirásek (n 15) 280–281.
51 Gramlich and others (n 44) 6–7.

52 Pedro Gomez and Dale Hardcastle, 'Scaling Voluntary Carbon Markets: A Playbook for Corporate Actions' [2023] World Economic Forum – White Paper 10 https://www3.weforum.org/docs/WEF_Scaling_Voluntary_Carbon_Markets_2023.pdf accessed 3 February 2025.
53 Johannes Sedlmeir and others, 'The transparency challenge of blockchain in organizations' (2022) 32(3) Electron Markets 1779 1788–1789 https://link.springer.com/article/10.1007/s12525-022-00536-0 accessed 3 February 2025; Marc Principato and others, 'Towards Solving the Blockchain Trilemma: An Exploration of Zero-Knowledge Proofs' [2023] International Conference on Information Systems ICIS 4–5.

Dominik Skauradszun and Sebastian Böhning

7 Applicable law in the supply chains of VCC tokens

Abstract: Whereas use cases of voluntary carbon credit tokens ('VCC tokens') surfaced several years ago, the legal framework remains surprisingly vague. The legal nature of voluntary carbon credits ('VCCs') has been subject to discussion across different legislations and national and supranational organisations, yet sufficient consensus across national borders is not in sight. The more recent development of VCC tokens as a decentralised instrument in a dynamic and, in parts, untransparent environment brings new opportunities to scale the market but entails new challenges for a legal analysis. In practice, market players face the difficulty of dealing with a subject associated with major legal uncertainties whilst the market is developing at a fast pace. From a legal perspective, the developing market environment harbours the appealing opportunity to accompany the developments and work towards a more certain legal framework in the future. The voluntary carbon market ('VCM') inherently presents itself as an international and supranational market as certain market models rely on cooperation across borders, for example, between investors from all over the globe and project developers located in the Global South. This situation naturally raises the question of the applicable law along the supply chains of VCC tokens. When addressing this question, the extensive discussion regarding the legal nature of VCC tokens constitutes a hurdle in the legal analysis, yet approaching VCC tokens from the perspective of Private International Law could also shed some light on the ongoing discussion and contribute to a better legal understanding of the VCM.

Keywords: Applicable law, Conflict of laws, Choice of law, Rome I Regulation, UNIDROIT DAPL

1 Introduction —— **152**
2 First insights into the use cases and their provisions regarding questions of Private International Law —— **152**
  2.1 International use cases which issue VCC tokens —— **153**
  2.2 German use cases which issue VCC tokens —— **154**
  2.3 Mere marketplaces for VCC tokens —— **155**
  2.4 Synopsis of accessible provisions regarding Private International Law —— **155**
3 Possible conflict of laws rules along the supply chain of VCC tokens —— **156**
  3.1 Conflict of laws rules within the Union and German legal framework —— **156**
  3.2 Conflict of laws rules in the UNIDROIT Principles on Digital Assets and Private Law —— **166**
  3.3 Conflict of laws rules in other jurisdictions —— **168**
4 Valuation of possible connecting factors in conflict of laws rules —— **169**
  4.1 *Lex rei sitae* —— **170**
  4.2 Habitual residence of the parties —— **170**

https://doi.org/10.1515/9783111706719-007

4.3 Closest connection — 171
4.4 *Lex libri siti* or statutory seat of the issuer or of the registry — 171
4.5 Choice of law by the parties — 171
5 Conclusions and brief proposal for a conflict of laws rule for VCC tokens — 172

1 Introduction

The VCM consists of a diverse variety of instruments with different technical and economic approaches. VCC tokens and their corresponding business models build upon this market and partially incorporate existing structures of the non-digital market. In order to assess the applicable law along the supply chains, a reasonable categorisation of the market players must be undertaken. In this sense, the current use cases shall be grouped according to common features with this analysis being limited to a select number of prominent use cases. Further, the analysis is restricted to VCC tokens as part of the VCM and shall not portray the entire VCM, even though recourses to traditional and non-digital VCCs are evident and necessary. When determining the applicable law, references to the legal nature[1] and regulatory aspects[2] of VCC tokens are only made when needed and those issues shall not be covered comprehensively. The analysis will start from a German point of view—which includes and primarily depends on the legal framework of the European Union ('EU')—and only partly touches on other jurisdictions such as England and Wales and the United States ('USA'). Special attention shall be paid to the UNIDROIT Principles on Digital Assets and Private Law[3] ('UNIDROIT DAPL', 'DAPL') as soft law, which can play an integral role when legally dealing with VCC tokens in the future. As a paper within the realm of Private International Law, the analysis shall be concluded by a discussion and evaluation of possible connecting factors and a proposal for a prospective mechanism to solve conflicts of laws in the future.

2 First insights into the use cases and their provisions regarding questions of Private International Law

As a first step, the following prominent use cases shall be subject to a brief analysis from the perspective of Private International Law. To determine the applicable law, a common basic understanding of the life cycle of VCC tokens from the legal perspective shall be conveyed and it will be examined whether the current use cases contain provisions regarding the applicable law as far as sources are accessible.

2.1 International use cases which issue VCC tokens

2.1.1 Toucan

The VCM is distinctly linked to verifiers for carbon credits such as Verra and Gold Standard, the most prominent and influential verifiers on the market. Verra, as a non-profit corporation under the laws of the District of Columbia, USA,[4] and the Gold Standard Foundation, as a non-profit foundation under Swiss law[5] are private entities that verify and certify carbon projects according to their own standards, that is, the 'Verified Carbon Standard' or the 'Gold Standard'. Carbon credits are issued to the supplier who can then sell the carbon credits to a buyer. The carbon credits are registered in the issuer's own registries, namely 'The Verra Registry' or 'The Gold Standard Registry'.

Toucan provides an infrastructure for the tokenised VCM and is—as far as one can tell—operated by the Toucan Protocol Association based in Switzerland.[6] The main component of the Toucan infrastructure is the 'Toucan Carbon Bridge', which connects registry systems such as the aforementioned with the so-called 'Toucan Registry' and tokenises carbon credits.[7] Presently, Toucan itself provides the 'Puro Carbon Bridge', which connects with the registry of the Puro Standard.[8] To use the Puro Carbon Bridge, the user must have an account with the Puro Standard and own carbon credits in the 'Puro Registry'. The carbon credits can then be tokenised and transferred to a blockchain address of the user. The created tokens can be traded in a variety of ways. The bridge works both ways so that the VCC tokens can also be detokenised again or retired on-chain. Toucan also provides 'Carbon Pools' for the pooling of VCC tokens and manages its own marketplace for those Carbon Pools.

According to its terms of service, Toucan offers the following services on its platform: Tokenisation of VCCs into VCC tokens, detokenisation of VCC tokens, deposit of VCC tokens into 'Carbon Pools', redemption of VCC tokens from 'Carbon Pools' by the destruction of 'Carbon Pool' tokens, and retirement of VCCs by way of retiring and burning of the corresponding VCC tokens.[9] The terms of service and any dispute or claim arising out of or in connection with the terms or their subject matter or formation shall be governed by and construed in accordance with the laws of England.[10]

2.1.2 Regen Network

Regen Network issues VCC tokens to project developers, operates its own registry, the 'Regen Registry', and provides a marketplace for VCC tokens. It registers tokens according to its own standard and is not linked to non-digital registries or standards like Verra or Gold Standard. Unlike Toucan, the tokens are issued directly on-chain. Regen Network as a standard, registry, and marketplace is not part of the trading contracts between sellers and buyers.[11] The marketplace provided may function as both a primary and secondary market, as tokens can be bought by project or sell order. Regen Network operates its own blockchain, the 'Regen Ledger'.[12]

Regen Network is controlled by Regen Network Development, PBC, a public-benefit corporation based in Delaware, USA.[13] According to their terms of service, the use of the offered services 'shall be governed and construed in accordance with the laws of the State of Delaware without regard to its conflict of law provisions.'[14]

2.2 German use cases which issue VCC tokens

2.2.1 Carbonstack

Carbonstack collaborates closely with carbon projects in Germany and issues VCC tokens for these projects, which can then be sold. The tokens are not registered with other prominent registries. The focus of Carbonstack's work is on supporting carbon projects from their inception with innovative technology and precisely calculating the carbon impact of these projects.[15] Information about the issuance and distribution of the VCC tokens is scarce. It can be assumed that there is no cooperation with the aforementioned players.

Carbonstack is operated by CarbonStack GmbH based in Germany.[16] Terms and conditions or other information regarding the applicable law are not accessible.

2.2.2 Goodcarbon

Goodcarbon issues tokens for carbon credits and provides a marketplace for them. The VCC tokens offered are also registered with a prominent registry such as Verra or Gold Standard. However, unlike Toucan, existing credits are not tokenised using a bridge; instead, when issuing the VCC tokens, they are also registered with the known standards.[17] According to their terms and conditions, the services 'shall be governed by the substantive laws of the Federal Republic of Germany excluding the application of private international law and UN sales law'.[18]

As another peculiarity, the VCC tokens are wrapped up in financial instruments and the German-based goodcarbon GmbH, which operates the platform, has been notified to the German Federal Financial Supervisory Authority ('Bundesanstalt für Finanzdienstleistungsaufsicht', 'BaFin') as a tied agent of a securities institute ('vertraglich gebundener Vermittler').[19] This constitutes an anomaly in the VCM and there is no other prominent use case with this special feature. There is no information accessible that further defines the peculiarities of Goodcarbon's products. Yet the available information leads to the conclusion that these products must be treated differently than the 'regular' VCC tokens from a legal perspective. In particular, regulatory matters come into play, which will not be covered by this analysis. Also, this touches on the core of the legal nature of VCC tokens. It can be assumed that the rights and claims under Goodcarbon's products are defined more clearly. Yet, as information about these products is not available, this use case shall not be the object of further analysis.

2.3 Mere marketplaces for VCC tokens

2.3.1 Senken

Senken offers a mere marketplace for VCCs and VCC tokens. For this purpose, it aggregates non-digital registries and blockchain registries such as Toucan or Regen Network into one marketplace. Buyers can trade VCC tokens from different registries on one platform. Senken is not a party to the exchange contracts concluded between users.[20]

The terms and conditions state that the law of the Federal Republic of Germany applies, excluding the UN Convention on Contracts for the International Sale of Goods, unless there are mandatory statutory provisions (especially consumer protection regulations) to the contrary.[21]

2.3.2 Kumo

Kumo operates a lending marketplace and matches funders and borrowers.[22] The loans given out via Kumo are backed by carbon credits, which may be VCC tokens. Borrowers must own VCCs or VCC tokens registered with an acknowledged standard.

Kumo is operated by Kumo Labs GmbH, based in Germany.[23] Their terms and conditions 'shall be governed by and construed in accordance with the laws of Rhineland-Palatinate, Germany, without regard to its conflict of law principles.'[24]

2.4 Synopsis of accessible provisions regarding Private International Law

To summarise, some of the use cases provide provisions regarding the governing law of the services offered. However, this is not the case for all use cases as far as sources are accessible.[25] More importantly, choice-of-law provisions in the use cases cannot convey a comprehensive picture of the applicable law along the supply chain. On the contrary, the provisions are only able to selectively determine the applicable law in one or a few steps of the life cycle and only under the condition that a choice of law is possible in the first place.[26] Due to the significant uncertainty surrounding their legal nature, the complex contractual or non-contractual relationships of several possible parties, and the given cross-border issues of VCC tokens, the question of the applicable law remains.

This brief introduction to the use cases and their business models and the found provisions shall be referenced in the following analysis of the different conflict of laws regimes. It will be assessed how the use cases can be treated under different conflict of laws rules and what part a choice of law can play in this regard.

3 Possible conflict of laws rules along the supply chain of VCC tokens

3.1 Conflict of laws rules within the Union and German legal framework

3.1.1 Rome I Regulation on the law applicable to contractual obligations

When opening proceedings before a German court, possible conflict of laws rules can be found in Union and national law. Private International Law is regulated in German law in the Introductory Act to the Civil Code[27] ('EGBGB'), *in concreto* in Part 1 division 2 (Art. 3–46e) EGBGB. According to Art. 3 EGBGB, the applicable law is to be determined by the provisions of the EGBGB unless immediately applicable rules of the EU or rules in international conventions, insofar as they have become directly applicable in national law, are relevant. Therefore, it must be assessed first whether an immediately applicable rule of the EU is relevant. Art. 3(1)(b) EGBGB explicitly mentions the Rome I Regulation on the law applicable to contractual obligations[28] ('Rome I'). Other rules such as the Rome II Regulation on the law applicable to non-contractual obligations[29] shall not be the subject of this analysis. Non-contractual obligations such as obligations arising out of torts or unjust enrichment are also conceivable in the context of VCC tokens.[30] Yet, from a preliminary perspective, the emergence of VCC tokens does not present entirely new challenges when determining the applicable law in this regard.[31]

3.1.1.1 Scope of the Rome I Regulation and no exclusion as negotiable instruments

As stated in Art. 1(1) Rome I, the Regulation shall apply, in situations involving a conflict of laws, to contractual obligations in civil and commercial matters. In accordance with the Brussels Ia Regulation ('Brussels Ia'),[32,33] a contractual obligation is to be understood as covering a situation in which there is an obligation freely assumed by one party towards another.[34] This is the case with VCC tokens, as the trading takes place voluntarily on a free market. It is important to note that only the contractual obligations are covered under this Regulation, and it is not applicable to proprietary rights or their transfer.[35]

According to Art. 1(2)(d) Rome I, obligations arising under bills of exchange, cheques and promissory notes and other negotiable instruments to the extent that the obligations under such other negotiable instruments arise out of their negotiable character are excluded from the scope of the Regulation. Consequently, in order to apply the Regulation, VCC tokens must not fall within this exclusion. As VCC tokens can be traded and can be seen as a financial investment for the buyer, the scope of the exclusion must be further assessed. The term 'negotiable instruments' is not defined in the Regulation[36] and there is no jurisprudence of the Court of Justice of the European Union ('CJEU') on the term with regard to Rome I. The term must also be interpreted autonomously without drawing upon national understandings.[37] The MiFID II[38] and the Prospectus Regulation[39] use the term 'transferable securities' and hence cannot be directly used for interpretation either.[40]

The exclusion of Art. 1(2)(d) Rome I is based on the development that several jurisdictions had incorporated specific conflict of laws rules in their Private International Law for bills of exchanges and cheques for several decades.[41] A characteristic of bills of exchanges and cheques is that the right represented by the document is transferred by the handover of the document. This characteristic is reflected in the scope exclusion as the exclusion is limited insofar as the obligations under a negotiable instrument must arise out of its negotiable character.[42] It must be analysed if a VCC token holds this characteristic or is at least sufficiently comparable to the explicitly mentioned instruments.

3.1.1.1.1 No obligations arising out of a negotiable character

It is conceivable to consider instruments that do not represent a right on a physical document but rather in digital form as negotiable instruments. There are compelling arguments to interpret the term in a contemporary manner and include electronic or blockchain-based securities in the term 'negotiable instrument'. For example, when transferring a blockchain-based security to a different blockchain address, the embodied claim against the issuer is transferred as well.[43]

When analysing a VCC token, it is already difficult to define its legal nature. A common understanding has not yet been reached on whether, and if so, which claims are represented by a VCC. One approach is to consider a VCC as a claim against a standard or registry to retire the carbon credit, hence, to take it out of circulation and consider its effect to be consumed.[44] When looking at a VCC token, there are two options to define its relationship to the carbon credit itself. In the use case of Toucan, an already existing VCC is tokenised. The resulting VCC token could therefore be considered as a right of access to the non-digital VCC, comparable to a utility token.[45] In the use cases of Regen Network, the VCC token is generated on-chain and there is no relationship to a non-digital VCC. Subsequently, there is no further object to consider and the VCC token itself could represent a claim.

However, even if considering a VCC token as a claim or a bundle of rights, there is no indication that obligations under a VCC token *arise out of its negotiable character*. Firstly, the negotiability is restricted insofar that at present there is no inter-operability between registries or standards. Secondly, when a VCC token is transferred, the trade must be filed with the registry, which only shows the holder of the VCC token. There are no provisions available that cover the relationship between sales contract, assignment of rights, transfer of tokens, and filing with the registry. In the absence of such provisions, for example, non-assignment clauses, the constitutive effect of filing with the registry or bona fide provisions, it must be assumed for now that all dealings with VCC tokens happen on a mere contractual basis at the free will of the parties. Therefore, there is no mechanism recognisable that a possible claim represented by a VCC token is automatically transferred along with the transfer of the token itself. It must be assumed that a possible transfer of claims can only be agreed upon by contract. Subsequently, obligations arising out of a negotiable character must be denied.

3.1.1.1.2 No sufficient comparability with bills of exchange or cheques

Furthermore, from a practical point of view, there is no sufficient comparability with the explicitly mentioned negotiable instruments such as bills of exchange or cheques. As mentioned above, tradability is limited as there is no inter-operability between different registries or standards. While most use cases only allow trading with VCC tokens under their own standard or refer to only one standard, like in the Toucan use case, marketplaces such as Senken do not change the picture. Even though they connect different registries, there is no actual inter-operability between the standards. Tokens cannot simply be swapped; rather, each transfer of a token must be filed with its specific registry. This constitutes an important difference to bills of exchange or cheques, which can and are traded simply by handing over the physical document that constitutes the right embodied.[46] In addition, there is a tremendous variety of carbon projects, ways of counting carbon offsets, and ways of packaging them for the market such as 'Carbon Pools'[47] or 'carbon forward tokens'.[48] In this sense, it is highly doubtful if there is reasonable standardisation of VCC tokens, which speaks against comparability to the instruments in Art. 1(2)(d) Rome I.

Another point to consider is the fact that VCCs were not originally designed to be financial instruments that can be traded for an unlimited time period. VCCs are characterised by the idea that they will be retired and that their effect will be consumed when taken out of circulation. This retirement can only be requested from the standard, which once again shows the prominent role the standards or registries play in the VCM. Even when considering a VCC token as a claim against the registry,[49] this claim does not constitute a financial asset in the conventional sense. The holder of a VCC token has—different from the compliance market—no direct monetary benefits from holding the token. VCCs are rather used to reach a positive eco-balance or 'net zero' regarding a company's carbon emissions. Naturally, this has some value for the company, but it is hard to measure financially and rather depicts the fulfilment of self-set compliance standards. The VCC token therefore constitutes a 'certificate' rather than a financial asset. Both aspects, no open market for different VCC tokens and the lacking characterisation as financial assets, speak against a comparability with the named negotiable instruments.

Therefore, VCC tokens are not covered by the exclusion of Art. 1(2)(d) Rome I, and the Rome I Regulation is applicable to contractual obligations in connection with VCC tokens.

3.1.1.2 Choice of law pursuant to Art. 3 Rome I Regulation

According to Art. 3(1) Rome I, a contract shall be governed by the law chosen by the parties. The article reflects the internationally respected principle of party autonomy. This principle is not overridden but only modified by other articles of the Rome I Regulation, such as Art. 6(2) (consumers), Art. 7(3) (insurances), or Art. 8(1) (employments), which depict protective measures for one party of the contract. The conflict of laws rules in Art. 4 Rome I apply only to the extent that the law applicable to the contract has not been chosen in accordance with Art. 3 Rome I. Some of the use cases include a clause regarding the governing law of their services. To elaborate on the constellations in the supply chain in which the law has been chosen, the provisions need to be further analysed. The pros and cons of a choice of law and their implications will be discussed below under Section 4.5.

The most detailed provision is accessible for the Toucan use case. According to their terms of service, the terms and any dispute or claim arising out of or in connection with these terms or their subject matter or formation (including non-contractual disputes or claims) shall be governed by and construed in accordance with the laws of England.[50] The services offered by Toucan are further defined as tokenisation of VCCs into VCC tokens, detokenisation of VCC tokens, deposit of VCC tokens into 'Carbon Pools', redemption of VCC tokens from 'Carbon Pools' by the destruction of 'Carbon Pool' tokens, and retirement of VCCs by way of retiring and burning of the corresponding VCC tokens.[51] Worth noting, Toucan shall in no event be liable to a user for any losses, claims, expenses, or damages arising out of or relating to the use of, or statements regarding, the VCCs, including claims arising out of or relating to ESG claims.[52] Hence, several steps along the life cycle of a VCC token are covered. Importantly, the issuance, sale, transfer, or exchange of VCC tokens is not mentioned as a service of Toucan. Toucan also explicitly states that they do not have custody or control over the contents of a user's registry account and have no ability to hold, transfer, acquire, retire, or cancel the VCCs in that account.[53] To conclude, the following main steps are covered by the choice of law provision: tokenisation, deposit of tokens in Carbon Pools, detokenisation, and retirement. Not covered by the provision are issuance of VCC tokens, sale of VCC tokens, transfer of VCC tokens, and trading on the secondary market.

Regen Network states in its terms of service that the terms shall be governed and construed in accordance with the laws of the State of Delaware without regard to its conflict of law provisions.[54] The services of Regen Network are not further specified, but the terms of service govern the use of the web pages and the 'Regen Registry'.[55] It is further stated that the 'Regen Registry' is a standard and certification system that provides certification of projects and the issuance or generation of products.[56] 'Regen Registry' is not a party to any agreement to a project or product between or among project developers, buyers, or any other parties. Interestingly, 'Regen Registry' claims not having any liability or obligation in connection with any project or product at any time.[57] Therefore, even if not completely unambiguous, it can be assumed that the tokenisation and issuance of VCC tokens are covered by the choice of law clause. The step of retirement of VCC tokens is not mentioned in the accessible sources but could also be considered as a possible service. Yet again, it can be concluded that the sale and transfer of VCC tokens and a possible trade on the secondary market are not covered.

Lastly, Senken states in their terms and conditions that the law of the Federal Republic of Germany applies.[58] It is said that Senken operates a marketplace via the platform for the exchange of tokenised carbon credits between users. Senken does not produce or tokenise these credits, and therefore does not assume responsibility for their quality, legality, or compliance with any standards.[59] The company acts as an intermediary between users and facilitates the exchange of credits at the instruction of the users, without any discretion or provision of advice. Senken is not a party to the exchange contracts concluded between users and does not have any role in the conclusion of the contract or the determination of its terms.[60] As a result, the choice of law clause only covers the usage of the platform as a marketplace. The actual sale or transfer of VCC tokens is not covered.

To summarise, the given choice of law provisions in the use cases only cover some steps in the life cycle of a VCC token. It is worth noting that the tokenisation or the issuance shall be covered by choice of law in the use cases. However, the sale and transfer of VCC tokens is not mentioned as the companies in the use cases are not party to the actual exchange contracts. Interestingly, all use cases state that they will not have any liability in connection with the actual VCC or carbon project. For the further analysis, it can be concluded that there are several steps in the life cycle of VCC tokens that are not covered under current choice of law provisions. Therefore, Art. 4 Rome I which determines the applicable law in the absence of choice must be analysed. The findings regarding choice of law provisions above will once again be considered in other conflict of laws regimes thereafter.

3.1.1.3 Habitual residence of the seller pursuant to Art. 4(1)(a) Rome I Regulation

Art. 4 Rome I contains an elaborated mechanism to determine the law governing a contract in cases where the law applicable to the contract has not been chosen. Art. 4 (1) Rome I entails rules for certain types of contracts. When applying Art. 4(1) Rome I, paragraphs (2) and (3) must also be considered. According to Art. 4(2) Rome I, paragraph (1) is only applicable if the elements of the contract are covered by one of the subparagraphs (a) to (h) of paragraph (1). According to Art. 4(3) Rome I, where it is clear from all the circumstances of the case that the contract is manifestly more closely connected with a country other than that indicated in paragraph (1), the law of that other country shall apply.

Art. 4(1)(a) Rome I covers a 'contract for the sale of goods'. The sale of a VCC token from the holder to a buyer on the primary or secondary market could constitute such a sale. This is only the case if a VCC token is to be considered a good in the sense of the article. According to Recital 17 Rome I, the concept of 'provision of services' and 'sale of goods' should be interpreted in the same way as when applying Art. 5 Brussels I Regulation (which today is Art. 7 Brussels Ia).

The German language version speaks of 'Verkauf *beweglicher* Sachen', which can be translated as 'sale of movables'. This alludes to an understanding that only physical objects are covered by the term.[61] However, this understanding is not depicted in other languages (French 'contract de vente de biens'; Spanish 'compraventa de mercaderías'). Also, the term may be subject to the change of times and with a more contemporary understanding, a physical aspect could be denied in the context of progressing digitalisation. The CJEU did not rule in this concrete matter. The resolution of this issue can be found in the telos of the Regulations' rules. The rules in both Regulations have territorial references. In Art. 4(1)(a) Rome I, the residence of the seller shall determine the applicable law. In Art. 7(1)(b) Brussels Ia, the place where goods are delivered determines the jurisdiction. The rules intend to make it easier for the parties to pursue their rights and reference places associated with the sale of the good.[62] This is not possible or helpful for a decentralised object such as a VCC token on a blockchain.[63] VCC tokens are not delivered at a specific place and are not bought at a store of the seller in the non-digital world. Therefore, there is no indication for such a broad interpretation and VCC tokens are not covered by the term 'goods' in the sense of Art. 4(1)(a) Rome I which, consequently, does not apply.[64]

3.1.1.4 Habitual residence of the service provider pursuant to Art. 4(1)(b) Rome I Regulation

According to Art. 4(1)(b) Rome I, a contract for the provision of services shall be governed by the law of the country where the service provider has his habitual residence. Certain steps within the life cycle of a VCC token could be considered as a provision of services. The term is not defined in the Regulation. Once again, Recital 17 refers to the Brussels I Regulation (now Brussels Ia) for a uniform interpretation of the term. Finding an exact definition of the term is challenging. However, the term should be interpreted in a broad sense.[65] A basic understanding of the provision of a service as carrying out a particular activity in return for remuneration[66] is sufficient for this analysis.

The individual steps in the life cycle must be inspected. When looking at VCC tokens, there are always certain ongoing activities involved. For example, maintaining the register or its own blockchain would constitute such activity. However, in order to apply Art. 4(1)(b) Rome I, the focus of a contractual obligation must be considered.[67] Not included in the provision of services is the sale and transfer of VCC tokens. When trading, the parties involved desire to transfer a VCC token in exchange for some kind of payment. The result of the transaction is the main objective of the parties and not the activity itself. The same applies to the tokenisation, issuance, and retirement of VCC tokens. Here, activities such as minting or burning of the token are essential parts of the agreement. Yet again, the parties' focus is not on the activity itself but rather on the final product. The user's objective is to hold the token or to retire it to remove it from circulation.[68] However, the use cases which constitute a mere marketplace can fall within Art. 4(1)(b) Rome I. As stated, e.g., in the terms and conditions of Senken, Senken is not a party to the exchange contracts concluded between users. It acts as an intermediary between users and facilitates the exchange of credits at the instruction of the users without any discretion or provision of advice.[69] This facilitating constitutes an activity in the sense of a provision of services. As Senken charges a transaction fee, a remuneration is given as well. Whereas Senken's service is governed by a choice of law clause as shown above, Art. 4(1)(b) Rome I would apply to comparable use cases which constitute a mere marketplace and act as an intermediary if no choice of law has taken place.

3.1.1.5 Residence of the party required to effect characteristic performance pursuant to Art. 4(2) Rome I Regulation

According to Art. 4(2) Rome I, where the contract is not covered by paragraph (1) or where the elements of the contract would be covered by more than one of subparagraphs (a) to (h) of paragraph (1), the contract shall be governed by the law of the country where the party required to effect the characteristic performance of the contract has his habitual residence. As shown above, besides the activity of a marketplace provider, the steps in the life cycle of a VCC token are not covered by Art. 4(1) Rome I. Therefore, the characteristic performance of each step must be further assessed. How the term 'characteristic performance' must be interpreted is not defined in the Regulation. Recital 19 sentence 2 Rome I states that the characteristic performance of the contract should be determined having regard to its centre of gravity. Literature further states that the characteristic performance enables a contract to be distinguished from other types of contracts.[70]

The characteristic performance of sale contracts, which do not fall within the scope of Art. 4(1)(a) Rome I but involve the exchange of a thing for some kind of payment, is the performance of the seller.[71] The payment with fiat money or another accepted currency does not constitute the characteristic performance. Therefore, the sale and the contractual obligations under a transfer agreement of VCC tokens can be covered by Art. 4(2) Rome I. The contract, consequently, shall be governed by the law of the country where the seller or former VCC token holder has their habitual residence.[72] Similar considerations apply to the issuance of VCC tokens.[73] The issuance is effected in exchange for some kind of fee. The purpose of the issuance is to enable the user to be the holder of the VCC, which is comparable to the sale of a VCC token. Therefore, the situations should be treated equally. However, the foregoing does not apply to the exchange of one VCC token for another or similar trades. Here, no characteristic performance can be defined. It is also conceivable that VCC tokens are issued for the 'payment' of transferring VCC tokens (back) to the issuer, where the same applies. These constellations are not covered by Art. 4(2) Rome I.

Lastly, the characteristic performance of the tokenisation and retirement of VCC tokens must be assessed. It is already problematic to determine whether separate tokenisation or retirement contracts are conceivable. The tokenisation could be considered as merely a prelude to the issuance of VCC tokens. The retirement could be regarded as a right of the VCC token holder and the request for retirement could lead to a unilateral legal obligation. These are questions that need to be further discussed. For the purpose of this analysis, it is sufficient to either consider tokenisation and retirement as a part of an aforementioned contract (issuance or sale of VCC token) which would not constitute the focus of the contract and hence would not change the applicable law or to imagine it as a separate contract. In the latter case, the characteristic performance would be the performance of the standard or registry and not the one of the user or holder of the VCC token. The user or holder only places the order and might pay a fee for the process, and the actual work is carried out by the other party. Therefore, the habitual residence of the standard or registry would determine the applicable law.

3.1.1.6 Law of the country which is most closely connected pursuant to Art. 4(4) Rome I

According to Art. 4(4) Rome I, where the law applicable cannot be determined pursuant to paragraphs (1) or (2), the contract shall be governed by the law of the country with which it is most closely connected. As shown above, there are scenarios imaginable where the characteristic performance cannot be defined. This is the case for an exchange of one VCC token against another or other transactions where there is no payment with an established currency, in particular. Art. 4(4) Rome I acts as a fallback clause and reflects the internationally established principle in Private International Law of the closest connection.[74] The term 'most closely connected' is not defined. Recital 21 Rome I only provides that in order to determine that country, account should be taken, *inter alia*, of whether the contract in question has a very close relationship with another contract or contracts. The closest connection cannot be determined in an abstract way but rather needs to be determined on a case-by-case basis.[75] Therefore, this analysis cannot provide a general prediction on how to treat use cases of VCC tokens when Art. 4(4) Rome I is applicable.

A variety of criteria come into play when determining the closest connection of a contract, of which some are useful with regard to VCC tokens, whereas some cannot be applied.[76] Due to the digital and decentralised nature of VCC tokens, for example, a place of fulfilment or a place of the conclusion of the contract can hardly be identified. Also, a *situs* of a VCC token cannot be defined as the blockchain is typically not located in one jurisdiction but its network rather operates globally. An applicable criterion is the habitual residence of the parties (cf Art. 4(1) and (2) Rome I) or in the case of VCC tokens, the statutory seat of the companies which are part of the contract. Yet, this criterion alone cannot determine the closest connection where the parties are located in different jurisdictions. As a new criterion for VCC tokens, the jurisdiction where the registry or standard has its seat comes into play, as a filing with the registry would be recommended even though no constitutive effect of an entry or bona fide rules are recognisable in the use cases. Lastly, even the language of the contract or the currency (even though not applicable when exchanging VCC tokens) could be considered when determining the closest connection of a contract.

In conclusion, no definite guideline can be given on how to apply Art. 4(4) Rome I when it comes to VCC tokens. The general principles are applicable, whereas the seat of the standard or registry can be considered as a new, but not necessarily decisive, criterion.

3.1.1.7 Conclusion for the conflict of laws rules in the Rome I Regulation

When briefly summarising the findings regarding the Rome I Regulation, it must be stressed once more that the Regulation only covers contractual obligations, whilst no rights *in rem* or proprietary rights are addressed. With Art. 3, the Rome I Regulation provides the option to determine the applicable law by choice of the parties, which was partly made use of in the given use cases. The services of marketplace providers are most likely to be considered a provision of services following Art. 4(1)(b) Rome I, and hence the habitual residence of the service providers, determines the applicable law in these cases. Whereas the sale of VCC tokens is not covered under Art. 4(1)(a) Rome I as a sale of goods, the issuance, sale, and transfer on the primary and secondary market can be covered under Art. 4(2) Rome I. As long as some kind of payment or fee is provided in a well-accepted currency, the performance of the issuer, seller, or party transferring the VCC token constitutes the characteristic performance. Hence, the habitual residence of this party determines the applicable law.

Yet, Art. 4(2) Rome I cannot be applied when the party required to effect the characteristic performance cannot be identified. This is the case, for example, when VCC tokens are exchanged for other VCC tokens or issued in exchange for other VCC tokens. In this instance, the applicable law is determined by the closest connection of the contract on a case-by-case basis in accordance with Art. 4(4) Rome I, which leads to legal uncertainty in such scenarios.

3.1.2 *Lex rei sitae* pursuant to Art. 43 German Introductory Act to the Civil Code

As mentioned above, German Private International Law is regulated by the German EGBGB. According to Art. 3 EGBGB, the applicable law is to be determined by the provisions of the EGBGB unless immediately applicable rules of the EU or rules in international conventions, insofar as they have become directly applicable in national law, are relevant. Whereas the Rome I Regulation covers contractual obligations in civil and commercial matters and the Rome II Regulation covers non-contractual obligations, Art. 43 EGBGB determines the applicable law to rights *in rem*. There are no applicable rules of the Union or rules in international conventions that cover the applicable law of rights *in rem*. The *lex rei sitae* principle in Art. 43 EGBGB further reflects the Union and international standard in Private International Law.[77] The EGBGB does not provide for a choice of law in the context of Art. 43 EGBGB[78] and the article is only limited by Art. 46 EGBGB, which states that if there is a substantially closer connection with the law of a state other than that which would apply under Art. 43, then that law shall apply.

According to Art. 43(1) EGBGB, rights *in rem* are governed by the law of the state in which the thing is situated. The scope and limits of Art. 43 EGBGB are not easy to define. Each jurisdiction may have different approaches to determine what factual or economic activities may constitute a right *in rem*.[79] For the purpose of this analysis, it is sufficient to define the scope of Art. 43 EGBGB as covering ownership, joint ownership, transfer of ownership, and interests in property such as pledges.[80] These questions also apply to VCC tokens; however, this analysis does not address whether VCC tokens are subject to ownership, nor how ownership is created or transferred.[81]

When considering Art. 43 EGBGB, it must first be analysed whether a VCC token can be considered a thing, which is covered by the article, according to the *lex fori*, which is German law. Therefore, a VCC token would need to be regarded as a 'thing' or '*res*' in the sense of the norm.[82] How this term should be interpreted is subject to discussion in the German legal literature.[83] Following a strict *lex fori* approach,[84] Sec. 90 of the German Civil Code[85] would apply, which explicitly states that only corporeal objects are things as defined by law. In this case, VCC tokens that are not corporeal, that is, physically perceivable, would not be considered a thing in the sense of the aforementioned article. A different approach advocates for an autonomous conflict of laws interpretation in borderline cases.[86] Yet, even when applying this approach, no different result is reached for VCC tokens. Art. 43 EGBGB depicts the *lex rei sitae* principle and hence rules that the law is applicable where the thing is situated. VCC tokens, which are digital and stored on a decentralised blockchain, can usually not be located geographically. Subsequently, the application of Art. 43 EGBGB would not be possible either way. Therefore, even with a broader understanding of Art. 43 EGBGB, VCC tokens do not constitute a thing in the sense of the article and Art. 43 EGBGB is not applicable.[87]

3.1.3 *Lex libri siti* pursuant to Sec. 17a Securities Deposit Act or Sec. 32 Electronic Securities Act

Besides the *lex rei sitae* principle, the *lex libri siti* principle is also an established approach in Private International Law. This principle is, for example, depicted in German law in Sec. 17a of the Securities Deposit Act[88] ('DepotG') and Sec. 32 of the Electronic

Securities Act[89] ('eWpG'). According to Sec. 17a DepotG, the deposition of securities that are registered with a registry or booked in an account with the effect that rights are created under this act are subject to the law of the state under whose supervision the registry is operated or in which the account-holding main or branch office of the custodian is located. However, it is already not recognisable in the use cases that when dealing with VCC tokens, the entry in the registry or the transfer of a VCC token to a user's blockchain address should have a constitutive or rights-creating effect. The terms of the use cases do not comment on this and since the use cases attempt to widely exclude liability with regard to the transfer or loss of VCC tokens, it can be assumed that the act of changing the registry entry or similar acts should have no legal effect.

According to Sec. 32 eWpG, rights in an electronic security and dispositions over an electronic security shall be governed by the law of the state under whose supervision the registry, in which the electronic security is registered, stands. If the registry is not under supervision, the statutory seat of the registry is decisive. If the statutory seat of the registry cannot be determined, the statutory seat of the issuer shall be decisive. Yet, a VCC token is already not an electronic security in the sense of the eWpG. According to Sec. 1 eWpG, the act applies to bearer bonds, registered shares, and bearer shares, if they are registered in a central registry. VCC tokens do not represent a share or a similar form of ownership of a company. They are also not similar to a loan and do not represent the promise of a later payment or performance either. Therefore, Sec. 17a DepotG and Sec. 32 eWpG and their reflected *lex libri siti* principle are not applicable to VCC tokens. However, the principle could also be considered for VCC tokens as they are centrally registered and such an approach would constitute a legally secure and predictable solution. The pros and cons of this approach will be discussed below.[90]

3.2 Conflict of laws rules in the UNIDROIT Principles on Digital Assets and Private Law

Conflict of laws rules can also be found in the UNIDROIT DAPL. UNIDROIT, the International Institute for the Unification of Private Law, is an intergovernmental organisation dedicated to harmonising international private law. Among its instruments are soft laws such as model laws or principles. In 2023, the Principles on Digital Assets and Private Law were published, addressing various aspects regarding the private law of digital assets. The principles (P) are accompanied by a commentary (C) providing guidance on interpreting or implementing each principle.

3.2.1 VCC tokens as digital assets according to Principle 2(2) UNIDROIT DAPL

In order to apply the UNIDROIT DAPL, VCC tokens must fall under the definition of digital assets according to P 2(2) DAPL. A digital asset is defined as an electronic record that is capable of being subject to control. An electronic record means information that is (i) stored in an electronic medium and (ii) capable of being retrieved. Despite the discussion regarding the legal nature of VCCs, a VCC token constitutes a kind of information. A VCC token contains information that can, for example, be traced back to the carbon credit reported itself. Howsoever a VCC token may be stored on a blockchain, in any case, it constitutes information to identify the token. Following C 2.1. DAPL, the term 'electronic medium' must be understood in a broad sense and intends to include any type of digital technology. The blockchain protocol is a digital technology and is further mentioned as an example of digital assets in C 2.8 DAPL. The information can also be perceived, for example, via a computer interface and is hence retrievable (C 2.1. DAPL). A VCC token must also be capable of being subject to control, which is defined in P 6 DAPL. According to P 6(1) DAPL, a person has control of a digital asset if (a) the digital asset, or the relevant protocol or system, confers on that person: (i) the exclusive ability to prevent others from obtaining substantially all of the benefit from the digital asset; (ii) the ability to obtain substantially all of the benefit from the digital asset; and (iii) the exclusive ability to transfer those abilities to another person; and (b) the digital asset, or the relevant protocols or system, allows that person to identify itself as having those abilities. Although the platforms mentioned work differently, VCC tokens are usually stored using wallets. For example, in the use cases of Toucan, Regen Network, and Senken, users have to connect a (third-party) wallet to use the platform.[91] In such cases, users have exclusive control over their private keys, which allows them to transfer the VCC token (cf C 2.8 DAPL). This feature gives the users the abilities mentioned in P 6(1)(a) DAPL and enables their identification as the holder of the VCC token. Therefore, VCC tokens are digital assets under the DAPL.

3.2.2 Applicable law for proprietary issues according to Principle 5 UNIDROIT DAPL

P 5 DAPL covers the applicable law regarding digital assets. It is important to note that P 5(1) DAPL only speaks of 'proprietary issues' in respect of a digital asset. The term is not further defined or explained in the commentary. It can be assumed that issues relating to proprietary rights are addressed. Issues merely relating to contractual relationships, for example, a sales contract in connection with a digital asset itself are hence not covered by the principle. This does not come as a surprise as conflict of laws rules regarding contractual obligations such as those set out in the Rome I Regulation are well-established. P 5(1) DAPL provides a waterfall mechanism for different factors when determining the applicable law. According to P 5(1)(a) DAPL, the applicable law is the law of the state expressly specified in the digital asset. With regard to VCC tokens, the law specified in the VCC token itself would be applicable. It is technologically possible to implement an applicable law clause in a token just like any other information. If such specification is not given, the applicable law is the domestic law of the state expressly specified in the system on which the digital asset is recorded (P 5(1)(b) DAPL). In the case of VCC tokens, such system would be the blockchain on which they are recorded. Therefore, the blockchain itself or—more precisely—the blockchain governance could specify the applicable law. Both P 5(1)(a) and (b) DAPL provide for a choice of law.

In the absence of a choice of law, the applicable law in relation to a digital asset of which there is an issuer is the domestic law of the state where the issuer has its statutory seat (provided that its statutory seat is readily ascertainable by the public) according to P 5(1)(c) DAPL. The term issuer is defined in P 5(2)(f) DAPL as a legal person (i) who put the digital asset in the stream of commerce for value; and (ii) who identifies itself as a named person, identifies its statutory seat and identifies itself as the person who put the digital asset into the stream of commerce for value. With regard to VCC tokens, the issuer is the person who gives out the VCC tokens for the first time. Besides the mere marketplace use cases, which are not issuers, this applies to all other use cases. Each platform gives out VCC tokens itself, no matter if non-digital carbon credits already exist, as shown in the Toucan use case. Hence, the statutory seat of those companies would determine the applicable law. Therefore, there is no scenario conceivable for P 5(1)(d) DAPL which states that, if none of the factors above apply, the applicable law is determined by the rules of Private International Law of the forum state.

It can be concluded that even though the UNIDROIT DAPL have not yet been implemented in any state, they convey interesting aspects when determining the applicable law of VCC tokens. It must be noted that the choice of law is on top of the 'waterfall' and seen as a suitable and decisive factor when determining the applicable law with regard to proprietary issues. Further, the statutory seat of the issuer is mentioned again, which shows that it can also be seen as an appropriate factor for a conflict of laws.

3.3 Conflict of laws rules in other jurisdictions

3.3.1 Conflict of laws rules in England and Wales

At present, there are no statutes regulating the applicable law of crypto assets in general or VCC tokens in particular. There is currently a project run by the Law Commission (England and Wales) to assess the challenges of digital assets and Private International Law titled: 'Digital assets and ETDs in private international law: which court, which law?'.[92] Yet, the project is still in its consultation phase and no conclusions can be drawn regarding the future legal framework at this stage. However, there is some case law relating to crypto assets and their applicable law worth mentioning. In two High Court decisions, it was ruled: '*lex situs* of a cryptoasset is where the person or company who owns it is domiciled'.[93] In another decision, it was ruled that the place of residence or business shall determine the applicable law, not domicile.[94] It should be noted that the rulings are not binding precedents.[95] Further, in each case, the claimant was an (alleged) victim and (among others) tort claims were filed.[96] It is possible that courts may rule differently in other cases when a victim of a tortious act cannot be identified. Also, the courts did not have to decide whether a choice of law would be allowed. Nonetheless, it is interesting to see that courts were able to define the *lex situs* of a decentralised crypto asset like Bitcoin in this case.

3.3.2 Conflict of laws rules in the US Uniform Commercial Code

It is also worth taking a look at US law. In 2022, the Uniform Law Commission implemented (among others) a new article in the US Uniform Commercial Code (UCC) covering 'controllable electronic records'. The UCC is a uniform act with the goal of harmonising the laws of sales and other commercial transactions across the USA. To date, several states have introduced or enacted the new article in their state law. For example, the State of Delaware has enacted the amendment whose laws shall be applicable in the Regen Network use case.[97] The new article includes a provision regarding the applicable law as Sec. 12–107 UCC provides for the 'Governing law'. To apply the article, VCC tokens must classify as 'controllable electronic records'. The term is defined in Sec. 12–102(a)(1) UCC as a record stored in an electronic medium that can be subject to control, whereas the term 'control' is further defined in Sec. 12–105 UCC. The definition is highly similar to the definition of digital assets in the UNIDROIT DAPL.[98] A VCC token, which is stored on a blockchain and connected to a private key that gives exclusive access to the token is a controllable electronic record in the sense of Art. 12 UCC.

Sec. 12–107(c) UCC provides for a waterfall mechanism as well. Following Sec. 12–107(c)(1) and (3) UCC, the controllable electronic record's jurisdiction is the one expressly provided by the controllable electronic record. If this does not apply, the jurisdiction is the one expressly provided by the rules of the system in which the controllable electronic record is recorded (Sec. 12–107(c)(2) and (4) UCC). In the case of VCC tokens, this would be the blockchain or protocol on which the token is stored. Again, the provision enables a comprehensive choice of law by the parties. If both factors do not apply, the jurisdiction of the District of Columbia is the applicable law according to the fall-back clause in Sec. 12–107(c)(5) UCC. It can be concluded once again that a choice of law is seen as the decisive element. Besides that, the UCC does not provide for any other connecting factors and only includes a fall-back clause for a specific jurisdiction.

4 Valuation of possible connecting factors in conflict of laws rules

As shown above, when examining the applicable law in the supply chain of VCC tokens, different statutes and case law can be considered. From a Union perspective, the applicable law concerning contractual obligations arising in relation to VCC tokens can be covered under the Rome I Regulation. Yet, as of the present date, there is no framework to determine the applicable law when looking at proprietary issues or rights *in rem* of VCC tokens in German or Union law. Further, there is no suitable provision in this regard for the applicable law of crypto assets in those jurisdictions which would cover VCC tokens. Such provisions are available in the US UCC and the UNIDROIT DAPL. Also, there is some case law regarding the applicable law in England and Wales. As a next step, the possible connecting factors that were touched upon in the different conflict of laws rules shall be evaluated to see how suitable they are when applied to VCC tokens.

4.1 *Lex rei sitae*

As a first connecting factor, the place where a thing is located comes into consideration (*lex rei sitae* principle). This principle can be found, for example, in Art. 43 EGBGB. However, the place where a crypto asset is located can usually not be reasonably determined due to its decentralised nature building on the distributed ledger technology and its storage, for example, on a blockchain. The rulings of the English High Court that the '*lex situs* of a cryptoasset is where the person or company who owns it is domiciled' must be approached *cum grano salis*. It can be assumed that the rulings were made to suit the specific cases and courts could rule differently in the future.

4.2 Habitual residence of the parties

Another connecting factor can be the habitual residence of the parties. This factor is reflected in Art. 4(1) and (2) Rome I. More specifically, the habitual residence of the seller, service provider, or the party that is required to effect the characteristic performance of the contract may determine the applicable law. This factor may lead to an appropriate solution and can often be precisely defined. In the case of VCC tokens, most transactions are covered by Art. 4(2) Rome I, whereas the characteristic performance is effected by the issuer or seller of VCC tokens. Yet, the underlying reasoning of Art. 4(1) and (2) Rome I or the connecting factor of the habitual residence of a party in general can only be applied with difficulty. As digital assets and crypto assets in particular have no geographical reference—other than goods that are sold in the store of a seller or delivered physically to the buyer—the transactions have no geographical reference either. As a result, the seller, for example, is not necessarily more closely 'connected' to the transaction. The factor may often provide a legally secure determination but does not guarantee appropriate solutions for each case.

4.3 Closest connection

A further connecting factor is the closest connection with a country, which is a fundamental principle in Private International Law. This factor is, *inter alia,* reflected in Art. 4(4) Rome I referring to the country with the closest connection to the contract. It can provide suitable solutions on a case-by-case basis. As each case may be treated differently, an appropriate treatment is guaranteed. However, this factor leads to a significant degree of legal uncertainty for the parties and the ruling by a court may not be foreseeable. Parties may struggle in determining the applicable law and may ultimately depend on the court's judgement. Therefore, this factor is best utilised as a fallback clause within a potential waterfall mechanism.

4.4 *Lex libri siti* or statutory seat of the issuer or of the registry

Furthermore, the statutory seat of the issuer or registry or the *lex libri siti* principle can be used as a connecting factor.[99] Even though this principle is not applicable to today's VCC tokens, it is reflected in various conflict of laws rules. German law implements this principle in Sec. 17a DepotG and Sec. 32 eWpG and the UNIDROIT DAPL also determine the statutory seat of the issuer as a connecting factor in P 5(1)(c) DAPL. Whereas different terms are mentioned in this context, in the case of VCC tokens, the connecting factor should be the seat of the issuer meaning the company which hands out the VCC tokens. This approach ensures a secure determination. The fact that issuers often provide their own registry and might even provide their own standard is not harmful. On the contrary, this highlights the importance of the issuer within the VCM. In the context of VCC tokens, where already existing non-digital carbon credits are tokenised like in the Toucan use case, the seat of the issuer (which also has its own registry) should be the determining factor and not the seat of the non-digital registry like Verra. On the downside, it could be argued that such conflict of laws rules would further strengthen the position of the already powerful issuers or registries. As the parties on the secondary market still rely on the original issuer, e.g., for filing with its registry when a sale is made, its position would be even more powerful if its seat also determined the applicable law. The parties of a contract might also have a closer connection to other jurisdictions and should not necessarily be bound to the country where the issuer has its seat.

4.5 Choice of law by the parties

Therefore, the choice of law by the free will of the parties appears to be an even better connecting factor when determining the applicable law for VCC tokens. The choice of law is part of most of the conflict of laws rules examined and is always put on top where a waterfall mechanism applies. This includes contractual obligations, such as in Art. 3 Rome I, as well as proprietary rights, such as in P 5 UNIDROIT DAPL. It is important to note that the choice of law happens differently in both scenarios. Whereas the parties of a sales contract, for example, agree upon the applicable law each time individually, the applicable law with regards to the proprietary right of a VCC token would need to be determined at the time of issuance and specified in the token itself.[100] One advantage of a choice of law is that it follows the principle of party autonomy and has the potential to assist with scaling the market for VCC tokens. This option would be an incentive for the parties on the market to determine the law to their liking on the one hand[101] and to ensure legal certainty on the other. This way, appropriate case-by-case solutions would be guaranteed as well. The downside of a choice of law, which is the possibility that the weaker party, for example, the consumer, could be overpowered by the stronger party, does not apply to the market for VCC tokens. At present, the market only provides for B2B transactions and hence no consumer is required to be protected with deviating provisions.

5 Conclusions and brief proposal for a conflict of laws rule for VCC tokens

The Private International Law of VCC tokens is, just as legal questions concerning VCC tokens in general, rather unsettled. Yet, an array of principles can be identified when looking at certain use cases and possible legal frameworks concerning the applicable law. Firstly, it can be concluded that most use cases lack comprehensive provisions regarding their Private International Law, as far as sources are accessible. One potential explanation for this situation is the still rather young market and the new business models in it. For instance, some use cases make use of very extensive exclusions of liability, and it is not always clear if there is any liability between the parties at all. Moreover, after the issuance of VCC tokens, the entities operating these use cases are typically not party to any subsequent sales contracts and only function as an intermediary or are not contractually involved at all. Finally, it must also be considered that a choice of law is not permitted in all areas of law as some statutes do not provide for this option in the first place.[102]

When looking at the applicable law from a German perspective, contractual obligations arising in the context of VCC tokens are, as of today, to be covered by the Rome I Regulation.[103] Today's VCC tokens are not to be considered negotiable instruments in the sense of Art. 1(2)(d) Rome I and therefore fall within the scope of the Regulation.[104] While Art. 3 Rome I allows for a choice of law, mere marketplaces for VCC tokens could be considered as providing services and hence fall within Art. 4(1)(b) Rome I. In this case, the contract is governed by the law of the country where the service provider has their habitual residence.[105] More importantly, the tokenisation, issuance, sale, and detokenisation can usually be covered by Art. 4(2) Rome I. Here, the habitual residence of the party required to effect the characteristic performance of the contract determines the applicable law. The characteristic performance is usually effected by the issuer or seller and not by the party that only pays a purchase price or fee for the transaction.[106] However, a characteristic performance cannot be identified in more complex transactions, for example, when VCC tokens are exchanged for other VCC tokens. In this case, the closest connection according to Art. 4(4) Rome I must be determined.[107] The German or Union legal framework does not provide for the applicable law in regard to rights *in rem* of VCC tokens. Yet, the UNIDROIT Principles on Digital Assets and Private Law as a soft law and the US Uniform Commercial Code include provisions for the applicable law regarding proprietary issues of digital assets or controllable electronic records. VCC tokens can be seen as such and therefore those conflict of laws rules are to be considered as a possible blueprint.

As today's law can—at least from a German perspective—not answer all questions of the applicable law in the supply chains of VCC tokens, it is worth considering how a possible conflict of laws rule for VCC tokens could be construed. For this undertaking, several connecting factors come into consideration. In order to provide for legal clarity and to assist the developing market,[108] a choice of law should be on top of a 'waterfall' when determining the applicable law. In instances where this does not apply, the statutory seat of the issuer of the VCC token shall be the determining factor. This provides for a clear and appropriate solution as the issuer is of paramount importance in the market.[109] Only as a fall-back clause, the closest connection of a country with the contract should come into play. If and how VCC tokens should be put in a legal framework needs to be intensely discussed at a global level. This analysis was able to demonstrate that certain aspects of the applicable law in the supply chains of VCC tokens can be addressed by the current law. However, not all aspects are adequately covered and various connecting factors warrant consideration when contemplating potential conflict of laws rules in the future.

Notes

1 See for the legal nature of VCC, e.g., UNIDROIT Study LXXXVI, Legal Nature of Verified Carbon Credits, current status and documents under https://www.unidroit.org/work-in-progress/verified-carbon-credits/ accessed 21 July 2025; ISDA, 'The Legal Nature of Verified Carbon Credits: France, Japan and Singapore' (2022) https://www.unidroit.org/work-in-progress/verified accessed 21 July 2025; ISDA, 'Legal Implications of Voluntary Carbon Credits' (2021) https://www.isda.org/a/38ngE/Legal-Implications-of-Voluntary-Carbon-Credits.pdf accessed 21 July 2025.

2 On 26.12.2024, Regulation (EU) 2024/3012 of the European Parliament and of the Council of 27.11.2024 establishing a Union certification framework for permanent carbon removals, carbon farming, and carbon storage in products (CRCR) [2024] OJ L3012/1 entered into force. However, the Regulation does not concern VCC tokens, nor does it stipulate a regulatory legal framework. Instead, a voluntary certification framework was created at Union level (see Hans-Peter Schwintowski, 'Die Zertifizierung von

CO_2-Entnahmen nach der CRCF-VO am Beispiel Wald' [2024] EWeRK Energie- und Wettbewerbsrecht in der Kommunalen Wirtschaft 87; see Section 2.1.1 for the certification process).

3 UNIDROIT Principles on Digital Assets and Private Law https://www.unidroit.org/wp-content/uploads/2024/01/Principles-on-Digital-Assets-and-Private-Law-linked-1.pdf accessed 21 July 2025.

4 Vera website https://verra.org/about/overview/#the-organization accessed 21 July 2025.

5 Gold Standard website https://www.goldstandard.org/faqs accessed 21 July 2025; https://www.geneve-int.ch/de/gold-standard-foundation-gsf-1 accessed 21 July 2025.

6 Cf https://toucan-protocol.notion.site/Legal-Notice-afbb0c7316734279a71c63b0e4ff0cef accessed 21 July 2025.

7 https://docs.toucan.earth/toucan/carbon-bridge accessed 21 July 2025.

8 https://docs.toucan.earth/toucan/carbon-bridge/puro-carbon-bridge accessed 21 July 2025; Puro Standard website https://puro.earth/ accessed 21 July 2025.

9 Toucan Terms of Service 4 https://toucan.earth/terms-of-service/ accessed 21 July 2025.

10 Toucan Terms of Service (n 9) 36.

11 Regen Network Terms of Service 4. https://www.regen.network/terms-service accessed 21 July 2025

12 https://docs.regen.network/ledger/ accessed 21 July 2025.

13 https://www.regen.network/faq/organization accessed 21 July 2025; Regen Network Whitepaper 24 https://regen-network.gitlab.io/whitepaper/WhitePaper.pdf accessed 21 July 2025.

14 Regen Network Terms of Service (n 11) 27.

15 https://carbonstack.de accessed 21 July 2025.

16 Carbonstack imprint https://carbonstack.de/#/de/imprint accessed 21 July 2025.

17 https://resources.goodcarbon.earth/blog/5m-pre-seed-funding accessed 21 July 2025.

18 Goodcarbon General Terms and Conditions 14.3 https://www.goodcarbon.earth/en/terms accessed 21 July 2025.

19 Goodcarbon Foundation imprint https://goodcarbonfoundation.org/imprint/ accessed 21 July 2025.

20 Senken Terms and Conditions 3., 7. https://www.senken.io/de/terms-and-conditions accessed 21 July 2025.

21 Senken Terms and Conditions (n 20) 16.

22 Kumo website https://www.kumo.earth/ accessed 21 July 2025.

23 Kumo imprint https://kumo.earth/imprint accessed 21 July 2025.

24 Kumo Terms & Conditions 8. https://kumo.earth/terms accessed 21 July 2025.

25 Matthias Lehmann, 'Kollisionsregeln für die Blockchain im Rechtsvergleich' (2023) 122 ZVglRWiss Zeitschrift für Vergleichende Rechtswissenschaft 269, 283 states that choice of law clauses can only seldomly be found on the crypto market.

26 E.g., this is not possible for *rights in rem* in several jurisdictions. See for Germany Art. 43 EGBGB (n 27), see Section 3.1.2.

27 Einführungsgesetz zum Bürgerlichen Gesetzbuch (EGBGB) 1900.

28 Regulation (EC) No. 593/2008 of the European Parliament and of the Council of 17 June 2008 on the law applicable to contractual obligations (Rome I) [2008] OJ L177/6.

29 Regulation (EC) No. 864/2007 of the European Parliament and of the Council of 11 July 2007 on the law applicable to non-contractual obligations (Rome II) [2007] OJ L199/40.

30 See for the civil law of VCC tokens Chapter 10, Sebastian Böhning and Dominik Skauradszun, 'VCC tokens' civil law - ownership, transfer and liability under Union and German Law'.

31 Cf for obligations arising out of torts or unjust enrichment in the context of tokens in general Dominik Skauradszun, 'Kryptowerte im Bürgerlichen Recht' (2021) 221 AcP Archiv für die civilistische Praxis 353, 369, 384.

32 Regulation (EU) No 1215/2012 of the European Parliament and of the Council of 12 December 2012 on jurisdiction and the recognition and enforcement of judgments in civil and commercial matters (Brussels Ia) [2012] OJ L351/1.

33 Recital 7 Rome I.
34 Case C-26/91 *Jakob Handte & Co. GmbH v Traitements Mécano-chimiques des Surfaces SA* [1992] ECR 1992 I-03967 para 15; Case C-51/97 *Réunion Européenne SA et al. v Spliethoff's Bevrachtingskantoor BV* [1998] ECR 1998 I-06511 para 17; Case C-334/00 *Fonderie Officine Meccaniche Tacconi SpA v Heinrich Wagner Sinto Maschinenfabrik GmbH* [2002] ECR 2002 I-7383 para 23.
35 Cf Section 3.1.2.
36 Recital 9 Rome I only states that bills of lading should also be covered to the extent that the obligations under the bill of lading arise out of its negotiable character.
37 Dieter Martiny in *MüKoBGB* (8th edn, C.H.BECK 2021) Rom I-VO Art. 1 para 59; Dominik Skauradszun, 'Das Internationale Privatrecht der Kryptowerte' [2022] ZfPW Zeitschrift für die gesamte Privatrechtswissenschaft 56, 68.
38 Directive 2014/65/EU of the European Parliament and of the Council of 15 May 2014 on markets in financial instruments and amending Directive 2002/92/EC and Directive 2011/61/EU [2014] OJ L173/349.
39 Regulation (EU) 2017/1129 of the European Parliament and of the Council of 14 June 2017 on the prospectus to be published when securities are offered to the public or admitted to trading on a regulated market, and repealing Directive 2003/71/EC [2017] OJ L168/12.
40 Cf for crypto assets and terms used in Union law Skauradszun, 'Das Internationale Privatrecht der Kryptowerte' (n 37) 68.
41 Andreas Spickhoff in *BeckOK BGB* (71st edn, C.H.BECK 01.08.2024) VO (EG) 593/2008 Art. 1 para 40; Michael Stürner in Harm P Westermann, Babara Grunewald and Gerog Maier-Reimer (eds), *Erman BGB* (17th edn, Otto Schmidt 2023) EGV 593/2008 Art. 1 para 13.
42 Ulrich Magnus in *Staudinger BGB* (Otto Schmidt De Gruyter 2021) ROM I Art. 1 para 65; Martiny (n 37) Art. 1 para 60.
43 Skauradszun, 'Das Internationale Privatrecht der Kryptowerte' (n 37) 68–69; contrary Björn Steinrötter in Philipp Maume and Lena Maute-Nguyen (eds), *Rechtshandbuch Kryptowerte* (C.H.BECK 2020) Sec. 3 para 38.
44 UNIDROIT Working Group on the Legal Nature of Verified Carbon Credits, 'Summary Report of the First Session, Study LXXXVI – W.G.1 – Doc. 3' (2024), 11–12.
45 According to Toucan, its tokens were considered utility tokens under the Swiss regulatory framework (Toucan, 'Public Consultation: Verra's Approach to Third-Party Crypto Instruments and Tokens. Response document by Toucan Protocol' (2022) 4 https://blog.toucan.earth/content/files/2023/01/Toucan_Verra_response.pdf accessed 21 July 2025); see for this issue Böhning and Skauradszun (n 30) and Chapter 8, Leon Krug and Walter Blocher, 'VCC tokenisation: Navigating legal frameworks and designing for regulatory compliance'.
46 Magnus (n 42) Art. 1 para 65; Martiny (n 37) Art. 1 para 59.
47 Carbon pools bundle carbon credits that share similar characteristics; see for further information https://docs.toucan.earth/toucan/carbon-pools accessed 21 July 2025.
48 See for further information about this instrument https://senken.medium.com/senken-is-launching-the-worlds-first-public-sale-of-carbon-forward-tokens-d48e8ea7005a accessed 21 July 2025.
49 Cf n 44.
50 Toucan Terms of Service (n 9) 36.1.
51 Toucan Terms of Service (n 9) 4.1.
52 Toucan Terms of Service (n 9) 23.6.
53 Toucan Terms of Service (n 9) 9.1.
54 Regen Network Terms of Service (n 11) 27.
55 Regen Network Terms of Service (n 11) 1.
56 Regen Network Terms of Service (n 11) 4.
57 Regen Network Terms of Service (n 11) 4.
58 Senken Terms and Conditions (n 20) 16.

59 Senken Terms and Conditions (n 20) 3.
60 Senken Terms and Conditions (n 20) 3.
61 Martiny (n 37) Art. 4 para 32; Spickhoff (n 41) VO (EG) 593/2008 Art. 4 para 7.
62 Cf Magnus (n 42) Art. 4 para 4; Reinhold Thode in *BeckOK ZPO* (53rd edn, C.H.BECK 01.07.2024) Brüssel Ia-VO Art. 7 para 13b.
63 This could be different for digital assets saved on a non-digital CD-ROM or other hard drive.
64 For crypto tokens in general Andreas Kerkemeyer, 'Blockchian-Transaktionen im Internationalen Recht' (2020) 184 ZHR Zeitschrift für das gesamte Handels- und Wirtschaftsrecht 793, 824; Lara Hanner, *Internationales Kryptowerterecht* (Nomos 2022) 177–183.
65 Martiny (n 37) Art. 4 para 38.
66 Case C-533/07 *Falco Privatstifung, Rabitsch v Weller-Lindhorst* [2009] ECR 2009 I-3369 para 29; Case C-9/12 *Corman-Collins SA v La Maison du Whisky SA* [2013] ECLI:EU:C:2013:860 para 37.
67 Martiny (n 37) Art. 4 para 46; Spickhoff (n 41) VO (EG) 593/2008 Art. 4 para 9.
68 Cf Hanner (n 64) 183–184.
69 Senken Terms and Conditions (n 20) 3.
70 Franco Ferrari in Ferrari and others (eds.), *Internationales Vertragsrecht* (3rd edn, C.H.BECK 2018) VO (EG) 593/2008 Art. 4 para 61; Spickhoff (n 41) VO (EG) 593/2008 Art. 4 para 55.
71 Spickhoff (n 41) VO (EG) 593/2008 Art. 4 para 67; Martiny (n 37) Art. 4 para 211.
72 Cf Hanner (n 64) 244–245.
73 Cf Hanner (n 64) 190.
74 Ferrari (n 70) para 78; Spickhoff (n 41) VO (EG) 593/2008 Art. 4 para 84.
75 Spickhoff (n 41) VO (EG) 593/2008 Art. 4 para 84.
76 See for the possible criteria Spickhoff (n 41) VO (EG) 593/2008 Art. 4 para 85.
77 Spickhoff (n 41) EGBGB Art. 43 para 4; Stürner (n 41) EGBGB Art. 43 para 1.
78 BGH NJW 1997, 461; Skauradszun, 'Kryptowerte im Bürgerlichen Recht' (n 31) 393; Spickhoff (n 41) EGBGB Art. 43 para 4.
79 Cf Spickhoff (n 41) EGBGB Art. 43 para 7; Heinrich Dörner in *Schulze BGB* (12th edn, Nomos 2024) EGBGB Art. 43 para 2.
80 Cf Dörner (n 79) para 2; Spickhoff (n 41) EGBGB Art. 43 para 10.
81 See for these issues Böhning and Skauradszun (n 30).
82 The German text speaks of 'Sache'.
83 Christiane Wendehorst in *MüKoBGB* (8th edn, C.H.BECK 2021) EGBGB Art. 43 para 11–13; Stürner (n 41) EGBGB Art. 43 para 10.
84 E.g., Karsten Thorn in *Grüneberg BGB* (83rd edn, C.H.BECK 2024) EGBGB Art. 43 para 1.
85 Bürgerliches Gesetzbuch (BGB) 1900.
86 E.g., Wendehorst (n 83) para 14–16.
87 Cf Hanner (n 64) 227; Derwis Dilek, 'IPR der Blockchains: Die Bestimmung des Sachstatus digitaler Werte – Ein Gesetzesvorschlag' in Sebastian Omlor and Florian Möslein (eds), *Blockchain und Recht* (Mohr Siebeck 2024) 188.
88 Gesetz über die Verwahrung und Anschaffung von Wertpapieren (Depotgesetzt – DepotG) 1937.
89 Gesetz über elektronische Wertpapiere (eWpG) 2021.
90 See Section 4.4.
91 Toucan Terms of Service (n 9) 3; Regen Network Whitepaper (n 13) 33.
92 Website https://lawcom.gov.uk/project/digital-assets-and-electronic-trade-documents-in-private-international-law/, accessed 21 July 2025.
93 *Ion Science Ltd v Persons Unknown and others* (unreported) 21.12.2020 (Comm*); Fetch.ai Ltd and others v Persons Unknown and others* [2021] EWHC 2254 (Comm) para 14.
94 *Tulip Trading Ltd v Van Der Laan and others* [2022] EWHC 667 (Ch) para 145; cf [2023] EWCA Civ 83 para 7.

95 Lehmann (n 25) 273.
96 Cf Lehmann (n 25) 273.
97 Regen Network Terms of Service (n 11) 27.
98 Cf Lehmann (n 25) 280.
99 For a detailed analysis of this connecting factor for digital assets in general Derwis Dilek, Sebastian Omlor and Dominik Skauradszun, 'A New Private International Law for Digital Assets' (2025) RabelsZ (forthcoming).
100 For the ways to implement a choice of law in the context of digital assets in general Dilek, Omlor and Skauradszun (n 99).
101 Cf C 5.4. UNIDROIT DAPL.
102 Cf n 26.
103 See Section 3.1.1.
104 See Section 3.1.1.1.
105 See Section 3.1.1.4.
106 See Section 3.1.1.5.
107 See Section 3.1.1.6.
108 See Section 4.5.
109 See Section 4.4.

Leon Krug and Walter Blocher

8 VCC tokenisation: Navigating legal frameworks and designing for regulatory compliance

Abstract: In this chapter, we will analyse the regulatory framework applicable to tokenised instances of VCCs. This necessitates a categorisation that can be used for VCC tokens and digital tokens in general. To this effect, digital tokens are to be examined as crypto-assets in blockchain environments. We will use the European Union's recently established Markets in Crypto-assets Regulation (MiCAR) as a legal basis, given its full applicability in the EU since 30 December 2024. MiCAR was drafted for the emerging market of crypto-assets, which is closely reminiscent of, but distinct from, the market of financial instruments. This is further substantiated by the observation of a close similarity between the legal nature of certain crypto-assets and financial instruments defined in the Markets in Financial Instruments Directives (MiFID and MiFID II).

We will assess the regulatory regime within the EU under which VCC tokens will fall, with a primary focus on MiCAR and MiFID II. In addition, given the increasing prevalence of VCCs and the likelihood of their regulation by legislators in the near future, we will also examine related legal acts that could influence their usage and determine the usefulness of their tokenisation. This chapter will encompass additional legislation to evaluate the European approach and demonstrate use cases where VCC tokens have been or are being used. Taking these use cases as examples, we identify the applicable regulation schemes and offer insights into the legal certainty for future scenarios.

The initial chapter will deal with the above-mentioned legal acts as well as relevant model law approaches (A.). The EU framework will be examined first (A. I.), followed by a comparison with other international policies that could be applicable to tokenised VCCs (A. II.). The subsequent examination will focus on key aspects of the relevant German law (A. III.) and insights from the UNIDROIT Working Groups for Digital Assets and Verified Carbon Credits (A. IV.). Finally, a selection of VCC tokens will be analysed in light of the applicable legal framework (B. and C.), and conclusions will be drawn (D.).

https://doi.org/10.1515/9783111706719-008

A Legal background — 180
I Legal frameworks — 180
II Comparison of non-European regulatory approaches with the European regulatory framework — 198
III Relevant German law — 204
IV UNIDROIT Principles — 205
B Case studies — 208
I Toucan — 208
II Nori — 209
III Crypto Carbon Company (C3) — 210
IV Coorest — 210
C Placing the use cases within the context of the relevant legislation — 211
I CHAR — 211
II Nori Regenerative Tonne and NORI — 213
III UBO and NBO tokens — 215
IV $CCO2, NFTrees and PoCC — 216
D Conclusion and outlook — 218

A Legal background

I Legal frameworks

1 MiFID and MiFID II

MiFID[1] and MiFID II[2] established the regulatory framework for financial instruments in the EU. Financial instruments are manifold, opaque, and of much importance for the financial well-being of consumers; they hereby need to be regulated by a precise framework of safety and transparency rules laid out by MiFID and further connected regulations.[3] Art. 4(15) MiFID II in connection with Annex I(C) of MiFID II defines financial instruments as any transferable securities, money-market instruments, units in collective investment undertakings, different kinds of derivatives and emission allowances recognised under the European Emissions Trading Directive[4] (EU ETSD). These instruments bear a great deal of financial responsibilities, thereby their issuers need to thoroughly inform their possible clients of any risks involved. The implications of the term 'financial instrument' are not easily defined, even though the categories are listed, leading to different implementations of MiFID II throughout the EU. Using Annex I(C) MiFID II, one can work out definitions of financial instruments.[5] Although MiFID II and MiCAR share some regulatory similarities, one must distinguish between them. Most of them do not involve VCCs or their tokens, with only a few describing similar financial instrument constructs—some of which will be discussed in the following. The specific market for crypto-assets has just arisen over the last few years and with it the need for regulation, resulting in MiCAR.

With the introduction of MiFID II, emission allowances in compliance with the EU ETSD are now being regulated. The reason for the amendment of the Directive into MiFID II was to increase the protection of investors in regard to the evolving fraud in the EU ETS, concerning the observed market abuse in the European carbon market, which was prohibited by making emission allowances fall under the Market Abuse Regulation (MAR) with their status as financial instruments.[6] As already established, the VCCs and VCC tokens cannot be used as an allowance to further emit carbon dioxide or equivalent gases (CO_2e) by any entity obliged under the EU ETSD.[7] Thus, they are not covered as emission allowances by the definitive list in Annex I(C)(11) MiFID II *per se*.

A VCC token could technically also be considered as a special derivative contract described in Annex I(C)(10) MiFID II.[8] These derivatives can relate to climatic variables, as it is often done by agricultural or energy-related undertakings to secure their upkeep in case of operations being obstructed by temperature, precipitation, drought, or other weather extremes.[9] VCC tokens are not necessarily reliant on any kind of variables. The only variability lies within their underlying VCC or, then again, in their underlying climate action and arises outside of the VCC tokens themselves. Their value should always stem from the agreed amount of emission reductions or removals stated (with possible additional values up to their purchasers). Financial derivatives as safeguards against risks related to climatic variables have to be evaluated differently due to their inherent variability and, thus, are regulated as financial instruments. VCCs and their tokens have no intentional variability and thereby should not be regarded as special derivative contracts according to Annex I(C)(10) MiFID II and to this effect not fall under MiFID II.

Even though MiFID II is drafted technologically neutral, we conclude that MiFID II is not decisive for the regulation of VCC tokens as these are not financial instruments.[10] Even in connection with the newly established Distributed Ledger Technology Pilot Regime (DLT Pilot Regime), which enables crypto-assets to qualify as financial instruments if their underlying asset is a financial instrument,[11] VCC tokens are not regulated by MiFID II.[12]

2 MiCAR

a) Classification of tokens

MiCAR is the newly enforced regime for crypto-assets in the EU. A crypto-asset as defined by Art. 3(1)(5) MiCAR is 'a digital representation of a value or of a right that is able to be transferred and stored electronically using distributed ledger technology or similar technology'. In the following, we will use the phrases tokens, digital assets, and crypto-assets interchangeably. Whilst this definition is open to many different interpretations, the main characteristic that classifies the token is the underlying 'value' and the stability established by it.[13] Similar to MiFID II, MiCAR differentiates between crypto-assets that encompass an intrinsic monetary value, and those that do not necessarily do so. The different categories of tokens are electronic money tokens (EMTs), asset-referenced tokens (ARTs), or 'other crypto-assets', that is, any other token that does not fall under the first two categories. According to Art. 3(1)(7) MiCAR, EMTs are similar to electronic money and are mainly used for payments with their value purporting stability as they are coupled to an official currency. Tokens that are asset-referenced on the other hand are linked to real asset values like gold, rights, or official currencies and mixes thereof (Art. 3(1)(8)). The main category is other crypto-assets which encases all tokens that are not ARTs or EMTs, with a few further exemptions, as stated by Recital 18 MiCAR. Considering their standing in MiCAR, their importance is underlined by being mentioned in Title II.

For our analyses, we assume that VCCs or in certain cases, their underlying climate actions, are the value of the tokens. As these are not official currencies by any definition,[14] they are not to be classified as EMTs and therefore Title IV MiCAR does not apply.

As VCCs could be an asset referenced to by a token, their tokenised version could possibly be an ART. For this to hold, the underlying VCC needs to be a value, a right, an official currency, or a combination thereof while not already being an EMT. The main difference to EMTs is the number of underlying assets and their possibility of combination. While there can only be one type of currency coupled to an EMT, ARTs can have multiple and different underlying values. Following this, VCCs could technically be categorised as a value as mentioned by MiCAR, because of their monetary value or their usage. But as their prices differ over time and in dependence on the applicable legislation, with some countries allowing the usage of VCCs in their cap-and-trade or carbon tax systems whereas others do not, they lack similarities to other assets underlying ARTs. The aforementioned assets are financial in nature, as they need to be able to hold a *stable* monetary value, such as official currencies, tangible and certain intangible assets, rights, or other crypto-currencies.[15] With ART, MiCAR mainly describes so-called stablecoins,[16] because of which Title III MiCAR most likely does not apply to VCC tokens.

The final category of MiCAR comprises other crypto-assets than EMTs or ARTs.[17] These can be described as the MiCAR category to encompass all tokens that should be regulated but are not or not as financial in nature as the other two.[18] Among other things, this term encompasses the already established currency and utility tokens. Security tokens, which are often mentioned alongside the aforementioned tokens, should be considered as tokenised securities and thereby fall under the provisions of MiFID II.[19] While the term currency token covers crypto-currencies such as Bitcoin and Ether, utility tokens 'only provide access to goods or services supplied by the issuer' (Art. 3(1)(9) MiCAR). With these utility tokens, the holders can collect or use the goods or services as laid out in the smart contract or an actual contract with the issuer. As VCCs embody the possibility or right to claim that a certain amount of emissions has been reduced or removed by another entity when they are retired, VCC tokens should embody the possibility to claim these reductions or removals have happened when they are burned. VCCs and their tokenised counterparts thus serve as evidence for their holders in some way, respectively. Since the claims are connected to a VCC, the underlying tokens should only enable the holder to back up these claims and not serve to enforce them against other persons or entities.[20] This may come from statements made by themselves or obligations allowing them to use VCCs to some extent.[21] The issuer merely acts as some sort of intermediary in these cases. VCC tokens can be classified as utility tokens if they are designed to be retired (or burned) and not as an investment option.[22] Hybrid cases are conceivable, in which a determination would be more difficult,[23] but as there is only a niche secondary market (as it is even more niche than the regular VCM), financial speculation should not be the main reason to buy VCC tokens. This can be up for change in the future, but as utility tokens are other crypto-assets under MiCAR and are therefore covered by Title II, critical cases, considering these hybrid tokens, will lead to the same regulation.

Thus, even if not considering the VCC as a good or service with the VCC token providing access to the VCC according to the legal definition set out by Art. 3(1)(9) MiCAR, VCC tokens can still be considered as other crypto-assets as established in Title II MiCAR. With regard to the obligations for entities wanting to offer VCC tokens or admit them to trading, the difference between utility tokens and other crypto-assets is almost negligible and only matters for a limited number of exempt cases and will be explained in the following.

b) Exemptions

As stated before, financial instruments, tokenised or not, fall under the regulations of MiFID II.[24] The same applies for different objects of other European legal acts that are mentioned by Art. 2(4) MiCAR. This encompasses (structured) deposits (b), funds (c), securitisation positions (d)[25], non-life or life insurance products (e),[26] pension products (f, g, h, i),[27] and social security schemes (j).[28] As VCCs do not fall under any of these definitions, these legal exemptions can be disregarded in the following analysis.

In accordance with Art. 2(3) MiCAR, regulations of MiCAR do not apply to crypto-assets that are unique and thus not fungible with other crypto-assets (NFTs).[29] Conversely, tokens need to be fungible to be relevant for the scope of MiCAR. Fungibility can be understood as the tradability of tokens with other tokens of their kind. While the term 'fungible' seems to be elusive to some extent,[30] the idea behind this exemption becomes clear in Recital 10 MiCAR: Tokens that are truly unique or backed by a truly unique asset cannot be traded fungibly considering their worth is subjective to their purchasers—just like art.[31] But according to MiCAR, NFTs, labelled as such, are not always NFTs in a technical sense, as most of them can be serialised or fractured into fungible assets. Serialised NFTs are fungible inside of their series. Whereas fractionalised NFTs are fungible inside of their fractionalisation. MiCAR regulations thus care for actual fungibility and not only claims of non-fungibility according to Recitals

10 and 11. This exemption is especially interesting considering the use case of VCC tokens. As more and more purchasers of VCCs are interested in the location and specific actions of the project developer who reduces or removes emissions, a sense of non-fungibility can be attributed to them.[32] If this non-fungibility holds, the MiCAR regime does not apply to these cases. This is where some non-fungibility designations of VCCs and VCC tokens fail, as most of them can at least be serialised. A distinctive tree farm in a specific forest holds a wide array of trees and delivers co-benefits to certain areas, workers, and communities around them. As every tree is unique in the way it can sequester CO_2e, depending on its specific kind, growth, and location, there are possibilities to either serialise different tree groups into fungible tonnes of CO_2e or to fractionalise the whole output (or rather intake) of the tree farm into fungible units of CO_2e. Further recommendations for the exemption of NFTs according to Art. 2(3) MiCAR were made by the European Banking Authority (EBA) and the European Securities and Markets Authority (ESMA) in accordance with Art. 142(2)(d) MiCAR.[33]

With the differentiation of true non-fungibility and fungibility laid out by MiCAR, the markets in crypto-assets get new guidelines considering the NFT bubble a few years ago. At least some of these NFTs should fall under either serialised or fractionalised NFTs, becoming fungible through the lens of MiCAR. For VCC tokens, this has to be considered on a case-by-case basis.

c) Obligations for offerors of crypto-assets and persons seeking admission to trading regarding VCC tokens

As we stated, VCC tokens can be considered as other crypto-assets (or in a few cases as utility tokens) specified by MiCAR. Title II (Art. 5–15 MiCAR) is therefore crucial for the regulation of their issuance. To comply, there are several steps an entity (offeror or person seeking admission to trading) has to take to either be able to offer the crypto-asset or to admit the crypto-asset to trading. There are a few differences between these two options regarding VCC tokens, which we will be looking at in the following.

aa) Offering a VCC token

According to Art. 4 MiCAR, the offeror of a crypto-asset has obligations to fulfil before he is allowed to offer any kind of other crypto-asset. The term 'offeror' is defined as 'a natural or legal person, or other undertaking, or the issuer, who offers crypto-assets to the public' (Art. 3(1)(13) MiCAR), and is broader than the term 'issuer', which refers only to those who issue the crypto-assets (Art. 3(1)(10) MiCAR). Disclosure requirements thus need to be fulfilled by the offerors (in the secondary market) and not only by the issuers (in the primary market).[34] These obligations are largely identical to those the entity must fulfil if it wishes to have its crypto-assets admitted to trading. Firstly, it has to be a legal person by the standards of EU law (a) and needs to work out a so-called crypto-asset white paper, notify to the national competent authority (NCA), and publish it (b–d). Furthermore, he may draft marketing communications and publish them in accordance with Art. 7 and 9 MiCAR (e, f). Lastly, he has to fulfil further obligations laid out in Art. 14 MiCAR, which deal with his commitment to transparency towards the potential purchasers and asset-holders. The white paper mentioned by MiCAR aims to mitigate the information asymmetries on the basis of the relationship between the entities obliged to publish it and possible holders. It is vastly different to any technical or other existing white paper before MiCAR came into force, which only explains the most basic information concerning the respective crypto-asset and is usually not standardised and therefore also misses mandatory contents.[35]

These obligations only come (partly) in effect for token offerings of a specific size and in accordance with their specific use case. If the crypto-asset is offered to less than 150 natural or legal persons per Member State (Art. 4(2)(a) MiCAR), the total consideration of the offer to the public does not exceed EUR 1,000,000 in respective currencies or crypto-currencies in the EU over the period of twelve months (b) or is only aimed at qualified investors as defined in Art. 3(30) MiCAR in connection with Annex II of MiFID II (c) no white paper has to be drafted and their marketing communications do not need to be published. This also has to be determined on a case-by-case basis for VCC tokens.[36]

The other exemption is connected to the specific use case of the crypto-asset in accordance with Art. 4(3)(a–d) MiCAR. If the offering of the asset is free ('airdrops'; a), the token acts as a reward for the maintenance of the DLT (b), the token is a utility token connected to a good that already exists or a service already in operation (c), or, if the holder has the right to exchange the token for goods and services only in a limited network of merchants contractually connected to the issuer (d), Title II MiCAR does not apply, as there is simply no consideration or investment character involved.[37] Classifying VCC tokens as utility tokens can lead to an exemption in connection with Art. 4(3)(c) MiCAR, in case the underlying VCC or climate action were to be considered a good or service already in existence or in operation—marking the special standing of utility tokens mentioned before. It is worth noting that none of the aforementioned exemptions are applicable, if the offerors or persons acting on their behalf communicate that they are seeking admission to trade these tokens in any way (Art. 4(4) MiCAR).

As VCC tokens are most likely purchased, only points (c) and (d) could be of relevance. As is sometimes the case, traditional and non-digital VCCs are connected to VCC tokens ('bridging')[38] on a blockchain (or via smart contracts). In this instance, the VCC token could be seen as the legal right to retire specific VCCs.[39] Confirming these VCCs as a good that already exists or a service that is in operation, their connected VCC token issuers would be exempted from the obligations of Title II. Considering the nature of VCCs, as not all of the reductions or removals have already completely taken place (e.g., tree farms can be destroyed—releasing all CO_2e back into the air), classification difficulties could arise as some of the 'goods' or 'services' exist, and some do not.[40] Alternatively, if VCCs are native on the blockchain, then the exemption would be more complicated to apply considering that the activities behind a VCC cannot easily be considered as a 'good existing' or a 'service in operation'.

If not exempted via point (c), both kinds of VCC tokens, bridged and native ones, could still be exempted according to point (d). As the underlying value of the VCC token stems from the possibility of claiming the existence of their CO_2e-reductions or -removals and not from claims against the offeror or the project developer (or other persons inside of a limited network), the usage of these assets is not necessarily limited to a specific network. Meanwhile, actions concerning the handling and eventually the burning of VCC tokens can only take place in the offeror's contractual network. The same holds true for the possibility of re-trading bridged VCC tokens into VCCs. Taking the limitation, the prerequisites for an exemption according to Art. 4(3)(d) MiCAR could still be present but would have to be evaluated case-by-case for specific VCC tokens. In this case, the question of exemption is determined by how the transaction and burning processes take place exactly (or how the specific smart contracts work). These processes could possibly stay inside or happen outside of the limited network of the offeror according to point (d). If certain emission systems allow for the use of VCCs and VCC tokens in a legal matter, the contractual network will no longer be limited to the offerors.

According to Art. 4(4) MiCAR, no exemptions are applicable if the offeror makes any communications regarding the admission of these crypto-assets to trading. As one of the main considerations for the tokenisation of VCCs is optimising the VCM's abilities to scale,[41] this should mostly be the case. Nevertheless, it is possible to structure VCC tokens in a way that exempts them from the regulatory scope of creating a white paper in the sense of MiCAR.

bb) Seeking admission to trading of VCC tokens

If a VCC token is to be traded, the entity must fulfil the obligations set out in Art. 5(1)(a–g) MiCAR, which are analogous to those in Art. 4(1)(a–g). There are no exemptions other than those laid down in Art. 5(4) MiCAR for crypto-assets that have already been admitted to trading on another trading platform within the EU (a) and for crypto-asset white papers that have been drawn up in accordance with Art. 6 (b) MiCAR. An offeror who desires their VCC tokens to be traded is therefore required to draft all the necessary documents.

d) Obligations of the offeror of crypto-assets

In the event that the offeror is obliged to fulfil the requirements of Title II MiCAR, it is necessary for him or them to draft and publish a crypto-asset white paper and to notify the NCA. A crypto-asset white paper shares several characteristics with a prospectus for securities.[42] Even though, the exact legal requirements differ in certain aspects, for example, white papers do not have to be authorised in accordance with Art. 20(1) of the Prospectus Regulation. Art. 6, 8, and 9 MiCAR, in conjunction with Annex I MiCAR, elucidate the information that must be included in the white paper. Moreover, the white paper serves as an official standardised information document,[43] a function that was not necessarily inherent to such documents prior to MiCAR.[44]

The white paper must include a preliminary statement of missing approval by any competent authority within the EU (Art. 6(3) MiCAR), furthermore, a summary that cautions against its own summarising function (Art. 6(7)(a) MiCAR), an indication of this statement's value in comparison to the entire white paper (b), the absence of connections to financial instruments (c), and a differentiation between the white paper and a regular prospectus (d).

As a prerequisite, the white paper must contain all relevant information about the offeror and, if applicable, also information concerning the issuer of the crypto-asset and the operator of the trading platform in cases where the platform draws up the crypto-asset white paper (Art. 6(1)(a–c) MiCAR). Furthermore, the crypto-asset project, the offer or the admission to trading itself, and the crypto-asset with its rights and obligations attached have to be defined specifically (d–g).

Finally, the technology underlying the crypto-asset, the risks associated with it, and the potential adverse effects of the consensus mechanism used must be provided (h–j). All of the aforementioned points must be presented in a concise manner and shall not be misleading (Art. 6(2) MiCAR). The crypto-asset white paper must not contain any assertions about the future value of the crypto-asset (Art. 6(4) MiCAR).

It is imperative to establish clarity regarding the crypto-asset, which may lose its value (Art. 6(5)(a) MiCAR), transferability (b), liquidity (c), or exchangeability against goods (d) and that there is no compensation or guarantee system in place (e, f). The white paper should be structured in a coherent manner (Art. 6(8) MiCAR), written in an official language of the home Member State or in a language that is customary in the sphere of international finance (Art. 6(9) MiCAR), and presented in a machine-readable format (Art. 6(10) MiCAR). In this way, the white paper becomes a crucial source of information regarding the crypto-asset in question. ESMA has developed a proof of concept for white paper creation, delineating the essential components of such documents in a structured manner.[45]

This is consistent with the fundamental premise of how VCCs should be used in the EU: In the wake of numerous allegations of greenwashing, prospective purchasers of VCCs have expressed a keen interest in acquiring a clear understanding of the assets that they are purchasing.[46] Given that these are currently largely unregulated, it is important that at least their tokenised counterparts are holistically structured and regulated.

In the event of a misleading white paper, the offerors, individuals seeking admission to trading, or even operators of trading platforms may be held liable (Art. 15 MiCAR). Analogously to the prospectus regulation, their liability should be assumed with a crypto-asset holder of average (crypto-)understanding.[47] The liability is considered to be indefinite as it is not stated otherwise, as the vagueness of Art. 15(1) MiCAR in terms of its liability statutes necessitates referral to other sources for interpretation.[48]

The information presented in the white paper is required to be complete, fair, clear, and not misleading. Any infringement of these criteria may result in liability. This is a notable aspect of MiCAR, as it directly established a liability clause in EU regulatory law.[49]

In the event of the drafting of a white paper, the offeror, person seeking admission to trading, or operators of trading platforms for crypto-assets are required to notify the NCA of their home Member State in accordance with Art. 8 MiCAR. The notifying entities are required to state the reasons why the crypto-asset is not to be considered as an ART, EMT, or any other instrument mentioned in Art. 2(4) MiCAR.

The notification process for a white paper includes the provision of information pertaining to the entity's operational domains within the EU Member States, the date of publication of the white paper, and the commencement date for the offer. Following the completion of this step, the white paper has to be publicised on the entity's website prior to the offering as outlined in Art. 9 MiCAR.

This is particularly relevant in the case of VCC tokens, where offerors, those seeking admission to trading, and operators of trading platforms may wish to communicate the value, considering any co-benefits or competitive advantages over traditional and non-digital VCCs and other VCC tokens. In doing so, the relevant entities are required to comply with the regulations set out in MiCAR; failure to do so may result in far-reaching legal consequences as outlined in Art. 15 MiCAR. Marketing communications must also be duly notified and published in a manner consistent with the white paper. Any alterations to the crypto-asset must be considered in the context of the white paper and the marketing communications. Changed attributes can establish an obligation to modify and notify any differences in the relevant documents to the NCA (Art. 12 MiCAR).

Furthermore, Art. 13 MiCAR establishes a right of withdrawal for retail holders of crypto-assets against the offeror or a crypto-asset service provider (CASP) for a period of 14 days with regard to transactions involving crypto-assets. Retail holders are defined in Art. 3(1)(37) MiCAR as natural persons acting outside of their trade, business, craft, or profession—meaning only small purchasers. It should be noted that this does not apply to cases in which the crypto-asset has already been admitted to trading, due to the reasonable consideration of price fluctuations.[50]

Subsequent to this triad, offerors, persons seeking admission to trading, and operators of trading platforms are permitted to offer or admit their crypto-assets to trading in the entire EU, without further information obligations in accordance with Art. 11 MiCAR. However, these rights are accompanied by additional obligations connected to activities related to crypto-assets. These obligations encompass the requirement to always act honestly, fairly, and professionally (Art. 14(1)(a) MiCAR), not in a misleading manner (b), in the best interest of the holders (c), and according to security standards upheld by the EU (d).

e) Crypto-asset service providers

Following the summary of the rights and obligations of offerors and persons seeking admission to trading for VCC tokens, the focus will now be turned towards entities that may be interested in offering services regarding these crypto-assets. These CASPs are obligated to fulfil certain requirements in order to operate within these ecosystems (Title V MiCAR). The term CASP is defined in Art. 3(15) MiCAR as

> a legal person or other undertaking whose occupation or business is the provision of one or more crypto-asset services to clients on a professional basis, and that is allowed to provide crypto-asset services in accordance with Article 59 [MiCAR].

This is followed by an enumeration of the various types of crypto-asset services, set forth in Art. 3(16) MiCAR, with further details being laid down in the following paragraphs. Crypto-asset services are all services surrounding crypto-assets: The custody and administration of crypto-assets (a), the operation of a trading platform (b), the exchange of crypto-assets for funds (c) or other crypto-assets (d), the execution of orders on behalf of clients (e), the placement of orders (f), the reception and transmission of orders on behalf of clients (g), the provision of advice (h), portfolio management (i), and transfer services on behalf of clients (j). Any entity contemplating the provision of one or more of these services is obligated to obtain a requisite authorisation, as stipulated in Art. 59–65 MiCAR.

aa) Authorisation of crypto-asset service providers

In order to become authorised in accordance with Art. 59 MiCAR and start operating as a CASP, legal persons or other undertakings need to submit an application to the NCA in their home Member State. In accordance with Art. 62(2) MiCAR, such entities have to provide the NCA with their contact data (a), legal form (b), articles of association (c), a description of their governance arrangements (f), the members of their management body (g), stakeholders or members with direct or indirect qualifying holdings (h), and proofs of their good repute and (collective) knowledge, respectively, including the absence of any criminal records referring to financial crimes or penalties imposed under the applicable commercial law (Art. 62(3) MiCAR). Furthermore, they are required to present a programme of operations, setting out the specific crypto-asset services they intend to provide (d), along with substantiated evidence that they are capable of fulfilling the mandatory security requirements, including prudential safeguards, internal control mechanisms, technical documentation of information and communication technology (ICT) and security systems, and detailed descriptions of their client fund segregation procedures and complaints-handling mechanisms (e), (i), (j), (k), and (l). Finally, they are required to specify the Member State in which they intend to provide their services, and whether they plan to offer any of the specific services listed in Art. 3(1)(16) (m–r) MiCAR.

Subsequent to the submission of an application, the NCA is obliged to notify the applicant within five working days of its receipt. The assessment of the application's completeness is to be conducted within a time span of 25 working days, with the NCA having the possibility to request further information if need be (Art. 63(1) and (2) MiCAR). Following the verification of additional safeguards by the NCA (Art. 63(6) MiCAR), the NCA evaluates the application and communicates its determination of approval or rejection. The application is to be refused according to Art. 63(10)(a–d) MiCAR under any of the following circumstances: Entities having direct or indirect influence on the applying CASP do not fulfil or can be expected not to fulfil their requirements (a–c); or the CASP does not fulfil any further requirement enacted on them (d).

The application process to become a CASP can be streamlined for established financial institutions (Art. 60 MiCAR). This is due to the fact that these entities have already been approved under other EU regulations, resulting in a shorter list of information needing to be submitted to the NCA, as most of the influential entities in these institutions are already considered trustworthy.

The authorisation of CASPs may be withdrawn or partially withdrawn by the NCA if they have been inactive for a period of nine months (Art. 64(1)(c) MiCAR), have not made use of their authorisation for a period of twelve months (a), or have expressly renounced it (b). In addition, in the event of irregular acquisition of the authorisation (d) or breach of the safeguards laid out by MiCAR and/or other legislation (Art. 64(1)(e–g), (2)), the NCA may also withdraw the authorisation.

Once authorised, CASPs are permitted to provide their services in their home Member State or in any other Member State of the EU in accordance with Art. 65 MiCAR. The provision of these services entails the fulfilment of general and specific obligations, which are outlined in the following section.

bb) Obligations for all crypto-asset service providers

When operating, CASPs must generally act honestly, fairly, and professionally in the best interests of their clients. This includes transparency regarding information, marketing communications, risks, pricing policies, and the possible adverse environmental impact of consensus mechanisms (Art. 66 MiCAR) as well as prudential safeguards (Art. 67 MiCAR). The management body and directly or indirectly influential stakeholders or members must be of sufficiently good repute and have appropriate knowledge, skills, and experience. This has to be on an individual and collective basis. They must also be free of convictions for financial crimes, including money laundering and terrorist financing. It lies within the CASP's responsibility to ensure that these conditions are met and that compliance with other European legislation is maintained (Art. 68 MiCAR).

The NCA must be notified of any changes in the management body (Art. 68 MiCAR). In the event of insolvency, the crypto-assets themselves and, in the case of 'other crypto-assets', the ownership rights of clients must be safeguarded (Art. 70(1) and (2) MiCAR). This means that the crypto-assets are only allocable to the clients' and not to the CASPs' capital.[51] The resolution of client complaints and the management of conflicts of interest must be conducted in accordance with clearly defined policies and templates that are accessible to relevant stakeholders (Art. 71 and 72 MiCAR).

CASPs are allowed to outsource services and activities to third parties, provided that they remain responsible and comply with the provisions of MiCAR (Art. 73 MiCAR). This must be documented in a contractual agreement with the outsourcing partner in a cooperative relationship with the NCA (Art. 73(3) and (4) MiCAR).

To carry out specific crypto-asset services in connection with Art. 75–82 MiCAR, CASPs must comply with additional specific regulations. These crypto-asset services are tiered into three classes (Annex IV MiCAR) pertaining to the minimum capital requirements in Art. 67(1)(a) MiCAR. While the operation of a trading platform (Art. 76 MiCAR) requires an amount of EUR 150,000 (Class 3), the provision of custody and administration and the exchange of crypto-assets, either for funds or for other crypto-assets (Art. 75 and 77 MiCAR) require EUR 125,000 and every other crypto-asset service (Art. 78–82 MiCAR) requires EUR 50,000 as minimum capital. This is closely connected to an underlying risk assessment.[52] These specific crypto-asset services are briefly introduced in the following sections.

cc) Provision of custody and administration of crypto-assets on behalf of clients

Pursuant to Art. 75 MiCAR, the provision of custody and administration of crypto-assets on behalf of clients, constitutes a specific crypto-asset service. 'Custody and administration' are defined in Art. 3(17) MiCAR as 'the act of safekeeping or controlling [...] crypto-assets or the means of access to such crypto-assets, where applicable in the form of private cryptographic keys'. In order to provide these services, the CASP and its clients must reach an agreement on the main points listed in Art. 75(1)(a–g). The CASP must maintain a registry to keep track of all their clients' rights to crypto-assets and their movements and facilitate the exercise of their clients' rights (Art. 75(2) and (4)).

In order to ensure the security of their clients' crypto-assets, CASPs must implement custody policies, provide information regularly and upon request, and establish systems to return crypto-assets as soon as possible (Art. 72(3), (5) and (6) MiCAR). CASPs have to keep their clients' crypto-assets separate from their own (Art. 75 (7) MiCAR). In addition, clients must be informed and give their consent before the CASP uses other CASPs to ensure the continued protection of their assets (Art. 75(9) MiCAR). CASPs may be held liable to clients in the event of a loss of crypto-assets or the means of accessing those assets, if an incident is deemed to be attributable to them, establishing a possibility to claim these losses on the clients' side. (Art. 75(8) MiCAR).

Companies, as a target customer group for VCC tokens, will have an interest in not handling their tokens themselves due to the costs involved. Rather, it is more likely that the custody and management of VCC tokens will become a widely used service, with CASP omnibus wallets and private keys linked to the company holding the tokens. Given the growing concern in the EU about the transparency of sustainability reporting and the drive to avoid any allegations of greenwashing, it is paramount that the VCC tokens remain accessible to the company at all times. The established liability will serve as a further safeguard for companies interested in VCC tokens.

dd) Operating a crypto-asset trading platform

Another example of a specific CASP is that of a crypto-asset trading platform operator. The act of operating a crypto-asset trading platform warrants a significant degree of responsibility for all customers engaged in trading activities on the platform. This crypto-asset service is similar to a multilateral trading facility (MTF) according to MiFID II and serves—in connection with the trading of crypto-assets (Art. 3(1)(19) and (20) MiCAR)—as a means to connect multiple sellers and buyers of crypto-assets.[53] The definition in Art. 3(1)(18) MiCAR is as follows:

> [T]he management of one or more multilateral systems that bring together or facilitate the bringing together of multiple third-party purchasing and selling interests in crypto-assets in the system and in accordance with its rules, in a way that results in a contract, either by exchanging crypto-assets for funds or by exchanging [...] for other crypto-assets.

Unlike in the case of Art. 75 MiCAR, CASPs do not have to engage in any contractual obligations with buyers according to Art. 76 MiCAR. Instead, Art. 76 MiCAR outlines the rules that CASPs must implement to ensure the fair and operational trading of crypto-assets in the language of their home Member State (Art. 76(1)(a–h) and (4) MiCAR). CASPs are also required to establish criteria for the exclusion of crypto-assets that may be used for illicit or fraudulent activities or that allow for the complete anonymisation of transactions (Art. 76(2) and (3) MiCAR). It should be noted that CASPs themselves are excluded from trading on their own platform, except in cases where they engage in matched principal trading (Art. 3(1)40 MiCAR in conjunction with Art. 4(1)(38) MiFID II). In such cases, they may act as the facilitator without financial benefit, provided that the clients have consented. Such matched principal trades have to be reported to the NCA (Art. 76(5) and (6) MiCAR). Transactions must be settled on the distributed ledger within 24 hours (Art. 76(12) MiCAR).

To ensure transparency, CASPs are required to make all bids and offers public on their website in a non-discriminatory manner. Furthermore, this must include the depth of trading interest and information on the price, volume, and time of transactions (Art. 76(9–11) MiCAR). Fee structures for transactions must be designed in a transparent, fair, and non-discriminatory manner so as to remove any incentive to place, modify, or cancel orders (Art. 76(13) MiCAR).

CASPs have to ensure that their systems are effective in terms of technical resilience and prevention of fraudulent behaviour, even under stress (Art. 76(7)(a–f)

MiCAR). They must be able to report to the NCA at any time, in particular in cases of market abuse, and keep records of all orders in crypto-assets for at least five years (Art. 76(8), (14), and (15) MiCAR). ESMA has established regulatory technical standards for the public display of the content of paragraphs (1), (9), and (10) and the presentation of the relevant data in paragraph (15) to the NCA on 3 July 2024 (Art. 75(16) MiCAR).[54]

Given that the majority of transactions in the VCM are currently conducted via over-the-counter (OTC) purchases facilitated by market participants, it is not implausible that new trading platforms for VCCs and especially for VCC tokens may emerge in the future. In light of the significant adverse selection problem arising from underlying information asymmetries,[55] which may be exacerbated by the additional layer of tokenisation, transparency obligations for trading platforms are particularly important. Establishing full transparency can be a first step to the prevention of market abuse.

With this long list of obligations to be met by CASPs and clients alike, operational and secure trading platforms can be established, which may help scale the (tokenised) VCM itself.

ee) Exchange of crypto-assets for funds or other crypto-assets

The exchange of crypto-assets for funds or other crypto-assets is defined in Art. 3(1)(19) and (20) MiCAR as 'the conclusion of purchase or sale contracts for crypto-assets with clients for funds [or "other crypto-assets"] using proprietary capital'. CASPs wishing to offer these services must adopt a non-discriminatory commercial policy with regard to the selection of their clients (Art. 77(1) MiCAR). The CASP shall publish a fixed price for the crypto-asset or the method for determining the price and any applicable limit set by the crypto-asset service provider on the amount to be exchanged (Art. 77(2) MiCAR). Orders shall be executed at the price displayed at the time of order (Art. 77(3) MiCAR) and information analogous to those of trading platforms in Art. 76(10) MiCAR (volume and prices of trades executed by the CASP) shall be publicly disclosed (Art. 77(4) MiCAR).

In conclusion, this obligation contributes to the development of new markets for VCC tokens and thus the whole VCM. Art. 77 MiCAR helps in establishing a fair exchange platform for VCC tokens to be traded for funds or other crypto-assets. In the future, trading unburned VCC tokens back into funds to use in other endeavours could be an important aspect of the VCM. Fair and level opportunities for all participants are the baseline for establishing and scaling the (secondary) market.

ff) Execution of orders for crypto-assets on behalf of clients

As defined in Art. 3(21) MiCAR, the execution of orders for crypto-assets on behalf of clients means 'the conclusion of agreements, on behalf of clients, to purchase or sell one or more crypto-assets or the subscription on behalf of clients for one or more crypto-assets, and includes the conclusion of contracts to sell crypto-assets at the moment of their offer to the public or admission to trading'. Similar to Art. 77 MiCAR, this covers a service on behalf of clients that, in this case, facilitates purchases and sales in the field of crypto-assets. CASPs wishing to provide such services are required to act in the best interests of their clients. This includes considerations of price, cost, speed, likelihood of execution and settlement, size, nature, custody conditions, and any other aspects relevant to the execution of the order in crypto-assets, unless the client gives contrary instructions (Art. 78(1) MiCAR).

In order to achieve the objectives set out in paragraph (1), it is necessary to establish and implement effective execution arrangements. These arrangements must be designed to ensure that the objective is achieved in a prompt, fair, and expeditious manner and in a manner that abuse is prevented (Art. 78(2) MiCAR). CASPs must provide appropriate and clear information regarding paragraph (2) and any changes thereto (Art. 78(3) MiCAR). The execution policy must be made available to clients or the NCA on request (Art. 78(4) MiCAR) and its effectiveness must be monitored by the CASP in order to identify any possible shortcomings (Art. 78(6) MiCAR). Clients must be duly informed and subsequently give their consent, before orders may be executed off-exchange (Art. 78(5) MiCAR).

The aim of Art. 78 MiCAR is to facilitate a process in which companies can commit to buying or selling VCC tokens, while ensuring that CASPs act in their best interests. The obligations set out by Art. 78 MiCAR are particularly significant for companies lacking expertise in DLT, tokenisation, or crypto-assets, as they help foster confidence in the process of buying or selling VCC tokens. Thus, they do not need to employ experienced DLT traders themselves to participate in the VCC token market but can still expect to receive the exact kind and amount of VCC tokens (or money) that meets their objectives. Furthermore, the possibility of establishing a subscription-like service can be of use for enterprises offsetting emissions that cannot feasibly be reduced.

gg) Placing of crypto-assets

Placing a crypto-asset according to Art. 3(22) MiCAR means 'the marketing [...] of the crypto-asset to purchasers' on behalf of an offeror. Contrary to Art. 77 and 78 MiCAR, this crypto-asset service is enacted on the supplier side. In order to place crypto-assets, CASPs must first enter into an agreement with a prospective offeror or person seeking admission to trading. This agreement must cover several key aspects, including the type of placement, the amount of transaction fees, the expected timing, process, and price, and the targeted purchasers. In the absence of such an agreement, CASPs are prohibited from placing crypto-assets (Art. 79(1)(a–d) MiCAR).

In addition to the rules on conflicts for all categories of CASPs in Art. 72(1) MiCAR, CASPs intending to place crypto-assets must also address conflict issues in their rules (Art. 79(2)(a–c) MiCAR).

The placement of crypto-assets could become an important undertaking for project developers in the traditional VCM space, who lack proper knowledge of DLT and crypto-assets, but still want to place their tokenised VCCs. CASPs operating in this space can facilitate the placement of these VCC tokens on behalf of project developers, further developing the digitalised ecosystem. It is crucial for project developers to work closely with CASPs at this stage, as they are possibly entering a completely new market with no best practices as a guideline other than the regulations of MiCAR.

hh) Reception and transmission of orders for crypto-assets on behalf of clients

Whenever a CASP acts on behalf of either side as an intermediary between the purchaser and the seller of crypto-assets, it offers the service of receiving and transmitting orders in accordance with Art. 3(23) MiCAR. Such orders can either occur as one-time purchases or in the form of a subscription model.

Pursuant to Art. 80 MiCAR, these specific CASPs must establish and implement procedures and arrangements to ensure the prompt and proper transmission of client orders (Art. 80(1) MiCAR). To ensure objectivity (Art. 80(2) MiCAR), they are prohibited from receiving any form of remuneration, discount, or non-monetary benefit when routing orders to specific trading platforms. They are also required to refrain from misusing any information relating to pending client orders and to take reasonable steps to prevent their employees from doing so (Art. 80(3) MiCAR).

This crypto-asset service is similar to the execution of orders for crypto-assets, but in this case, these executions are carried out by a third party.[56] The CASP can act as an intermediary, either on the side of the client interested in purchasing VCC tokens, or on the side of the client wishing to sell, in a specific market of other CASPs or with the execution carried out by other CASPs.

In particular, small companies or even individuals without sufficient knowledge or experience who wish to offset through the use of VCC tokens can benefit from these CASPs. The CASPs themselves are obliged to act fairly, without accepting any or following any incentives from the other party or trading platforms regarding their routing, and to support their clients in their endeavours.

ii) Providing advice on crypto-assets and providing portfolio management of crypto-assets

Both the provision of advice on crypto-assets and the management of crypto-asset portfolios on behalf of clients are regulated in Art. 81 MiCAR. While the provision of advice may be considered a secondary service, the active management of client portfolios represents a more principal service of CASPs.

The term 'providing advice' is defined as 'offering, giving, or agreeing to give personalised recommendations to a client, either at the client's request or on the initiative of the [CASP]' (Art. 3(24) MiCAR). The management of portfolios 'means managing portfolios in accordance with mandates given by clients on a discretionary client-by-client basis' (Art. 3(25) MiCAR).

A so-called suitability assessment has to be a feature of both services (Art. 81(1) MiCAR), which bears a strong similarity to the suitability assessment enforced by

MiFID I for financial instruments.[57] CASPs must assess their clients' knowledge, experience, investment objectives, risk tolerance, and financial situation, including their ability to bear losses. They must also implement appropriate policies and procedures to inform their clients of the results of the suitability assessment (Art. 81(8) and (10) MiCAR). In addition, they are required to carry out assessments of their clients on a regular basis (Art. 81(12) MiCAR).

Where CASPs intend to provide advisory services, they are obliged to inform prospective clients in a timely manner of the extent to which their services are independent from third parties and the scope and depth of the advice to be provided (Art. 81(2) MiCAR). As a general rule, they have to inform their clients of all costs and charges associated with the advice they provide (Art. 81(4) MiCAR). If they claim to act independently, they must also draw from a sufficient range of crypto-assets available on the market, which must be adequately diverse and not provided by that same CASP, and may not accept or retain any fees from any third party or any person acting on behalf of a third party in relation to the provision of the service to clients (Art. 81(3)(a) and (b) MiCAR).

In addition to the suitability assessment mentioned above, CASPs managing portfolios on behalf of clients must ensure their independence by not accepting or retaining any fees, commissions, or other benefits from any entity related to the service (Art. 81(5) MiCAR). They must also provide their clients with regular updates on their portfolios at intervals of no more than three months, except if a client has access to the information through an online system (Art. 81(14) MiCAR).

Both of these categories of CASPs must warn their clients of the risks associated with changes in value, potential losses, and illiquidity of the crypto-asset (Art. 81(9)(a–e) MiCAR). In addition, they are prohibited from recommending crypto-assets or crypto-asset services to their clients and from commencing the provision of associated portfolio management until the suitability of the crypto-assets and/or services has been determined or decided against (Art. 81(11) MiCAR).

With regard to services related to VCC tokens, advice may be of particular value to companies that wish to acquire VCC tokens as part of their sustainability agenda without having sufficient knowledge.[58] In addition, portfolio management is a potential avenue for CASPs seeking to provide an integrated solution for the use of VCC tokens. In either case, CASPs need to obtain and review all relevant information regarding the suitability of various VCC tokens or services related to them in order to further their clients' objectives. By providing regular updates on their advice or portfolios, companies can use this information for their sustainability reporting, particularly if the CASPs already have expertise in the sustainable management of VCCs or VCC tokens.

jj) Placing transfer services for crypto-assets on behalf of clients

The final category of specific CASPs in Title V, Chapter 3 MiCAR refers to CASPs that facilitate transfer services on behalf of their clients. They are defined in Art. 3(26)

MiCAR as 'providing services of transfer, on behalf of a natural or legal person, of crypto-assets from one distributed ledger address or account to another'. In essence, they move crypto-assets to different blockchain addresses for their clients.[59]

In order to provide these services, an agreement must be concluded with the client, setting out the duties and responsibilities of the service provider (Art. 82(1)(a–d) MiCAR). Given the relatively simple nature of the service, the agreement referred to in paragraph (1) is the only requirement. According to paragraph (2), ESMA, in cooperation with EBA, was responsible for issuing additional guidelines on procedures, policies, and the delineation of client rights in the context of transfer services, which they have done on 17 December.[60]

Providing the management of transactions from a company's address is a very basic crypto-asset service that a CASP could offer and thus will most likely be coupled to further crypto-asset services. Companies will need to work out efficient and beneficial arrangements with these CASPs to keep the right VCC tokens in their 'possession', especially if they are already retired (if they are still tradable at this point) to keep them accountable in any voluntary or even compliance schemes.

f) Other European legislation on VCC tokens

As VCCs and VCC tokens can be used for the same purposes, it is possible to burn VCC tokens to claim that CO2e has been reduced or removed. This may be covered by some of the European legislation that has been enacted or is in the proposal stage. As the primary use case is the act of making environmental claims in relation to the production of goods or the provision of services, the EU has provided clear guidance on how to make reliable environmental claims. Directives such as the Corporate Sustainability Reporting Directive (CSRD)[61] and the Consumer Empowerment Directive (CED)[62] indicate that the EU intends to impose tighter restrictions on companies claiming to be 'climate neutral'.

The CSRD amended the Accounting Directive[63] to extend its scope to a wider range of companies. It also added the need for sustainability reporting by subjected companies on their impact on the environment and the impact of the environment on their business activities, respectively. It added Art. 19a and 29a Accounting Directive, mandating entities of public interest to report on their sustainability issues. With the support of a delegated regulation enacted through Art. 1(8) CSRD and its established European Sustainability Reporting Standard (ESRS),[64] the companies concerned are required to comply with a table of rules to draft their sustainability reporting. The reports need to be clearly defined in order to avoid any misrepresentation of information to (potential) stakeholders. The ESRS contains a set of rules defining the usage of CO_2e offsetting, which addresses VCCs and VCC tokens as forms of offsetting. Paragraph (61) of the ESRS E1 requires companies making public claims of CO_2e neutrality to explain how these claims are linked to emission reduction targets (a), whether and how the reliance on VCCs hinders their target to become net zero (b), and how they ensure the integrity of the VCCs used (c). Companies will have to separate their emission reduction pathways from their use of VCCs to ensure compliance with their neutrality targets.

The CED is a competition law measure aimed to ensure fair competition through empowering consumers to hold companies liable for unlawful 'environmental claims' as defined in Art. 1(1)(b) CED. It amends the Unfair Commercial Practices Directive (UCPD)[65] to provide a legal definition of 'environmental claim' that is accessible to competition law. In the context of the ESRS, environmental claims relating to the inappropriate use of VCCs may result in significant penalties under competition law.

The definition of environmental claims will be further clarified by the Green Claims Directive (GCD),[66] which is currently in the proposal stage. In particular, Art. 3 (h) GCD will require companies to justify any explicit environmental claim in terms of the separation and clear definition of the offsetting and thus VCCs and VCC tokens used in such claims. Therefore, all VCCs used to achieve net-zero commitments must be fully documented and explained when used for marketing statements.

Another important piece of legislation is the Carbon Removal and Carbon Farming Regulation (CRCF),[67] which was adopted on 27 November 2024. Although the CRCF primarily focuses on one specific type of VCCs, removal credits, it nevertheless aims to establish a framework for the certification of high-integrity (removal) VCCs. The potential use of high-integrity removal credits in the EU ETS has also been considered and is addressed in Recital 4 CRCF. It is clear that a significant amount of documentation will be required to maintain the integrity of these removal credits.

Likewise, the potential utilisation of high-integrity VCCs in the European Carbon Border Adjustment Mechanism (EU CBAM) may only be possible with sufficient documentation.[68]

As we have briefly described, a short analysis of the various European legal acts relating to VCCs reveals a clear need for high-integrity and well-documented VCCs. In relation to VCC tokens, it is possible to create them in a way that prevents any subsequent changes to their inputs and to finalise transactions relating to them—this includes creation, trading, and burning. As long as there are VCCs that comply with these regulations to some extent, tokenisation can help in maintaining their integrity while increasing their availability by scaling tradability, improving transparency, and ensuring immutability to a certain extent. For anything happening before the creation of the VCC token, other processes ensuring the quality of the underlying VCC or climate action have to be in place. Tokenisation can help in some aspects, but it is not a comprehensive solution for all problems of the VCM.

II Comparison of non-European regulatory approaches with the European regulatory framework

In view of the extensive nature of the provisions of MiCAR, it is important to consider other legal frameworks that may also be applicable to VCC tokens.

1 Regulation of VCC tokens in the USA

In the USA, the financial regulatory system is divided between two main institutions: The Securities Exchange Commission (SEC) and the Commodity Futures Trading Commission (CFTC). The SEC oversees securities, while the CFTC is responsible for commodities and their derivatives. As VCC tokens, and crypto-assets in general, are not explicitly defined as one or the other, the institutions are in a competitive relationship over the regulatory scope.

The SEC works with the definition of a security, which is defined in 15 U.S. Code § 77b. As this definition originates from sources long before DLT and blockchains, it does not mention any type of digital assets. The definition covers several different types of securities and various catch-all phrases, such as investment contracts, transferable shares or 'certificates of interest of participation in a profit-sharing agreement'.[69] Because of the list of definitions being quite broad, the SEC uses a concept derived from the 1946 case SEC v. W. J. Howey Co.[70] to define what falls under the term 'investment contract'. The SEC applies this so-called Howey test to determine whether various unregulated items fall within its jurisdiction and thus whether their offerors must be registered and authorised to offer them.

For an item to fall under the SEC's regulatory oversight, there must be an investment of money (1.) in a common enterprise (2.) with an expectation of profits (3.), primarily derived from the efforts of others (4.). All four prongs of this test must be satisfied for an item to qualify as an investment contract and thus as a security. As the definition, and in particular the Howey test, was created without DLT, blockchains, crypto-assets, or VCC tokens in mind, the SEC has drafted a non-binding framework on how to assess digital assets in light of the Howey test.[71] This leads to a dynamic and legally uncertain situation around crypto-assets, as the framework contains a non-exhaustive list of more than 60 factors that influence the determination of whether a digital asset is a security or not, which needs to be considered on a case-by-case basis.[72]

If items are not securities, they may be commodities and fall under the purview of the CFTC. Art. 1a Commodity Exchange Act (CEA) defines commodities as a list of specific 'goods and articles [...] and all services, rights and interests [...] in which contracts for future delivery are presently or in the future dealt in'. As this is again a broad definition that does not mention crypto-assets or VCC tokens, the CFTC will need to further define its scope. In previous cases, the CFTC has stated that virtual currencies such as Bitcoin fall under its oversight.[73]

As they are primarily focused on regulating derivatives, the existence of a commodity in an OTC market does not empower the CFTC to regulate crypto-assets in the form of crypto-currencies, but it does enable the regulation of their derivatives.[74] Since VCC tokens are closely related to their underlying VCCs, a different assessment must be made. In the eyes of the CFTC, traditional, non-digital VCCs can be declared as 'environmental commodities'.[75] VCCs and their tokenised versions that are traded in a manner analogous to crypto-currencies, futures, or derivative financial instruments thus may also be considered commodities.[76]

Given the considerable diversity of VCC tokens (and crypto-assets in general), there cannot be a single clear definition under the dual regulatory regime of the SEC and the CTFC. While VCC tokens can be designed to fit either definition, it remains uncertain whether these definitions will align with specific use cases of VCC tokens. Ultimately, as crypto-assets, VCC tokens may be securities, commodities, both, or nothing at all, leading to tremendous legal uncertainty.[77]

There are several ongoing attempts to regulate crypto-assets in the USA, but these have yet to be voted on and passed into law. Amongst these attempts are the Digital Commodities Act of 2022,[78] the Lummis-Gillibrand Responsible Financial Innovation Act of 2023,[79] and the Financial Innovation and Technology for the 21st Century Act, also of 2023.[80] These laws aim to define crypto-assets as commodities, giving the CFTC the ability to regulate them. This would lead to further restraints on the SEC, which seems to have overstretched its regulatory activities (as seen in the *SEC v Ripple Labs, Inc.* case in 2023).[81] A full assessment can only be made once legislation is in place.[82]

The federal structure of the USA may preclude the possibility of comprehensive regulation of voluntary carbon offsets. Some states have enacted minor regulations that allow the use of locally sourced VCM to exceed the emissions cap established by a cap-and-trade system, such as the Regional Greenhouse Gas Initiative or the Western Climate Initiative. As in the EU, the VCM is mainly voluntary.

In its Joint Policy Statements on the VCM, published in May 2024, the US Government outlined the importance of maintaining the integrity of the VCM.[83] The use of blockchain technology in conjunction with VCC tokens may facilitate the implementation of several mentioned principles, including accurately reflecting climate actions (Principle 5 Joint Policy Statement), reducing transaction costs (Principle 7 Joint Policy Statement), and may help to facilitate obligations set forth by the CFTC and/or the SEC. Considering this possibility, it is evident that the USA is not confident of the exact classification of VCC tokens.

The future of both regimes may be up for major changes, not least due to plans by the second Trump administration.

2 Regulation of VCC tokens in the United Kingdom

In the UK, the Financial Conduct Authority (FCA) is the regulatory authority responsible for overseeing financial matters. In this role, the FCA regulates all activities listed in the Financial Services and Markets Act 2000 (FSMA 2000). Due to the absence of an initial definition of crypto-assets under FSMA 2000, the FCA has developed a series of guidelines and statements on the implementation of such assets.

The FCA's final guidance on crypto-assets in 2019 stated that only certain tokens would need to be regulated under FSMA 2000.[84] In particular, these were e-money tokens and security tokens, while exchange tokens (crypto-currencies) and utility tokens would not require regulation.

As this has evolved and given that the UK's regulatory approach is primarily focused on activities rather than the underlying assets themselves, HM Treasury, the UK's economic and financial affairs ministry, has undertaken further consultations. According to these consultations, regulatory law shall apply to all types of tokens if they are or can be used in regulated activities in accordance with the FSMA 2000.[85]

The activities covered by Section 22 FSMA 2000 are primarily specified investment transactions. The newly amended Section 22(4) FSMA 2000 includes crypto-assets as a possible part of these activities. Crypto-assets are legally defined as 'any cryptographically secured digital representation of value or contractual rights' that can be transferred, stored, or traded electronically (a), and use technology that supports the recording and storage of data, such as DLT (b). These FSMA 2000-specified investments are further refined by an enumeration in the FSMA 2000 (Regulated Activities) Order 2001 (RAO).

In its final guidance, the FCA provides further clarification on whether crypto-assets could be considered specified investments. Structured rights or entitlements similar to those of financial instruments, tradability on exchanges, payment flows, or a directly stated investment-like character may indicate characteristics of specified investments. More precise definitions are not applicable due to the complexity of crypto-assets.[86] As these regulated activities are generally prohibited under Art. 19 FSMA 2000, companies wishing to offer crypto-assets used for any of these activities under Section 22 FSMA 2000 must obtain authorisation from the FCA or be otherwise exempted from the general prohibition.

To provide further protection for consumers investing in crypto-assets, the FCA has issued a series of guidance papers on the promotion of crypto-assets, resulting in amendments to the Financial Promotion Order 2005 (FPO), which regulates the promotion of financial products and services, to include crypto-assets. These guidelines also address the issue of unregulated crypto-assets, which are still considered high-risk investments.[87]

Under paragraph 26F of Schedule 1 FPO, which sets out the FPO's regulated activities, crypto-assets are deemed to be regulated if they are fungible (1)(a) and transferable (b). Furthermore, they are not qualified if they are a controlled investment (2)(a), electronic money (b), fiat currency (c), fiat currency issued in digital form (d), or a crypto-asset that can only be transferred or sold by way of redemption with the issuer and can only be used in a limited way to obtain the underlying goods and services from the issuer or a limited network connected to the issuer (e). The last exception is similar to that of Art. 4(3) MiCAR.

As the FCA states in its policy paper, there is no need for a different classification of token types (e.g. utility tokens), as the compliance costs of the FPO do not differ significantly between them.[88] Those involved in the promotion of crypto-assets have a duty to ensure that the information provided is fair, clear, and not misleading. It is noteworthy that there is no obligation to publish a white paper as in the EU. Rather, the UK is seeking to encourage all crypto-asset issuers to promote their services in a consumer-friendly manner.

Detailed information on how to act in accordance with the FPO is provided in the form of non-handbooks or guidance documents.[89] With a new Discussion Paper dating from December 2024, the FCA aims to further develop a holistic market abuse regime for crypto-assets (MARC) and a crypto-asset admissions and disclosures regime (A&D).[90]

In regard to VCCs, the UK is considering the potential inclusion of specific VCCs in the UK ETS to incentivise the development of carbon removal technologies in line with its 2050 net-zero emissions target.[91] First, with the Law Commission's Final Report on Digital Assets[92] and, since 11 September 2024, with a new Bill,[93] VCCs and their digitalised forms can be considered as personal property, not falling into the two categories established by English common law (things in possession and things in action), but into a third category.

Similar to the other mentioned approaches, VCC tokens will need to be assessed on a case-by-case basis as to whether they can be characterised as a security-like investment falling under the FSMA 2000 and the FPO, as only a qualifying crypto-asset falling under the FPO or as an unqualified crypto-asset under Section 26F(3) of Schedule 1 to the FPO. As their initial design is not yet subject to a best practice, they can be created in a way that suits any of the three options above. The proposed regimes regarding crypto-assets (MARC and A&D) will help in clarifying any uncertainties and structure the framework for crypto-assets holistically in the future.

3 Comparison of the different regulatory approaches

The three different approaches have one thing in common: they distinguish security (-like) tokens from non-security-like tokens. Although all three approaches treat security tokens as securities due to their inherent financial implications, they differ in the employed classification systems. The USA uses a dynamic framework centred on the Howey test, which allows for considerable leeway in the interpretation of legislation to classify different crypto-assets as securities. If the Howey test is satisfied, the SEC assumes the role of a determinative authority with far-reaching obligations. If one of the prongs of the Howey test is not applicable, the crypto-asset is likely to be considered a commodity under the jurisdiction of the CFTC and CEA. Presumably, the majority of VCC tokens should be subject to commodity regulation, which still includes anti-money laundering and anti-terrorist financing provisions.

In the case of the UK, the FCA is responsible for determining which activities fall as specified investments within the scope of FSMA 2000. These specified investments centred on tokens fall under the general prohibition of section 19 FSMA 2000. As most VCC tokens are unlikely to have the characteristics of these investments, they will not fall under the regulatory framework of FSMA 2000. However, as they could be classified as crypto assets under the remit of the FPO, they could still fall under its financial promotion regime. With an enactment of the MARC and A&D regime, most crypto-assets—also VCC tokens—will need to comply with a holistic framework.

The FPO does not apply a stringent classification of tokens, so the majority of VCC tokens (unless exempted in a manner comparable to MiCAR) will have to comply with the advertising obligations. In general, the UK's approach is focused on consumer protection in this regard, similar to that of MiCAR. This can be attributed to the UK's ongoing internalisation of European law, even after Brexit. In particular, this concerns MiFID II and the Prospectus Regulation, which also served as the basis for MiCAR.

The EU classifies more tokens than just security tokens and non-security tokens. MiCAR currently distinguishes between four groups of tokens: Tokenised securities (MiFID II), ARTs (Title III MiCAR), EMTs (Title IV MiCAR), and other crypto-assets (Title II MiCAR). In the context of VCC tokens, as reasoned in the beginning, it is particularly important to consider them as other crypto-assets defined in Title II MiCAR, which serves as the main category of the regulation. With the addition of obligations for CASPs, this approach attempts to regulate the entire crypto-asset ecosystem in the most holistic manner. In general, the EU aims to provide a comprehensive framework for all matters related to crypto-assets and is the first jurisdiction to do so. Whether this will facilitate a sustainable growth of the crypto-asset space or hinder innovation can only be answered in the future.

A further common feature of the various regulatory frameworks is the lack of direct regulation of VCCs (and thus VCC tokens). The lack of regulation governing the creation of these tokens allows for a greater degree of flexibility in their design, thereby allowing to avoid the more stringent obligations typically associated with securities. It is therefore crucial to ensure that potential purchasers are adequately informed, even in cases where the VCC tokens in question are not classified as securities. Furthermore, it is possible to disregard white paper requirements entirely, as demonstrated by non-investment utility tokens that provide access to pre-existing unregulated VCCs that are not traded.

If the predictions for the VCM prove to be accurate, it is likely that the demand for VCCs and VCC tokens will increase in line with the approach of net-zero targets, stimulating the growth of a secondary market. With a real and well-functioning secondary market, connecting holders with other holders or potential holders may make VCCs, and thus VCC tokens, increasingly more akin to securities due to financial incentives like speculation. It is reasonable to assume that frameworks allowing for dynamic interpretation, particularly the Howey test in the USA, may ultimately lead to quicker results in regard to delineating investment-like VCC tokens and others.

III Relevant German law

Following our analyses of the European regulatory framework and comparisons with alternative approaches, we would like to address a rather specific case of the transposition of European law into national law in the German context. As MiCAR is drafted as a European regulation, it is generally applicable in all EU Member States according to Art. 288 of the Treaty on the Functioning of the European Union (TFEU). To this end, Germany—like every Member State—must enact new legislation and amend existing legislation in line with MiCAR. In the specific case of Germany, this was done through the enactment of the Financial Markets Digitalisation Act (*Finanzmarktdigitalisierungsgesetz*; FinmadiG), which established the new Crypto Markets Supervision Act (*Kryptomärkteaufsichtsgesetz*, KMAG) and amended the main financial supervisory laws (most notably the *Kreditwesengesetz*; KWG). The KMAG has since been enacted on 27 December 2024.

The KMAG regulates all aspects of the authorisation of the NCA. In the case of Germany, this is the domain of the Federal Financial Supervisory Authority (*Bundesanstalt für Finanzdienstleistungsaufsicht*, BaFin). With the KMAG, the German legislator attempted to make the same clear distinction between financial instruments and crypto-assets as the European legislator.[94] However, the KMAG overlooks important points regarding other crypto-assets as defined by MiCAR. Art. 2(4) KMAG lists all institutions under the regulatory framework as offerors or persons seeking admission to trading for ARTs (1.) and EMTs (2.) or as CASPs (3.). Surprisingly, Title II MiCAR seems to also have been overlooked—deliberately or not. This could lead to the initiation of infringement proceedings by the European Commission.[95] As VCC tokens are likely to fall into the category of other crypto-assets, this omission does not contribute to clarifying the regulatory framework for VCC tokens in German law.

Until the amendment was enacted, crypto-assets were categorised as financial instruments and regulated by Section 1 (1a) sentence 4 KWG as

> digital representations of a value, which is not emitted or guaranteed by any central bank or public authority and which does not have the legal status of currency or money, but is accepted by natural or legal persons as a means of exchange or payment by agreement or custom or for investment purposes and which can be transferred, stored and traded electronically.

In addition, the German legislator excluded e-money and certain digitised monetary values such as vouchers or cash cards (Section 1 (1a) sentence 5 KWG). As cryptocurrencies are electronically tradable and accepted by natural or legal persons but are not issued or guaranteed by any of the institutions mentioned, they could have been considered as financial instruments similar to MiFID II.[96] Utility tokens could not be fully categorised as financial instruments, as the German legislator considered them to be a simple way of redeeming certain goods and services from the issuer, thus not making them financial instruments in the German regulatory framework and keeping them unregulated.[97] Other crypto-assets established by MiCAR could have been encased by this definition.

With the FinmadiG amendment to the KWG, the term crypto-asset has been changed to 'cryptographic instruments' (*Kryptographische Instrumente*). For the new definitions of crypto-assets, the KWG will refer to the definitions of MiCAR. The 'new' cryptographic instruments (as they keep the old definition) should apparently act as a catch-all element for crypto-assets that do not fall under the main MiCAR category of other crypto assets, nor under the ART or EMT categories, and which are not financial instruments under MiFID II. At present, this does not seem convincing, as there does not appear to be any applicable cases for cryptographic instruments.[98] Exemptions from crypto-assets such as Art. 2(3) MiCAR (NFTs) or Art. 4(3) MiCAR (crypto-assets not subject to Title II MiCAR) are also not added by the amended KWG.[99] Only utility tokens similar to Art. 4(3)(c) MiCAR, which represent the definition of a redeemable voucher for goods and services that already exist or are in operation, are explicitly excluded from the scope of the amended KWG by Section 1 (11) sentence 5.[100]

A possible scope of cryptographic instruments could be exactly the other crypto-assets exempted by MiCAR. These would be airdrops, crypto-assets issued for the maintenance of a blockchain or crypto-assets that can only be traded in a limited network of the provider (Art. 4(3)(a), (b), and (d) MiCAR). Even if the material scope allows this approach, the legislation around the cryptographic instruments could be incompatible with EU legislation, making any further consideration at this point more or less negligible.[101]

The German approach appears to be an incomplete transposition of MiCAR into German regulatory law, with some errors or omissions regarding the regulation of other crypto-assets in Title II MiCAR. As mentioned before, Title II is the main scope of VCC tokens, as they are not EMTs or ARTs. The exemptions in MiCAR appear to be only partially mirrored in the German KWG, with the result that the newly created definition of cryptographic instruments is not suitable for VCC tokens (or any other crypto-asset). The thought of pre-emptively encompassing crypto-assets not covered by MiCAR (real NFTs or VCC tokens created as voucher-like utility tokens) led the German legislator to create an empty shell of a definition. The main difficulty lies in the fact that VCCs themselves are not regulated in German law. If they were, there would be no need to regulate tokens for existing VCCs. With all of the regulations mentioned above, the VCC tokens in Germany exist in a regulatory vacuum until Title II MiCAR is transposed accordingly.

IV UNIDROIT Principles

The International Institute for the Unification of Private Law (UNIDROIT) is an independent intergovernmental organisation dedicated to the unification and modernisation of Private International Law. Its 65 member states represent a wide variety of legal, economic, and political systems. UNIDROIT strives to standardise various aspects of legislation throughout the world by advocating and creating model private law instruments.

The UNIDROIT instruments that are most relevant in this context are the Principles on Digital Assets and Private Law (DAPL),[102] and the Draft Principles on the Legal Nature of Verified Carbon Credits along with related works. While UNIDROIT focuses on private law aspects, some of its definitions and approaches may be helpful in the area of regulatory law, which we will explore further.

1 UNIDROIT Principles on Digital Assets and Private Law

The DAPL, published by UNIDROIT in 2023, are designed to be technologically neutral and to reflect the transitional nature of the evolving digital assets landscape. The Working Group behind these Principles met between November 2020 and May 2023. The Principles are intended to serve as best practice guidelines for digital-asset legislation. They are issued with accompanying commentary to assist with their interpretation. Explicitly, they do not cover regulatory approaches (Comment 1.1. DAPL). 'Digital assets' are defined in Principle 2 DAPL and can be targets of proprietary rights. In general, the definition of 'digital assets' as laid out in Principle 2 should encompass VCC tokens as well.[103]

Furthermore, Principle 4 aims at defining a 'linked asset'. This is also a digital asset that can be subject to proprietary rights according to Principle 3(1) DAPL. It is questionable if VCCs created as (utility) tokens linked to traditional and non-digital VCCs can be defined as 'linked assets'. Linked assets, according to Principle 4, are digital assets that are 'linked to another asset'. These 'other assets' may be tangible, intangible, or even digital assets. The existence, requirements, and legal effect of the established link are to be determined by 'other law'.[104] Commentary 4.2. DAPL mentions enabling transactions of the other asset in concordance with the digital asset as one of the main reasons for linkage, which is one of the aims for tokenising VCCs as well.[105] While the reasons for the existence of such a link and its legal effect come from other law, the existence of the link is a question of fact (Commentary 4.4.–4.6). As will be seen in the use cases later on, most bridged VCC tokens are connected to specific VCCs via digital identifications. Thus, VCC tokens created as utility tokens enabling access in accordance with Art. 3(1)(9) MiCAR can be considered as linked assets according to Principle 4 DAPL. Linking digital assets to a VCC in this case would lead to the governance of private law concerns through the scope of the laws regulating a VCC. As VCCs are largely unregulated, Principle 4 DAPL would be difficult to apply. Other laws as defined in Principle 2(4) DAPL, in the form of the aforementioned EU legislation on VCCs, could change this in the future.

For now, this means that (utility) tokens may be subject to proprietary rights, just as the Principles would establish for native VCC tokens. Differences in regulatory law between utility tokens acting as redeemable vouchers and other crypto-assets are not recognised in the Principles.[106] The laws governing the link between digital assets and other assets (tangible, intangible, or digital) are to be determined by national legislation. This leads back to regulatory laws, or rather the, lack thereof, as VCCs themselves are not regulated and VCC tokens only have the chance to be regulated under crypto-asset regulations.

As stated before, the DAPL do not offer explicit information on regulatory aspects, but show further evidence for the need to treat certain VCC tokens as utility tokens due to the aspect of linking.

2 Draft UNIDROIT Principles on the Legal Nature of Verified Carbon Credits

Similar to the Working Group on Digital Assets and Private Law, the Working Group on the Legal Nature of Verified Carbon Credits[107] aims to summarise best practices for the treatment of these credits under private law in the form of Principles. The Working Group met in October 2023, April and September 2024, January and April 2025 with further meetings planned for September 2025 and thereafter. Finalisation is planned for the first half of 2026.

The term 'Verified Carbon Credits' stems from discussions between the first and the second meeting, as the legal nature of these credits will be determined before they are used voluntarily (VCCs) or in compliance markets (e.g., emission allowances).[108] Since the Working Group has yet to meet, no Principles have been finalised, but the group has produced a draft set of initial Principles (VCC Draft Principles).

In this draft, the definitions in Principle 2 immediately establish that VCCs should be treated as intangible assets (Commentary 2.2 VCC Draft Principles). In conjunction with the Principles on Digital Assets and Private Law, VCCs can form the basis of a linked digital asset, confirming the notion that certain VCC tokens are linked assets or even utility tokens.

UNIDROIT states in Principle 2(1)(c) and (d) VCC Draft Principles that uniqueness is a mandatory attribute for the creation of VCCs, as they require a 'unique identifier' in a registry. This is reminiscent of the idea of VCC tokens being NFTs, as all linked VCCs would need to have a unique serial number. As noted before, the simple description of being unique does not satisfy the requirement of being an NFT under MiCAR, which would lead to minor discrepancies between the VCC Draft Principles and MiCAR when it comes to VCC tokens. It is questionable if the mere hash value of tokens on a blockchain would meet the requirements of Principle 2(1)(c) and (d) VCC Draft Principles, as this should not suffice for the requirements of non-fungibility of MiCAR (as most tokens would then be NFTs).

Both Principles will be of relevance in relation to VCC tokens. While further work on the legal nature of Verified Carbon Credits will help to determine the applicable private law in respect to their underlying digital asset transactions, the Principles on Digital Assets and Private Law will aid in the private law aspects of the tokens themselves. Furthermore, the thought of including tokenisation as part of their Principles will help to enlighten this analysis.[109] It remains unknown whether, and to what extent, legislators will take inspiration from these Principles.

B Case studies

To gain a practical overview of VCC tokens and the legal requirements to be observed when dealing with them, a number of use cases can be examined that use tokenised VCCs to a certain extent. The objective of this examination is to evaluate the category of tokens created and whether or not they are subject to the regulatory framework outlined above.

We selected these use cases because they offer a comprehensive representation of VCC tokens, while also exemplifying distinct differences between them. In the subsequent discussion, the impact of these variations on the applicable legal framework will be addressed.

I Toucan

The Toucan Protocol Association (Toucan)[110] is a Swiss technology firm specialising in the creation of blockchain-based solutions for the scaling of the VCM by bridging in terms of efficiency, integrity, and speed. The initial instance of bridging by Toucan concerned VCCs from the two largest registry systems, 'Verra'[111] and 'Gold Standard'.[112] In order to avoid double-counting, the respective VCC was retired first and then a token connected to the retired VCC was created on the blockchain to make it tradable again (minting). However, in 2022, both Verra and Gold Standard prohibited the tokenisation of (retired) VCCs. Currently, both parties are seeking to independently advance these systems themselves.[113] To further support the scaling of the VCM in the meantime, Toucan has undertaken new efforts with other registries. Together with Puro.earth,[114] they claim to have created the first liquid market for biochar[115] credits (CHAR).

The creation of CHARs occurs through a two-way bridging system whereby different eligible projects by Puro.earth are tokenised. The projects get VCCs credited by removing CO_2e through the establishment and maintenance of biochar projects. The Toucan Carbon Bridge is utilised for tokenisation, and following this process, VCC tokens (TCO2) are minted on the underlying blockchain. As TCO2 tokens are all related to their vintage and their underlying projects, they are non-fungible (in a broad sense, not necessarily according to MiCAR) and get pooled together with comparable tokens. Through the means of pooling, fungible units of CHAR can be drawn out of the pool.

In a partnership with 'Neutral',[116] an exchange for environmental assets, Toucan introduced a 'Pool Health Fee' to ensure that projects within the pool do not monopolise and project diversity can be maintained. CHARs are labelled as 'vouchers that provide access to the underlying asset'[117] and are minted on the Ethereum-based Celo blockchain. These tokens can be traded via Uniswap, a decentralised exchange based on the Ethereum blockchain. To retire the VCCs, holders of CHARs must redeem their tokens for specific TCO2 tokens inside the pool via the Toucan interface. These TCO2 tokens, which are managed by holders, can be burnt, thereby retiring the underlying VCCs in the Puro.earth registry.

II Nori

Nori Inc. was a Seattle-based company operating within the domain of traditional carbon removal since 2017. In 2019, the company unveiled the 'Nori Removal Tonne', subsequently rebranded as the 'Nori Regenerative Tonne' (NRT). The NRT was a digital asset designed to indicate carbon removal for a minimum of 10 years, primarily facilitated through carbon farming practices in the USA.[118] These digital assets were issued on the Ethereum blockchain within the Nori application. In contradistinction to Toucan's CHARs, NRTs were required to be retired immediately following their purchase, thereby signalling the retirement of their underlying removals. The primary rationale for utilising an application on the Ethereum blockchain was to circumvent the occurrence of double-counting of retired units.[119]

Initially, there was a proposal to introduce an additional crypto-asset, the NORI token, with the objective of creating a tradable commodity for the purpose of trading carbon and establishing a carbon pricing mechanism.[120] Farmers seeking to adopt sustainable practices in accordance with Nori's standards in collaboration with external entities would have received NRTs, which could be traded on the Nori marketplace to companies and individuals seeking to offset their CO2e emissions over a period of at least ten years (as these farmers had committed to maintaining these practices for a minimum of ten years). Upon purchase, the NRTs would have been retired immediately and should not have been tradable to circumvent any aspirations of double-counting tonnes of CO2e. The NORI token could have been traded further instead.[121]

Subsequently, in 2023, Nori introduced an additional sustainable investment option: The 'Nori Net Zero Tonne'. As outlined in an informational white paper (not in the sense of MiCAR), this product is designed to integrate fast-cycling CO2e removals (as previously described) with carbon removals that can be stored for up to 1000 years, as these long-lasting removal options become increasingly available in the future. It is noteworthy that this product does not incorporate any blockchain-based technologies other than the incorporated NRT. Consequently, these 'Net Zero Tonnes' would not have raised any additional concerns with regard to crypto-assets regulation.

Nori Inc. closed down in 2024, as the new CEO, Matt Trudeau, labelled the 'challenges of a stagnant Voluntary Carbon Market and tough funding environment' as too demanding for Nori. This was communicated through *LinkedIn* by Nori co-founder Alexsandra Guerra.[122]

III Crypto Carbon Company (C3)

Crypto Carbon Company (C3) is a decentralised platform that created a bridging system for VCCs similar to Toucan's for the registries of Verra and Gold Standard (2022). In conjunction with Verra's and Gold Standard's disapproval of tokenisation of their VCCs, C3 announced plans to expand their standards to include American Carbon Registry (ACR),[123] Climate Action Reserve (CAR),[124] and Plan Vivo.[125]

The C3 bridge is created as a permissionless protocol, meaning it is open for everyone to create VCC tokens, but to do so, they need to retire their VCCs in the first place. To avoid double-counting, each minted NFT receives a unique hash that corresponds to the metadata of the retired VCC. These, again, get fractionalised into ERC-20 tokens, becoming fungible. These tokens are then aggregated into one of C3's carbon pools, categorised by their VCC's underlying methodology, either in the 'Universal Basic Offset Pool' (UBO Pool) or in the 'Nature-Based Offset Pool' (NBO Pool). A further pool, the 'Afforestation and Restoration-based Offsets' (ARBO Pool), is scheduled for launch in the future, according to C3.

It is noteworthy that UBO or NBO tokens that exit the bridge are fully fungible and can be further traded by their holders. An important difference between C3's and Toucan's bridge for CHAR is that, in the case of C3, VCCs need to be retired before they can be submitted to the bridge. This is reminiscent of Toucan's first attempt at a carbon bridge.[126]

A further token, the C3 token, is utilised for governance, fees, and growth incentives, with further utility implementations planned in the future. These can be obtained through bridging, staking, and providing liquidity. As these C3 tokens do not directly relate to VCCs, except for being obtained through specific actions related to VCC tokens, they fall outside the scope of our analysis.

IV Coorest

Coorest OÜ, a company founded in Estonia in 2021, claims to have created the 'first certified standard for blockchain-based CO_2 compensation powered by smart contracts and satellite data'—the Coorest Carbon Standard (CCS). Projects eligible under the CCS are able to generate '$CCO2 tokens' ($CCO2) or 'NFTrees' according to their additional activities that sequester CO_2e. These tokens can be traded in a decentralised application on the Polygon blockchain, which is monitored by Coorest.[127]

There are two different kinds of NFTrees that can be purchased from Coorest. As the name suggests, these tokens are NFTs connected to specific trees. The underlying trees may be fruit-bearing or not. Upon planting of the actual trees, the connected NFTrees commence the minting of $CCO2, equivalent to the calculated amount of CO_2e sequestered by the respective tree in accordance with the standards and methodologies established by Coorest. Fruit-bearing trees possess an additional function in that the holder receives a proportionate compensation for the fruits of the trees linked to their NFTrees. However, these remunerations are not part of the present analysis due to them being unrelated to VCC tokens.[128]

The $CCO2 earned from NFTrees can be held, transferred, or burned by their holders, with each crypto-asset representing one kilogram of CO2e sequestered by real-world trees. Claims of carbon neutrality through compensation can only be substantiated through their on-chain burning. Subsequent to the burning of $CCO2, an NFT in accordance with the ERC-721 standard is minted and transferred to the wallet of the entity that performed the burn. The burning process serves as a proof of carbon compensation, resulting in the creation of a certificate (Proof of Carbon Compensation; PoCC) that contains data pertaining to the reason for compensation, the amount, the date, and the name of the entity responsible for the burning given by the holder burning the $CCO2.

In contrast to the aforementioned three on-chain tokens, which are related to traditional and non-digital VCCs, Coorest offers several on-chain tokens that do not share this characteristic. Instead, they function through a process of bridging real-world trees, facilitating the creation of native VCC tokens. It is noteworthy that all of the aforementioned tokens issued by Coorest can be regarded as VCC tokens, as they each represent a distinct phase in the lifecycle of a VCC.[129]

C Placing the use cases within the context of the relevant legislation

I CHAR

As Toucan has articulated, CHARs are voucher-like tokens and thus can act as utility tokens according to MiCAR. CHARs have to be linked to project-related TCO2 and these again have to be linked to certain VCCs.

The exemption of both the TCO2 tokens and their underlying VCCs from Title II MiCAR can be granted under Art. 4(3)(c) MiCAR, provided that the TCO2 tokens and their underlying VCCs are regarded as 'goods and services that exist or are in operation'. The definition of a VCC is pivotal in determining this status. If the TCO2 token is classified as a good or service that exists or is in operation, CHARs could be exempted from Title II MiCAR. Consequently, this would exempt Toucan from drafting and notifying a crypto-asset white paper. Negating any characteristics of this exemption from MiCAR would lead to the categorisation of CHARs as other tokens subjected to Title II MiCAR.

The question remains, however, whether the dynamic nature of the TCO2 pool, which undergoes changes with each deposit, affects the existence or operational status of the underlying assets or services of CHARs. If this can be negated or affirmed, it would be crucial to determine whether CHARs and TCO2 tokens would be obliged to comply with Title II MiCAR. It can be deduced that if the TCO2 inventory is altered, the value of the TCO2 tokens and, consequently, the value of specific CHARs will fluctuate. This fluctuation would suggest that the underlying goods or services of the CHAR cannot be defined as existing or operational, and a white paper would be required. This is further dependent on the functioning of the 'Pool Health Fee', which regulates the inventory of the pool. In any case, further elaboration of the fee is necessary, which in turn highlights the need for additional information from the purchaser.

In addition to their resemblance to vouchers, these tokens could be exempted by Art. 4(3)(d) MiCAR, on the basis that the burning process (the original destiny of these tokens) can only be performed within the limited network of Toucan in conjunction with the Puro.earth registry, another merchant in Toucan's contractual network. It cannot be performed elsewhere, for example, through the use of different services or applications on other blockchains, or even outside of the technical layer. This again can lead to the exemption from Title II MiCAR.

Art. 4(4) MiCAR can act as an exemption from the exemptions when the offeror communicates any thoughts of admitting their tokens into trading, consequently making CHARs subject to Title II once again. Toucan's promotion of CHARs as 'the first liquid market for biochar credits'[130] and their availability for trading on Uniswap, a prominent decentralised exchange, appears to endorse Art. 4(4) MiCAR, thereby rendering Title II MiCAR applicable again. In order to be compliant with it, Toucan must fulfil the requirements set out in Art. 4 and 5 MiCAR, namely the creation, notification, and publication of a white paper (and marketing communications) in accordance with Art. 6–9, 12, and 15 MiCAR. Furthermore, Toucan is obliged to fulfil all other obligations stipulated in Title II and Title V MiCAR regarding the crypto-asset services they are offering.

Non-fungibility of TCO2 according to MiCAR should not be a cause for concern, as these tokens can be readily pooled and made fungible, not falling within the narrow scope of non-fungibility of MiCAR.

In accordance with US security law, CHARs are expected to fail the Howey test, as they are not acquired with the primary objective of profit (third prong). However, this dynamic may shift as the market gains traction, the value of CHARs and their underlying VCCs increases over time, and their supply does not meet demand. The precise outcome of the Howey test by the SEC is unclear. Nonetheless, there is a possibility that the market's future growth may categorise the purchase of CHAR as an investment contract.

The remaining prongs of the test are expected to hold, given the necessity of purchasing CHARs (first prong) and the subsequent pooling of funds into a common enterprise to remunerate project developers (second prong), with any profit incentive derived from the performance of others (fourth prong). However, given the Howey test's dynamic and ambiguous nature, resulting in a wide margin for interpretation, it remains challenging to make a conclusive statement.

Given the capacity of CHARs to be traded similarly to other crypto-assets that fall under the remit of commodity laws, it is conceivable that they could be regarded as commodities. In the event that CHARs were considered securities, Toucan would be required to register with the SEC and comply with their regulatory jurisdiction. However, this would not be necessary if CHARs were only classified as commodities due to the absence of regulatory oversight over spot markets for commodities by the CFTC.[131] This would again change if the CFTC were to conclude CHAR to be a derivative of a VCC (a commodity).

In the UK, the conditions for the applicability of security regulations are more narrowly defined. Therefore, CHARs should not fall under the FSMA 2000, as they are not used in a specified investment according to Part III of the RAO. This can only be derived from an investment character akin to one described in the list, which is up for interpretation to some extent. However, this should not be the case with CHARs. Nevertheless, it is conceivable that they could be classified as qualifying crypto-assets under the FPO, which would necessitate Toucan's adherence to promotional laws due to their fungibility and tradability.

Section 26F(2)(e) of Schedule 1 to the FPO functions analogously to the exemption of specific utility tokens traded within a restricted network of the issuer as set out in MiCAR. This suggests the potential for promotions of CHARs to be exempt from the promotional guidelines stipulated by the FPO. The latter would apply, for example, if CHARs were to be exclusively available for sale and use within the issuer's network. Even if they could only be redeemed and utilised within the Toucan interface, they could still be traded outside of the offeror's network. Consequently, the exemption would not apply, and Toucan would be obliged to adhere to promotional laws when advertising their CHARs in the UK.

II Nori Regenerative Tonne and NORI

As NRTs demonstrated a considerable similarity to CHARs, albeit with an alternative focus on other VCCs, the majority of the observations previously made can also be applied in this context. The primary distinction is that the tokens became untradeable following their acquisition. The exemption (from the exemptions) set out in Art. 4(4) MiCAR would not apply in such a case, as the NRTs in question were not designed for further trading, and the offeror did not make any statements indicating their intention to seek admission to trading them (simply because they are no longer tradeable). The plausibility of considering NRTs as utility tokens exempt from Title II MiCAR is considerably higher than that of CHARs. Negating their nature as utility tokens leads to NRTs being considered as an other crypto-asset subject to Title II MiCAR.

The existence of a market is questionable, as the NRTs were distributed to the project developers (or farmers in this case), which can be defined as the primary market. The farmers could simply retire their crypto-assets for themselves, if they wanted to. The secondary market would then be constituted by transactions between purchasers and NRT-holders.[132] It is possible that the primary market would already fall within Art. 4(4) MiCAR.

In the context of MiCAR, the concept of non-fungibility is not applicable, as the diverse tokenised activities, in accordance with Nori's standards and methodologies, can be integrated within the framework of NRTs, thereby resulting in fungibility.

Again—considering the limits of the exemptions of Art. 4(3) MiCAR—NRTs could have been utility tokens exempted from Title II MiCAR or other crypto-assets subject to Title II MiCAR. In both cases, Nori would act as a CASP, thus being subject to Title V MiCAR.

The Howey test, which posits an expectation of profit, would have likely failed in this case, as the NRTs were not tradable and thus no profit could be attained. In their primary market, these tokens were not purchased but traded for CO_2e-sequestration actions. This is not a direct purchase, but rather a trade, and yet it could still have been considered as an 'investment of money' as defined by the Howey test.[133] Further prongs of the Howey test are difficult to assess, as Nori Inc. ceased their services and there is a lack of information on how project developers sold their NRTs to individuals. According to US law, NRTs could have also been classified as a commodity since tradability is not explicitly stipulated as a prerequisite by the CEA.

The absence of any indication that the NRTs constituted a specified investment prevented them from falling within the purview of the FSMA 2000. As they were crypto-assets, it is possible that they could have fallen under the scope of the FPO; however, as previously mentioned, they lacked the essential characteristic of tradability. According to 26F(1)(a) to Schedule 1 FPO, they would not have qualified as crypto-assets needing promotional regulation, thus the promotional laws of the UK would not have been applicable to NRTs.

The intention of Nori founder Paul Gambill was to establish a carbon trading system, and therefore it is evident that the NORI tokens should have been created as a means of making NRTs tradable.[134] This would result in an analysis analogous to that of CHAR tokens. It is stated that one NORI token would have been equivalent to one unit of the NRT pool. This would have resulted in the tokens being considered tradable and fungible. The evaluation according to UK legislation would have been comparable to that of CHAR.

III UBO and NBO tokens

It is evident that UBO and NBO tokens are fundamentally similar in nature. Both of these concepts rely on a traditional and non-digital VCC and the retirement is a prerequisite for tokenisation. The distinguishing factor between these tokens is the underlying methodologies employed. This analysis will adopt a similar approach for both of these crypto-assets.

The fundamental distinction between these VCC tokens and the other use cases lies in the prerequisite for the creation of a UBO/NBO token, which necessitates the retirement of the underlying VCC. In the aforementioned cases, the VCC is retired with the token (either linked or blockchain-native). This modification to the narrative is marginal, yet it contributes to the delineation of an existing good or service in operation underlying these tokens.

As previously mentioned, the linkage between a traditional VCC and its tokenised counterpart is flexible; the retirement of the former on the traditional registry helps the link to become more static, thus underpinning the definition of utility tokens. Again, negating this leads to the conclusion that a UBO/NBO token is an other crypto-asset according to MiCAR. However, it should be noted that, given the intention of UBO/NBO tokens to be traded further, any exemption does not apply according to Art. 4(4) MiCAR. The fungibility of these VCC tokens is facilitated by their reasonable pooling, which aligns with the principles outlined in MiCAR. It is therefore reasonable to conclude that UBO and NBO tokens should both fall under the regulatory scope Title II MiCAR and C3 tokens under the regulatory scope of Title V MiCAR regarding their offered services.

In the context of the two VCC tokens, the Howey test is expected to be unsuccessful on two grounds: The expectation of profit and the reliance on the work of others. Even if the profit-seeking characteristic could be confirmed, the profit should not be reliant on the work of others, as their underlying VCCs are already retired. The value of these tokens is no longer dependent on the actions of the underlying VCCs (e.g., the maintenance of tree farms or the prevention of reversals) or on the integrity of the registry. Consequently, it can be deduced that these tokens would likely fail the Howey test. However, if the maintenance of the utilised blockchain is considered a prerequisite for this prong to be met, the Howey test itself could be deemed satisfactory, thereby classifying UBO and NBO tokens as securities. Furthermore, they could be regarded as commodities, akin to other crypto-assets.

Given the unlikelihood of being designated as an investment, comparable to other analysed crypto-assets, and the additional point of their value-creating underlying VCC being retired upon their creation, UBO and NBO tokens should not be subject to the FSMA 2000. As tradable and fungible crypto-assets, they are subject to regulation by promotional laws according to the FPO.

IV $CCO2, NFTrees and PoCC

The three crypto-assets established by Coorest are all distinctly different, as are the conclusions that can be drawn from them. This analysis will primarily focus on the $CCO2 token, which is most analogous to the other tokens analysed, while the NFTrees allow for interesting insights. While these tokens differ in the amount of CO_2e underlying them (one kilogram compared to one tonne), their main use case should not deviate too much.

Given the direct link between $CCO2 and the performance of NFTrees, it can be deduced that the latter is an underlying good or service in operation in a broader sense. The distinguishing factor is that the tree, within the context of its lifecycle, is still in a growth phase, meaning that the service is not yet complete. Conversely, the sequestered CO_2e can be considered the underlying asset of the NFTree. This complicates the application of MiCAR's definition of the 'goods existing or service in operation'. In this case, the service can either be in operation as the NFTree sequesters CO_2e, or the sequestered CO_2e can already exist as a good.[135] The exemption of Title II MiCAR is contingent upon the linked asset. This is debatable in this instance. However, given the communication of $CCO2 tokens as tradable outside of their infrastructure, the exemptions of Art. 4(3)(d) MiCAR should not apply. Consequently, the $CCO2 falls within the scope of MiCAR, either as another crypto-asset or a non-exempted utility token.

In terms of the relevant legislation in the USA and the UK, it is anticipated that the results will be analogous to those observed in the analysis of other tokens. Indeed, $CCO2 should not be regarded as an investment contract but most likely as a commodity in the USA. Furthermore, it is subject to promotional laws according to the FPO in the UK. The primary distinction between these tokens and the others discussed lies in the quantity of sequestered CO_2e, with the $CCO2 seemingly focusing on more exact offsetting.

A more intriguing analysis is that of NFTrees, which are designed to be linked to real trees at a 1:1 scale (disregarding the 10% of extra trees planted by Coorest) and are observable via satellite. This suggests that they should also be considered as non-fungible according to MiCAR, a notion further reinforced by the fact that the only fungible aspect (their output, or rather intake) is a separate token—the $CCO2. As fungibility is a necessary characteristic for the MiCAR definition, NFTrees should not be obliged to comply with MiCAR.

As the Howey test allows for a broad definition of securities, NFTrees could fall under the regulatory law for securities in the USA. Since NFTrees can be purchased using fiat or crypto-currencies, the first prong should be satisfied. The NFTrees can only fulfil their objective of generating $CCO2 if the underlying trees are maintained and cared for. This is primarily achieved through the efforts of individuals employed by or working with Coorest, who receive compensation for their services rendered in the form of the proceeds from NFTree sales. This provides a basis for a common enterprise (second prong). The expectation of profits (third prong), which has hitherto been unsuccessful for most other tokens, can be present in this case. The generated $CCO2 may be monetised through sale, potentially incentivising initial purchases of NFTrees. This phenomenon is further accentuated in the context of fruit-bearing NFTrees, whose produce can be sold for profit. This resemblance is reminiscent of the original Howey case, wherein the Howey Co. engaged in investments in citrus grove development. Coorest themselves have stated that these fruit-bearing trees recoup their purchase price in profits in about five years.[136] Furthermore, these profits primarily rely on others (fourth prong), as Coorest must meticulously oversee, nurture, and maintain their trees to ensure the generation of these returns.

The Howey test, as subjective as it may be, can be fulfilled for NFTrees. This would classify them as securities within the US regulatory system. The method of sale, which is analogous to an ICO, further reinforces this. As ICOs are frequently regarded as security offerings, their security-like character is accentuated, although further trading can mitigate this for some crypto-assets.[137] Consequently, Coorest would be required to register and obtain approval in the USA to sell their NFTrees under the oversight of the SEC.

By contrast, the regulatory framework in the UK is comparatively less extensive, resulting in NFTrees not being classified as specified investments. They are not subject to the FSMA 2000, and due to their non-fungible nature, the promotional laws do not apply to them.

As Proofs of Carbon Compensations (PoCCs) are the certificates of burned $CCO2, they could also be considered as VCC tokens. PoCCs are the crypto-assets that enable individuals and companies to claim and display their offsetting activities, and they encase means to ensure that $CCO2 cannot be double-counted and used more than once. The fungibility of PoCCs is obstructed by the specific information exhibited and hashed into the tokens. As they possess no inherent value other than a certificate that a specific entity has offset a certain amount of CO2e at a certain time, their fungibility is missing. This should hold for MiCAR's standard of non-fungibility. Thus, MiCAR should not be applicable to PoCCs according to Art. 2(3) MiCAR.

The Howey test should once again fail on the grounds that the PoCCs are not purchasable. Indeed, they can only be created by burning amounts of $CCO2. Thus, the first prong, namely the fulfilment of the requirement, should not be met. This assertion can be discussed further, as the burning of $CCO2 for the PoCC to be created can also be regarded as an investment of money in a broader sense. If the PoCCs' creation by the underlying blockchain can be regarded as constituting a common enterprise, the expectation of attaining profit cannot be satisfied. PoCCs should not be declared as securities, even with their restricted fungibility, but they could still be considered commodities.

PoCCs are not used in specified investments, so any expectations of them being regulated should not be met. Due to their missing fungibility, they are also not required to comply with promotional laws in the UK.

D Conclusion and outlook

At least the EU regulatory framework, as outlined by MiCAR, appears to explicitly encompass all VCC tokens that have been examined by us. Discrepancies in terms of fungibility, token classification, and use cases do not allow for a general circumvention of the regulatory scope of MiCAR. While it is still possible to create VCC tokens in a manner that avoids MiCAR's regulatory scope at least partially, doing so would alter their use cases to such an extent that a regulatory framework would no longer be necessary. MiCAR's exemption from its exemptions has far-reaching implications for all tradeable crypto-assets, a category that should encompass nearly all VCC tokens on the market. The absence of a clear definition of what constitutes a traditional and non-digital VCC means that their tokenised versions can be classified as either other crypto-assets or, in some cases, utility tokens. The final categorisation relies on the nature of the underlying VCC—either as a good, a service, a right, a claim, or merely as evidence for the expenditure of money for climate action taken by another party. Furthermore, all services offered by the legal persons in these use cases fall under one or more of the crypto-asset services regulated by Title V MiCAR.

The regulatory frameworks of the USA and the UK that do not directly regulate VCC tokens, but rather employ a dynamic analysis of the underlying action, seem to leverage regulatory uncertainty. A less stringent regulatory framework may facilitate the scaling of the VCM—regulatory uncertainty definitely will not. EU Member States, such as Germany, are obligated to implement MiCAR by modifying national regulatory frameworks, notably laws concerning financial instruments, which have the potential to over-regulate the creation of tokens. For instance, the implementation of KMAG in Germany appears to underestimate the significance of the main classification of other crypto-assets in a manner that is not consistent with MiCAR.

Legislation pertaining to the VCM and VCCs around the world has emphasised the importance of having a compatible regulatory framework on a global scale. Many of these attempts require clear and transparent documentation of any kind of offsetting. MiCAR can help by requiring standardised and fair white papers for VCC tokens and binding CASPs to enact fair measures. Furthermore, MiCAR and its improvement of regulatory stability can offer a paradigm for a comprehensive regulation of crypto-assets in general and VCC tokens in particular. Regulatory certainty will facilitate the evolution of the VCM, a process that will be further advanced by policymakers and participants developing blockchain-based approaches to VCCs. A potential outcome of such developments could be the creation of best practices, which may then be evaluated by more dynamic approaches. This is further underlined by the regulatory changes in progress, such as the bills introduced in the USA and the MARC and A&D regimes in the UK. These changes will help to make the regulatory frameworks in both countries more reliable.

The pursuit of technological solutions to existing problems, in addition to the fulfilment of net-zero goals and climate ambitions, which are imperative in combating climate change, is hindered by regulatory uncertainties. The classification of existing VCC tokens within existing frameworks demonstrates the efficacy of MiCAR in combating such uncertainties by providing an encompassing category of other crypto-assets in Title II. Subsequent steps will include the acceleration of participants' involvement in and acceptance of blockchain-based technologies, thereby fostering their participation in the market expansion. The transfer of 'good' VCCs can be facilitated with fewer intermediaries than is the case with conventional VCCs, due to the main features of decentralisation through tokenisation. Ensuring the quality of underlying VCCs is a separate issue that must be addressed at its roots. As long as there are at least some VCCs that can be regarded as high quality, it would be a valid step in the positive development of the VCM to ensure their quality and mitigate the risk of double-counting through the use of tokenisation.

Notes

1 Directive 2004/39/EC of the European Parliament and of the Council of 21 April 2004 on markets in financial instruments amending Council Directives 85/611/EEC and 93/6/EEC and Directive 2000/12/EC of the European Parliament and of the Council and repealing Council Directive 93/22/EEC.
2 Directive 2014/65/EU of the European Parliament and of the Council of 15 May 2014 on markets in financial instruments and amending Directive 2002/92/EC and Directive 2011/61/EU (recast).
3 MiFID II is closely connected to the Regulation (EU) 2017/1129 of the European Parliament and of the Council of 14 June 2017 on the prospectus to be published when securities are offered to the public or admitted to trading on a regulated market, and repealing Directive 2003/71/EC (Prospectus Regulation) and the Regulation (EU) No 596/2014 of the European Parliament and of the Council of 16 April 2014 on market abuse (market abuse regulation) and repealing Directive 2003/7/EC of the European Parliament and of the Council and Commission Directives 2003/124/EC, 2003/125/EC and 2004/72/EC (Market Abuse Regulation).
4 Directive (EU) 2023/959 of the European Parliament and of the Council of 10 May 2023 amending Directive 2003/87/EC establishing a system for greenhouse gas emission allowance trading within the Union and Decision (EU) 2015/1814 concerning the establishment and operation of a market stability reserve for the Union greenhouse gas emission trading system.
5 Susanne Kalss and Fabian Aubrunner in Susanne Kalss, Christoph Krönke and Oliver Völkel (eds), *Crypto-Assets* (C. H. Beck 2024), Art. 4 MiFID II para 31–32.
6 European Commission, 'Ensuring the integrity of the European carbon market' (2020) https://climate.ec.europa.eu/eu-action/eu-emissions-trading-system-eu-ets/ensuring-integrity-european-carbon-market_en accessed 31 January 2025.
7 Cf Carsten Mueller and Leah Kling, 'Tokenising the Voluntary Carbon Credit Market: Harnessing Opportunities for Sustainable Development' in this book.
8 Dimitrios Linardatos, 'Finanzinstrumente im Digitalzeitalter – Teil II -' [2024], WM Zeitschrift für Wirtschafts- und Bankrecht 1685, 1689.
9 For more definitions of derivatives in MiFID II, cf Susanne Kalss and Fabian Aubrunner, in Susanne Kalss, Christoph Krönke and Oliver Völkel (eds), *Crypto-Assets* (C. H. Beck 2024), Art. 4 MiFID II para 28.
10 Cf Thorsten Voß, 'Non-fungible Token auf CO_2-Zertifikate – Eine kapitalmarkt- und aufsichtsrechtliche Einordnung' [2022], BKR 620; Dimitrios Linardatos, 'Finanzinstrumente im Digitalzeitalter – Teil

I -' [2024], WM, 1633; Linardatos, 'Finanzinstrumente im Digitalzeitalter – Teil II -' [2024], WM Zeitschrift für Wirtschafts- und Bankrecht 1685, 1689; Susanne Kalss and Fabian Aubrunner, in Susanne Kalss, Christoph Krönke and Oliver Völkel (eds), *Crypto-Assets* (C. H.Beck 2024), Art. 4 MiFID II para 38–42.

11 Susanne Kalss and Fabian Aubrunner, in Susanne Kalss, Christoph Krönke and Oliver Völkel (eds), *Crypto-Assets* (C. H. Beck 2024), Vor MiFID II para 22.

12 See also Sebastian Böhning and Dominik Skauradszun, 'VCC Tokens' Civil Law – Ownership, Transfer and Liability under Union and German Law' in this book.

13 Oliver Völkel in Susanne Kalss, Christoph Krönke and Oliver Völkel (eds), *Crypto-Assets* (C. H. Beck 2024), Art. 3 MiCAR para 23–24.

14 Especially considering Art. 3(8) MiCAR, see Matthias Lehmann in Susanne Kalss, Christoph Krönke and Oliver Völkel (eds), *Crypto-Assets* (C. H. Beck 2024), Art. 3 MiCAR para 65.

15 Oliver Völkel in Susanne Kalss, Christoph Krönke and Oliver Völkel (eds), *Crypto-Assets* (C. H. Beck 2024), Art. 3 MiCAR para 41–44.

16 Philipp Maume, 'Die Verordnung über Märkte für Kryptowerte (MiCAR) – Zentrale Definitionen sowie Rechte und Pflichten beim öffentlichen Angebot von Kryptowerten' [2022], RDi 461, 464.

17 These are not legally defined but mentioned under Title II MiCAR.

18 Christopher Rennig in Susanne Kalss, Christoph Krönke and Oliver Völkel (eds), *Crypto-Assets* (C. H. Beck 2024), Art. 4 MiCAR para 2.

19 Philipp Maume and Alireza Siadat, 'Struktur, Definitionen und Anwendungsfälle der Kryptoregulierung' [2023], NJW Neue Juristische Wochenschrift 1168; Susanne Kalss and Fabian Aubrunner in Susanne Kalss, Christoph Krönke and Oliver Völkel (eds), *Crypto-Assets* (C. H. Beck 2024), Art. 4 MiFID II para 34.

20 Principle 2 No 1 of the draft UNIDROIT Principles on the Legal Nature of Verified Carbon Credits; UNIDROIT Working Group on the Legal Nature of Voluntary Carbon Credits, Summary Report of the Second Session, Study LXXXVI – W.G.2 – Doc. 3 rev. (June 2024), 23 https://www.unidroit.org/wp-content/uploads/2024/07/Study-LXXXVI-W.G.2-Doc.-3-rev.-Summary-Report.pdf accessed 31 January 2025; for further discussion about claims established by VCCs and VCC tokens, see Sebastian Böhning and Dominik Skauradszun, 'VCC Tokens' Civil Law – Ownership, Transfer and Liability under Union and German Law' in this book.

21 E.g., Singapore allows to offset up to 5% of taxable emissions with high-quality international carbon credits, see National Climate Change Secretariat Singapore, 'Carbon Tax' (2023) https://www.nccs.gov.sg/singapores-climate-action/mitigation-efforts/carbontax/ accessed 31 January 2025.

22 Oliver Völkel in Susanne Kalss, Christoph Krönke and Oliver Völkel (eds), *Crypto-Assets* (C. H. Beck 2024), Art. 3 MiCAR para 75.

23 Oliver Völkel in Susanne Kalss, Christoph Krönke and Oliver Völkel (eds), *Crypto-Assets* (C. H. Beck 2024), Art. 3 MiCAR para 74.

24 European Securities and Markets Authority, 'Final Report – Guidelines on the conditions and criteria for the qualification of crypto-assets as financial instruments' (2024).

25 In accordance with Art. 2(1) of Regulation (EU) 2017/2402 of the European Parliament and of the Council of 12 December 2017 laying down a general framework for securitisation and creating a specific framework for simple, transparent and standardised securitisation, and amending Directives 2009/65/EC, 2009/138/EC and 2011/61/EU and Regulations (EC) No 1060/2009 and (EU) No 648/2012.

26 Annexes I and II to Directive 2009/138/EC of the European Parliament and of the Council of 25 November 2009 on the taking-up and pursuit of the business of Insurance and Reinsurance (Solvency II) (recast).

27 In accordance with Directive (EU) 2016/2341 of the European Parliament and of the Council of 14 December 2016 on the activities and supervision of institutions for occupational retirement provision (IORPs) (recast), Directive 2009/138/EC (Solvency II Directive) or Art. 2(2) of Regulation (EU) 2019/1238 of the European Parliament and of the Council of 20 June 2019 on a pan-European Personal Pension Product (PEPP).

28 In accordance with Regulation (EC) No 883/2004 of the European Parliament and of the Council of 29 April 2004 on the coordination of social security systems and Regulation (EC) No 987/2009 of the European Parliament and of the Council of 16 September 2009 laying down the procedure for implementing Regulation (EC) 833/2004 on the coordination of social security systems.

29 Further regulation concerning 'real' NFTs can still follow as the EU still sees their importance, according to Georg Lorenz, 'MiCAR – Markets in Crypto-Assets Regulation' [2024], ZIP Zeitschrift für Wirtschaftsrecht 58, 66.

30 Philipp Maume, 'Die Verordnung über Märkte für Kryptowerte (MiCAR) – Zentrale Definitionen sowie Rechte und Pflichten beim öffentlichen Angebot von Kryptowerten' [2022], RDi 461, 465; Philipp Maume, 'The Regulation on Markets in Crypto-Assets (MiCAR): Landmark Codification, or First Step of Many, or Both?' [2023], ECFR European Company and Financial Law Review 243, 259.

31 Cf Ben-Benedict Hruby in Susanne Kalss, Christoph Krönke and Oliver Völkel (eds), *Crypto-Assets* (C. H. Beck 2024), Art. 2 MiCAR para 36–39.

32 Jiehong Lou, Nathan Hultman, Anand Patwardhan and Yueming Qiu, 'Integrating sustainability into climate finance by quantifying the co-benefits and market impact of carbon projects', (2022) communications earth & environment 3:137 https://www.nature.com/commsenv accessed 31 January 2025; Jiehong Lou, Nathan Hultman, Anand Patwardhan and Irving Mintzer, 'Corporate motivations and co-benefit valuation in private climate finance investments through voluntary carbon markets' (2023) npj Climate Action 2:32 https://www.nature.com/npjclimataction/ accessed 31 January 2025; Groom and Venmans, 'The social value of offsets' [2023], Nature 768; Leho Tedersoo and others, 'Towards a co-crediting system for carbon and biodiversity' [2024], PPP Plants People Planet 6, 18.

33 European Securities and Markets Authority, 'Final Report – Guidelines on the conditions and criteria for the qualification of crypto-assets as financial instruments' (2024) Guideline 8.

34 Philipp Maume, 'Die Verordnung über Märkte für Kryptowerte (MiCAR) – Zentrale Definitionen sowie Rechte und Pflichten beim öffentlichen Angebot von Kryptowerten' [2022], RDi 461, 465.

35 Alireza Siadat, 'Markets in Crypto Assets Regulation – erster Einblick mit Schwerpunktsetzung auf Finanzinstrumente' [2021], RdF Recht der Finanzinstrumente 12, 17.

36 For more details regarding Art. 4(2) MiCAR see Christopher Rennig in Susanne Kalss, Christoph Krönke and Oliver Völkel (eds), *Crypto-Assets* (C. H. Beck 2024), Art. 4 MiCAR para 15–25.

37 Philipp Maume, 'The Regulation on Markets in Crypto-Assets (MiCAR): Landmark Codification, or First Step of Many, or Both?' [2023], ECFR 243, 263.

38 For more details regarding the bridging of VCCs see Carsten Mueller and Leah Kling, 'Tokenising the Voluntary Carbon Credit Market: Harnessing Opportunities for Sustainable Development' in this book.

39 Alireza Siadat, 'Regulierte Finanzinstrumente mit Schwerpunktsetzung auf NFT' [2023], RdF 4, 9; for a more critical view, see Sebastian Böhning and Dominik Skauradszun, 'VCC Tokens' Civil Law – Ownership, Transfer and Liability under Union and German Law' in this book.

40 Philipp Maume, 'Die Verordnung über Märkte für Kryptowerte (MiCAR) – Zentrale Definitionen sowie Rechte und Pflichten beim öffentlichen Angebot von Kryptowerten' [2022], RDi 461, 464.

41 For more considerations regarding tradability, see Georg von Wangenheim and Leon Krug, 'VCCs Tokenisation and the EU CBAM: Some Microeconomics of VCCs' in this book.

42 According to the Prospectus Regulation.

43 Christopher Rennig in Susanne Kalss, Christoph Krönke and Oliver Völkel (eds), *Crypto-Assets* (C. H. Beck 2024), Art. 6 MiCAR para 3.

44 Petra Buck-Heeb, 'Whitepaper-Haftung nach MiCAR' [2023], BKR Zeitschrift für Bank und Kapitalmarktrecht 689, 690.

45 European Securities and Markets Authority, 'MiCA white papers PoC' (2024), https://www.esma.europa.eu/document/mica-white-papers-poc accessed 31 January 2025.
46 For counterintuitive incentives to buy VCCs and VCC tokens, see Georg von Wangenheim and Leon Krug, 'VCCs, Tokenisation and the EU CBAM: Some Microeconomics of VCCs' in this book.
47 Christopher Rennig in Susanne Kalss, Christoph Krönke and Oliver Völkel (eds), *Crypto-Assets* (C. H. Beck 2024), Art. 15 MiCAR para 13.
48 Petra Buck-Heeb, 'Whitepaper-Haftung nach MiCAR' (2023), BKR 689, 695.
49 Philipp Maume, 'The Regulation on Markets in Crypto-Assets (MiCAR): Landmark Codification, or First Step of Many, or Both?' (2023), ECFR 243, 264; Christopher Rennig in Susanne Kalss, Christoph Krönke and Oliver Völkel (eds), *Crypto-Assets* (C. H. Beck 2024), Art. 15 MiCAR para 7.
50 Philipp Maume, 'Die Verordnung über Märkte für Kryptowerte (MiCAR) – Zentrale Definitionen sowie Rechte und Pflichten beim öffentlichen Angebot von Kryptowerten' (2022), RDi 461, 468.
51 Dominik Skauradszun, Selina Schweizer and Jeremias Kümpel, 'Das Kryptoverwahrgeschäft und der insolvenzrechtliche Rang der Kunden – Aussonderung oder Insolvenzquote' (2022), ZIP 2101, 2113.
52 Renate Prinz, Annabelle Rau and Oliver Völkel in Susanne Kalss, Christoph Krönke and Oliver Völkel (eds), *Crypto-Assets* (C. H. Beck 2024), Vor Art. 75 ff. MiCAR para. 3.
53 Oliver Völkel in Susanne Kalss, Christoph Krönke and Oliver Völkel (eds), *Crypto-Assets* (C. H. Beck 2024), Art. 3 MiCAR para 128–132.
54 European Securities and Markets Authority, 'Final Report – Draft Technical Standards specifying certain requirements of the Markets in Crypto Assets Regulation (MiCA) – second package' (2024).
55 For a more detailed discussion of the information asymmetry problems, see Georg von Wangenheim and Leon Krug, 'VCCs, Tokenisation and the EU CBAM: Some Microeconomics of VCCs' in this book.
56 Oliver Völkel in Susanne Kalss, Christoph Krönke and Oliver Völkel (eds), *Crypto-Assets* (C. H. Beck 2024), Art. 80 MiCAR para 4.
57 Philipp Ley in Susanne Kalss, Christoph Krönke and Oliver Völkel (eds), *Crypto-Assets* (C. H. Beck 2024), Art. 81 MiCAR para 2–3.
58 Philipp Ley in Susanne Kalss, Christoph Krönke and Oliver Völkel (eds), *Crypto-Assets* (C. H. Beck 2024), Art. 81 MiCAR para 5.
59 Oliver Völkel in Susanne Kalss, Christoph Krönke and Oliver Völkel (eds), *Crypto-Assets* (C. H. Beck 2024), Art. 82 MiCAR para 4.
60 European Securities and Markets Authority, 'Final Report – Guidelines specifying certain requirements of the Markets in Crypto Assets Regulation (MiCA) on investor protection – third package' (2024).
61 Directive (EU) 2022/2464 of the European Parliament and of the Council of 14 December 2022 amending Regulation (EU) No 537/2014, Directive 2004/109/EC, Directive 2006/43/EC and Directive 2013/34/EU, as regards corporate sustainability reporting.
62 Directive (EU) 2024/825 of the European Parliament and of the Council of 28 February 2024 amending Directives 2005/29/EC and 2011/83/EU as regards empowering consumers for the green transition through better protection against unfair practices and through better information.
63 Directive 2013/34/EU of the European Parliament and of the Council of 26 June 2013 on the annual financial statements, consolidated financial statements and related reports of certain types of undertakings, amending Directive 2006/43/EC of the European Parliament and of the Council and repealing Council Directives 78/660/EEC and 83/349/EEC (Accounting Directive).
64 Commission Delegated Regulation (EU) 2023/2772 of 31 July 2023 supplementing Directive 2013/34/EU of the European Parliament and of the Council as regards sustainability reporting standards.
65 Directive 2005/29/EC of the European Parliament and of the Council of 11 May 2005 concerning unfair business-to-consumer commercial practices in the internal market and amending Council Direc-

tive 84/450/EEC, Directives 97/7/EC, 98/27/EC and 2002/65/EC of the European Parliament and of the Council and Regulation (EC) No 2006/2004 of the European Parliament and of the Council.
66 Proposal for a Directive of the European Parliament and of the Council on substantiation and communication of explicit environmental claims (Green Claims Directive), COM(2023) 166 final (22.3.2023).
67 Regulation (EU) 2024/3012 of the European Parliament and of the Council of 27 November 2024 establishing a Union certification framework for permanent carbon removals, carbon farming and carbon storage in products.
68 For the evaluation on using VCCs for the EU CBAM, see Georg von Wangenheim and Leon Krug, 'VCCs, Tokenisation and the EU CBAM: Some Microeconomics of VCCs' in this book.
69 Program on International Financial Systems, 'A Review of Cryptoasset Market Structure and Regulation in the United States' (2023).
70 *SEC v Howey Co.* [1946] 328 U.S. 293, https://supreme.justia.com/cases/federal/us/328/293/ accessed 31 January 2025.
71 Cf U.S. Securities and Exchange Commission, 'Framework for 'Investment Contract' Analysis of Digital Assets' (2024), https://www.sec.gov/about/divisions-offices/division-corporation-finance/framework-investment-contract-analysis-digital-assets accessed 31 January 2025.
72 Program on International Financial Systems, 'A Review of Cryptoasset Market Structure and Regulation in the United States' (2023).
73 *CFTC v Coinflip Inc., d/b/a Derivabit, and Francisco Rioardan* [2015] CFTC Docket No 15–29; Commodity Futures Trading Commission, 'Digital Assets' (2024), https://www.cftc.gov/digitalassets/index.htm accessed 31 January 2025.
74 Program on International Financial Systems, 'A Review of Cryptoasset Market Structure and Regulation in the United States' (2023).
75 *CFTC v CQC Impact Investors LLC* [2024], CFTC Docket No 24–37; Congressional Research Service, 'Voluntary Carbon Credit Markets and the Commodity Futures Trading Commission' (2024), https://crsreports.congress.gov/product/pdf/R/R48095 accessed 31 January 2025.
76 Federal Register, 'Commission Guidance Regarding the Listing of Voluntary Carbon Credit Derivative Contracts' (2024), https://www.federalregister.gov/documents/2024/10/15/2024-23105/commission-guidance-regarding-the-listing-of-voluntary-carbon-credit-derivative-contracts accessed 31 January 2025.
77 Program on International Financial Systems, 'A Review of Cryptoasset Market Structure and Regulation in the United States' (2023); Program on International Financial Systems, 'Implementing an Effective Cryptoasset Regulatory Framework in the United States' (2024).
78 Digital Commodities Consumer Protection Act of 2022.
79 Luummis-Gillibrand Responsible Financial Innovation Act of 2023.
80 Financial Innovation and Technology for the 21st Century Act of 2023.
81 *SEC v Ripple Labs, Inc., Bradley Garlinghouse, and Christian A. Larsen* [2024] 20 Civ. 10832 (AT).
82 Program on International Financial Systems, 'Implementing an Effective Cryptoasset Regulatory Framework in the United States' (2024).
83 US Government, 'Voluntary Carbon Markets Joint Policy Statement and Principles' (2024).
84 Financial Conduct Authority, 'Guidance on Cryptoassets – Feedback and Final Guidance to CP 19/3' (2019).
85 HM Treasury, 'Future financial services regulatory regime for cryptoassets – Consultation and call for evidence' (2023); HM Treasury, 'Future financial services regulatory framework for cryptoassets – Response to the consultation and call for evidence' (2023).
86 Financial Conduct Authority, 'Financial promotion rules for cryptoassets – Policy Statement PS23/6' (2023).
87 Financial Conduct Authority, 'Financial promotion rules for cryptoassets – Policy Statement PS23/6' (2023).

88 Financial Conduct Authority, 'Financial promotion rules for cryptoassets – Policy Statement PS23/6' (2023).
89 Financial Conduct Authority, 'Finalised non-handbook guidance on Cryptoasset Financial Promotions – FG23/3' (2023).
90 Financial Conduct Authority, 'Regulating cryptoassets: Admissions & Disclosures and Market Abuse Regime for Cryptoassets – Discussion Paper DP 24/4' (2024).
91 UK Government, Welsh Government, Scottish Government and Department of Agriculture, Environment and Rural Affairs for Northern Ireland, 'Integrating Greenhouse Gas Removals in the UK Emissions Trading Scheme – A joint consultation of the UK Government, the Scottish Government, the Welsh Government and the Department of Agriculture, Environment and Rural Affairs for Northern Ireland' (2024).
92 Law Commission, 'Digital assets: Final report' (2023).
93 Property (Digital Assets, etc.) Bill [HL] (HL Bill 31—EN).
94 Dimitrios Linardatos, 'Finanzinstrumente im Digitalzeitalter – Teil II -' [2024], WM 1685, 1686; Florian Möslein and Christopher Rennig, 'Das Finanzmarktdigitalisierungsgesetz (FinmadiG) im europäischen Kontext (2024), RDi 145, 147.
95 Dimitrios Linardatos, 'Finanzinstrumente im Digitalzeitalter – Teil II -' [2024], WM 1685, 1686.
96 Philipp Maume '§ 12 Finanzdienstleistungsaufsicht' in Maume and Maute (eds), Rechtshandbuch Kryptowerte (1st edn, C. H. Beck 2024), para 7–8; Dimitrios Linardatos, 'Finanzinstrumente im Digitalzeitalter – Teil II -' [2024], WM 1685, 1686; Matthias Terlau, '§ 36 DLT-basiertes Geld im Währungs-, Aufsichts-, Geldwäsche-, Wertpapierrecht' in Florian Möslein and Sebastian Omlor (eds), FinTech-Handbuch (2nd edn C. H. Beck 2024), para 168.
97 Philipp Maume '§ 12 Finanzdienstleistungsaufsicht' in Philipp Maume and Lena Maute (eds), Rechtshandbuch Kryptowerte (1st edn, C. H. Beck 2024), para 26–27; Matthias Terlau, '§ 36 DLT-basiertes Geld im Währungs-, Aufsichts-, Geldwäsche-, Wertpapierrecht' in Florian Möslein and Sebastian Omlor (eds), FinTech-Handbuch (2nd edn C. H. Beck 2024), para 168.
98 Dimitrios Linardatos, 'Finanzinstrumente im Digitalzeitalter – Teil II -' [2024], WM 1685, 1687–1691.
99 Dimitrios Linardatos, 'Finanzinstrumente im Digitalzeitalter – Teil II -' [2024], WM 1685, 1691.
100 BT-Drucksache 20/10280 (2024), 164.
101 Dimitrios Linardatos, 'Finanzinstrumente im Digitalzeitalter – Teil II – '[2024], WM 1685, 1691.
102 UNIDROIT, 'Principles on Digital Assets and Private Law' https://www.unidroit.org/work-in-progress/digital-assets-and-private-law/ accessed 31 January 2025.
103 For a more defined evaluation of Principle 2 DAPL, see Dominik Skauradszun and Sebastian Böhning, 'Applicable Law in the Supply Chains of VCC Tokens' in this book.
104 According to Principle 2(4) DAPL, 'other law' refers to the existing law of the states looking to apply the Principles.
105 Tokenisation can help trading VCCs in some ways, see Georg von Wangenheim and Leon Krug 'VCCs, Tokenisation and the EU CBAM: Some Microeconomics of VCCs' in this book.
106 E.g., in German law, see BT-Drucksache 20/10280 (2024), 164.
107 UNIDROIT, 'Draft Principles on the Legal Nature of Verified Carbon Credits' (2025) https://www.unidroit.org/work-in-progress/verified-carbon-credits/ accessed 31 January 2025.
108 UNIDROIT, 'Summary Report of the second session' (2024), 4.
109 This was to be discussed at the meeting in April 2025; UNIDROIT, 'Issues Paper' (2025), 52.
110 Toucan Protocol Association https://toucan.earth/ accessed 31 January 2025.
111 Verra https://verra.org/ accessed 31 January 2025.
112 Gold Standard https://www.goldstandard.org/ accessed 31 January 2025.
113 Gold Standard, 'Conditions for consenting to tokenisation of Gold Standard-issued credits' (2022) https://www.goldstandard.org/consultations/conditions-for-consenting-to-tokenisation-of-gold-stan

dard-issued-credits accessed 31 January 2025; Verra, 'Verra Addresses Crypto Instruments and Tokens' (2022) https://verra.org/verra-addresses-crypto-instruments-and-tokens/ accessed 31 January 2025.
114 Puro.earth https://puro.earth/ accessed 31 January 2025.
115 Biochar refers to the act of capturing CO_2e in biomass through pyrolysis; for an in-depth article on biochar's properties, see Hamed Sanei and others, 'Assessing biochar's permanence: An inertinite benchmark' (2024), International Journal of Coal Geology 104409.
116 Neutral https://www.neutralx.com/ accessed 31 January 2025.
117 Sander DiAngelis, 'The world's first liquid market for biochar' (*Toucan*, 2024) https://blog.toucan.earth/onchain-climate-action-char/ accessed 31 January 2025.
118 Nori's websites are no longer accessible, cf Haje Kamps, 'Immune to irony, Nori puts a carbon market on the blockchain' (*TechCrunch*, 2022) https://techcrunch.com/2022/02/24/nori-series-a-carbon-blockchain/ accessed 31 January 2025.
119 Haje Kamps, 'Immune to irony, Nori puts a carbon market on the blockchain' (*TechCrunch*, 2022) https://techcrunch.com/2022/02/24/nori-series-a-carbon-blockchain/ accessed 31 January 2025.
120 Paul Gambill, 'How to save the planet and make climate change 'just go away' using blockchain and cryptocurrency' (*Medium*, 2020) https://medium.com/nori-carbon-removal/how-to-save-the-planet-and-make-climate-change-just-go-away-using-blockchain-and-cryptocurrency-f6e33917089d accessed 31 January 2025.
121 Paul Gambill, 'How to save the planet and make climate change 'just go away' using blockchain and cryptocurrency' (*Medium*, 2020) https://medium.com/nori-carbon-removal/how-to-save-the-planet-and-make-climate-change-just-go-away-using-blockchain-and-cryptocurrency-f6e33917089d accessed 31 January 2025.
122 Cf Lisa Stiffler, 'Nori, a Seattle-based carbon removal marketplace that raised $17M, shuts down after 7 years' (*Geekwire*, 2024) https://www.geekwire.com/2024/nori-a-seattle-based-carbon-removal-marketplace-that-raised-17m-shuts-down-after-7-years/ accessed 31 January 2025.
123 American Carbon Registry https://acrcarbon.org/ accessed 31 January 2025.
124 Climate Action Reserve https://www.climateactionreserve.org/ accessed 31 January 2025.
125 Plan Vivo Foundation https://www.planvivo.org/ accessed 31 January 2025.
126 C3.app, 'C3 Documentation' https://docs.c3.app/ accessed 31 January 2025.
127 Coorest, 'Coorest Carbon Standard' (2022) https://coorest.io/carbon-standard/ accessed 31 January 2025.
128 Coorest, 'Coorest Whitepaper 3.0' (2023) https://coorest.gitbook.io/coorest-whitepaper-3.0 accessed 31 January 2025.
129 For more details on the Lifecycle of VCCs, see Jonathan Lautenschlager, Marike Reinelt, Vincent Schaaf and Nils Urbach, 'From Project Design to Retirement: The Role of Blockchain along the Voluntary Carbon Credit Lifecycle' and Valeriya Arnold, Vincent Schaaf, Nils Urbach and Jonathan Lautenschlager, 'Designing a framework for a blockchain-based Carbon Credit Lifecycle' in this book.
130 Toucan, 'The first liquid market for biochar credits' (2024) https://toucan.earth/char/ accessed 31 January 2025.
131 Program on International Financial Systems, 'Implementing an Effective Cryptoasset Regulatory Framework in the United States' (2024).
132 Cf UNIDROIT, 'Summary Report of the first session' (2023), 5.
133 U.S. Securities and Exchange Commission, 'Framework for 'Investment Contract' Analysis of Digital Assets' (2024), https://www.sec.gov/about/divisions-offices/division-corporation-finance/framework-investment-contract-analysis-digital-assets accessed 31 January 2025.
134 Paul Gambill, 'How to save the planet and make climate change 'just go away' using blockchain and cryptocurrency' (*Medium*, 2020) https://medium.com/nori-carbon-removal/how-to-save-the-planet-and-make-climate-change-just-go-away-using-blockchain-and-cryptocurrency-f6e33917089d accessed 31 January 2025.

135 Coorest, 'FAQ' https://coorest.io/about/faq/ accessed 31 January 2025.
136 Coorest, 'Coorest NFTree' (2023) https://coorest.gitbook.io/coorest-whitepaper-3.0/coorest-nftree accessed 31 January 2025.
137 Program on International Financial Systems, 'A Review of Cryptoasset Market Structure and Regulation in the United States' (2023).

Florian Möslein and Frieda Mainka

9 Voluntary carbon credits and digital product passports: Similarities and differences

Abstract: The dual imperatives of addressing climate change and promoting sustainability have driven the development of innovative mechanisms such as voluntary carbon credits (VCCs) and digital product passports (DPPs). While these tools serve different purposes, they are united by their reliance on digitalisation to ensure trust, transparency, and compliance with sustainability goals. VCCs enable the voluntary offsetting of greenhouse gas (GHG) emissions through rigorously certified projects and operate within an evolving legal framework, exemplified by the European Union's (Union; EU) Carbon Removals and Carbon Farming Certification Regulation (CRCFR).[1] Mandated by the Union's Ecodesign for Sustainable Products Regulation (ESPR),[2] DPPs integrate regulatory requirements into product lifecycle management, promoting traceability, resource circularity, and compliance throughout supply chains. This chapter examines the environmental objectives, issuance processes, technical structures, and legal underpinnings of VCCs and DPPs, highlighting their common reliance on robust data frameworks and legal mechanisms to combat greenwashing and promote accountability. Despite their differences—such as the voluntary nature and project-based focus of VCCs versus the mandatory implementation and product-level integration of DPPs—both instruments address complementary aspects of environmental governance. Together, they demonstrate the potential for coherent legal and regulatory strategies to drive systemic change, promote climate neutrality, and transform sustainability into an enforceable business practice.

Keywords: voluntary carbon credits, CRCFR, digital product passports, ESPR, market-based mechanism

1 Introduction: Trust in sustainability —— 228
2 Fundamental characteristics —— 228
  2.1 Ecological background and objectives —— 228
  2.2 Issuance process ('Lifecycle') —— 229
  2.3 Technical nature and content —— 230
3 Legal framework —— 231
  3.1 Carbon removals and carbon farming certification regulation —— 231
  3.2 Ecodesign for sustainable products regulation —— 232
4 Comparison —— 233
  4.1 Similarities —— 233
  4.2 Differences —— 234
5 Conclusion —— 235

https://doi.org/10.1515/9783111706719-009

1 Introduction: Trust in sustainability

Climate change poses a complex and urgent challenge that necessitates a multifaceted response. From market-based approaches and innovative technologies to legal frameworks, a wide array of instruments must be deployed in concert to curb emissions, transition to sustainable practices, and safeguard the planet's future. Among these tools, VCCs and DPPs stand out as emerging mechanisms that operate at the crossroads of sustainability and digitalisation.

At first glance, these two mechanisms may seem unrelated, connected only by their shared reliance on digital technologies to advance environmental objectives. VCCs provide a solution for offsetting GHG emissions, allowing businesses and individuals to compensate for their environmental impact by funding projects that reduce or remove GHG emissions. DPPs, by contrast, offer a data-centric framework for tracing the lifecycle of products, including their sustainability attributes, thus promoting transparency and enabling circular economy practices.

Despite these apparent differences in purpose and application, a closer examination reveals intriguing parallels between the two. Both are built on the premise that digital tools can transform how we quantify, manage, and communicate sustainability efforts. Both aim to bridge gaps—between actions and impacts, between stakeholders in supply chains, and between abstract sustainability goals and measurable outcomes. Furthermore, both face similar challenges, such as ensuring data integrity, addressing regulatory complexities, and achieving widespread adoption. Finally, both instruments play a crucial role in fostering trust in sustainability. VCCs rely on robust verification mechanisms to assure stakeholders that the credits represent genuine GHG emission reductions or removals, while DPPs enhance transparency and accountability by providing verifiable data about a product's environmental credentials.

This chapter seeks to explore the deeper connections between VCCs and DPPs. By examining their shared reliance on digitalisation, their potential for driving systemic change, their ability to build trust, and their complementary roles in fostering sustainability, the analysis aims to illuminate whether these tools, often viewed in isolation, might together form part of a cohesive strategy for climate action.

2 Fundamental characteristics

2.1 Ecological background and objectives

VCCs emerged as a market-based mechanism to address climate change, allowing entities to offset their GHG emissions.[3] The approach originates from the idea that the emission of GHG in one region can be compensated by removing or reducing GHG emissions elsewhere, ideally leading to climate neutrality thus curbing climate change.[4] VCCs play a particularly pivotal role in relation to GHG emissions that can hardly be avoided.[5] Distinct from compliance systems, such as the Union's Emissions Trading System,[6] VCCs aim to encourage voluntary private sector engagement in addressing global emission reduction targets.[7] By providing funding for projects that reduce or remove GHG emissions, they incentivise and reward their development and implementation. Furthermore, with the projects predominantly taking place in developing countries, VCCs enable money flows to be directed to these, driving further benefits such as creating employment and enhancing biodiversity.[8] Companies voluntarily purchasing VCCs are empowered to promote their climate performance, helping them to achieve sustainability targets, whereas consumers are enabled to compensate for their individual climate impact.[9] If VCCs are created by employing rigorous certification standards and if transparency in their issuance and trade is ensured, they play a vital role in fostering trust in climate action.

Like VCCs, DPPs are a market-based mechanism for tackling climate change.[10] However, DPPs take a different approach, attempting to curb climate change by transitioning to a circular economy,[11] thus recognising the critical role of products in achieving climate neutrality. By providing standardised and digitised information about a product's lifecycle, DPPs aim to increase product traceability and supply chain transparency, as well as to improve resource circularity and efficiency, leading to a reduction of GHG emissions from the outset, and strengthening supply chain governance. They empower stakeholders, including consumers, manufacturers, and regulators, to make informed and sustainable decisions, whether in purchasing, repairing, recycling, or policymaking.[12] In this way, consumers are enabled to fulfil their 'basic duty of ecological proportionality'[13] by choosing more sustainable options. Companies are enabled to differentiate products in a competitive market by highlighting their commitment to sustainability. Further, DPPs help them meet environmental standards and comply with evolving environmental regulations, reducing the risk of legal complications. Conversely, DPPs facilitate official supervision in this respect.[14] By avoiding issues such as greenwashing, DPPs, like VCCs, seek to build trust in sustainability claims through accessible, verifiable, and reliable data.[15]

2.2 Issuance process ('Lifecycle')

The lifecycle of a VCC typically begins with the development of a project aiming to reduce or remove GHG emissions. Potential projects span a variety of areas, including renewable energy development, reforestation, methane capture, and energy efficiency initiatives. Upon the project proponent's or developer's request, an authorised validation/verification body (VVB) conducts a baseline assessment of the project plan and validates the project's compliance with the methodology of a carbon crediting body's internationally recognised GHG crediting programme like Verra's Verified Carbon Standard (VCS) as well as the expected level of reduction or removal of GHG emissions over a specified verification period. After the project's implementation, monitoring, and management to achieve the expected emission reductions, the VVB audits and verifies the actual performance of the project over the verification period, and reports its results in a verification report. The project proponent or developer can now request the acceptance of the verification report and, following that, the issuance of one VCC per verified removed or reduced GHG emissions equivalent to one metric ton of carbon dioxide equivalent (CO_2e) of a carbon crediting body. Following the VCC's issuance and assignment of a serial number, it is recorded in a VCC registry. The VCC can be traded and retired, allowing the entity on whose behalf the VCC is retired to claim the associated offset benefits. Once retired, the VCC is no longer tradable or usable, hence, retirement marks the end of a VCC's lifecycle.[16]

The lifecycle of a DPP is tied to the lifecycle of the underlying product, spanning production, use, recycling, and end-of-life stages.[17] The first step to the issuance of a DPP involves collecting information from across the product's lifecycle and supply chain, covering raw material sourcing, manufacturing processes, and distribution channels. This information is standardised according to guidelines issued by regulatory bodies or industry consortia, ensuring its interoperability and comparability, and digitised, creating a set of data specific to the product—its DPP. Each product is then assigned a unique identifier and a data carrier, linking it to its DPP and allowing stakeholders to access relevant information throughout the product's lifecycle.[18] In the Union, the European Commission will set up and manage a web portal enabling stakeholders to access, search, and compare the data included in a DPP.[19] The DPP is continuously updated to reflect changes, such as repair, maintenance, or recycling activities.[20] It cannot be traded independently of the underlying product. The DPP must be available for at least a period corresponding to the expected life span of the product.[21]

2.3 Technical nature and content

From a technical perspective, VCCs are records in a database. The database is usually digital and can be a blockchain. From a material point of view, the content of a VCC differs from one crediting programme to another. However, a typical VCC includes detailed information about the underlying project, such as its location, methodology, and baseline data, as well as certification details, the respective validation and verification reports, and the VCC's unique identifier. The information is compound to the serial number assigned to a VCC during its issuance process.

DPPs, from a technical point of view, are a set of data specific to a product based on a data storage and access system and recorded on and accessible through a data carrier (such as a QR code or RFID chip) embedded in the underlying product or its packaging.[22] From a material perspective, a DPP typically contains information about the product's identity, including its unique identifier, its material composition, details of its manufacturing process, and lifecycle information encompassing use, maintenance, and recycling. Additionally, DPPs often include records of compliance with environmental standards and certifications, as well as information on the contributions of various stakeholders within the supply chain. By aggregating this data, DPPs provide a comprehensive and transparent overview of the product's (sustainability) attributes creating its digital twin.[23]

3 Legal framework

3.1 Carbon removals and carbon farming certification regulation

Distinct from products traded under compliance systems such as emission allowances traded under the Union's Emissions Trading System, VCCs emerged independently of any regulatory framework. To this date, there is no Union or German legal framework explicitly implementing mandatory requirements for VCCs.[24] In 2024, however, the Union introduced the CRCFR, establishing a comprehensive voluntary certification framework for carbon removals and soil emission reductions, directly applicable across all Union Member States from December 2024.[25] It covers permanent carbon removals, carbon farming, and carbon storage in products carried out in the Union.[26]

Project developers or proponents[27] planning to operate a carbon mitigation project can apply to an independent certification scheme recognised by the European Commission[28] for certification of the project's outcome under the CRCFR. An outcome is eligible for certification, if it is independently verified in accordance with the Regulation and qualifies as a carbon removal or soil emission reduction generated by an activity falling within the scope of the Regulation and meeting its QU.A.L.ITY criteria by applying a recognised method, meaning the activity must be quantified, additional, long-term stored, and sustainable.[29] The recognised methods are set by delegated acts of the European Commission.[30]

The certification process begins with the project proponent's or developer's application and the subsequent submission of an activity plan, including evidence of the activity's compliance with the QU.A.L.ITY criteria as well as the expected benefit and a monitoring plan, to an accredited certification body appointed by the certification scheme.[31] The certification body conducts an *ex-ante* certification audit, verifying the submitted information's accuracy and reliability as well as the activity's compliance with the QU.A.L.ITY criteria, with a successful verification leading to the issuance of a certification audit report and a certificate of compliance. Both are reviewed and made publicly available in a registry established and maintained by the certification scheme or, once established, in the Union CRCF registry,[32] by the certification scheme. Where necessary to protect commercially sensitive information, the certification audit report may be published in a summarised form.[33]

Approximately every year to five years, the activity's correct implementation and the actual outcome must be reconfirmed *ex-post* in a re-certification audit conducted by the certification body, resulting in the issuance of a re-certification audit report and an updated certificate of compliance. Both will again be reviewed and made publicly available (if necessary, in a summarised form) in a registry by the certification scheme, ensuring transparency and traceability.[34] Based on the updated certificate of compliance, the registry will issue and register the status of certified units, which, that is, can be traded on the voluntary carbon market.[35] The certified unit's validity depends on the expected duration of storage and possible risks of reversal.[36]

The CRCFR aims to foster trust in the certification of carbon removals and soil emission reductions by promoting their environmental integrity, quality, and transparency, leading to a positive climate impact and avoiding greenwashing. Thereby, it incentivises the development of GHG mitigation projects and helps entities back their voluntary claims on carbon removals and soil emission reductions.[37]

To conclude, the Union's implementation of the CRCFR is an important step along the way to a climate-neutral economy. Ensuring the independence of parties involved in the certification process and mandating disclosure of information regarding VCCs promotes not only trust in VCCs but also in sustainability in general, by mitigating risks such as greenwashing. However, being a voluntary framework, the CRCFR's success largely depends on its acceptance by market players such as carbon crediting bodies as well as project proponents and developers.

3.2 Ecodesign for sustainable products regulation

The Union's DPP is established through the ESPR.[38] The Regulation implements a comprehensive framework for setting ecodesign requirements, directly applicable across all Union Member States from July 2024.[39] The ESPR covers all physical goods, components, and intermediate products placed on the market or put into service, focusing on critical sectors such as iron and steel, textiles, detergents, chemicals, and electronics.[40] The Regulation applies to all economic operators involved in placing covered products on the market or initiating their use, including manufacturers, importers, and distributors.[41]

The ESPR requires the provision of a DPP for each product within its scope.[42] DPPs must contain essential information about the product, such as its materials, repairability, recyclability, carbon footprint, and any substances of concern. The specific requirements are set by delegated acts of the European Commission.[43] The responsibility for ensuring the accuracy, completeness, and accessibility of this data lies with manufacturers, importers, and distributors.[44] To enhance transparency, the data will be maintained in a digital format linked to a unique product identifier and accessible via data carriers such as QR codes or digital watermarks embedded in the product.[45] Importantly, the DPP must remain accurate and accessible for at least the expected lifetime of the product.[46] Failure to comply with the requirements of the Regulation can result in significant penalties, such as fines or restrictions on market access.[47] Companies are therefore strongly encouraged to implement advanced data collection and management systems to ensure readiness and compliance.

Access to information within a DPP is differentiated according to the needs of different stakeholders, such as consumers, regulators, repairers, and recyclers. The system aims to facilitate informed decision-making and compliance checks, while protecting intellectual property and sensitive business information.[48]

In line with the European Green Deal and the Circular Economy Action Plan, the ESPR aims to promote a sustainable and competitive market, contributing to the achievement of the Union's climate, energy, and wider environmental targets. By integrating lifecycle considerations into product design, the Regulation seeks to accelerate the transition to a circular economy while significantly reducing waste and products' energy footprints, ensuring 'the performance of frontrunners in sustainability'[49] to become progressively the norm.[50] In line with the general objectives of DPPs, the Union's DPP plays a key role in operationalising these objectives by aiming to enhance the traceability of products and materials throughout their entire lifecycle; to promote transparency by providing consumers and other stakeholders with information enabling sustainable decision-making; and to support compliance and innovation by providing regulatory and market opportunities for businesses to innovate and align with Union sustainability objectives.[51] The Regulation requires the development of technical specifications for DPPs to ensure interoperability and consistency across sectors.[52] By the introduction of a DPP registry,[53] the ESPR seeks to enable the European Commission, customs, and market surveillance authorities to monitor and enforce the compliance of products with its requirements.[54] To complement the DPP system, the Regulation aligns with existing Union laws, such as the REACH Regulation[55] and the SCIP database for tracking hazardous substances, established under the Waste Framework Directive.[56]

In conclusion, the Union's DPP initiative represents a landmark shift in sustainable product governance. By mandating comprehensive lifecycle data disclosure, it not only promotes transparency but also strengthens the foundation for a climate-neutral, resource-efficient economy. Stakeholders across the supply chain are urged to engage proactively, recognising compliance not merely as an obligation but as an opportunity to drive innovation and foster sustainability.

4 Comparison

4.1 Similarities

VCCs and DPPs are two separate instruments for promoting sustainability, each addressing different but related aspects of environmental governance. Despite their differences, they share some similarities in purpose, methodology, and their role in building trust in sustainability initiatives. Both VCCs and DPPs serve as tools to verify compliance with legal and sustainability requirements, and both aim to combat climate change and promote sustainable practices. VCCs enable companies to demonstrate their contribution to GHG emission reduction efforts and to offset their GHG emissions by funding projects that reduce or eliminate GHG emissions, such as reforestation or renewable energy initiatives. DPPs, on the other hand, provide detailed information on product sustainability, enhancing transparency and accountability throughout supply chains. They focus on enhancing product lifecycle management by improving traceability, resource circularity, and supply chain transparency. While VCCs directly address emissions, DPPs target the environmental impact of products throughout their lifecycle, from raw material sourcing to recycling.

Digital technologies underpin both instruments, with VCCs relying on digital registries to track certified emission reductions and removals and DPPs using data carriers such as QR codes or RFID chips to store and share detailed product information. These technologies not only enable efficient data management but also play a crucial role in building trust. For VCCs, the maintenance of registries increases transparency and traceability and avoids issues such as double counting, while DPPs provide verifiable and accessible data to increase transparency and combat greenwashing.

Another common feature is their ability to empower stakeholders through reliable information. VCCs enable companies and individuals to address their carbon footprint and support climate-neutrality goals, while DPPs provide consumers, manufacturers, and regulators with the data needed to make informed decisions about purchasing, repair, and recycling. Both tools respond to regulatory and market demands, encouraging innovation and compliance with evolving sustainability standards.

4.2 Differences

In spite of these similarities, the differences between the two instruments underline the unique role of each. VCCs are tradable certificates that function independently of physical products. They follow a project-based lifecycle, starting with project development and ending with the retirement of credits for offsetting emissions. In contrast, DPPs are non-tradable digital records that are intrinsically linked to physical products, providing a continuous flow of data throughout the products' lifecycle.

Unlike the voluntary nature of VCCs, which are governed by private schemes and emerging frameworks such as the CRCFR, DPPs are mandated under the ESPR and come with strict compliance requirements and penalties. Even though legal frameworks now exist for both instruments, VCCs existed prior to the issuance of the CRCFR, which was developed in response to the ongoing evolution and application of these credits. In contrast, the Union's DPP was introduced explicitly by the ESPR, marking a deliberate regulatory initiative to create a new mechanism for fostering sustainability. More importantly, the establishment of VCCs under the CRCFR is voluntary, allowing entities to participate based on their individual sustainability strategies and market preferences. This approach emphasises flexibility and market-driven solutions. On the other hand, the creation of DPPs under the ESPR is mandatory, requiring compliance from relevant stakeholders. This mandatory nature underscores the Union's commitment to integrating sustainability into product design and lifecycle management on a more systemic and enforceable basis.

Both instruments serve transparency objectives, although they differ in their focus on information. VCCs provide project-specific data, including location, type, and emission reduction impact, while DPPs provide detailed product-level information, including material composition, lifecycle impacts, and compliance records. In addition, DPPs are integrated into physical products, acting as digital twins that reflect their sustainability attributes, while VCCs operate independently as digital assets.

5 Conclusion

VCCs and DPPs complement one another by addressing distinct yet interconnected aspects of sustainability. VCCs mitigate emissions at a macro level, while DPPs enhance transparency and circularity at a product level. Together, they contribute to a cohesive strategy for combating climate change, fostering trust, and driving innovation in sustainable practices. Both VCCs and DPPs are defined by rigorous issuance processes, robust technical content, and a reliance on digital tools to ensure credibility and transparency. These characteristics not only make them effective instruments for advancing sustainability goals but also foster trust among stakeholders. By aligning participants with reliable and accessible information, VCCs and DPPs offer complementary pathways to drive systemic change and support meaningful climate action beyond the Union's borders. Additionally, both legal frameworks align with the broader Union sustainability initiative, reflecting the political dedication to advancing environmental goals through innovative legal and regulatory measures. By addressing different aspects of sustainability, both instruments collectively contribute to the Union's overarching strategy for fostering a greener, more resilient economy.

Notes

1 Regulation (EU) 2024/3012 of the European Parliament and of the Council of 27 November 2024 establishing a Union certification framework for permanent carbon removals, carbon farming and carbon storage in products [2024] OJ L2024/3012.

2 Regulation (EU) 2024/1781 of the European Parliament and of the Council of 13 June 2024 establishing a framework for the setting of ecodesign requirements for sustainable products, amending Directive (EU) 2020/1828 and Regulation (EU) 2023/1542 and repealing Directive 2009/125/EC [2024] OJ L2024/1781.

3 Cf Andrew A Bernstein, 'The Perfect is the Enemy of the Good: Carbon Credits and Funding for Decarbonization in Developing Countries' (2023) 35 NE J of Public Policy Art 4, 2f, 6; Haut Comité Juridique de la Place financière de Paris (Legal High Committee for Financial markets of Paris; HCJP), *Report on the Legal and Regulatory Aspects of Voluntary Carbon Credits* (2024) 9f. For an early account, cf Michael P Vandenbergh and Anne C Steinemann, 'The Carbon-Neutral Individual' (2007) 82 NYU L Rev 1673, 1718 (listing examples of companies that offer offsets in n 206).

4 Cf Nicole Franki, 'Regulation of the Voluntary Carbon Offset Market: Shifting the Burden of Climate Change Mitigation from Individual to Collective Action' (2022) 48 Col J of Environmental L 177, 179; Bernstein (n 3) 6.

5 Cf Recital 2 CRCFR; Bernstein (n 3) 3, 7, 9; The World Bank, 'State and Trends of Carbon Pricing: International Carbon Markets 2024' (2024) 15, available at https://blogs.worldbank.org/en/climatechange/state-and-trends-of-carbon-pricing--international-carbon-markets accessed 5 February 2025.

6 For further information on the differences of VCCs and emission allowances created under the Union's Emissions Trading System, see HCJP (n 3) 14f.

7 Cf Bernstein (n 3) 2f; HCJP (n 3) 10.

8 Cf United Nations' High-Level Expert Group on the Net Zero Emissions Commitments of Non-State Entities, *Integrity Matters: Net Zero Commitments by Businesses, Financial Institutions, Cities and Regions* (2022) 19; Bernstein (n 3) 2f, 16f; Klas Wetterberg, Jane Ellis and Lambert Schneider, 'The Interplay between Voluntary and Compliance Carbon Markets: Implications for Environmental Integrity' (2024) OECD Environment Working Papers No 244, 14, 16, 100, available at https://www.oecd.org/en/publications/the-interplay-between-voluntary-and-compliance-carbon-markets_500198e1-en.html accessed 5 February 2025; HCJP (n 3) 9; The World Bank (n 5) 15; see also Recital 20 CRCFR.

9 Cf Harry Fearnehough and others, 'Future Role for Voluntary Carbon Markets in the Paris Era – Final Report, Project No (FKZ) 3718 42 006 0 – Report No FB000420/ENG' (2020) 44 Climate Change (Umweltbundesamt (German Environment Agency)) 33; Franki (n 4) 180; Bernstein (n 3) 3f; HCJP (n 3) 9f; Wetterberg and others (n 8) 11; The World Bank (n 5) 13.

10 Cf Florian Fuchs-Zeitner, 'Der Digitale Produktpass (DPP) nach der Neuen ÖkodesignVO – Klarheit erst durch Geplantes Tertiärrecht' [2024] ZUR Zeitschrift für Umweltrecht 534, 535.

11 For detailed information on the concept of a circular economy, see David J Langley and others, 'Orchestrating a Smart Circular Economy: Guiding Principles for Digital Product Passports' (2023) 169 J of Business Research 114259, 2ff.

12 Cf Recital 1 ESPR; Thomas Götz and others, 'Digital Product Passport: the Ticket to Achieving a Climate Neutral and Circular European Economy?' [2022] CISL and the Wuppertal Institute 10ff.; Langley and others (n 11) 1, 4; Simon D Meyer, 'Neue EU-Ökodesign-Verordnung Kommt – Produkte Sollen Nachhaltiger Werden' [2024] DB Der Betrieb 1258, 1261.

13 Gerd Winter, 'Rechtsprobleme im Anthropozän: Vom Umweltschutz zur Selbstbegrenzung' [2017] ZUR Zeitschrift für Umweltrecht 267, 275 ('Grundpflicht ökologischer Verhältnismäßigkeit'); see also Fuchs-Zeitner (n 10) 534.

14 Meyer (n 12) 1261; Götz and others (n 12) 11.

15 Cf Fuchs-Zeitner (n 10) 535; Götz and others (n 12) 14, 19.

16 Cf Fearnehough and others (n 9) 32f; Bernstein (n 3) 3f; HCJP (n 3) 9f, 12; UNIDROIT Working Group on the Legal Nature of Verified Carbon Credits, 'Summary Report of the Third Session, Study LXXXVI – W.G.3 – Doc. 4' (2024) para 72f.

17 Christiane Plociennik and others, 'Towards a Digital Lifecycle Passport for the Circular Economy' (2022) 105 Procedia CIRP 122f.

18 Cf Art. 10(1)(a), (d) ESPR; Langley and others (n 11) 5; Monika Menz, '§ 7 Digitaler Produktpass' in Jens Nusser and Marthe-Louise Fehse (eds), *Das Neue Ökodesign–Recht: Ökodesign–Verordnung für nachhaltige Produkte (ESPR)* (Nomos 2025) para 1, 10. In the Union, the unique product identifiers will be recorded in a DPP registry, set up and managed by the European Commission. Where considered

appropriate, the European Commission can determine further data from a product's DPP to be recorded in the DPP registry (Art. 13 ESPR; see also Recital 41 ESPR).

19 Art. 14 ESPR; see also Recital 42 ESPR.

20 Cf Menz (n 18) para 18; see also Recital 32 ESPR.

21 Art. 9(2)(i) ESPR.

22 See Art. 2(28) ESPR; Recital 41 ESPR; Menz (n 18) para 10; Tobias Burchert and Mia Weber, 'EU–Ökodesign–Verordnung – Verschärfungen durch das Europäische Parlament?' [2023] ESG Zeitschrift für nachhaltige Unternehmensführung 104, 108. The data system should be decentralised (Recital 41 ESPR).

23 Cf Art. 7, Annex III ESPR; Götz and others (n 12) 11; Menz (n 18) para 1, 13; Anne-Christin Mittwoch, 'Der Digitale Produktpass der Ökodesign–Verordnung: Passierschein zur erfolgreichen Zwillingstransformation im Produktrecht?' [2024] RDi Recht Digital 62, 63.

24 At international level, different supra-national organisations have addressed VCCs. The International Institute for the Unification of Private Law (UNIDROIT) is developing the UNIDROIT Principles on the Legal Nature of Verified Carbon Credits, addressing private law issues in the context of Verified Carbon Credits. The International Organization of Securities Commissions (IOSCO) has developed a set of Good Practices that focusses on the integrity and structure of the voluntary carbon market. Being soft-law, both instruments are not directly applicable in the Union or Germany.

25 Art. 1(1) sentence 2, 19 CRCFR; Art. 288(2) Treaty on the Functioning of the European Union (TFEU); see also Antonia vom Dahl, 'Die Zertifizierung von CO_2-Entnahmen – Grünes Licht für „Net Zero" oder nur heiße Luft?' [2023] EnWZ Zeitschrift für das gesamte Recht der Energiewirtschaft 359, 363.

26 Art. 1(1) sentence 2(a) and Art. 2(3) CRCFR; Q&A on the provisional agreement on the Regulation establishing an EU-wide voluntary framework for certifying permanent carbon removals, carbon farming and carbon storage in products (CRCF Regulation) (2024) version 1.0 1 available at https://climate.ec.europa.eu/document/download/a8abe1c4-a3c6-4c94-be0e-4b76f7fd0308_en?filename=policy_carbon_faq_crcf_regulation_en.pdf accessed 5 February 2025. For exceptions, see Art. 1(3) CRCFR.

27 The CRCFR uses the terms 'operator' or 'group of operators' defined in Art. 2(5), (6) CRCFR.

28 Art. 11(1),(2), 13 CRCFR; Recital 33f CRCFR. Already existing as well as new private or public certification schemes, such as carbon crediting bodies, can voluntarily apply for recognition as a certification scheme under the CRCFR by the European Commission. The recognition is valid for five years (Art. 13(1) CRCFR; Recital 5 CRCFR; Q&A on the provisional agreement on the CRCFR (n 26) 4; see also vom Dahl (n 25) 361). The recognition is, however, not mandatory for a certification scheme to be allowed to operate in the Union (Recital 5 CRCFR).

29 Art. 3–7 CRCFR; vom Dahl (n 25) 360f.

30 The European Commission is empowered to adopt such delegated acts in accordance with Art. 16 CRCFR by Art. 8(2) CRCFR.

31 Art. 9(1) and Art. 10(1) CRCFR; Q&A on the provisional agreement on the CRCFR (n 26) 5. A certification body operates legally and financially independent from (groups of) operators, in the public interest and under the Union Member States supervision (Art. 10(2)(b), (c), (4) CRCFR; Recital 32 CRCFR).

32 The Union CRCF registry is a registry to be established by the European Commission by December 2028 making information in relation to the certification process publicly accessible by using automated systems, limiting the risk of fraud and double counting (Art. 12(1) CRCFR; Recital 36 CRCFR).

33 See Art. 9(2), 11(3) and 12(3) CRCFR; Recital 29 CRCFR; Q&A on the provisional agreement on the CRCFR (n 26) 5.

34 Art. 9(3) CRCFR; Recital 36 CRCFR; Q&A on the provisional agreement on the CRCFR (n 26) 5.

35 Art. 9(3) subpara 3 CRCFR; Recital 42 CRCFR; Q&A on the provisional agreement on the CRCFR (n 26) 5. The CRCFR distinguishes four types of certified units: permanent carbon removal units (Art. 2(19) CRCFR), soil emission reduction units (Art. 2(20) CRCFR), carbon farming sequestration units (Art.

2(22) CRCFR) and carbon storage in product units (Art. 2(23) CRCFR) (cf Q&A on the provisional agreement on the CRCFR (n 26) 2).
36 Recital 22 CRCFR.
37 Recital 3–5, 7, 43 CRCFR; European Commission, 'Proposal for a Regulation of the European Parliament and of the Council Establishing a Union certification Framework for Carbon Removals' COM (2022) 672 final 1; Q&A on the provisional agreement on the CRCFR (n 26) 6; vom Dahl (n 25) 359.
38 Art. 1(1) subpara 2 ESPR; see also Recital 32 ESPR; Götz and others (n 12) 15; Menz (n 18) para 1; Meyer (n 12) 1258. Similar requirements apply to digital battery passports as provided for in Art. 77f Regulation (EU) 2023/1542 of the European Parliament and of the Council of 12 July 2023 concerning batteries and waste batteries, amending Directive 2008/98/EC and Regulation (EU) 2019/1020 and repealing Directive 2006/66/EC [2023] OJ L2023/191.
39 Art. 1(1) subpara 1, 80 ESPR; Art. 288(2) TFEU; see also Meyer (n 12) 1261; Frank Petersen and Marie Massow, 'Die EU-Ökodesign-Verordnung und das „Warenvernichtungsverbot" – Gefährdet die „Nachhaltige Klimapolitik" die Kreislaufwirtschaft?' [2023] ZUR Zeitschrift für Umweltrecht 67, 67ff; Jens Nusser, '§ 1 Einleitung – die Ökodesign-Verordnung im Überblick' in Jens Nusser and Marthe-Louise Fehse (eds) (n 18) para 1, 18. Art. 79 ESPR implements transitional provisions for specific product groups (for more information, see Nusser (n 39) para 18).
40 Art. 1(2) sentence 1, Art. 18(5)(a), (c), (f), (i), and (k) ESPR; see also Recital 13 ESPR; Nusser (n 39) para 15. For exceptions, see Art. 1(2) sentence 2 ESPR.
41 Art. 2(46) ESPR; Nusser (n 39) para 17.
42 Art. 9(1) ESPR.
43 Cf Art. 9(2) ESPR; the European Commission is empowered to adopt such delegated acts in accordance with Art. 72 ESPR by Art. 4(1) ESPR.
44 According to Art. 9(1) sentence 2 ESPR, the data in the DPP shall be 'accurate, complete and up to date'; see also Recital 32 ESPR and, with regard to the obligations of distributors, Art. 30 ESPR.
45 For details, see Art. 10 ESPR.
46 Art. 9(1), (2)(a)(b)(i) ESPR.
47 See Art. 74 ESPR.
48 Recital 32 ESPR; Menz (n 18) para 19. The European Commission is empowered to determine the access to the DPPs data granted to different stakeholders in delegated acts in accordance with Art. 72 ESPR (Art. 9(2)(f), 4(1) ESPR).
49 Recital 6 ESPR.
50 Recital 2, 6, 9f ESPR; see also Götz and others (n 12) 15.
51 Cf Recital 2f, 28, 32 ESPR.
52 Recital 39 ESPR.
53 See n 18.
54 Recital 41 ESPR; see also Menz (n 18) para 29.
55 Regulation (EC) No 1907/2006 of the European Parliament and of the Council of 18 December 2006 concerning the Registration, Evaluation, Authorisation and Restriction of Chemicals (REACH), establishing a European Chemicals Agency, amending Directive 1999/45/EC and repealing Council Regulation (EEC) No 793/93 and Commission Regulation (EC) No 1488/94 as well as Council Directive 76/769/EEC and Commission Directives 91/155/EEC, 93/67/EEC, 93/105/EC and 2000/21/EC [2006] OJ L396/1.
56 Directive 2008/98/EC of the European Parliament and of the Council of 19 November 2008 on waste and repealing certain Directives [2008] OJ L312/3.

Sebastian Böhning and Dominik Skauradszun

10 VCC tokens' civil law – ownership, transfer and liability under Union and German law

Abstract: Whereas the potential of the VCM is seen as bright and it is forecast to reach a market value of tens of billions of USD, it is essential for the VCM that big market players like financial institutions join the market to further drive it. With the entry of institutional players, the market could live up to its potential and create a wide impact economically and environmentally. A crucial question for these and other market participants is whether and how they are able to report VCC tokens in their balance. If the balancing is sound and accepted by auditors, VCC tokens become even more interesting assets to invest in. Closely connected to and partly at the core of those questions is the civil law of VCC tokens. To answer such questions, it is important to grasp the legal nature of VCC tokens and to comprehend the transfer from one market player to another. Only if the transfer can be traced back and explained in a legally sound way can proprietary rights in VCC tokens be claimed by the relevant acquiring person. This analysis aims to assess certain aspects of VCC tokens' civil law to give potential answers to the questions raised and nurture a common understanding of civil law issues from a Union and German law point of view. Whereas a first glance into non-EU jurisdictions serves as the starting point of the analysis, the analysis is focused on ownership, transfer, and liability under Union and German law. Under each keyword, different categories will be discussed and the analysis will show that while certain questions can be answered more definitely, others remain subject to further discussion in academia and in practice.

Keywords: Civil law, legal nature, Market in Crypto-assets Regulation, UNIDROIT DAPL, proprietary rights

1 Glance at the legal nature of VCCs and crypto-assets across different jurisdictions —— 240
- 1.1 Growing discussion regarding the legal nature of VCCs in different jurisdictions —— 240
- 1.2 Legal nature of crypto-assets and questions of property across different jurisdictions —— 241

2 Legal nature of VCC tokens under Union and German law —— 241
- 2.1 Categorisation of VCC tokens under the Markets in Crypto-Assets Regulation —— 242
- 2.2 Is a VCC token a claim against another person? —— 244
- 2.3 Ownership according to Art. 70(1) MiCAR and Principle 3(1) UNIDROIT DAPL? —— 245
- 2.4 VCC tokens and their categorisation under German civil law —— 246

3 Transfer of VCC tokens —— 249
- 3.1 Change of control as one form of transfer —— 250
- 3.2 Transfer solely within the law of obligations? —— 250
- 3.3 Transfer by agreement and delivery comparable to movable things? —— 251
- 3.4 Transfer by way of assignment comparable to the assignment of rights —— 251

4 Statutory obligations in the context of VCC tokens —— 252
- 4.1 Claims arising from the loss of physical possession? —— 253

https://doi.org/10.1515/9783111706719-010

4.2 Claim for removal of an interference with an absolute right — 253
4.3 Claim for compensation for damages according to tort law — 254
4.4 Claim to surrender on the basis of unjust enrichment — 254
5 Conclusions — 255

1 Glance at the legal nature of VCCs and crypto-assets across different jurisdictions

The VCM presents itself as an international market. As carbon projects depend on certain environmental circumstances, the carbon project and the investor are not necessarily located in the same jurisdiction and cross-border matters are common.[1] This analysis is focused on the Union and German perspective, yet a short look into US and English law will contribute to a deeper understanding of the matter and indicate the trends on the international stage concerning legal issues regarding VCC tokens as well.

1.1 Growing discussion regarding the legal nature of VCCs in different jurisdictions

Currently, and as far as we can see, the legal nature of VCC tokens has not been explicitly regulated by lawmakers around the globe.[2] Yet there are sources dealing with the legal nature of (traditional and non-digital) VCCs that state that VCC tokens could be treated equally.[3] Besides documents by market players[4] or affiliated law firms,[5] only studies by supra-national organisations have profoundly analysed the legal nature of traditional and non-digital VCCs in certain jurisdictions.[6] A discussion in the German or English academic legal literature cannot be identified, again with the caveat that all legal literature from all jurisdictions can hardly have been reviewed. It is largely accepted that VCCs can be seen as commodities under US law.[7] This is plausible due to the very broad definition of the term set out in Section 1a(9) of the Commodity Exchange Act.[8] It is also stated that VCCs can be interpreted as intangible property under French law.[9] Similarly, there are assessments considering VCCs as intangible property under English law.[10] In both cases, parallels to the legal nature of EU emission allowances are drawn.

It is doubtful that the legal nature of VCC tokens can be decided upon by solely looking at the parallel discussion regarding traditional and non-digital VCCs. The digital manifestation of VCC tokens could be an important difference when assessing their legal nature. However, the findings that other jurisdictions are open to include VCCs in their judicial framework and consider them as some kind of property or subject to proprietary rights need to be kept in mind for the further analysis.

1.2 Legal nature of crypto-assets and questions of property across different jurisdictions

As already mentioned, when discussing the legal nature of VCC tokens, the legal nature of crypto-assets plays an important role. Due to their digital manifestation, VCC tokens could be seen as crypto-assets and hence categorised in the same way. At the EU level, the discussion is influenced by Union (regulatory) legislation such as the Markets in Crypto-Assets Regulation (MiCAR).[11] However, such regulatory legislation inherently does not (fully) determine the civil law of crypto-assets on a national level. Most importantly, Union law must be neutral towards the property law of its Member States (cf. Art. 345 TFEU).[12] Further, the Union legislation, in principle, looks at crypto-assets from a regulatory point of view and is only concerned with specific questions, for instance, those of consumer protection. The civil law of crypto-assets remains widely non-codified and is disputed in academia across different legislations. A prominent example of such a debate was the Law Commission consultation of England and Wales on digital assets.[13] Its work led to a draft bill, which was recently introduced by the UK Government and provides that digital assets can be considered to be personal property under the laws of England and Wales.[14] Already before the consultation, English courts ruled that crypto-assets can be considered property under English law.[15] Under US law, while lacking a nationwide codification, the view that crypto-assets are property seems to be predominant across state borders.[16] Further, there are European civil law legislations that treat some crypto-assets at least partly as property.[17]

To conclude, there is a strong tendency on a global level to consider crypto-assets as property or proprietary rights. The recent English approach is likely to further nourish this development. The analysis will continue to examine whether VCC tokens can be categorised as crypto-assets and which conclusions are to be drawn in this regard from a Union and German law perspective.

2 Legal nature of VCC tokens under Union and German law

After a brief glance at the legal nature of VCCs and crypto-assets under different jurisdictions, the focus will be shifted towards VCC tokens under Union and German law. It will be discussed how VCC tokens fit into various existing categories in law with a focus on proprietary matters and it will be asked what VCC tokens are or embody at their very core.

2.1 Categorisation of VCC tokens under the Markets in Crypto-Assets Regulation

To gain a comprehensive understanding of the legal nature of VCC tokens and to define the legal landscape of crypto-assets, it is advisable to look at existing definitions in this area. However, it needs to be kept in mind that definitions do not lead to legal consequences by themselves. This is especially the case in the context of civil law as definitions may originate from regulatory legal frameworks.

2.1.1 VCC tokens as financial instruments under MiFID II?

In 2023, the EU introduced MiCAR as a comprehensive regulatory framework for crypto markets, placed next to the MiFID II[18] regime and therefore designed to establish an either-or-framework. This is why MiCAR does not apply to financial instruments (Art. 2(4)(a) MiCAR) or other instruments listed in Art. 2(4) MiCAR, which shall be largely governed by the co-regime, the MiFID II. According to Art. 3(1)(49) MiCAR, the term 'financial instrument' consequently means financial instruments as defined in Art. 4(1)(15) MiFID II. MiFID II does not define financial instruments in an abstract way but specifies those instruments in Section C of Annex I. Importantly, Art. 4(1)(15) MiFID II explicitly states since its latest amendment by the DLT Pilot Regime[19] that instruments issued by means of distributed ledger technology are included.

The most debatable category which could apply to VCC tokens is 'transferable securities'.[20] This category is further defined in Art. 4(1)(44) MiFID II and means

> those classes of securities which are negotiable on the capital market, with the exception of instruments of payment, such as: (a) shares in companies and other securities equivalent to shares in companies, partnerships or other entities, and depositary receipts in respect of shares; (b) bonds or other forms of securitised debt, including depositary receipts in respect of such securities; (c) any other securities giving the right to acquire or sell any such transferable securities or giving rise to a cash settlement determined by reference to transferable securities, currencies, interest rates or yields, commodities or other indices or measures.

Whereas VCC tokens are indeed negotiable on a comparable (small) market, it is already questionable whether the market is part of the 'capital market' in the sense of Art. 4(1)(44) MiFID II. Further, the wording of the article itself could oppose such an understanding. VCC tokens, unlike shares or bonds, do not embody a certain claim (see Section 2.2 below for this question), yet this could be a common understanding of the term 'security' in general. However, both aspects can be left aside, since, most importantly, VCC tokens do not give 'the right to acquire or sell any such transferable securities as shares or bonds or give rise to a cash settlement' in the sense of Art. 4(1)(44) MiFID II. Consequently, the precise and rather narrow definitions of 'transferable security' and 'financial instrument' are not applicable. This finding can be supported by the fact that EU emission allowances which have some common characteristics with VCC tokens are listed *separately* in Section C of Annex I and not mentioned in Art. 4(1)(44) MiFID II. To conclude, VCC tokens are not financial instruments in the meaning of MiFID II and hence could be crypto-assets under MiCAR.[21]

2.1.2 VCC tokens as crypto-assets according to Art. 3(1)(5) MiCAR

The key term of MiCAR is 'crypto-asset' as defined in Art. 3(1)(5) MiCAR. It means 'a digital representation of a value or of a right that is able to be transferred and stored electronically using distributed ledger technology or similar technology'. As explicitly stated in Recital (16) MiCAR, the term 'should be defined as widely as possible'. Further, Recital (2) MiCAR states that the meaning of value can be subjective and based only on the interest of the purchaser of the crypto-asset. Whilst the value or right represented by a VCC token needs to be further discussed below, it can already be decided at this point whether a VCC token can be subsumed as a crypto-asset under MiCAR.

As VCC tokens are purchased and traded, they represent a value of some kind. A crucial question is whether VCC tokens are transferable as demanded by MiCAR. The transfer is further illustrated by Recital (17) MiCAR. It states that 'digital assets that are accepted only by the issuer or the offeror and that are technically impossible to transfer directly to other holders should be excluded from the scope of this Regulation'. As an example, loyalty schemes are mentioned. Interoperability between different platforms on the market for VCC tokens is not given (yet). Also, the technical transfer of the VCC token itself often demands an action of the trading platform or registry (see Section 3 for the question, whether and how claims, rights, or other things in the context of VCC tokens can be transferred). Yet, this is the case for many crypto-assets. Moreover, VCC tokens are usually held using a (third-party) wallet in the same way as other known crypto-assets like Bitcoin, Ether, or Tether and can be transferred into a wallet and from one blockchain address to another.[22] Likewise, VCC tokens are not only accepted by the issuer or the offeror but by several market participants, for example, a buyer on the secondary market. Therefore, a transfer within the meaning of MiCAR takes place. VCC tokens are also electronically stored using distributed ledger technology. VCC tokens are therefore crypto-assets as defined in Art. 3(1)(5) MiCAR.

MiCAR defines different categories of crypto-assets. Most prominent is the distinction mentioned in Recital (18) MiCAR between electronic money tokens (Art. 3(1)(7) MiCAR), asset-referenced tokens (Art. 3(1)(6) MiCAR), and other crypto-assets (Title II MiCAR), including utility tokens (Art. 3(1)(9) MiCAR). Utility tokens are defined as crypto-assets that are 'only intended to provide access to a good or a service supplied by its issuer'. Whereas the (self-)categorisation as utility tokens was in vogue to bypass regulatory requirements before MiCAR,[23] today's clear definition limits the scope of the term. Although VCC tokens have been described as utility tokens in the past as well,[24] this categorisation could fail under the MiCAR definition. As will be shown below, there are services connected to holding VCC tokens to be considered, like for instance the retirement of the VCC token. Yet, VCC tokens are not *only* intended to provide a service supplied by its issuer, like a voucher or coupon.[25] VCC tokens have a value by themselves and the holder may decide the fate of a VCC token. Hence, VCC tokens do not seem to be utility tokens as defined in Art. 3(1)(9) MiCAR.[26]

2.2 Is a VCC token a claim against another person?

2.2.1 Claims in the context of traditional and non-digital VCCs

One crucial question when discussing the legal nature of VCC tokens is whether they are, embody or represent claims against involved parties. The studies regarding the legal nature of traditional and non-digital VCCs discussed a so-called bundle of rights approach.[27] More specifically, it was discussed whether a VCC represents a claim against the standard setter or registry to retire the carbon credit, that is, to take it out of circulation and consider its effect to be consumed. Yet, this approach was not further followed, as it was not able to fully characterise the legal nature of VCCs. Even further, it was stated that VCCs themselves are not claims against another person.[28]

This view is convincing. A VCC serves a different function from an economic perspective. A holder of a VCC wishes to gain a 'green' or 'sustainable' image towards its customers or the market in general by compensating for its own emissions, for example. They might also have the desire to trade with VCCs as an investment vehicle. Yet, the holder does not desire to pursue a claim in the future or to claim a future right against another person.[29] A VCC does not work as a voucher or coupon and has its own inherent value. Further, it is unlikely that such a 'claim' could be used to make use of a right of retention or set-off. This, however, would (usually) be possible with a claim in a legal sense.

Leaving the technical aspects aside, these considerations are transferable to VCC tokens as well. VCC tokens serve, in general, the same economic function as VCCs. The wish to compensate for emissions is guiding for the holder rather than having a (future) claim against another person. Furthermore, when reviewing the use cases, it is even unclear whether the holder of a VCC token would have an enforceable claim against the standard setter or registry as discussed above. The parties involved try to make use of extensive disclaimers to not be liable whatsoever.[30] The comparison with VCCs therefore speaks against the view that VCC tokens are or represent claims.

2.2.2 Claims in the context of crypto-assets in general

When looking at VCC tokens primarily as crypto-assets, the picture does not change. Crypto-assets do not inherently represent a claim against another party.[31] A crypto-asset may be used to reflect the actual non-digital legal situation and ideally the content of the blockchain does not contradict with underlying contractual agreements. However, the crypto-asset itself (typically) does not embody a claim against another person. Exceptions to this general rule are possible. For example, it is possible to issue securities in an electronic form as the German Electronic Securities Act[32] ('eWpG') shows. In this case, similar to bills of exchanges or cheques, the digital 'paper' embodies the claim itself. The claim is only transferred when transferring the digital 'paper'.[33]

However, similar provisions or economic considerations are not reflected in the use cases for VCC tokens. For example, non-assignment clauses are not part of the terms of VCC tokens. The blockchain can be used to trace back the history of a VCC token and further information can be stored. But this information does not give rise to claims and is not by itself enforceable by law. Therefore, VCC tokens themselves—similar to most crypto-assets in general—are not and do not represent claims. The fact that a holder of a VCC token has contractual claims against involved parties due to the underlying contractual framework needs to be considered separately and will be discussed below. The VCC token itself is not a representation of such claims. This is consistent with the understanding that VCC tokens fall under the category of intrinsic tokens.[34]

2.3 Ownership according to Art. 70(1) MiCAR and Principle 3(1) UNIDROIT DAPL?

2.3.1 Art. 70(1) MiCAR and ownership rights

The finding that a VCC token does not represent a claim does not mean that it is automatically to be considered a 'nothing' in the legal sense. Just as any other object, it could still be subject to proprietary rights or transferred with legal effect. Property law is in general determined by the national law of the Member States of the European Union (Art. 345 TFEU).[35] Yet, as VCC tokens are to be considered crypto-assets under MiCAR, it needs to be analysed if MiCAR comments on ownership rights or other property issues. According to Art. 70(1) MiCAR, 'crypto-asset service providers that hold crypto-assets belonging to clients or the means of access to such crypto-assets shall make adequate arrangements to safeguard the ownership rights of clients'.

This provision indicates that MiCAR assumes that ownership rights regarding crypto-assets persist. However, it does not state that crypto-assets are to be considered property. This is consistent as the system of property ownership is, as already mentioned and shown in Art. 345 TFEU, subject to the national law of the Member States. Besides the fact that MiCAR acts on the assumption that ownership rights persist, no further consequences can be drawn from Art. 70(1) MiCAR in this regard.[36] Nevertheless, it is important to notice that the European legislator is at least open to this concept and leaves it up to the Member States to regulate ownership (or similar rights) in the context of crypto-assets.

2.3.2 Principle 3(1) UNIDROIT DAPL and proprietary rights for digital assets

Principle 3(1) UNIDROIT DAPL[37] states that 'a digital asset can be subject of proprietary rights.' A digital asset is defined in Principle 2(2) UNIDROIT DAPL and means 'an electronic record which is capable of being subject to control'. As a VCC token contains information stored on a blockchain and can be held and transferred using a wallet, it is a digital asset within the meaning of Principle 3(1) UNIDROIT DAPL. According to Commentary 3.4., 'proprietary rights' must be understood in a broad sense and is not necessarily congruent with the term 'ownership' across different jurisdictions. Commentary 3.2. states that 'whether digital assets can be the subject of proprietary rights (a legal consequence) must be distinguished from the categorisation of digital assets'.

As the UNIDROIT DAPL represent soft-law, they are by definition not able to settle the current legal situation. Also, UNIDROIT, as a supra-national organisation is particularly sensitive about differentiating legal frameworks around the globe, including different concepts of proprietary rights. Yet, it is clearly shown and explicitly stated in Commentary 3.1. that UNIDROIT 'advise[s] states to increase legal certainty on this issue and make explicit that digital assets can be the subject of proprietary rights'. This finding corresponds with the concept of ownership rights under MiCAR and indicates that different institutions are not only open to proprietary rights in the context of crypto-assets but even recommend a codification of this approach.

2.4 VCC tokens and their categorisation under German civil law

After examining Union law and the abstract question of whether a VCC token represents a claim against another person (*quod non*), a categorisation of VCC tokens under German civil law shall be undertaken. It was shown that Union law is not able to determine proprietary issues of its Member States and that national law must be examined in this regard. Looking at those and other issues, different categories with varying legal consequences come into play.

2.4.1 VCC tokens and corporeal objects

When discussing the legal nature of digital assets, a first path to consider is the comparability to corporeal objects. Whereas civil law jurisdictions such as Germany and Switzerland[38] have codified rules regarding corporeal objects, the common law system distinguishes between two types of personal property, that is, choses in possession and choses in action.[39] The former only applies to corporeal objects. German property law is often concerned with the term 'thing' (German text: 'Sache') defined in Sec. 90 German Civil Code[40] ('BGB'). For example, Sec. 903 BGB, which describes the powers of the owner, mentions 'the owner of a thing'. Sec. 929 BGB describes 'the transfer of the ownership of a movable thing'. Therefore, it must be analysed whether VCC tokens are things as defined in Sec. 90 BGB.

Sec. 90 BGB states that 'only corporeal objects are things as defined by law'. The definition demands corporeality. Non-corporeal objects are not things within the meaning of Sec. 90 BGB. While corporeality is not further defined by law, there is a common understanding that a thing within the meaning of the section needs to be sensuously perceivable and spatially delimited.[41] This is not the case for VCC tokens, which only exist in digital form. There is a prevailing understanding in German legal literature that crypto-assets are not corporeal objects.[42] This leads to the prevailing view that Sec. 90 BGB cannot be applied (directly) to crypto-assets.

Yet, it is argued that corporeality within the meaning of Sec. 90 BGB needs to be understood in a functional way emphasising controllability and differentiability.[43] Such characteristics could be fulfilled by VCC tokens as well. This view might lead to a stronger legal position for the holder of a VCC token as German property law would apply. A functional understanding could simplify the treatment of crypto-assets under German law at first glance but might give rise to difficult interpretations of provisions on the law of things and property that were never designed for tokens. The question remains if such a strong functional approach would not only push the boundaries of the wording to its limit but rather exceed them. A decision by the German courts or the legislator on this matter remains desirable but is currently not in sight.

There are authors who advocate for treating crypto-assets like things applying Sec. 90 BGB mutatis mutandis.[44] However, whether the numerous counter-arguments can be overcome remains questionable. Firstly, the provisions of the BGB are based on the understanding that things are corporeal. A functional view would lead to friction with the manifold provisions concerning (corporeal) things. For example, provisions relating to the transfer of things or *bona fide* acquisitions could hardly be suitable for crypto-assets.[45] Secondly, the German legislator had the opportunity to update the traditional understanding of a thing within the meaning of Sec. 90 BGB over the last years in several instances.[46] Nevertheless, it decided to stick with such understanding and rather implement a provision like Sec. 2(3) eWpG. It states 'an electronic security is deemed to be a thing within the meaning of Sec. 90 BGB.' Instead of changing Sec. 90 BGB itself (or allowing an application mutatis mutandis), the German legislator decided to codify a legal fiction for (only) a specific instrument. To conclude, VCC tokens are not things according to Sec. 90 BGB and are not to be treated as such.

2.4.2 VCC tokens as intangible assets

The term intangible asset is not uniformly defined and may vary from jurisdiction to jurisdiction. Yet, in the context of VCCs and VCC tokens, it is a crucial term as it, generally speaking, suggests a value and a tradability of an object. The term intangible asset is not codified in German civil law. German sales law is once again centred around the term 'things' as the core provision of Sec. 433 BGB shows, which speaks of 'the seller of a thing'. Still, the provisions regarding purchase agreements in Sec. 433ff BGB do not only apply to things. This is depicted in Sec. 453(1) sentence 1 BGB, which states that 'the provisions governing the purchase of things apply accordingly to the purchase of rights and other objects'. VCC tokens themselves are not rights in the understanding of German sales law. With a similar reasoning to that above, a VCC token as pure digital information does not embody a claim or another right within the meaning of the provision. However, 'object' (German text: 'Gegenstand') is another key term in German civil law, which therefore needs to be further examined. If VCC tokens were objects under German law, *inter alia*, the provisions regarding purchase agreements would be applicable.

The term is not defined by law. It is important to notice that the term 'object' has a catch-all function in German civil law and German sales law in particular.[47] If VCC tokens were not considered as objects, they would be considered as a legal nullity under German *sales* law as codified in Sec. 433ff BGB. The fact that market participants acquire VCC tokens in exchange for a digital or non-digital payment would oppose such a consideration. Objects, *inter alia*, are intangible assets.[48] Intangible assets have the characteristics that they are tradable and have an economic value.[49] VCC tokens are traded on certain platforms and have a value as they are purchased with money or other currencies or can be exchanged. Consequently, VCC tokens are intangible assets and, hence, objects within the meaning of Sec. 453(1) sentence 1 BGB as well.[50] This finding is further supported by the newly integrated Sec. 453(1) sentence 2 BGB, which states that a digital content can be subject of a sales contract. A VCC token as digital information on the blockchain is comparable with a digital content from a technical point of view. In light of the aforementioned findings, it is possible to conclude legally effective sales contracts regarding VCC tokens as they are considered intangible assets under German civil law.

2.4.3 VCC tokens as absolute rights

Another essential part of civil law is tort law. Generally speaking, tort law (amongst other things) secures in particular the integrity of absolute rights. German tort law, *inter alia*, is covered by Sec. 823ff BGB. A core provision is Sec. 823(1) BGB, which states: 'A person who, intentionally or negligently, unlawfully injures the life, limb, health, freedom, property, or some other right of another person is liable to provide compensation to the other party for the damage arising therefrom.' A VCC token could be considered as an 'other right' within the meaning of Sec. 823(1) BGB. The term is not further defined by law. It must be defined from a tort law perspective and is not necessarily congruent with the usage of 'right' in Sec. 453(1) sentence 1 BGB. An 'other right' must be an absolute right, that is, a legal position which is also protected or recognised by provisions outside of tort law.[51] Such absolute rights are characterised as follows: The right must be allocated to a specific person, the owner of the right must be able to use the right independently of the will of others and the owner must be able to exclude others from the right.[52]

A VCC token is held by a specific person as the holder. This is usually done by storing the VCC token on the blockchain address of the holder and further indicated by an entry in a register. That does not change when the client engages a crypto custodian, as a crypto-asset service provider shall make adequate arrangements to safeguard the ownership rights of its clients according to Art. 70(1) MiCAR.[53] When the VCC token is allocated to the blockchain address of the holder or crypto custodian, only the person who has the private key may transfer the VCC token. Only the holder/client is able to freely use the right, for example, to request the retirement of the VCC token. Further, only the holder/client can exclude others from the right as no other person is able to transfer or impact the VCC token.

That digital information—as VCC tokens constitute such digital information—is also protected and recognised by provisions outside of tort law is shown by Sec. 303a German Criminal Code[54] ('StGB'), which penalises the deletion, suppression, rendering, or altering of data,[55] and Sec. 327ff BGB, which deal with digital products.[56] Therefore, a VCC token could be considered an absolute right and an 'other right' in the meaning of Sec. 823(1) BGB.[57] The integrity of a VCC token is, in general, protected under German tort law (see Section 4.3 for compensation for damages, etc.).

3 Transfer of VCC tokens

After the legal nature of VCC tokens has been examined, the transfer of VCC tokens shall be analysed from a legal perspective. Transfer is closely connected with property or proprietary rights and therefore the examination of national law is required. Yet, as shown below, the UNIDROIT DAPL and MiCAR also comment on some kind of transfer, namely the change of control. Whereas the further analysis is centred around the German point of view, the underlying concepts of transfer could be transferred to other jurisdictions as well and the broad lines of thought are universally applicable.

3.1 Change of control as one form of transfer

The discussion regarding the transfer of VCC tokens is usually centred around the transfer of ownership or proprietary rights. However, due to the factual and legal characteristics of VCC tokens and digital assets, it must be kept in mind that already the change of control over a VCC token can be followed by legal consequences. Whether proprietary rights are transferred is a separate question to be answered. The UNIDROIT DAPL do not comment on the transfer of proprietary rights in a digital asset and leave it to the 'law of a State', that is, national legislation (Commentary 2.26. and 6.5). Nevertheless, the change of control plays an important part when dealing with digital assets. For example, the change of control is one condition of a *bona fide* acquisition according to Principle 8(1)(a) UNIDROIT DAPL. In order to qualify as an innocent acquirer, a transferee must, *inter alia*, obtain control of the digital asset. 'Control' is defined in Principle 6(1) UNIDROIT DAPL and according to Commentary 6.1 and 6.2., is a purely factual matter rather than a legal concept. Hence, a change of control is also of a factual nature and not (necessarily) a legal act. Similarly, MiCAR speaks of 'control' and 'controlling' of crypto-assets (e.g., Art. 3(1)(17), Art. 75(3)), especially with regard to crypto-asset service providers. As the EU legislator is neutral towards the systems of property ownership of its Member States, the use of different concepts is needed (see Section 2.3.1 for more details).

This change of control does not necessarily go hand in hand with the transfer of ownership. However, certain legal consequences may be linked to the transfer of control. For dealing with VCC tokens, this leads to the conclusion that particular attention needs to be paid to the control aspects of VCC tokens. While today's market for VCC tokens is not as elaborate and crypto-asset service providers do not shape the image of the market, the situation might change in the future. Likewise, it is possible that national or other lawmakers may gravitate to a more practical change of control approach when regulating civil law aspects of crypto-assets like VCC tokens in the future.

3.2 Transfer solely within the law of obligations?

When analysing the transfer of VCC tokens, the discussion regarding the transfer of crypto-assets in general needs to be considered. There are authors who advocate for the view that crypto-assets are and can only be transferred within the law of obligations.[58] This is insofar plausible as crypto-assets are not considered corporeal objects and cannot be physically delivered. For example, VCC tokens are currently not considered things within the meaning of Sec. 90 BGB (see Section 2.4.1) and Sec. 929 BGB for the transfer of movable things is not (at least not directly) applicable.

However, a view that solely looks at the law of obligations and demands only a contractual agreement does not reflect the factual process of how a VCC token is transferred. Besides a transfer agreement, at least some kind of factual or legal act regarding access to the VCC token must be considered. The transfer via the blockchain or the factual access to the VCC token cannot be completely ignored. From a German perspective, such a view also contradicts the German abstract system of title transfer (German: Abstraktionsprinzip), which separates the obligation (*causa*) to transfer an object and the conveyance of the legal title to such object. Those processes need to be treated separately (or abstractly) and one does not affect the other. Therefore, a transfer solely within the law of obligations is hardly convincing under German civil law.[59] Besides this matter of German civil law, it is questionable whether a sole obligational agreement that omits the issues of control over the VCC token is suitable to describe the transfer of VCC tokens comprehensively.

3.3 Transfer by agreement and delivery comparable to movable things?

While VCC tokens cannot be physically delivered, one could still argue that VCC tokens should be transferred comparable to the transfer of movable things. The delivery could be seen in using the private key to a wallet to start the technical process of transferring a VCC token from one blockchain address to another. In German law, a mutatis mutandis application of Sec. 929 sentence 1 BGB could be considered.[60] Sec. 929 sentence 1 BGB states that 'the transfer of the ownership of a movable thing requires the owner to deliver the thing to the acquirer and both to agree that ownership is to pass'.

However, said acts by the holder of the VCC token are not able to effect a 'delivery' sufficiently similar to the corporeal delivery of a movable thing. The usage of the private key only initiates a process in which several parties are involved and on which the technical transfer depends. Besides a possible action required by the registry, the verification in the network of the blockchain (e.g., a proof of work or a proof of stake) and the consensus of its members are required to transfer the VCC token. Only when this verification and consensus take place is the transaction logged into the blockchain. Consequently, in the context of VCC tokens, there is no sufficient equivalent to the delivery by the owner (or holder) as stipulated by Sec. 929 sentence 1 BGB. A transfer comparable to the transfer of movable things, for example, applying Sec. 929 BGB mutatis mutandis under German law, is hence not suitable for VCC tokens.

3.4 Transfer by way of assignment comparable to the assignment of rights

As a third way, besides a sole obligational agreement and a transfer comparable to the transfer of movable things, the transfer by way of assignment could be considered.[61] In German law, the assignment of rights is dealt with in Sec. 413, 398 BGB.

Since VCC tokens are intangible assets (see Section 2.4.3.), they are 'other rights' within the meaning of Sec. 413 BGB.[62] According to Sec. 398 BGB, the transfer to another person takes place 'by contract with that person (assignment)'. The transfer is completed 'when the contract is concluded.' Hence, the assignment itself effects the transfer of the right. However, such transfer by sole assignment cannot be construed for VCC tokens. The assignment is not able to fully effect the transfer of the VCC token as already stated above. Besides the assignment, the verification in the network is needed to log the transaction into the blockchain. The sole assignment, under German law according to Sec. 413, 398 BGB, is therefore not sufficient to effect the transfer of the VCC token.[63]

However, this problem could be solved by a peculiarity of the assignment agreement. Such peculiarity according to a mutual agreement is covered by the freedom of contract and does, at least under German law, not contradict the law of assignments. Moreover, Sec. 398 and 399 BGB provide for the option of a different agreement between the parties. Sec. 399 second alternative BGB states that 'a claim [or an other right] may not be assigned [. . .] if the assignment is excluded by agreement with the obligor [or the other party]'. This provision applies accordingly to the transfer of other rights according to Sec. 413 BGB, as well. Whereas the parties are not interested in excluding the assignment, it is accepted under German civil law that agreements other than the full exclusion of assignment are possible.[64] As a consequence, under German law an assignment is permitted where parties agree to transfer rights exclusively via a specific blockchain. This view reflects the technical process of transferring a VCC token on a blockchain and suits the commercial practice of transferring VCC tokens in an appropriate way. Therefore, a VCC token is transferred by way of assignment with the peculiarity that the parties agree to transfer the VCC token exclusively on the blockchain used. Under German law, this transfer can be construed by applying Sec. 413, 398, 399 second alternative BGB accordingly.[65]

4 Statutory obligations in the context of VCC tokens

After examining the legal nature of a VCC token and analysing its transfer from a legal perspective, aspects of liability in the context of VCC tokens shall be discussed. The market for VCC tokens is based on several contractual agreements between the participating parties. Issues of liability are manifold and to be considered within each contractual relationship. As this analysis is focused on VCC tokens rather than traditional and non-digital VCCs, questions regarding the risks of carbon projects or the validity of (external) auditing statements shall not be discussed. In this regard, VCC tokens do not necessarily pose a new challenge to legal practitioners. Instead, the consequences of the findings regarding the legal nature of VCC tokens shall be further analysed, namely the statutory obligations in the context of VCC tokens.

4.1 Claims arising from the loss of physical possession?

Statutory obligations are closely connected to the findings above regarding the legal nature of VCC tokens. Under German law, VCC tokens are (currently) not considered things within the meaning of Sec. 90 BGB (see Section 2.4.1). Therefore, several statutory obligations regarding things in German civil law do not apply. This is the case for statutory obligations or claims in connection with the 'possession' of a thing. Claims on account of deprivation of or interference with possession according to Sec. 861 and 862 BGB cannot be pursued, as they require the possession of a thing within the meaning of Sec. 90 BGB.[66] This also applies to the claim of the former possessor according to Sec. 1007(1) or (2) BGB since it also requires the possession of a movable thing, as stated by the norm itself.

Similarly, the claim to surrender according to Sec. 985 BGB is not applicable as it requires the ownership of a thing within the meaning of Sec. 90 BGB.[67] Consequently, claims regarding emoluments or damages according to Sec. 987ff BGB do not exist either, as they require the ownership of a thing, too. An application of these provisions mutatis mutandis is not indicated as the legal position of the holder of a VCC token is protected by law through other means, as shown below. Furthermore, the above considerations could be transferable to other jurisdictions as well. As VCC tokens are not corporeal objects, physical possession could be denied in other jurisdictions in the same manner.

4.2 Claim for removal of an interference with an absolute right

Whereas a person has no physical possession in a VCC token, other ways are defined by law to defend against interferences for the holder. Sec. 1004(1) BGB states: 'If the ownership is interfered with by means other than removal or retention of possession, the owner may demand that the disturber remove the interference. If there is the concern that further interferences will ensue, the owner may seek a prohibitory injunction.' As already stated, VCC tokens are other rights within the meaning of Sec. 823(1) BGB. It is accepted by German courts and legal literature that such other rights as absolute rights are protected by the application of Sec. 1004(1) BGB mutatis mutandis.[68]

Applying this to VCC tokens, it is conceivable that the control over a VCC token is interfered with. This could be the case if the functionality of or the disposing over a VCC token is restricted, especially by technical means. It is imaginable that access to a holder's wallet is restricted or hindered or that the blockchain itself or the function to log in further information is affected. In this case, the removal of the interference can be demanded mutatis mutandis Sec. 1004(1) sentence 1 BGB.[69] Prohibitory injunctions according to Sec. 1004(1) sentence 2 BGB are conceivable in the context of VCC tokens, as well, if an interference is to be expected.

4.3 Claim for compensation for damages according to tort law

Other important statutory claims to consider are such arising from tort law. Sec. 823 (1) BGB states, *inter alia*, that who unlawfully injures an other right of another person is liable to provide compensation to the other party for the damage arising therefrom. As shown above, a VCC token qualifies as an other right within the meaning of the norm and hence Sec. 823(1) BGB can, in principle, be applied to VCC tokens. A VCC token can be 'injured' if the digital 'substance' of the VCC token is damaged. This could be the case if the VCC token's content was deleted or the network of the blockchain is attacked to the point of non-functionality. In these cases, compensation for damages could be claimed.

Likewise, Sec. 823(2) BGB could be applied. It states that 'the same duty is incumbent on a person who commits a breach of a statute that is intended to protect another person'. Instead of an injury of an absolute right, the breach of a protective statute is required. Here, Sec. 303a(1) StGB constitutes such a statute which states that 'whoever unlawfully deletes, suppresses, renders unusable or alters data (Sec. 202a(2) StGB) incurs a penalty of imprisonment for a term not exceeding two years or a fine'. The statute intends to protect the holder of any kind of data.[70] The holder of a VCC token is therefore protected under this law as well. If one of the listed actions occurred in the context of a VCC token, for example, a VCC token was manipulated to the extent of non-functionality, the holder would be entitled to compensation for their damages.

4.4 Claim to surrender on the basis of unjust enrichment

Lastly, a claim to surrender on the basis of unjust enrichment could be considered in the context of VCC tokens as well. This claim is defined in Sec. 812(1) BGB which reads:

> A person who obtains something as a result of the performance of another person or otherwise at that person's expense without legal grounds for doing so is under a duty to surrender to that person what has been obtained. This duty also exists if the legal grounds later cease to exist or if the result intended to be achieved by an act of performance in accordance with the substance of the legal transaction does not materialise.

'Something' within the meaning of Sec. 812(1) BGB can be any benefit that has some asset value.

Holding or having control over a VCC token constitutes such a benefit as a VCC token has an economic value. It is traded for a certain price and usually acquired in exchange for a payment. The obtaining of such a position (i.e., holding or having control over the VCC token) could occur by accidentally transferring the VCC token or fraudulently obtaining control over it, for example, by gaining access to the rightful owner's wallet. Each alternative of Sec. 812(1) BGB can be applicable depending on the relationship between the parties. For example, while an accidental transfer could be the result of the performance of another person, fraudulently obtaining control could be seen as otherwise obtaining at the other person's expense. The legal consequence of Sec. 812(1) BGB is the claim to surrender what has been obtained, in this case, the control over a VCC token, for instance.

5 Conclusions

Several different areas of civil law were the subject of this analysis. Similar to traditional and non-digital VCCs, the legal discussion concerning the civil law of VCC tokens is still at an early stage. When analysing VCC tokens, some considerations regarding traditional or non-digital VCCs can be drawn upon. This is, in particular, the case when discussing whether a VCC token itself is a claim against another person. It could be shown that VCC tokens as VCCs alike are not and do not represent a claim against another person. When diving deeper into questions of civil law, the similarities to traditional and non-digital VCCs decrease and crypto-assets in general move into focus. While other jurisdictions such as the United Kingdom are close to codifying some civil law aspects of the legal nature of crypto-assets, this is not necessarily the case for Union or German law. Union law and the UNIDROIT DAPL refrain from interfering with the property law of its Member States, respectively of national jurisdictions. Yet, both are open to ownership or proprietary rights regarding crypto-assets and the UNIDROIT DAPL even advise national legislators to increase legal certainty on this issue and make explicit that digital assets can be the subject of proprietary rights.

While VCC tokens are not corporeal objects and hence not 'things' within the meaning of German civil law, they are to be considered intangible assets and absolute rights under German law. Regarding the legal transfer of VCC tokens, those findings and the technical aspects of VCC tokens lead to the conclusion that they are transferred by way of assignment comparable to the assignment of rights with the peculiarity that the parties agree to exclusively transfer the VCC token on the blockchain used. An appealing concept is the change of control approach in the UNIDROIT DAPL (and MiCAR as well), which says that not only the change of proprietary right could lead to (severe) consequences but the change of control, too. The legal nature of VCC tokens further leads to various statutory obligations under German civil law. VCC tokens are protected by law and claims under tort law or on the basis of unjust enrichment are possible.

To summarise, already today VCC tokens can be integrated into German civil law and do not constitute a legal nullity. On the contrary, VCC tokens are intangible assets and absolute rights and protection by law are guaranteed. Nevertheless, it seems advisable to further codify issues concerning VCC tokens and crypto-assets in general to create more legal certainty for legal practitioners in the future. It remains to be seen whether the future of civil law on VCC tokens will be developed in accordance with the civil law of crypto-assets, or if a comprehensive framework for VCCs, which also includes VCC tokens, will eventually see the light of day.

Notes

1 See for the question of the applicable law Chapter 7, Dominik Skauradszun and Sebastian Böhning, 'Applicable Law in the Supply Chains of VCC Tokens'.

2 On 26.12.2024, Regulation (EU) 2024/3012 of the European Parliament and of the Council of 27.11.2024 establishing a Union certification framework for permanent carbon removals, carbon farming, and carbon storage in products (CRCR) [2024] OJ L3012/1 entered into force. However, the Regulation does not stipulate a regulatory legal framework. Instead, a voluntary certification framework was created at Union level (see Hans-Peter Schwintowski, 'Die Zertifizierung von CO_2-Entnahmen nach der CRCF-VO am Beispiel Wald' [2024] EWeRK Energie- und Wettbewerbsrecht in der Kommunalen Wirtschaft 87).

3 UNIDROIT Working Group on the Legal Nature of Verified Carbon Credits, 'Summary Report of the First Session, Study LXXXVI – W.G.1 – Doc. 3' (2024) 14 https://www.unidroit.org/wp-content/uploads/2024/01/Study-LXXXVI-W.G.1-Doc.-3-Report.pdf accessed 21 July 2025.

4 Toucan, 'Public Consultation: Verra's Approach to Third-Party Crypto Instruments and Tokens – Response document by Toucan Protocol' (2022) https://blog.toucan.earth/content/files/2023/01/Toucan_Verra_response.pdf accessed 21 July 2025.

5 Sim Ting, Adrian Ang and Tay Yong Seng, 'The Legal Character of Voluntary Carbon Credits: A Way Forward' (2024) https://genzero.co/wp-content/uploads/2024/03/The-Legal-Character-of-Voluntary-Carbon-Credits-report.pdf accessed 21 July 2025.

6 UNIDROIT Study LXXXVI, Legal Nature of Verified Carbon Credits, current status and documents under www.unidroit.org/work-in-progress/verified-carbon-credits/ accessed 21 July 2025; ISDA, 'The Legal Nature of Voluntary Carbon Credits: France, Japan and Singapore' (2022) https://www.isda.org/a/PlcgE/Legal-Nature-of-Voluntary-Carbon-CreditsFrance-Japan-and-Singapore.pdf accessed 21 July 2025; ISDA, 'Legal Implications of Voluntary Carbon Credits' (2021) https://www.isda.org/a/38ngE/Legal-Implications-of-Voluntary-Carbon-Credits.pdf accessed 21 July 2025.

7 Congressional Research Service, 'Voluntary Carbon Markets and the Commodity Futures Trading Commission' (2024) 2 https://crsreports.congress.gov/product/pdf/R/R48095 accessed 21 July 2025; ISDA, 'Legal Implications of Voluntary Carbon Credits' (n 6); Ben McQuhae & Co, 'The Legal Nature of Carbon Credits' (2023) https://bmcquhae.com/en/2023/03/15/the-legal-nature-of-carbon-credits/ accessed 21 July 2025.

8 Sec. 1a(9) of the Commodity Exchange Act (CEA): 'The term commodity means wheat, cotton, rice, corn, oats, barley, rye, flaxseed, grain sorghums, mill feeds, butter, eggs, Solanum tuberosum (Irish potatoes), wool, wool tops, fats and oils (including lard, tallow, cottonseed oil, peanut oil, soybean oil, and all other fats and oils), cottonseed meal, cottonseed, peanuts, soybeans, soybean meal, livestock, livestock products, and frozen concentrated orange juice, and all other goods and articles, except onions (as provided by section 13–1 of this title) and motion picture box office receipts (or any index, measure, value, or data related to such receipts), and all services, rights, and interests (except motion picture box office receipts, or any index, measure, value or data related to such receipts) in which contracts for future delivery are presently or in the future dealt in'.

9 ISDA, 'The Legal Nature of Voluntary Carbon Credits: France, Japan and Singapore' (n 6) 7.

10 ISDA, 'Legal Implications of Voluntary Carbon Credits' (n 6) 13; Ben McQuhae & Co (n 7).

11 Regulation (EU) 2023/1114 of the European Parliament and of the Council of 31 May 2023 on markets in crypto-assets and amending Regulations (EU) No 1093/2010 and (EU) No 1095/2010 and Directives 2013/36/EU and (EU) 2019/1937 [2023] OJ L150/40.

12 Dominik Skauradszun and Thi Minh Ngoc Nguyen, 'MiCAR, UNIDROIT Principles on Digital Assets and Private Law, and their Insolvency Principles' (2024) 123 ZVglRWiss Zeitschrift für Vergleichende Rechtswissenschaft 261, 267. Art. 345 TFEU reads 'The Treaties shall in no way prejudice the rules in Member States governing the system of property ownership.'

13 Law Commission of England and Wales, Project on Digital Assets, status and documents under https://lawcom.gov.uk/project/digital-assets/ accessed 21 July 2025.

14 Property (Digital Assets, etc.) Bill [HL].

15 E.g., AA v Persons Unknown [2019] EWHC 2556 (Comm); cf Sebastian Omlor, 'Digitales Eigentum an Blockchain Token – rechtvergleichende Entwicklungslinien' (2020) 119 ZVglRWiss Zeitschrift für Vergleichende Rechtswissenschaft 41, 47; Sophia Schwemmer, 'Das Tokensachstatut – Zur kollisionsrechtlichen Behandlung der Übertragung von Bitcoin, Kryptowertpapieren und anderen Kryptotoken' [2022] IPRax Praxis des Internationalen Privat- und Verfahrensrechts 331, 334.

16 Cf IRS, Digital assets https://www.irs.gov/businesses/small-businesses-self-employed/digital-assets accessed 21 July 2025; Jason G Allen, Michel Rauchs, Apolline Blandin and Keith Bear, 'Legal and Regulatory Considerations for Digital Assets' (2020) 22 https://www.jbs.cam.ac.uk/wp-content/uploads/2020/10/2020-ccaf-legal-regulatory-considerations-report.pdf accessed 21 July 2025; Schwemmer (n 15) 334; Frederick Rieländer, 'Eigentum an digitalen Vermögenswerten – Auf dem Weg zu einem sachenrechtlichen Zuordnungsregime für Krypto-Assets' [2024] ZEuP Zeitschrift für das Europäische Privatrecht 769, 777; Jason G Allen, Henry Wells and Marco Mauer, 'Cryptoassets in Private Law: Emerging Trends and Open Questions from the First 10 Years' (2022) SMU Centre for AI & Data Governance Research Paper No. 06/2022 11f; Joseph Jasperse, '50-State Review of Cryptocurrency and Blockchain Regulations' (2022) Stevens Center for Innovation in Finance https://stevenscenter.wharton.upenn.edu/publications-50-state-review/#_ftnref1 accessed 21 July 2025.

17 France has acknowledged ownership rights for security tokens, Sophia Schwemmer (n 15) 334; Lichtenstein has at least implicitly acknowledged ownership rights for crypto tokens, Omlor, 'Digitales Eigentum an Blockchain Token – rechtvergleichende Entwicklungslinien' (n 15) 54–57; Sophia Schwemmer (n 15) 334–335; Germany introduced the Electronic Securities Act in 2021 which treats crypto securities similar to traditional securities and states in Sec. 2(3) that an electronic security is deemed to be an object according to Sec. 90 German Civil code (see for details 2.4.1), cf Dominik Skauradszun and Selina Schweizer, 'Corporate Financing through Crypto Securities and Financial Restructuring in the Case of Company Distress' [2024] NIBLeJ Nottingham Insolvency and Business Law eJournal 1, 3ff.

18 Directive 2014/65/EU of the European Parliament and of the Council of 15 May 2014 on markets in financial instruments and amending Directive 2002/92/EC and Directive 2011/61/EU [2014] OJ L173/349.

19 Regulation (EU) 2022/858 of the European Parliament and of the Council of 30 May 2022 on a pilot regime for market infrastructures based on distributed ledger technology, and amending Regulations (EU) No 600/2014 and (EU) No 909/2014 and Directive 2014/65/EU [2022] OJ L151/1.

20 Dimitrios Linardatos, 'Finanzinstrumente im Digitalzeitalter – Teil II -' [2024] WM Zeitschrift für Wirtschafts- und Bankrecht 1685, 1689 mentions other derivate contracts according to point (10) of Section C of Annex I as a category worth discussing as well.

21 ISDA, 'The Legal Nature of Voluntary Carbon Credits: France, Japan and Singapore' (n 6) 5, 7; cf Linardatos (n 20) 1689; see for the regulatory and compliance matters regarding VCC tokens in detail Chapter 8, Leon Krug and Walter Blocher, 'VCC tokenisation: Navigating legal frameworks and designing for regulatory compliance'.

22 See as examples Toucan Terms of Service 3 https://toucan.earth/terms-of-service/ accessed 21 July 2025; Regen Network Whitepaper 2021, 33 https://regen-network.gitlab.io/whitepaper/WhitePaper.pdf accessed 21 July 2025.

23 Cf Anika Patz, 'Überblick über die Regulierung von Kryptowerten und Kryptowertedienstleistern' [2021] BKR Zeitschrift für Bank und Kapitalmarktrecht 725, 727.

24 Cf Toucan, 'Public Consultation: Verra's Approach to Third-Party Crypto Instruments and Tokens. Response document by Toucan Protocol' (n 4) 4; PWC, 'Carbon offset token' (2022) https://www.pwc.in/assets/pdfs/emerging-tech/carbon-offset-tokens.pdf accessed 21 July 2025.

25 There are other crypto-assets on the VCM related to VCC tokens that could constitute utility tokens. This is especially the case for 'carbon forward tokens' offered by Senken. By acquiring a carbon forward token, the right to purchase a future carbon credit for a discounted price is acquired. This allows pre-funding of carbon projects similar to futures. See for more details https://www.senken.io/blog/senken-has-launched-the-worlds-first-public-sale-of-carbon-forward-tokens accessed 21 July 2025.

26 See for the regulatory and compliance matters regarding VCC tokens in detail Blocher and Krug (n 21).

27 UNIDROIT Working Group on the Legal Nature of Verified Carbon Credits, 'Summary Report of the First Session, Study LXXXVI – W.G.1 – Doc. 3' (n 3) 11.

28 Principle 2(1) DRAFT UNIDROIT Principles on the Legal Nature of Verified Carbon Credits; UNIDROIT Working Group on the Legal Nature of Verified Carbon Credits, 'Summary Report of the Second Session, Study LXXXVI – W.G.2 – Doc. 3 rev.' (2024) 23 https://www.unidroit.org/wp-content/uploads/2024/07/Study-LXXXVI-W.G.2-Doc.-3-rev.-Summary-Report.pdf accessed 21 July 2025.

29 This is the case notwithstanding the manifold claims that could arise due to the underlying contractual relationship and obligations, see Section 4 for this matter.

30 E.g., Regen Network Terms of Service 4 https://www.regen.network/terms-service accessed 21 July 2025; Toucan Terms of Service (n 22) 23.6.

31 Dominik Skauradszun in Heinz Beck, Carl-Theodor Samm, Axel Kokemoor (eds), *Kreditwesengesetz mit CRR* (239th edn, C.F.Müller 2024) Kryptowerte im Bürgerlichen Recht, Internationalen Privatrecht und Bilanzrecht, III para 10; Dominik Skauradszun, 'Kryptowerte im Bürgerlichen Recht' (2021) 221 AcP Archiv für die civilistische Praxis 353, 365; Ursula Kleinert and Volker Mayer, 'Elektronische Wertpapiere und Krypto-Token' [2019] EuZW Europäische Zeitschrift für Wirtschaftsrecht 857, 859.

32 Gesetz über elektronische Wertpapiere (eWpG) 2021.

33 Christoph Gleske and Nikolaus Bunting in Klaus J Hopt and Christoph H Seibt (eds), *Schuldverschreibungsrecht* (2nd edn, Otto Schmidt 2023) Sec. 2 eWpG para 8–10.

34 Dominik Skauradszun and Sebastian Böhning, 'Voluntary Carbon Credits Token in der Insolvenz' [2025] KTS Zeitschrift für Insolvenzrecht 139, 150.

35 Skauradszun and Nguyen (n 12) 267.

36 Cf Paula Moffatt and Dominik Skauradszun, 'Conference in European Restructuring and Insolvency Law (CERIL) Statement 2023-3 on Crypto-assets in Restructuring and Insolvency' (2023) https://www.ceril.eu/news/ceril-statement-2023-3-on-crypto-assets-in-restructuring-and-insolvency accessed 21 July 2025; Skauradszun and Nguyen (n 12) 267.

37 UNIDROIT Principles on Digital Assets and Private Law https://www.unidroit.org/wp-content/uploads/2024/01/Principles-on-Digital-Assets-and-Private-Law-linked-1.pdf accessed 21 July 2025.

38 See, e.g., Art. 713 Swiss Civil Code.

39 E.g., Benedikt Bartylla, 'Der Vorschlag zur (Neu-)Regelung des Token-Eigentums im englischen Recht' [2024] RDi Recht Digital 201, 202.

40 Bürgerliches Gesetzbuch (BGB) 1900.

41 E.g., Malte Stieper in *Staudinger BGB* (Otto Schmidt De Gruyter 2021) Sec. 90 para. 9; Jörg Fritzsche in *BeckOK BGB* (72nd edn, C.H.BECK 01.11.2024) Sec. 90 para. 5.

42 E.g., Skauradszun, 'Kryptowerte im Bürgerlichen Recht' (n 31) 363; Lisa M Guntermann, 'Non Fungible Token als Herausforderung für das Sachenrecht' [2022] RDi Recht Digital 200, 203; Gerald Spindler and Markus Meyer, 'Digitale Assets im Deliktsrecht' [2023] MMR Zeitschrift für IT-Recht und Recht der Digitalisierung 907, 908; Sebastian Omlor, 'Blockchain-Token im Zivilrecht' [2023] JURA Juristische Ausbildung 661, 667; Johannes Meier and Hendrik K W Vormwald, 'Kryptowerte im System der Drittwiderspruchsklage' (2024) 224 AcP Archiv für civilistische Praxis 98, 119; Aurelia P Birne, *Das Allgemeine Privatrecht der Blockchain-Token* (Mohr Siebeck 2023) 63; different von Anjuli Hülst, *Absoluter Schutz von Blockchain-Token* (Mohr Siebeck 2024) 219.
43 Von Hülst (n 42) 99ff, 219–220.
44 E.g., Philipp Koch, 'Die „Tokenisierung" von Rechtspositionen als digitale Verbriefung' [2018] ZBB 359, 362–363.; Andreas Walter, 'Bitcoin, Libra und sonstige Kryptowährungen aus zivilrechtlicher Sicht' [2019] NJW Neue Juristische Wochenschau 3609, 3613; Birne (n 42) 100.
45 E.g., Birne (n 42) 100 advocates for an application of Sec. 90 BGB mutatis mutandis but does not want to apply the provisions concerning the transfer of things.
46 Skauradszun in *Kreditwesengesetz mit CRR* (n 31) para 6; Skauradszun, 'Kryptowerte im Bürgerlichen Recht' (n 31) 363.
47 Florian Faust in *BeckOK BGB* (71th edn, C.H.BECK 01.08.2024) Sec. 453 para 24; Ivo Bach in *Staudinger BGB* (Otto Schmidt De Gruyter 2024) Sec. 453 para 85.
48 E.g., Roland M Beckmann in *Staudinger BGB* (Otto Schmidt De Gruyter 2013) Sec. 453 para. 37.
49 Skauradszun, 'Kryptowerte im Bürgerlichen Recht' (n 31) 363; cf Felix Maultzsch in *MüKoBGB* (9th edn, C.H.BECK 2024) Sec. 453 para 9.
50 For crypto-assets, e.g., Skauradszun, 'Kryptowerte im Bürgerlichen Recht' (n 31) 356; Guntermann (n 42) 207; Spindler and Meyer (n 42) 910; Omlor, 'Blockchain-Token im Zivilrecht' (n 42) 669; Birne (n 42) 55; Skauradszun in *Kreditwesengesetz mit CRR* (n 31) para 14.
51 Cf Gerhard Wagner in *MüKoBGB* (9th edn, C.H.BECK 2024) Sec. 823 para 344.
52 Wagner (n 51) para 346; Johannes Hager in *Staudinger BGB* (Otto Schmidt De Gruyter 2017) Sec. 823 para B 124; Skauradszun, 'Kryptowerte im Bürgerlichen Recht' (n 31) 368.
53 Skauradszun and Nguyen (n 12) 266.
54 Strafgesetzbuch (StGB) 1872.
55 Stefan Möllenkamp in Thomas Hoeren, Ulrich Sieber and Bernd Holznagel (eds), *Handbuch Multimedia-Recht* (60th edn, C.H.BECK 2023) 13.6 para. 46; Birne (n 42) 152.
56 Spindler and Meyer (n 42) 907; cf Patrick Ehinger and Julia Hugendubel, 'NFT-Produkte – Verwertungsrechte und neue Nutzungsarten' [2023] GRUR Gewerblicher Rechtsschutz und Urheberrecht 1065, 1074.
57 For crypto-assets, e.g., Katja Langenbucher, 'Digitales Finanzwesen' (2018) 218 AcP Archiv für die civilistische Praxis 385, 408–409; Skauradszun, 'Kryptowerte im Bürgerlichen Recht' (n 31) 369; Spindler and Meyer (n 42) 911; Skauradszun in *Kreditwesengesetz mit CRR* (n 31) para 16; different view, e.g., Omlor, 'Blockchain-Token im Zivilrecht' (n 42) 668; Meier and Vormwald (n 42) 105; Birne (n 42) 150.
58 For crypto-assets, e.g., David Paulus and Robin Matzke, 'Smart Contracts und das BGB – Viel Lärm um nichts?' [2018] ZfPW Zeitschrift für die gesamte Privatrechtswissenschaft 431, 451; Leonid Shmatenko and Stefan Möllenkamp, 'Digitale Zahlungsmittel in einer analog geprägten Rechtsordnung' [2018] MMR Zeitschrift für IT-Recht und Recht der Digitalisierung 495, 499.
59 For crypto-assets, e.g., Skauradszun, 'Kryptowerte im Bürgerlichen Recht' (n 31) 372.
60 For crypto-assets Koch (n 44) 362; Gerald Spindler and Martin Bille, 'Rechtsprobleme von Bitcoins als virtuelle Währung' [2014] WM Zeitschrift für Wirtschafts- und Bankrecht 1357, 1363.
61 For crypto-assets, e.g., Peter Zickgraf, 'Initial Coin Offerings – Ein Fall für das Kapitalmarktrecht?' [2018] AG Die Aktiengesellschaft 293, 299.
62 Cf Wolfgang Rosch in *jurisPK-BGB* (10th edn, juris 01.02.2023) Sec. 413 para 4.

63 For crypto-assets Skauradszun, 'Kryptowerte im Bürgerlichen Recht' (n 31) 374; Spindler and Bille (n 60) 1360; Walter (n 44) 3611.
64 Jan Busche in *Staudinger BGB* (Otto Schmidt De Gruyter 2022) Sec. 399 para. 53; cf Mathias Rohe in *BeckOK BGB* (71st edn, C.H.BECK 01.08.2024) Sec. 399 para 18.
65 For crypto-assets, e.g., Skauradszun, 'Kryptowerte im Bürgerlichen Recht' (n 31) 379; similar Omlor, 'Blockchain-Token im Zivilrecht' (n 42) 666; different, e.g., Guntermann (n 42) 207.
66 For cypto-assets, e.g., Martin Gutzeit in *Staudinger BGB* (Otto Schmidt De Gruyter 2018) Sec. 861 para 5.
67 For crypto-assets Skauradszun, 'Kryptowerte im Bürgerlichen Recht' (n 31) 363.
68 Frank Ebbing in Harm P Westermann, Babara Grunewald and Gerog Maier-Reimer (eds), *Erman BGB* (17th edn, Otto Schmidt 2023) Sec. 1004 para. 10; Hans Schulte-Nölke in *Schulze BGB* (12th edn, Nomos 2024) Sec. 1004 para 1; Christian Berger in Rolf Stürner (ed), *Jaurnig BGB* (19th edn, C.H.BECK 2023) Sec. 1004 para 2; Silke Bayer in *jurisPK-BGB* (9th edn, juris 2020) Sec. 1004 para 55.
69 For crypto-assets Skauradszun in *Kreditwesengesetz mit CRR* (n 31) para 16.
70 Walter Kargl in Urs Kindhäuser, Ulfrid Neumann, Hans-Ullrich Paeffgen, Frank Saliger (eds), *StGB* (6th edn, Nomos 2023) Sec. 303a para 3; Brunhild Wieck-Noodt in *MüKoStGB* (4th edn, C.H.BECK 2022) Sec. 303a para 2.

Valeriya Arnold, Vincent Schaaf, Nils Urbach, and Jonathan Lautenschlager

11 Designing a framework for a blockchain-based voluntary carbon credit lifecycle

Abstract: Voluntary Carbon Credits (VCCs) are essential tools in combating climate change, enabling carbon offsetting and incentivising sustainable investments. However, their traditional lifecycle is hindered by challenges such as limited verifiability, transparency, and trust, which compromise effectiveness and market integrity. This research introduces a blockchain-based framework that leverages immutability, transparency, and efficiency. Using the Design Science Research (DSR) methodology, we developed a holistic framework incorporating smart contracts, decentralised file systems, and oracles to optimise key lifecycle processes. We defined ten Design Objectives (DOs) for the pre-issuance phase, post-issuance phase, and the entire VCC lifecycle, addressing challenges and requirements like privacy and regulatory compliance. The evaluation confirmed that all DOs were met, demonstrating significant potential for improving transparency, efficiency, and accountability. However, further research is needed to explore the most suitable blockchain type, advanced technologies like Zero-Knowledge Proofs for privacy or rollups for scalability, as well as business model considerations such as cost and pricing structures to ensure financial stability and practical viability.

Keywords: Voluntary Carbon Market (VCM), Voluntary Carbon Credit (VCC) lifecycle, blockchain, tokenisation, prototype

1 Introduction —— **261**
2 Background —— **263**
  2.1 Understanding VCC market —— **263**
  2.2 Blockchain and tokenisation of VCCs —— **265**
3 Method —— **266**
4 Problem identification and design objectives —— **268**
5 Design and development —— **273**
  5.1 Prototype architecture: Stakeholders and components —— **273**
  5.2 Prototype functionalities: VCC lifecycle —— **275**
6 Evaluation —— **280**
7 Discussion and conclusion —— **283**

1 Introduction

Voluntary Carbon Credits (VCCs) have emerged as a crucial instrument in global sustainability efforts, offering a market-based mechanism for mitigating greenhouse gas emissions.[1] Given the urgent and existential threat posed by climate change, VCCs fa-

https://doi.org/10.1515/9783111706719-011

cilitate the offsetting of carbon footprints by enabling entities to invest in projects aimed at carbon reduction or sequestration.[2] The increased stringency of emission reduction targets under international frameworks such as the Paris Agreement has further amplified the importance of VCCs.[3] These credits serve not only as a tool for environmental accountability but also as a driver of investment in sustainable practices and technologies, thereby integrating economic incentives with ecological preservation.

Despite their potential, VCCs face significant challenges related to verifiability, transparency, and trust.[4] The verifiability of VCCs is compromised by the complexities involved in accurately measuring and validating the emissions reductions achieved by offset projects.[5] The VCC markets are often lacking transparency due to different standards and platforms, leading to questions about the legitimacy and efficacy of certain credits. Consequently, trust in VCCs is undermined by instances of fraud and the circulation of credits that fail to deliver genuine environmental benefits.[6] An investigation into Verra, the leading certifier for forest carbon offsets, revealed that over 90% of their rainforest offset credits are 'phantom credits', meaning they do not result in actual carbon reductions and may exacerbate global warming.[7] The study, conducted by The Guardian, Die Zeit, and SourceMaterial, found significant discrepancies between Verra's claims and the actual impact on deforestation, raising serious concerns about the validity of offsets used by major corporations like Disney, Shell, and Gucci. These issues undermine the credibility of the VCC system and hinder its effectiveness as a tool for carbon mitigation.

Against this backdrop, blockchain technology presents promising affordances for addressing some of these fundamental problems of VCCs. By providing an immutable and transparent ledger, blockchain can enhance the traceability of carbon credits, ensuring that each credit corresponds to measurable emission reductions.[8] Tokenisation of VCCs, being the digital representation of an asset on a blockchain, could facilitate more efficient trading and reduce administrative overhead, thus improving market efficiency.[9] These integrations are essential to realise the full potential of blockchain in creating a robust and reliable VCC system.

Despite the potential blockchain might offer with tokenisation, existing VCC tokens have yet to achieve substantial market adoption. Due to failed initiatives and negative publicity of projects such as the Toucan Protocol, which involved tokenised retired credits, the market has recently seen a decline.[10] This observation is corroborated by academic literature, highlighting the fragmented and often deficient design of current VCC token solutions. For example, studies on initiatives like KlimaDAO reveal significant shortcomings, including inadequate lifecycle management, poor interoperability, and a lack of regulatory compliance.[11] These deficiencies underscore the necessity for more comprehensive and integrative design approaches to VCC tokenisation. As blockchain technology is not a panacea, it often requires integration with complementary technologies such as decentralised file systems for secure and scalable file storage[12] or trusted oracles that provide accurate and reliable off-chain data.[13]

Consequently, the objective of our research is to propose a holistic VCC token concept that addresses the entire lifecycle of carbon credits, leveraging blockchain technology and integrating additional technologies as needed. Our aim is to resolve the prevalent issues of verifiability, transparency, and trust, thereby enhancing the efficacy and reliability of the VCC market. By designing a comprehensive system that integrates these elements, we aim to create a more reliable and effective market for VCCs, thereby enhancing their role in global sustainability efforts. Concretely, this book chapter strives to answer the following research question:

RQ: How to design a blockchain-based VCC token system to comprehensively address the lifecycle of carbon credits and enhance verifiability, transparency, and trust in the VCC market?

Our approach is grounded in the Design Science Research (DSR) methodology.[14] We begin by collecting requirements for a successful VCC token design from relevant literature and industry standards. Utilising these requirements, we design our artefact and evaluate it against predefined design objectives (DOs) to ensure its practical relevance and effectiveness. The structure of the remaining chapter is as follows: After a brief dive into the background of VCC markets and the tokenisation, we review existing literature to identify key challenges and requirements; subsequently, we present our proposed design; this is followed by an evaluation of its performance; and finally, we discuss the implications of our findings and propose directions for future research.

2 Background

2.1 Understanding VCC market

VCCs have emerged as an important tool in global efforts to reduce carbon emissions, offering a market-based approach for organisations and individuals to offset their carbon footprint. As certificates representing the reduction of one ton of CO_2, they can be voluntarily purchased by individuals or organisations to offset their emissions.[15] This process involves a comprehensive lifecycle with six phases: project design, registration, monitoring-reporting-verification (MRV), issuance, transaction, and retirement.[16] During the initial *design* phase, developers planning environmental projects conduct a comprehensive feasibility assessment to evaluate the potential impact of their proposed carbon reduction efforts.[17] Based on the outcomes of this assessment, developers select an accredited standard provider, such as Verra or the Gold Standard, and submit the project during the *registration* phase to ensure compliance with the methodologies and criteria established by the respective standard-setter.[18] Once registered, the project enters the *MRV* phase, where project developers measure and report key metrics on the development of the project and third-party auditors verify the accuracy of emissions reductions and confirm that the project is meeting its environmental commitments.[19] Upon successful completion of the MRV phase, carbon credits are issued to the project developers within the *issuance* phase.[20] These validated carbon credits can then be traded in carbon markets during the *transaction* phase.[21] Developers may choose to sell the credits directly in over-the-counter (OTC) transactions or via intermediaries, such as brokers, who may either sell them directly to end buyers or aggregate them into portfolios for broader market distribution.[22] Ultimately, end buyers, such as corporations or individuals aiming to offset their carbon emissions, can enter the *retirement* phase of the carbon credits by permanently removing them from circulation, thereby fulfilling their carbon offset obligations.[23]

As illustrated by the lifecycle, standard-setting programs play a pivotal role in maintaining the reliability and integrity of carbon credits by rigorously verifying their achievement of intended environmental and sustainability objectives. However, the market's supply side remains highly fragmented due to the presence of multiple, often divergent standards. Prominent organisations such as Verra and the Gold Standard are key players in this space. Although both organisations aim to ensure the quality, transparency, and positive impact of carbon credits, they differ in their specific areas of focus, programs, and methodologies.[24] Verra emphasises advancing sustainable development and climate action, while the Gold Standard is particularly renowned for its stringent integration of environmental impacts with the social and economic benefits of carbon offset projects.[25] Beyond Verra and the Gold Standard, a variety of other registries operate, including the American Carbon Registry (ACR), Climate Action Reserve (CAR), Carbon Trust, Plan Vivo Standard, and the Climate, Community & Biodiversity (CCB) Standard.[26] These organisations also provide certification and validation of carbon credits, ensuring their quality and transparency. Each registry offers a unique focus, whether it be on community development, biodiversity conservation, or specific regional initiatives, contributing to the diversity of the carbon offset certification landscape.

This fragmented market landscape has significantly increased the demand for enhanced transparency, liquidity, and integrity. In response, several initiatives have emerged to introduce standardisation across various stages of the carbon credit lifecycle, aiming to address these challenges effectively. A notable example is the EU Carbon Removal Certification Framework, adopted in 2024.[27] This framework seeks to establish rigorous certification and verification standards for carbon removal projects across European markets and to implement a uniform registry that enhances transparency in emission reductions while preventing double-counting, which occurs when the same credit is claimed more than once within or across markets.[28] The London Stock Exchange's Voluntary Carbon Market Designation is another key initiative aimed at creating a standardised framework for reporting processes that entities must adhere to qualify for market participation. This designation ensures that only entities meeting strict reporting standards can participate, thereby enhancing the market's reliability and transparency. Additionally, there is a global push to standardise trading mechanisms, as presented by initiatives such as Japan's GX League and Australia's Carbon Exchange.[29] These efforts include the creation of centralised trading platforms that facilitate the buying and selling of carbon credits, making transactions more efficient and transparent. There are also initiatives, such as the Voluntary Carbon Markets Initiative, which, among other efforts, focus on developing guidelines for claiming carbon offsets, especially during the retirement phase.[30] This standardisation is crucial for preventing greenwashing and ensuring that companies provide clear, accurate information about their carbon reduction efforts. However, many of these initiatives are concentrated on specific regions or stages of the carbon credit lifecycle, leaving significant gaps in the broader market. The World Bank's Carbon Assets Tracking System (CATS) seeks to address this issue by offering an ambitious international solution designed to integrate both voluntary and compliance carbon markets.[31] The main goal of CATS is to create a transparent and reliable platform for the issuance, recording, and tracking of emissions reductions across all standard programs throughout the entire VCC lifecycle on a global scale. At this moment in time, however, CATS is in development and limited to World Bank climate finance programs, such as the Forest Carbon Partnership Facility, restricting its applicability in the broader international VCC market. Finally, while the ongoing standardisation efforts work to unify the market, an alternative technological solution gaining momentum is the blockchain-based tokenisation of carbon credits, which also seeks to continuously improve the transparency, traceability, liquidity, and integrity of the market.

2.2 Blockchain and tokenisation of VCCs

Blockchain technology is a decentralised and fault-tolerant distributed ledger technology, which has significantly reshaped various industries by utilising public key cryptography and consensus protocols to ensure secure and transparent transactions.[32] Its append-only structure, linking blocks with hash pointers, creates an immutable ledger that fosters trust and eliminates the need for a central authority.[33] This technology underpins systems like Bitcoin and Ethereum, enabling secure cryptocurrency transactions and facilitating applications such as tokenisation. Tokenisation, which represents real-world assets as digital tokens, enables fractional ownership, enhances transaction efficiency through smart contracts, and promises to democratise access to assets. The integration of blockchain and tokenisation is thereby revolutionising traditional finance and ownership paradigms, promoting decentralisation, transparency, and efficiency.[34]

The underlying asset of a token can encompass blockchain-native assets in the form of cryptocurrencies as well as off-chain assets, which exist outside of the blockchain, such as traditional financial assets like stocks, bonds, or real estate.[35] As outlined in the previous section, one off-chain asset that has seen both investigation and practical implementation as a token is the VCC. Tokenising VCCs has the potential to address several key challenges by leveraging blockchain technology, whose core characteristics directly align with these challenges. In a tokenised system, VCCs are represented as digital tokens on a blockchain.[36] Consequently, this system can use smart contracts to automate and streamline processes, such as validating carbon offset projects and ensuring compliance with regulations, thus reducing the risk of fraud and improving market confidence. Furthermore, blockchain provides a transparent and tamper-proof ledger, which can mitigate issues related to the verification and tracking of carbon credits.[37] By ensuring that every transaction is recorded immutably, blockchain technology can enhance trust among participants and reduce the administrative burden associated with carbon credit trading.[38] Additionally, tokenisation can increase market accessibility and liquidity, enabling more participants to engage in the VCC market and facilitating 24/7 trading without the need for intermediaries.

The market has already recognised all the mentioned benefits of tokenising carbon credits, leading to the development of various tokens.[39] Among them is Toucan's CO2 token (TCO2), which is based on the Verra methodology and operates on both the Polygon and Celo blockchains. Similarly, Gold Standard CO2 token (GCO2) is developed by Flowcarbon and offers an alternative tied to the standards set by Gold Standard. Moss CO2 token (MCO2) is another notable token, issued under the methodology for Reducing Emissions from Deforestation and Forest Degradation. However, this diversity of tokens highlights that the issue of market fragmentation remains unresolved, as it introduces additional complexity. Moreover, the implementation of blockchain technology presents its own set of challenges that must be carefully addressed. The integration of blockchain technology into the VCC market requires significant technical expertise and infrastructure investment, which can be a barrier for smaller organisations. Furthermore, the regulatory environment for blockchain and digital assets is still evolving, and uncertainties in legal frameworks can pose risks to the adoption of tokenised VCCs. Additionally, the environmental impact of blockchain, particularly proof-of-work systems, raises concerns about the sustainability of using such technology for environmental purposes.

In conclusion, while blockchain and tokenisation offer significant opportunities to enhance the VCC market by addressing challenges related to transparency, efficiency, and security, a comprehensive approach is needed to tackle the technical, regulatory, and environmental issues, as well as to mitigate the additional fragmentation they may introduce.

3 Method

In the development of a holistic VCC token concept, we adhered to the DSR methodology, as illustrated in Figure 11.1.[40] The goal of DSR is to address identified real-world problems through a build-and-evaluate process, leading to the creation of purposeful design artefacts and the generation of actionable and generalisable knowledge.[41] These artefacts can take various forms, such as constructs, models, methods, and instantiations, with prototypes being typical instantiations.[42] The DSR methodology is known for its systematic approach, which encompasses the iterative processes of building, evaluating, and refining artefacts.[43] This makes it an effective framework for tackling the complex challenges associated with VCC tokenisation. Our approach was informed by specific aspects of the DSR methodology, which helped ensure a structured and rigorous development process. DSR typically involves identifying a problem, designing a solution, and evaluating its effectiveness.[44] By adhering to these principles, we integrated insights from both practical examples and blockchain literature to inform our prototype development. This iterative process allowed us to derive generalisable knowledge through a structured evaluation, addressing the deficiencies of existing VCC mechanisms and tokenisation efforts.

The motivation for our research stemmed from the lack of comprehensive design concepts for VCC tokens and their practical applicability. Traditional carbon credit mechanisms and initial blockchain-based solutions, such as tokenised credits, currently suffer from issues related to verifiability, transparency, and trust.[45] These challenges underscore the need for a solution that leverages blockchain's capabilities while addressing its limitations. Our research was guided by the goal of developing a more effective blockchain-based solution to enhance the VCC market. To address these identified challenges, we derived DOs based on literature pertaining to carbon credits, blockchain technology, and past tokenisation efforts. In our technical analysis of current blockchain-based VCC concepts, we developed and refined identified DOs further, which finally guided the creation and evaluation of our VCC token..[46] By iteratively refining the prototype, we adhered to the DSR principle of continuous improvement, ensuring that it effectively addressed verifiability, transparency, and trust issues in VCC tokenisation. This process established a solid foundation for both practical applications and future development.

We finally conducted a thorough, logical analysis to evaluate our prototype, ensuring that the DOs were fulfilled. This evaluation provided valuable insights into the effectiveness of our reference implementation and the application of blockchain technology for VCC tokens. The iterative process was crucial for refining the prototype, ensuring its practical relevance and generalisability. This approach allowed us to transition from an instance-specific solution to a broader, more abstract framework, aligning with the DSR goal of producing generalisable knowledge.

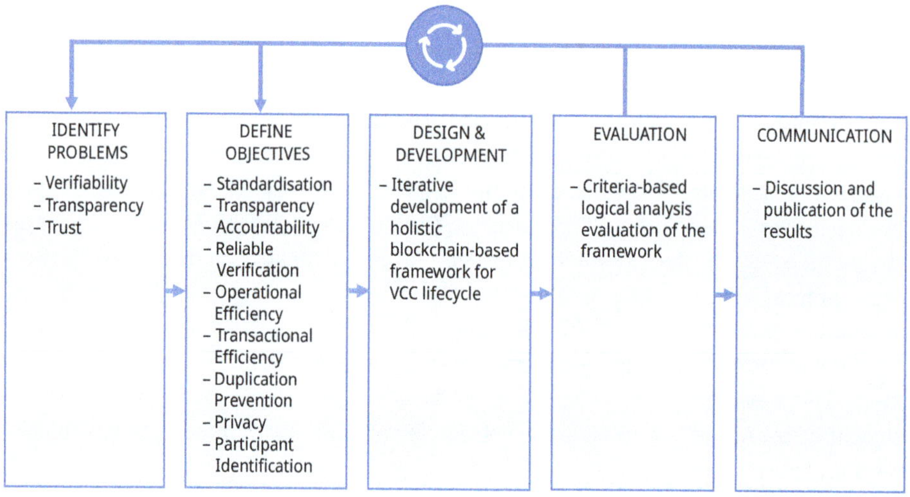

Figure 11.1: Our DSR Research Process.

4 Problem identification and design objectives

As previously outlined, the DSR process commences with the identification of relevant challenges that the designed prototype seeks to address. A comprehensive understanding of these challenges is crucial to establishing clear DOs that will systematically guide the development process, ensuring that the prototype effectively meets its intended purposes. To derive these DOs in a structured manner, this section follows the VCC lifecycle, with the findings summarized in Table 11.1. Initially, we conduct an analysis of the challenges associated with the entire VCC lifecycle to formulate overarching lifecycle DOs. Subsequently, we examine the pre–VCC-issuance phase (lifecycle steps 1–3), where the project design is developed and verified, followed by an exploration of the post-VCC-issuance phase (lifecycle steps 4–6), during which the VCC is issued, traded, and retired.

The first thing that stands out when analysing the existing standards in the VCC market is the fragmentation of the market itself. Although the overall VCC lifecycle follows a similar structure, different standards and methodologies are applied during the initial stages of the lifecycle, depending on the provider, such as Verra, Gold Standard, or the ACR. While Verra and ACR for example focus primarily on carbon reduction, with ACR concentrating exclusively on projects in the USA, the Gold Standard places a strong emphasis on delivering additional social and environmental co-benefits.[47] Based on the standards set by each institution, the MRV process, as well as the pool of verifiers, can vary. Additionally, the different registries and trading platforms further contribute to market fragmentation. As a result, trading occurs across multiple, often disconnected platforms or in OTC transactions, which makes it difficult for buyers and sellers to connect and leads to inconsistent pricing, higher transaction costs, and reduced liquidity.[48] Consequently, a holistic VCC concept necessitates the consideration of diverse perspectives and the implementation of a *standardised process* that facilitates participation by all standard-setting organisations without barriers. Initiatives such as the London Stock Exchange Voluntary Carbon Market or the EU Carbon Removal Certificates proposal already aim to standardise processes, but they often fall short in terms of ensuring the transparency and integrity of the carbon credits themselves.[49]

The demand for transparency arises, especially within the initial pre–VCC-issuance phase. Although VCC programs have made several efforts to make project information and plans more publicly accessible, significant gaps remain, especially in the availability and accuracy of data.[50] For instance, while geospatial site boundaries are theoretically accessible through many offset programs, numerous projects fail to provide this information or supply corrupted or inaccurate data, undermining the credibility of the submitted project and the related VCCs. Moreover, the procedures for emission reduction measurements and the verification processes within the MRV have been subject to considerable criticism due to their opacity.[51] Therefore, the holistic VCC concept should incorporate full *transparency* in the initial pre–VCC-issuance phase, ensuring the information regarding project design, registration, and MRV process is clear and accessible.

However, transparency alone is not enough. It is imperative that the information provided during the initial phase is not only accessible but also immutable, thereby reinforcing the principle of transparency.[52] This means that once data is submitted, it should be securely stored in a way that prevents any alterations. The implementation of tamper-proof data systems is critical for safeguarding the integrity of the process, as it guarantees that all stakeholders are held accountable for the information they provide and the commitments they make.[53] Therefore, another key DO for the holistic VCC concept is establishing mechanisms that ensure rigorous *accountability* of all participants during the initial pre–VCC-issuance phase, ensuring the reliability of the provided data.

While ensuring that data is tamper-proof and transparent is essential, it does not inherently guarantee the integrity of the project design and the data themselves. In the conventional lifecycle of a VCC project, independent third parties play a critical role in validating and verifying the legitimacy of a project and its actual contribution to emission reduction.[54] These entities are also responsible for ensuring that the data presented in monitoring reports are accurate and that the project's commitments to emission reduction are faithfully adhered to throughout its operational period. However, significant concerns persist about the accuracy of data collection, the methodologies employed for measuring carbon emissions, and the overall verification process.[55] Critics have questioned whether the methods employed by verifiers are rigorous enough to ensure the credibility and accuracy of the projects, arguing that some may exaggerate or misrepresent their environmental impact by exploiting the complexity and opacity of the verification process to appear more sustainable than they truly are.[56] Consequently, as another DO, it is essential to establish a *reliable verification process* that thoroughly assesses the legitimacy of the project, ensures the accuracy of the data in monitoring reports, and verifies that the project's commitments to emission reduction are genuinely met.

To build on the previously outlined DOs, it is crucial to supplement them with additional focus on operational efficiency. While transparency, accountability, and rigorous verification processes are fundamental to the integrity and success of the VCC lifecycle, these objectives must be reinforced by an efficiency requirement to ensure their practical implementation. Despite efforts by VCC programs to improve speed and efficiency, many processes remain hindered by outdated, manual methods like Excel spreadsheets and PDFs for data tracking.[57] These inefficiencies result in costly and time-consuming audits and verifications.[58] The reliance on such labour-intensive methods not only slows down the entire lifecycle but also increases the risk of human error, complicates data management, and creates unnecessary bottlenecks.[59] Hence, as an additional DO for the pre–VCC-issuance phase, incorporating *operational efficiency* is essential.

As the VCC lifecycle progresses into the post-issuance phase, the need for efficiency extends further, with a particular emphasis on optimising trading processes. After the issuance of VCCs, the traditional trading process frequently depends on financial intermediaries, such as brokers and carbon exchanges, which operate within formal hierarchies and can impose barriers that restrict accessibility to smaller projects and buyers in the carbon market.[60] Furthermore, the dependency on intermediary processes not only slows down the pace of trading but also drives up transaction costs, with commission fees ranging from 3% to 8%.[61] To enhance market liquidity by reducing entry barriers, transactional frictions, and costs, it is additionally necessary to introduce *transactional efficiency* as a further DO.

Furthermore, strengthening the connection to the earlier discussion on market fragmentation brings to light additional implications for the post-issuance phase that warrant further examination. The market's heterogeneity, coupled with the lack of established mechanisms that allow carbon credits to be recognised and utilised across various platforms and frameworks, makes effective interaction between these markets particularly challenging.[62] This lack of interoperability impedes the seamless exchange of carbon credits and diminishes market efficiency, which in turn complicates efforts to meet global climate goals. Therefore, it is vital to introduce *interoperability* as another core DO to facilitate global integration and ensure that carbon credits are consistently recognised and utilised across all platforms.

In addition to the challenges posed by the lack of carbon credit exchange among different platforms, the heterogeneity of markets significantly increases the risk of doubling carbon credits across various industrial and regional markets in the post-issuance VCC phase.[63] This issue arises when the same credit is counted and/or claimed more than once, either within a single market or across multiple markets, which can undermine the integrity and effectiveness of global climate mitigation efforts. While the introduction of interoperability DO also partly addresses the issue of double-counting by requiring connected and harmonised markets, this objective is not specifically focused on the doubling issue. To ensure that the final prototype thoroughly addresses the risks associated with double-counting and double-claiming across different markets, it is essential to additionally introduce a DO specifically dedicated to *duplication prevention*.

At the same time, while the transparency requirement in the pre-issuance phase can be extended to the post-issuance phase to maintain the credibility of the VCCs, its scope of impact should be partially restricted. In this latter stage, openly sharing trading and transaction details across stakeholders may lead to concerns about confidentiality, competitive advantages, and market manipulation.[64] Balancing the need for transparency with the protection of sensitive information becomes crucial to maintaining trust and efficiency in the trading process while avoiding potential obstacles that could hinder market participation and effectiveness.[65] Consequently, a *privacy* DO is vital in the VCC transaction phase to safeguard sensitive information without compromising the overall transparency of the market.

Finally, it is essential to ensure that privacy measures do not obscure the identities of market participants, particularly when it comes to compliance and retirement purposes. The clear identification of all participants is crucial to prevent any entities from exploiting anonymity to misuse carbon credits, such as by fraudulently claiming multiple credits, engaging in money laundering, or financing illicit activities, which could undermine the market's integrity.[66] While it is important to maintain the confidentiality of negotiation details and trade specifics among the parties directly involved, this privacy must not extend to the point where it compromises regulatory oversight. Regulatory bodies responsible for compliance, such as anti-money laundering (AML) or counter-terrorist financing (CTF), must have full visibility into the identities of all participants to ensure that the market operates transparently and securely. This *participant identification* DO is the concluding one, providing a safeguard against any potential misuse of the system while balancing the need for privacy.

Table 11.1: Derivation of Design Objectives.

VCC – Lifecycle	Design Objectives	Description
Entire lifecycle	Standardised Process	A standardised framework is needed to harmonise the diverse standards and methodologies across the VCC market, ensuring consistency and accessibility without creating an entry barrier.[67]

Table 11.1 (continued)

VCC – Lifecycle	Design Objectives	Description
Pre–issuance phase	Transparency	Transparency in the initial pre–VCC-issuance phase is crucial for credibility. Persistent gaps in data availability and accuracy highlight the need for full transparency in project design, registration, and MRV processes to ensure clarity for stakeholders.[68]
	Accountability	The information provided during the initial pre–VCC-issuance phase must be immutable to ensure accountability. Tamper-proof data systems are essential to maintain data integrity and to hold all participants responsible.[69]
	Reliable verification process	Due to persistent concerns regarding data accuracy, carbon measurement methods, and the rigor of verification, a reliable process is essential to validate project legitimacy, ensure accurate monitoring, and verify adherence to emission reduction commitments.[70]
	Operational efficiency	Inefficient manual processes result in costly audits, human errors, and data management challenges, highlighting the need to enhance operational efficiency.[71]
Post–issuance Phase	Transactional efficiency	The reliance on financial intermediaries often restricts market access for small businesses, increases costs, and slows trading, thus highlighting the need for improved market liquidity, reduced frictions, and lower costs.[72]
	Interoperability	Interoperability is needed to address the lack of cross-platform recognition for carbon credits, facilitating seamless exchanges, improving market efficiency, and ensuring their consistent use across various platforms.[73]
	Duplication prevention	The heterogeneity of markets increases the risk of double-counting and double-claiming carbon credits across sectors and regions. Therefore, implementing duplication prevention is crucial to safeguard the integrity of global climate mitigation efforts.[74]
	Privacy	Sharing transaction details in the post-issuance phase can raise concerns over confidentiality and competitive advantage, underscoring the need for privacy measures to protect sensitive information while maintaining overall market transparency.[75]
	Participant identification	Regulatory visibility is crucial for AML and CTF compliance, necessitating clear participant identities to prevent misuse like fraud or money laundering while maintaining a balance with privacy.[76]

5 Design and development

Building on the identified DOs, we developed a holistic, conceptual blockchain-based framework for the VCC lifecycle. To enhance comprehension, the textual concept is supported by a visual illustration.[77] A logical view, shown in Figure 11.2 and discussed in the first subsection, clarifies stakeholders and components, while a procedural view, represented in Figures 11.3, 11.4, *and* 11.5 and covered in the second subsection, depicts the VCC lifecycle itself.

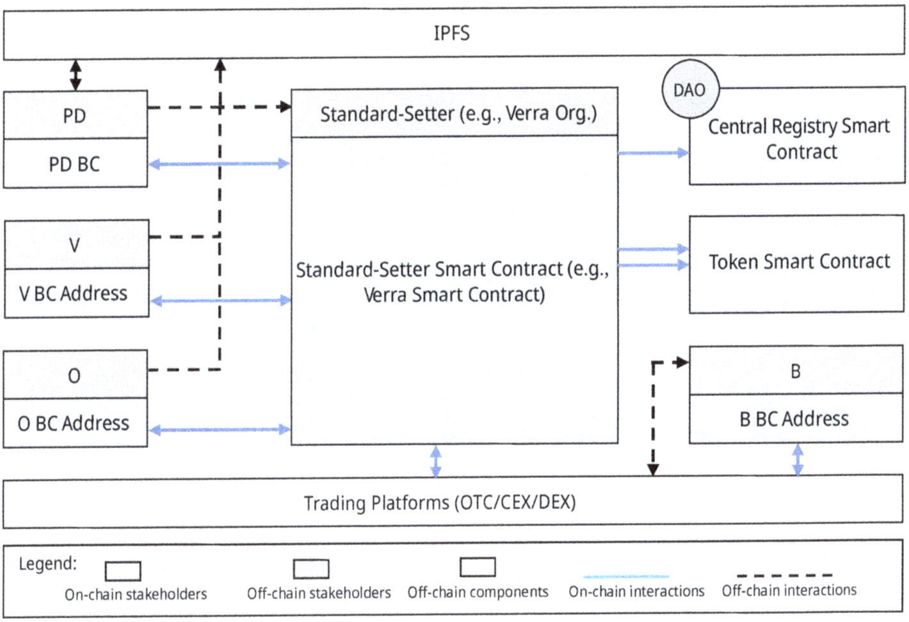

Figure 11.2: Logical View of Architectural Stakeholders and Components.

5.1 Prototype architecture: Stakeholders and components

Figure 11.2 illustrates all real-world actors in grey, while their corresponding blockchain addresses and general smart contracts are shown in light blue. The white-coloured boxes indicate actors and systems that operate outside the blockchain. Furthermore, the black dashed lines represent interactions that occur off-chain, while the thick blue lines represent interactions that occur on-chain with the corresponding stakeholders and components. The key stakeholders in this framework include *project developers (PD), verifiers (V),* the *standard-setters,* such as Verra Org., and the final *offset buyers (B).* To offer trading flexibility and diverse access options for buyers, our trade flow supports multiple forms of trading, including OTC trade, central exchanges

(CEX), and decentralised exchanges (DEX), all grouped under the *Trading Platforms (OTC/CEX/DEX)* category. This approach allows buyers and project developers to choose the right trading method based on their individual preferences.

In addition to the regular stakeholders, *oracles (O)* are integrated to provide off-chain data, such as satellite imagery, to ensure that the blockchain-based concept has access to real-world information. Oracles act thereby as bridges between the blockchain and external data sources, enabling the system to automatically verify and incorporate relevant off-chain information.[78] Furthermore, since standard-setters in a traditional VCC lifecycle handle large volumes of project-related documents and information, which would be too costly to store directly on the blockchain, we integrated the *InterPlanetary File System (IPFS)* to manage this data efficiently. IPFS is a distributed peer-to-peer file storage system that enables PDs and Vs to upload files, which can be distributed across nodes, ensuring data integrity and availability.[79] The file must first be uploaded to an IPFS node and pinned to ensure it remains accessible. During the upload process, IPFS splits the file into smaller chunks, hashes each chunk, and combines them into a single Content Identifier (CID). This CID acts as the address linking all related chunks. Because the CID is content based, any change to the file will result in a new CID, enabling easy verification of the file's integrity. To finally retrieve the file, users such us final buyers or other standard-setters can simply request it using the CID, and IPFS will locate and deliver the file from any node storing it, ensuring data integrity and providing a cost-efficient, decentralised storage solution.

By utilising the outlined off-chain components such as IPFS, key stakeholders can optimise the three types of on-chain smart contracts, namely: the Standard-Setter Smart Contract (SC), the Token SC, and the Central Registry Smart SC. *The Standard-Setter SC*, such as the Verra SC, incorporates core VCC lifecycle functions that should be consistent across all Standard-Setter SCs for the standardisation DO. These functions include project and report submission through CID provision, verifier assignment, verification, and registration of the credits. Simultaneously, it provides standard-setters with the necessary flexibility to customise the contract according to the specific methodologies and requirements, thereby reducing barriers to adaptation while maintaining standardisation requirement. For instance, standard-setters can decide whether they require more functions or whether verifier assignments occur automatically based on predetermined rules, or through a competitive application process, depending on their specific needs and preferences.

Another key standardisation feature integrated into the registration function of the Standard-Setter SC is the automatic initiation of the *Token SC* upon execution. The Token SC manages the project-specific token and includes standardised functions such as transfer and retirement, with the option to add custom features as needed. This approach ensures flexibility while maintaining a consistent framework for token management. To enhance traceability and duplication prevention, we opt for the use of standards that allow both fungible and non-fungible token (NFT) within the same contracts such as ERC-1155.[80] This standard enables the creation of unique tokens, each with a distinct value, making it ideal for representing VCCs, where each project has its own unique characteristics and attributes. Additionally, the ability to support fungibility and fractionalisation is valuable for VCCs, as it allows credits to be divided into smaller units and traded more flexibly, increasing accessibility and liquidity for buyers and sellers. It is also further important to note that the Token SC must be set up in a way that allows initiation during the registration phase to allow trading of pre-issued VCCs. Since the subsequent MRV phase is lengthy and costly for PDs, they often seek funding early in the process.[81] By issuing the Token SC at this stage, PDs can trade VCCs to secure financing for their projects, effectively transforming them into issued VCCs after a successful MRV. Additionally, given that initial emission calculations are prone to risks like miscalculations or unforeseen environmental impacts, we also recommend incorporating buffer functions into the Token SC, following the model of the World Bank's CATS Program.[82] This feature helps protect against project underperformance, mitigates risks for buyers, and enhances the overall credibility of the VCC market.[83]

Finally, the standardised functions mentioned earlier are essential for *the Central Registry SC*, which acts as a central hub connecting the standard-setters' smart contracts. This connection is established through key functions of Standard-Setter SCs such as the submitting function, which automatically reports submitted projects to the central registry, or the registry function, which records the address of the initiated Token SC. By consolidating these functions' results in a single location, the Central Registry SC promotes transparency, simplifies traceability for all participants across various standards, and helps to prevent double-counting. To additionally ensure fairness, the Central Registry SC should be governed as a Decentralised Autonomous Organisation (DAO), where VCC owners hold governance rights and decide for example upon majority votes or a two-third majority, which standard-setters are to be included in this system. This governance model prevents standard-setters from monopolising or restricting entry to the central registry to limit competition. In contrast, VCC owners have an incentive to increase competition, as it fosters higher-quality standards.

5.2 Prototype functionalities: VCC lifecycle

Building on the previously discussed prototype components, the procedural view in Figures 11.3 *to* 11.5 provides a structured framework for analysing the system's functionality. The operational aspects of the design are divided into lifecycle phases and are examined using Verra as a practical example of a standard-setter, facilitating a step-by-step exploration of the VCC lifecycle. To further maintain visual consistency and easy reference, Figures 11.3 *to* 11.5 follow the same colour coding as Figure 11.2.

First and foremost, identifying all stakeholders through a KYC procedure is essential to ensure compliance with regulations such as AML and CFT, as formalised by the partitioner identification DO. This process is conducted off-chain, where key partici-

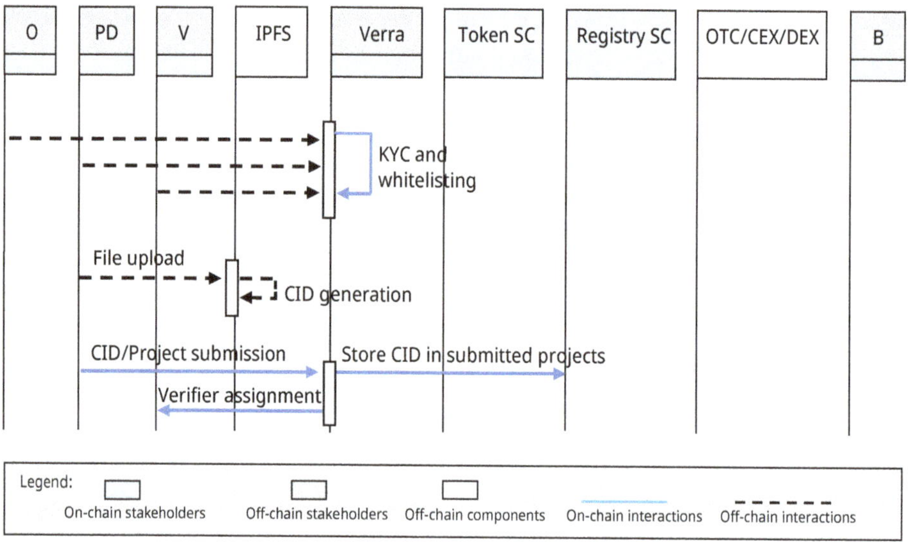

Figure 11.3: Whitelisting and Project Submission.

pants, such as the PD and V, must engage with the standard-setter, like Verra. Once verified, Verra whitelists these participants by linking their blockchain addresses to the Verra SC, granting them access to their role-specific system functionalities. Additionally, since oracles are permitted to provide external data, it is essential to verify the trustworthiness of these data providers. Consequently, for an oracle to be allowed to supply data, it must also undergo verification and it must be whitelisted by Verra as a legitimate off-chain data provider, allowing PDs to select the oracle as needed in the further procedures. After being whitelisted and conducting a feasibility study, PDs can submit their project to Verra. Within the proposed framework, the PD must first upload the project file to IPFS to generate the corresponding CID. Using their blockchain address, the PD can then submit the project through the designated function of the Verra SC by providing the CID as input, which will then automatically communicate the CID to the Central Registry SC for transparency and accountability purposes. This ensures that all submitted projects, regardless of the standard-setter, can be easily accessed and verified. Following submission, a verifier is assigned to the project. This can happen automatically based on predefined criteria or by allowing verifiers to apply for the task. Verra selects the most appropriate method depending on the specific needs and characteristics of the used methodologies.

In the next step, assigned verifiers can use the submitted CID to securely retrieve the project file from IPFS, ensuring a tamperproof transfer. In a typical VCC lifecycle, verifiers manually review the document, assess the project's feasibility, and decide whether to approve its registration.[84] However, the developed concept also allows for the integration of oracles into this process. For instance, PDs can include present and/

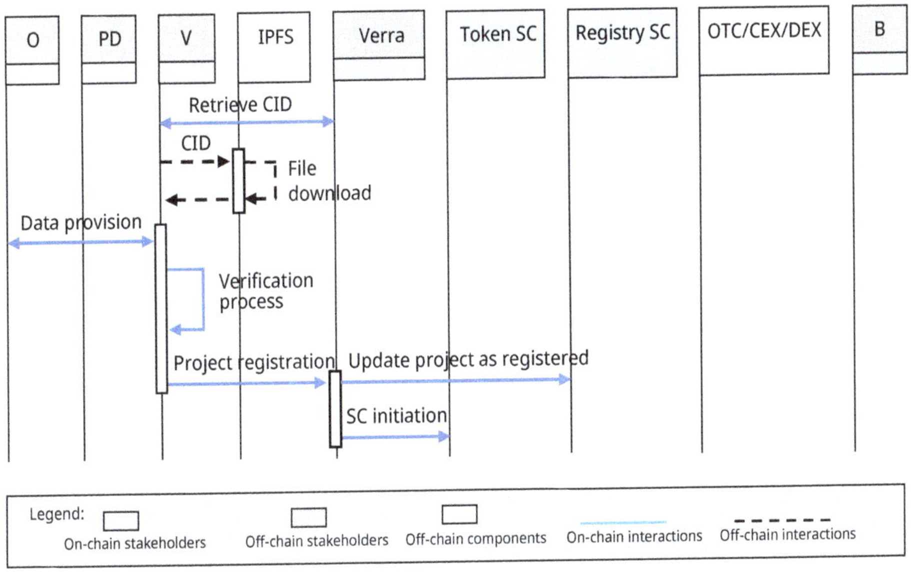

Figure 11.4: Project Registration and Verification.

or historical satellite images of a forest, which demonstrate their efforts to reduce carbon emissions. This integration can enhance efficiency and improve the reliability of the verification process by providing objective, real-time data that complements manual checks, reducing the potential for human error and improving data accuracy. Once verification of the registration is complete, verifiers can use the appropriate registration function to finalise the project's registration. This also triggers two further transactions from the Verra SC: One to the Central Registry SC for adding a new project and one that initiates the Token SC.

In the subsequent phase, PDs are responsible for demonstrating the integrity of their project over its lifecycle. This is achieved by utilising monitoring methods that were determined during the initial phase. These methods may include a variety of techniques, such as satellite imagery or other specific data sources, to track key indicators like carbon sequestration, forest health, or biodiversity levels, depending on the project's goals. PDs must compile these findings into a monitoring report, which is then submitted similarly to the first phase, as shown in Figure 11.4, by uploading it to IPFS and providing the CID to Verra SC. Assigned verifiers can then retrieve the reports and either conduct a manual review or as mentioned earlier, enhance the process by integrating oracles to improve the accuracy and efficiency of the verification. Once the verifiers approve the MRV, the Verra SC automatically notifies the Central Registry SC and updates the token status in the Token SC from pre-issued to issued. Since the report submission and verification are similar to the previous phase, we refer to Figure 11.4 in this phase.

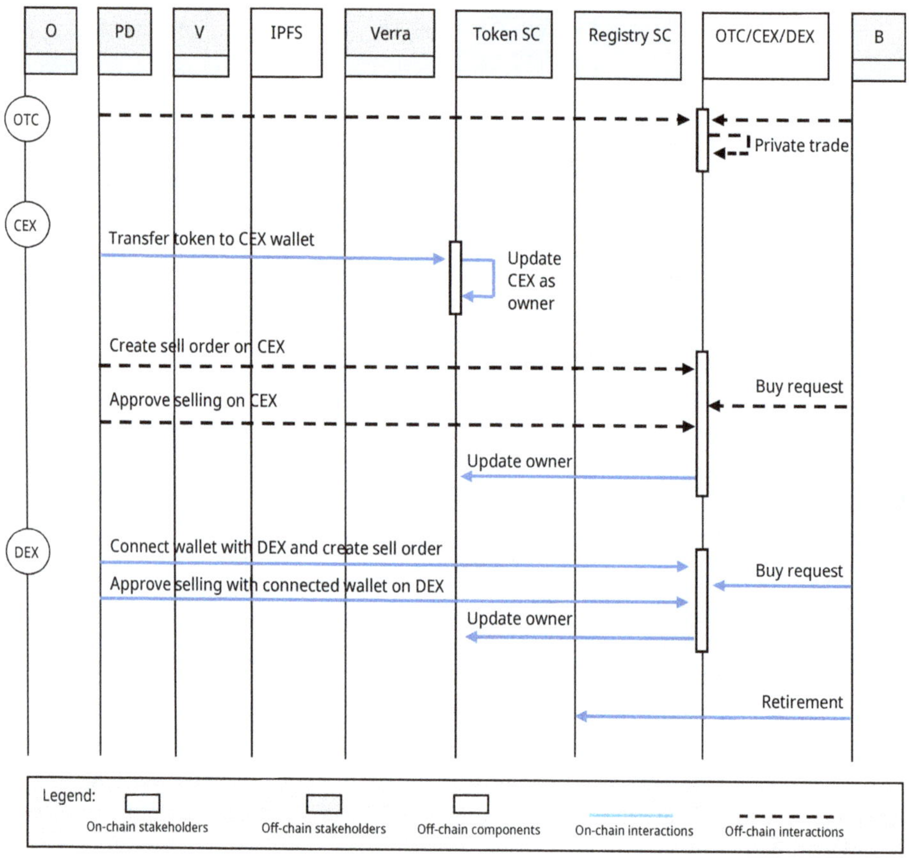

Figure 11.5: Transaction and Retirement.

As outlined in the previous section, token trading can start as soon as the Token SC is initiated. The process remains the same regardless of whether pre-issued or issued tokens are traded or whether it is the initial trade between PD and B or a secondary trade between the current owner and another B. This stage of the VCC lifecycle offers great flexibility, allowing PDs and buyers to select their preferred trading platform and determine how they want to negotiate and process payments. For instance, PD and B can choose OTC trading, where the PD transfers ownership rights directly to the buyer's blockchain address, while payment and negotiation can either happen personally off-chain or on-chain.

Alternatively, they may opt to use a CEX as an intermediary, which provides a regulated environment for transactions. In this case, the PD deposits their VCC tokens into a CEX wallet, meaning the CEX takes custody of the tokens and becomes the registered owner in the Token SC. Once deposited, the PD can trade off-chain within the CEX platform. When a deal is finalised, the CEX updates its internal ledger. Afterwards, the PD can withdraw fiat currency to their bank account, and the buyer can withdraw the tokens. The CEX then updates the Token SC on-chain to transfer ownership to the buyer using the smart contract's transfer function.

Additionally, PDs and buyers can use a DEX for direct wallet-to-wallet trading without an intermediary, using blockchain-native tokens for payment, which makes it the most efficient transaction option. Unlike a CEX, where tokens are held by the exchange, a DEX allows users to retain full control of their assets by trading directly from their wallets. To trade on a DEX, the PD connects their wallet to the platform and creates a sell order through a smart contract. The buyer selects the order, and the DEX automatically facilitates the exchange, transferring tokens directly between wallets on-chain, with the Token SC immediately reflecting the new ownership.

All three options are valid within the system, allowing users to choose based on their preferences. Furthermore, each platform fulfils the necessary regulatory requirements, such as KYC, AML, or CFT, and is therefore not included in the transaction function of the Token SC. Additionally, each option offers thereby varying degrees of transactional privacy. On a DEX, transaction amounts are fully public, while CEX and OTC transactions can keep the transferred amounts concealed. It is, however, important to highlight that blockchain addresses remain visible across all trading options, as ownership is tracked in the Token SC. For traceability and transparency purposes, this visibility is the default setting of the smart contract, but some companies may prefer to obscure their identities for competitive reasons. A challenge with blockchain in this regard is its pseudonymity. While blockchain addresses do not reveal personal details directly, they can still be linked to real-world identities through transaction patterns or external data.[85] However, there are emerging technologies designed to protect user identities, such as stealth addresses or ring signatures.[86] These tools allow users to create unlinkable addresses for increased privacy. However, since these technologies are still evolving and there is no perfect solution yet, it is up to buyers to choose the privacy-enhancing tools that best suit their needs and risk tolerance.

Finally, the last buyer claims the carbon emission reduction by retiring the tokens, using the retire function, which flags the corresponding tokens, making them immovable but still visible for record-keeping. This ensures that the credits are removed from active circulation, thus preserving double spending while maintaining a clear audit trail. Additionally, the retire function allows the buyer to add a comment or metadata, such as a description of what the retired tokens were used for, like financial reporting in a specific year or for a particular project. This added functionality helps the buyer track the purpose of the retired credits, providing a detailed record that can be used for internal reporting, external audits, or regulatory compliance.

6 Evaluation

Since the primary objective of this chapter was to develop a holistic blockchain-based VCC-Lifecycle framework to address several real-world challenges, this section focuses on evaluating its effectiveness by analysing the fulfilment of the defined DOs.[87] To assess how and why the framework meets these objectives, we employ an artificial evaluation approach, leveraging theoretical reasoning to validate the design and establish a foundation for further enhancements.[88]

As outlined earlier, the fulfilment of the *standardisation DO* evolves around the Central Registry SC and its connection with Standard-Setter SCs. Thereby, to enable a seamless connection, the central registry defines key processes that must be standardised by all standard-setters in their smart contracts. This standardisation effort focuses on core functions common to all standard-setters, such as submission and registration. At the same time, the framework offers flexibility, allowing standard-setters to customise specific smart contract functions. This adaptability not only accommodates variations in detailed processes but also lowers entry barriers for participation. Moreover, linking standard-setters to the central registry also enhances the *interoperability DO* by consolidating all participants onto a single platform. This functional integration reduces market fragmentation and fosters a more connected ecosystem.

Additional advantage of the framework comprising of the Central Registry SC, the Standard-Setter SCs, and the Token SCs, is an enhanced visibility within an already transparent blockchain infrastructure. By automatically updating all projects and their corresponding tokens in the registry, the system minimises the opacity commonly found in traditional systems, where information is scattered across multiple platforms, as well as the potential opacity that could arise from having different disconnected smart contracts for various standards on the blockchain. Besides this, the main driver of the fulfilment of the *transparency DO* is, however, the inherent transparency of a blockchain itself, where all transactions are accessible to participants.[89] In this context, transparency means that every transaction, such as project submission or registration, is recorded on a ledger, visible and verifiable by all participants, ensuring no information is hidden.

Moreover, the framework leverages the tamper-resistant nature of blockchain, ensuring that once data is transparently recorded, it cannot be altered or deleted, holding data providers accountable for the integrity of their information.[90] This tamper resistance contributes directly to the *accountability DO* and is primarily achieved through cryptographic hashing. Hashing works by generating a unique 'fingerprint' from the data in each block. Even the slightest change in the data will result in a completely different hash, making any tampering immediately detectable.[91] This is further combined with a decentralised consensus mechanism, which ensures that no single entity can control or alter the blockchain, making manipulation extremely difficult. These characteristics ensure that all data retrieved from oracles or stored on

IPFS becomes tamper-resistant when referenced on the blockchain, even though IPFS and oracles do not inherently provide the same level of infrastructure.

Besides transparency and accountability, the advantages of a blockchain-based infrastructure, combined with the developed framework, also contribute significantly to achieving the *duplication prevention DO* and the *reliable verification DO*. The technology offers a secure method for tracking submitted projects and their progression across various markets within a single, unified location—the Central Registry SC. This unified approach enhances visibility for standard-setters, auditors, and external observers, ensuring comprehensive awareness of all existing projects. Consequently, the risk of double-counting is minimised not only through blockchain's inherent transparency features[92] but also through the framework's construction. Similarly, double-claiming is effectively prevented by leveraging both the technology itself and the linkage of each Token SC to the central registry, enabling participants to track existing tokens, the projects they represent, and their current status.[93] Beyond duplication prevention, the framework also enables traceability in the project verification process, allowing stakeholders to review and audit the steps involved in the typically opaque MRV process. While verification remains largely performed by third-party entities, the integration of oracles, which provide trustworthy off-chain data signed using cryptographic keys, significantly improves the validity of project information by reducing reliance on data submitted solely by PDs.[94]

Furthermore, oracles not only enhance the verification process but also play a key role in achieving the *operational efficiency DO*. By integrating oracles into smart contracts, the system can automatically retrieve relevant data for verification, significantly improving speed and enabling thresholds for automated checks. For example, smart contracts can be programmed to automatically verify whether a forest has grown in a predetermined area based on data provided by oracles. This capability underscores automation as one of the core strengths of smart contracts, enabling the seamless execution of processes with precision and efficiency.[95] Beyond their use with oracles, this automation extends to several standardised functions, such as the creation of Token SCs and the automatic reporting of projects to the Central Registry SC. By automating these processes, the framework reduces reliance on manual operations, minimising human errors and improving overall functional efficiency.[96] Additionally, the flexibility of the Standard-Setter SCs allows them to incorporate further automation into their processes as needed, enabling even greater efficiency.

The *transactional efficiency DO* is also supported by automated processes, such as the automatic update of ownership after tokens are sold. However, the primary driver of transactional efficiency lies in the reduced or eliminated involvement of financial intermediaries in the trade process, depending on the chosen trading platform.[97] As a result, transactional efficiency is inherently tied to the flexibility of platform choice. For example, if a seller and buyer decide to use an OTC platform or a DEX for trading, they eliminate the need for financial intermediaries,[98] which often create entry barriers in a regular VCC lifecycle through high transaction fees and slow processes, ultimately reducing efficiency.[99] In contrast, trading on a CEX involves financial intermediaries, which may reduce transactional efficiency. Nonetheless, using a CEX must remain an option to ensure inclusivity, particularly for participants who do not own the native cryptocurrency and prefer trading on platforms that accept fiat currencies or offer advanced custodial services, like a CEX.

The different trade platforms also support *the trade-specific aspects of the participant identification DO*, besides the *VCC-specific aspects*, which are achieved through the whitelisting procedures implemented by standard-setters and their smart contracts at the initial stage. These identification processes are essential for meeting regulatory requirements such as KYC, AML, and CFT compliance.[100] While standard-setters address the regulatory requirements for the VCC market, each trade platform implements participant identification in its own way to comply with trade-specific regulatory obligations.[101] For instance, CEXs inherently require all participants to identify themselves as part of their operational model. This allows the exchange to conduct KYC checks, monitor transactions, and ensure compliance with AML and CFT regulations. In contrast, platforms like DEXs or blockchain-based OTC trades often rely on external mechanisms for compliance, including the use of CEXs for identity verification.[102] Some DEXs also integrate smart contract-based KYC or AML verification, requiring users to complete identity checks before accessing specific trading functionalities.[103] These advancements enhance compliance while preserving the decentralised nature of these platforms. Furthermore, for OTC transactions conducted outside blockchain-based mechanisms, regular bank accounts provide a practical alternative. They apply standard KYC and AML processes enforced by private banks, ensuring the same level of regulatory compliance.

Finally, the achievement of the *privacy DO* is also closely linked to the selection of the trading platform. As outlined earlier, privacy in this context consists of two aspects: privacy of the transaction amount and identity privacy. On DEXs, transaction amounts are fully visible, while CEXs and OTC trades can obscure this information. However, blockchain addresses remain publicly visible regardless of the platform, as they are tracked within the Token SCs. While the addresses themselves do not directly reveal the real identity behind them, they can potentially be linked to real-world identities through clustering techniques that analyse transactional patterns.[104] This pseudonymity is an intentional feature of the framework, designed to balance privacy with the transparency and traceability benefits discussed earlier. Nevertheless, technologies such as stealth addresses and ring signatures, offer the potential to enhance the privacy DO by enabling unlinkable addresses and providing stronger protection for user identities.[105] Yet, as these tools are still evolving and no perfect solution currently exists, users must independently select additional privacy-enhancing measures that best align with their individual privacy needs and preferences.

In conclusion, the holistic blockchain-based VCC lifecycle framework addresses several inefficiencies and challenges inherent in the traditional VCC lifecycle by fulfilling the defined DOs and offering stakeholder-specific flexibility. Additionally, for this framework to function effectively, it provides strong incentives for different stakeholders to participate. Standard-setters, for instance, can be attracted by the enhanced visibility of their services to potential project developers and offset buyers, while increasing efficiency and retaining their unique specifications through the flexibility offered by the framework. Additionally, project developers and buyers holding VCCs at different stages of their lifecycle benefit from the inclusion of DAO governance functionality of the Central Registry SC. This feature incentivises participation by promoting fairness and granting stakeholders greater influence over market governance. In summary, the framework not only addresses inefficiencies in the traditional VCC lifecycle but also fosters a collaborative and transparent ecosystem where all stakeholders are empowered to contribute meaningfully, ensuring the long-term sustainability and scalability of the VCC market.

7 Discussion and conclusion

VCCs play a notable role in global efforts to combat climate change, providing a mechanism for offsetting carbon emissions while driving investments in sustainability and innovation. However, the effectiveness of VCCs is undermined by persistent challenges such as the lack of verifiability, transparency, and trust.[106] These issues hinder the credibility of the VCC market and limit its potential to deliver genuine environmental benefits. In this discussion, blockchain-based tokenisation of VCCs is often highlighted as a promising solution to address key challenges, owing to its inherent characteristics like transparency and tamper resistance. Building on this foundation, our research explores the potential of blockchain combined with complementary technologies such as decentralised file systems and trusted oracles to design a robust and reliable holistic VCC token framework.

This process was guided by the DSR methodology.[107] After identifying DOs for all VCC-lifecycle phases through a thorough literature review, we developed a holistic framework that was refined through an iterative cycle of evaluation and improvement, ensuring its practical applicability and effectiveness. At its core, the framework integrates key stakeholders through a set of interconnected smart contracts: the Standard-Setter SC, the Token SC, and the Central Registry SC. These contracts together mirror the essential lifecycle processes, such as project submission, verification, token issuance, and retirement. Thereby, the Central Registry SC acts as the central connecting hub for all standard-setters, enhancing transparency and traceability across all participants and preventing issues like double-counting through standardised reporting and registration. Complementing the blockchain infrastructure, the framework incorporates off-chain components, such as IPFS for decentralised storage of project-related documents, and oracles to bridge the gap between the blockchain and external data sources. In addition, the framework supports multiple trading options, including

OTC, CEX, and DEX, allowing participants to select their preferred methods based on their individual needs. Finally, the concluding evaluation demonstrates that the proposed blockchain-based VCC lifecycle framework effectively fulfils the defined DOs, addressing challenges related for example to standardisation, transparency, accountability, and efficiency.

Yet, although the concept offers a feasible solution to the primary challenges associated with VCCs, several technological, regulatory, and business-related aspects remain open and require further exploration and refinement. One key consideration is the choice of blockchain type for implementing the proposed design. We advocate for a highly transparent solution, such as a public permissionless blockchain like Ethereum, to maximise transparency and security.[108] However, public blockchains often face scalability challenges, leading to slower processes and increased costs, which could negatively impact both operational and transactional efficiency.[109] Considering these limitations, public permissioned blockchains may offer a more practical alternative by addressing scalability concerns.[110] However, this approach introduces trade-offs in decentralisation, as permissioned blockchains restrict participation through predetermined rules, potentially limiting openness.[111] Another viable solution could involve employing a public permissionless blockchain in conjunction with scalability-enhancing technologies such as rollups, which process transactions off-chain to improve efficiency.[112] While promising, these technologies are still in their early stages and often raise additional questions that require further evaluation. Given these complexities, our research has deliberately focused on developing a conceptual framework rather than specifying a particular technological implementation. By prioritising the conceptual view, we aimed to establish a flexible foundation that enables a more detailed technological analysis in the future.

Furthermore, several questions regarding the appropriate business implementation remain unresolved and warrant further research, particularly in the development of viable business models that effectively address cost and revenue structures. These models are essential to ensure the long-term sustainability of such designs. For example, it remains unclear how costs associated with blockchain transactions, such as gas fees, will be managed and fairly distributed among stakeholders. Equally critical is determining how revenue streams will be structured, whether through transaction fees or subscription-based services. Additionally, the framework's flexibility to accommodate diverse stakeholders, including standard-setters, project developers, verifiers, and buyers, necessitates a clear definition of their roles and financial responsibilities within the system. The inclusion of complementary technologies, such as oracles and decentralised file systems, further complicates the cost structure, introducing additional expenses that must be integrated into the business model. Addressing these considerations, which are strongly interconnected with technology choices, is crucial for creating a financially sustainable and equitable framework that aligns stakeholder incentives with operational efficiency.

Beyond the technical and business considerations, the developed design must also remain adaptable to evolving regulatory landscapes. As a relatively new technology, blockchain continues to be the focus of dynamic regulatory discussions at both national and international levels. While the proposed framework incorporates key regulatory requirements, a more detailed legal analysis will be necessary to refine and adjust the smart contracts to specific jurisdictions. In conclusion, the presented design provides a strong foundational framework for addressing the most pressing challenges in the VCC market. However, unlocking the full potential of this framework will require addressing the remaining questions and refining its components through collaborative effort and continuous adaptation. With further exploration, this design has the potential to play a key role in establishing a transparent, efficient, and trustworthy VCC ecosystem that aligns with global sustainability goals.

Notes

1 Charlotte Streck, 'How voluntary carbon markets can drive climate ambition' (2021) 39(3) Journal of Energy & Natural Resources Law 367 367–371.

2 Gregor Spilker and Nick Nugent, 'Voluntary carbon market derivatives: Growth, innovation & usage' (2022) 22 Borsa Istanbul Review 109 110–111; Streck (n 1) 370.

3 Gregor Spilker and Nick Nugent (n 2) 110.

4 Nicolas Kreibich and Lukas Hermwille, 'Caught in between: credibility and feasibility of the voluntary carbon market post-2020' (2021) 21(7) Climate Policy 939 944–945.

5 Michal Jirásek, 'Klima DAO: a crypto answer to carbon markets' (2023) 12(4) Journal of Organization Design 271 272–273.

6 Philippe Delacote and others, 'Strong transparency required for carbon credit mechanisms' (2024) 7(6) Nature Sustainability 706 706–709; Kreibich and Hermwille (n 4) 942–943.

7 Delacote and others (n 6) 706–707.

8 Adam Sipthorpe and others, 'Blockchain solutions for carbon markets are nearing maturity' (2022) 5(7) One Earth 779 783.

9 Derek Sorensen, 'Tokenized Carbon Credits' (2023) 8 Ledger 77–78.

10 CarbonCredits, 'Verra Bans Tokenizing Retired Carbon Credits, Proposes Immobilizing Credits' (CarbonCreditsCom 2022) https://carboncredits.com/verra-suspension-carbon-credits-proposes-immobilizing-credits/ accessed 10 February 2025.

11 Jirásek (n 5) 280–281.

12 Dennis Trautwein and others, 'Design and evaluation of IPFS: A Storage Layer for the Decentralized Web' [2022] ACM SIGCOMM 2022 Conference 2.

13 Hamda Al-Breiki and others, 'Trustworthy Blockchain Oracles: Review, Comparison, and Open Research Challenges' (2020) 8 IEEE Access 85675 85676.

14 Ken Peffers and others, 'A Design Science Research Methodology for Information Systems Research' (2007) 24(3) Journal of Management Information Systems 45 45–74.

15 Moss, 'Moss Carbon Credit MCO2 Token White Paper' (2024) 7–9 https://v.fastcdn.co/u/f3b4407f/54475626-0-Moss-white-paper-eng.pdf accessed 10 February 2025.

16 Jirásek (n 5) 272.

17 Jirásek (n 5) 272.

18 Global Carbon Fund, 'The Carbon Credit Lifecycle' (2022) https://globalcarbonfund.com/carbon-news/the-carbon-credit-lifecycle/ accessed 10 February 2025.
19 Raymond Song, Ainjing Li and Caroline Ott, 'How to Build a Trusted Voluntary Carbon Market' (2022) https://rmi.org/how-to-build-a-trusted-voluntary-carbon-market/ accessed 10 February 2025.
20 Global Carbon Fund (n 18); Jirásek (n 5) 272.
21 Jirásek (n 5) 273.
22 Jirásek (n 5) 273.
23 Global Carbon Fund (n 18); Jirásek (n 5) 273.
24 Axel Michaelowa and others, 'Overview and comparison of existing carbon crediting schemes' [2019] Nordic Initiative for Cooperative Approaches (NICA) 1 10–16.
25 Axel Michaelowa and others (n 24) 14.
26 Carbon.Credit, 'What Are the Largest Carbon Credits Registries?' (2023) https://blog.carbon.credit/2023/01/04/what-are-the-largest-carbon-credits-registries/ accessed 10 February 2025.
27 Regulation (EU) 2024/3012 of the European Parliament and of the Council of 27 November 2024 establishing a Union certification framework for permanent carbon removals, carbon farming and carbon storage in products [2024] OJ L3012/1.
28 Allegra Dawes, Cy McGeady and Joseph Majkut, 'Voluntary Carbon Markets: A Review of Global Initiatives and Evolving Models' (2023) https://www.csis.org/analysis/voluntary-carbon-markets-review-global-initiatives-and-evolving-models accessed 10 February 2025.
29 Dawes, McGeady and Majkut (n 28).
30 Dawes, McGeady and Majkut (n 28).
31 World Bank, 'Operational Guidelines CATS (Carbon Assets Tracking System): KP Emission Reduction Transaction Registry (P172241)' [2024] 1 10–11.
32 Karl Wust and Arthur Gervais, 'Do you Need a Blockchain?' [2018] Crypto Valley Conference on Blockchain Technology (CVCBT) 45 45–46.
33 Bert-Jan Butijn, Damian A Tamburri and Willem-Jan van den Heuvel, 'Blockchains: A Systematic Multivocal Literature Review' (2021) 53(3) ACM Computing Surveys 1 4–5.
34 Yifeng Tian and others, 'Finance infrastructure through blockchain-based tokenization' [2020] Frontiers of Engineering Management 458 486–487.
35 Vincent Gramlich and others, 'A multivocal literature review of decentralized finance: Current knowledge and future research avenues' (2023) 33(1) Electron Markets 1 8–19.
36 Sorensen (n 9) 77.
37 Oscar Golding and others, 'Carboncoin: Blockchain Tokenization of Carbon Emissions with ESG-based Reputation' [2022] 2022 IEEE International Conference on Blockchain and Cryptocurrency (ICBC) 1–2.
38 Oscar Golding and others (n 37) 1–2.
39 Sorensen (n 9) 79.
40 Peffers and others (n 14) 45–74.
41 Shirley Gregor and Alan R Hevner, 'Positioning and Presenting Design Science Research for Maximum Impact' (2013) 37(2) MIS Quarterly 337 336–338.
42 Salvatore T. March and Gerald F. Smith, 'Design and natural science research on information technology' (1995) 15(4) Decision Support Systems 251 253.
43 Gregor and Hevner (n 41) 349–351.
44 Peffers and others (n 14) 58.
45 CarbonCredits (n 10).
46 Jonathan Lautenschlager, Marike Reinelt, Vincent Schaaf, Nils Urbach, and Valeriya Arnold, 'From Project Design to Retirement: The Role of Blockchain along the Voluntary Carbon Credit Lifecycle' 133.
47 Axel Michaelowa and others (n 24) 16–17.

48 Melvin Tjon Akon, 'The role of market operators in scaling up voluntary carbon markets' (2023) 18(2) Capital Markets Law Journal 259.
49 Dawes, McGeady and Majkut (n 28).
50 Delacote and others (n 6) 707; Song, Li and Ott (n 19).
51 Patrick Greenfield, 'Revealed: more than 90% of rainforest carbon offsets by biggest certifier are worthless, analysis shows' https://www.theguardian.com/environment/2023/jan/18/revealed-forest-carbon-offsets-biggest-provider-worthless-verra-aoe accessed 10 February 2025.
52 World Bank Group, 'Blockchain and Emerging Digital Technologies for Enhancing Post-2020 Climate Markets' [2018] 14–17.
53 Sipthorpe and others (n 8) 780.
54 Jirásek (n 5) 280–281.
55 Junghoon Woo and others, 'Applying blockchain technology for building energy performance measurement, reporting, and verification (MRV) and the carbon credit market: A review of the literature' (2021) 205 Building and Environment 108199 2–3.
56 Greenfield (n 51).
57 Michael J Ashley and Mark S Johnson, 'Establishing a Secure, Transparent, and Autonomous Blockchain of Custody for Renewable Energy Credits and Carbon Credits' (2018) 46(4) IEEE Engineering Management Review 100 101.
58 Ashley and Johnson (n 57) 101.
59 dClimate, 'MRV: the Key to Unlocking the Voluntary Carbon Market' *Medium* (2024) https://dclimate.medium.com/mrv-the-key-to-unlocking-the-voluntary-carbon-market-fe2d25a10621 accessed 10 February 2025.
60 Laura Franke, Marco Schletz and Søren Salomo, 'Designing a Blockchain Model for the Paris Agreement's Carbon Market Mechanism' (2020) 12(3) Sustainability 2–3; Jirásek (n 5) 273.
61 Soheil Saraji and Mike Borowczak, 'A Blockchain-based Carbon Credit Ecosystem: White Paper' 4.
62 Ibid 3–4; Sipthorpe and others (n 8) 782–786.
63 Kreibich and Hermwille (n 4) 944–946; Franke, Schletz and Salomo (n 60) 1.
64 Woo and others (n 55) 5–6.
65 World Bank Group (n 52); Vincent Gramlich and others, 'In Decentralized Finance Nobody Knows You Are a Dog' [2024] Proceedings of the 57th Hawaii International Conference on System Sciences (HICSS).
66 Tim Adams and others, 'Taskforce on Scaling Voluntary Carbon Markets: Final Report' [2021] 1 103–105.
67 Axel Michaelowa and others (n 24) 16–17; Tjon Akon (n 48) 259.
68 Delacote and others (n 6) 705–707; Yu Bai and others, 'Construction of Carbon Trading Platform using Sovereignty Blockchain' [2020] International Conference on Computer Engineering and Intelligent Control (ICCEIC) 149 150.
69 Sipthorpe and others (n 8) 780; World Bank (n 31) 14–17.
70 Greenfield (n 51); Jirásek (n 5) 280–281; Woo and others (n 55) 2–3.
71 Ashley and Johnson (n 57) 101.
72 Franke, Schletz and Salomo (n 60) 2–3; Jirásek (n 5) 280–281.
73 Saraji and Borowczak (n 61) 3–4; Sipthorpe and others (n 8) 780.
74 Kreibich and Hermwille (n 4) 944–946; Sipthorpe and others (n 8) 782–786.
75 Woo and others (n 55) 5–6.
76 Adams and others (n 66) 103–105.
77 P. B Kruchten, 'The 4+1 View Model of architecture' (1995) 12(6) IEEE Softw 42 43–35.
78 Al-Breiki and others (n 13) 85676.
79 Trautwein and others (n 12) 2–3.

80 Witek Radomski and others, 'ERC-1155: Multi Token Standard' (2018) https://eips.ethereum.org/EIPS/eip-1155 accessed 10 February 2025.
81 Verra, 'Early Finance Carbon Unit – Public Consultation' (2020) https://verra.org/early-finance-carbon-unit-public-consultation/ accessed 10 February 2025.
82 World Bank (n 31) 30.
83 World Bank (n 31) 30.
84 Jirásek (n 5) 272–273.
85 Shivani Jamwal and others, 'A survey on Ethereum pseudonymity: Techniques, challenges, and future directions' (2024) 232 Journal of Network and Computer Applications 2.
86 Jamwal and others (n 85) 6–8.
87 Peffers and others (n 14) 45–74.
88 John Venable, Jan Pries-Heje and Richard Baskerville, 'FEDS: a Framework for Evaluation in Design Science Research' (2016) 25(1) European Journal of Information Systems 77 80.
89 Wust and Gervais (n 32) 45–46.
90 Roman Beck and others, 'Blockchain Technology in Business and Information Systems Research' (2017) 59(6) Business & Information Systems Engineering 381 381–382.
91 Beck and others (n 90) 381–382; Wust and Gervais (n 32) 45.
92 Sipthorpe and others (n 8) 783–786.
93 Sipthorpe and others (n 8) 783–786.
94 Matthias Babel and others, 'Enabling end-to-end digital carbon emission tracing with shielded NFTs' (2022) 5(S1) Energy Inform 1 6.
95 Weiqin Zou and others, 'Smart Contract Development: Challenges and Opportunities' (2021) 47(10) IEEE Trans Software Eng 2084 2084–2085.
96 Zou and others (n 95) 2084–2085.
97 Simon Feulner and others, 'Shedding light on the blockchain disintermediation mystery: A review and future research agenda' [2022] Thirtieth European Conference on Information Systems (ECIS 2022) 3–5.
98 Feulner and others (n 97) 3–5.
99 Saraji and Borowczak (n 61) 4.
100 Adams and others (n 66).
101 Directive (EU) 2018/843 [2018] OJ L156/43.
102 Gramlich and others (n 35) 11–12.
103 Gramlich and others (n 35) 11–12.
104 Jamwal and others (n 85) 5–6.
105 Jamwal and others (n 85) 6–10.
106 Kreibich and Hermwille (n 4) 941–942.
107 Peffers and others (n 14) 45–74.
108 Sana Zeba, Preetam Suman and Kanishka Tyagi, 'Chapter 4 – Types of blockchain' in Rajiv Pandey, Sam Goundar and Shahnaz Fatima (eds), *Distributed Computing to Blockchain* (Academic Press 2023) 55–68.
109 Yannis Bakos and Hanna Halaburda, 'Permissioned vs Permissionless Blockchain Platforms: Trade offs in Trust and Performance' [2021] NYU Stern School of Business working paper 20–21.
110 Bakos and Halaburda (n 109) 20–21.
111 Zeba, Suman and Tyagi (n 108) 55–68.
112 L. Thibault, Sarry T. and Hafid A. 'Blockchain Scaling Using Rollups: A Comprehensive Survey' (2022) 10 IEEE Access 93039 93040.

List of figures

Figure 1.1 Comparison of Total Cumulative Carbon Emissions Versus Carbon Emissions Covered Under a Government Compliance Scheme for 1990–2022 —— **6**
Figure 1.2 Representation of Country Income Groupings by Total Emissions, Emissions Under Government Compliance Mechanisms, and Voluntary Carbon Credits —— **6**
Figure 1.3 Lifecycle of a Typical Voluntary Carbon Credit —— **9**
Figure 1.4 Process of Carbon Credit Tokenisation —— **9**
Figure 1.5 Verra Voluntary Carbon Credits Tokenised —— **11**
Figure 1.6 Comparison of Verra Credit Portfolio Between Toucan Tokenised Credits and All Verra Issued Credits Between 2009 and 2022 —— **12**
Figure 3.1 Heatmap of Averaged Percentage of Respondents Affected by Grouped Challenges Across Market Stages in the Voluntary Carbon Market —— **52**
Figure 3.2 Verra VCUs Tokenised by the Three Major Carbon Bridges —— **57**
Figure 3.3 Process of Tokenising Verra's VCUs Used by Toucan, Moss, and C3 —— **58**
Figure 4.1 Idealised market for VCC when information is assumed to be complete and symmetric —— **75**
Figure 4.2 Structure of market for VCCs acknowledging information asymmetries and their remedies —— **77**
Figure 6.1 VCC Lifecycle Stages —— **136**
Figure 11.1 Our DSR Research Process —— **268**
Figure 11.2 Logical View of Architectural Stakeholders and Components —— **273**
Figure 11.3 Whitelisting and Project Submission —— **276**
Figure 11.4 Project Registration and Verification —— **277**
Figure 11.5 Transaction and Retirement —— **278**

https://doi.org/10.1515/9783111706719-012

List of tables

Table 5.1 Overview of key insight areas, sub-aspects, and the future academic and practical avenues within —— **118**
Table 6.1 BLC Value propositions in the VCC context —— **138**
Table 11.1 Derivation of Design Objectives —— **271**

https://doi.org/10.1515/9783111706719-013

Index

Admissions and disclosures regime (A&D) 202–203, 218
Afforestation and Restoration-based Offsets (ARBO) 210
Air Carbon Exchange 11
Akerlof, George A. 76, 80
Algorand 55, 65
American Carbon Registry (ACR) 48, 137, 210, 264
Anti-money laundering (AML) 144, 146, 202, 271, 275, 282
Applicable law, VCCs
- conflict of laws rules 168–169
- German use cases 154–155
- international use cases 153–154
- mere marketplace 155
- private international law 155–156
- supply chain 156–166
- UNIDROIT DAPL 166–168
Asset-referenced tokens (ART) 182, 188, 203–205
Asymmetric-information 15, 74, 76, 79–83, 90

Behr, Patrick 26
Bi-directional approach 100
Bitcoin 55, 83–84, 135, 169, 243, 265
Blockchain technology 13, 27–28, 48–49, 61, 120, 135–136, 230, 265–266
- accessibility and adoptions 124–125
- carbon markets 49–50, 56
- energy consumption and carbon footprint 49
- error-free settlement 19
- global governance 41
- innovations 54–56
- interoperability 122–123
- ledger databases 53–54
- market accessibility and design 66–68
- market dynamics and financial stability 125–126
- new markets 23–25
- operational approach 97, 125
- Regen network 103–106
- registries on-chain 68
- Senken 109–110
- technical, interoperability, and volatility 101
- technological innovations 22–23
- tokenisation 8, 65
- transaction 21, 54, 125
- transparency and trust 15–19
Bloomberg 11

Cap-and-trade system 5, 200
Carbon Assets Tracking System (CATS) 265, 275
Carbon border adjustment mechanism (CBAM)
- certificates 89
- climate change 73–74
- emissions 74
- reduction and removal 89
- VCC markets 79–83, 88–89
Carbon bridge 8–9, 98–99, 210
$CCO_2 Tokens ($CCO_2) 22, 210–211, 216–217
Carbon credits 4, 42, 112. *See also* voluntary carbon credits (VCCs)
- certified credits 77–78
- forward contracts 25, 40, 43, 119, 125
- lifecycle 8, 16, 19
- pooling protocols 14
- portfolio 12–13, 16, 26
- quality and pricing 22–23, 51–52
- sustainability 22
- taxes and proliferation 4
- tokenisation (*see* carbon tokenisation)
- tradability of 85–87
- transparency and trust 16
- Verra 12
Carbon emission 5, 74, 88, 137
- climate change 135
- compliance mechanisms 5–6, 28
- energy consumption 65
- global efforts 263
- greenhouse gas (GHG) 48
- scientific methodologies 51
- verification process 269
CarbonPlus Grasslands Methodology 106, 123
Carbon pools 19, 99, 153, 158, 159
Carbon pricing 3, 4, 88, 209
Carbon Removal and Carbon Farming Regulation (CRCFR) 198, 231–232
Carbonstack 140, 154–155
Carbon storage in products (CRCR) 231
Carbon tokenisation 9, 10, 28. *See also* tokenisation
- carbon credit 8–9
- diversification benefits 26

https://doi.org/10.1515/9783111706719-014

- efficiency and scalability 19–22
- innovation and new markets 22–26
- liquidity 14–15
- market efficiency and access 11, 13–15
- transparency and trust 15–19
- Verra 12–13
- voluntary carbon credits (VCCs) 8–9

Carbon TradeXchange 14, 20

Celo blockchain 18, 98, 122, 266

Central exchanges (CEX) 273–274, 282, 284

CHAR token 18, 208–214

Choice of law 155–156, 165, 168
- Art. 3 Rome I regulation 159–160
- by parties 171–172

Civil law, German VCCs token
- absolute rights 248–249
- and corporeal objects 246–247
- crypto-assets 240–241
- intangible assets 248
- legal nature of 241–252
- statutory obligations 252–255

Clean Development Mechanism (CDM) 2, 4

Climate, Community & Biodiversity (CCB) Standard 264

Climate Action Reserve (CAR) 137, 210, 264

Climate change 2, 28, 38, 135, 219, 228, 234, 261–262
- global stocktake 3
- global temperatures 48
- greenhouse gas 73–74
- historical progression 3–4

CO_2 and its equivalents (CO_2e) 5, 25, 28, 50, 181, 184–186, 197, 208–211, 214, 216

Collateralized Basket Token (CBT) 25

Commodity Exchange Act (CEA) of 1936 199, 202, 214

Commodity Futures Trading Commission (CFTC) 27, 199–200, 202, 213

Compliance carbon markets (CCM) 3, 5, 36, 265

Conference of the Parties (COP) meetings 2–3

Conflict of laws
- Art. 43(1) EGBGB 164–165
- choice of law 171–172
- closest connection 171
- in England and Wales 168–169
- German legal framework, and within union (*See* Rome I regulation)
- habitual residence 170
- *lex libri siti* principle 171
- *lex rei sitae* principle 170
- Sec. 17a, Securities Deposit Act (DepotG) 165–166
- Sec. 32, Electronic Securities Act (eWpG) 165–166
- UNIDROIT principles 166–168
- in US Uniform Commercial Code (UCC) 169
- valuation 169–172

Consumer Empowerment Directive (CED) 197

Coorest 11, 21–22, 210–211, 217

Coorest Carbon Standard (CCS) 22, 210

CORCs (CO_2 removal credits) 18–19

Core Carbon Principles (CCPs) 18, 38, 111, 118

Corporate social responsibility (CSR) 5, 15–16, 23–24

Corporate Sustainability Reporting Directive (CSRD) 111, 197

CORSIA offsetting 100–101

Cosmos ecosystem 98, 103, 122

Countering the financing of terrorism (CFT) 144, 146, 275, 279, 282

Court of Justice of the European Union (CJEU) 157, 161

Crypto-asset service provider (CASP) 188–197, 203, 214, 218

Crypto-assets Regulation 27, 56, 209. *See also* Markets in Crypto-assets Regulation (MiCAR)
- Art. 3(1)(5) MiCAR 243–244
- Art. 4(1)(15) MiFID II 242–243
- claims 244–245
- clients 193–194
- custody and administration 191–192
- European legislation 197–198
- financial instruments 204
- funds/crypto-assets 193
- German regulatory framework 204–205
- offering 184–186
- offeror, obligations 186–188
- placing 194–195
- platform operator 192–193
- service providers 189–197
- trading 186
- transfer services 196–197
- VCC tokens as financial instruments 242–243

Crypto Carbon Company (C3) 8, 11, 56–60, 210, 215

Cryptocurrencies 8, 17, 22, 54, 55, 108, 115, 117, 135, 204, 265, 282

Crypto Markets Supervision Act (KMAG) of 2024 204

Cumulative carbon emissions 5–6

Data integrity 62, 101, 107–108, 117, 123–124, 274
Data transparency 15–19, 142, 146
Decentralised autonomous organisations (DAOs) 11, 16, 67, 105, 107, 112, 142, 275, 283
Decentralised exchanges (DEXs) 68, 124, 209, 212, 274, 279, 284
Decentralised finance (DeFi) 97, 101, 112
Design objectives (DO) 268–272, 280–282
- duplication prevention 281
- prototype architecture 273–275
- prototype functionalities 275–279
- reliable verification 281
- standardisation 280
- transactional and operational efficiency 281–282
Design Science Research (DSR) methodology 263, 266–268, 283
Digital Assets and Private Law (DAPL) 206
Digital monitoring, reporting, and verification (dMRV) 21–22, 64
Digital product passports (DPPs)
- certification process 231–232
- ecodesign 232–233
- lifecycle 229–230
- market-based mechanism 228–229
- sustainability 228
- technical nature and content 230–231
- *vs.* voluntary carbon credits (VCCs) 233–234
Distributed ledger technology (DLT) 7–8, 15, 38, 49, 135, 137, 170, 181, 194, 199, 201, 242–243, 265
- Pilot Regime 181
Diversification 13, 26, 66
Double-counting 3, 7, 17, 36–38, 56, 63, 79, 96, 98, 103, 106, 118, 141, 142, 208–210, 234, 264, 271, 275, 283
Double-spending 80, 82, 137, 142

Ecodesign for Sustainable Products Regulation (ESPR) 232–233
Ecological state protocols (ESPs) 103–104, 232–235
Electronic money tokens (EMT) 182, 188, 203–205
Electronic Securities Act (eWpG) of 2021 165–166, 171, 245, 247
Emissions trading systems (ETSs) 4, 5, 37, 74, 88, 181, 202, 229, 231
End-to-end solutions 13, 20–21, 28, 103
ERC-20 standards 18, 115, 210
Ethereum 19–20, 22, 54, 83–84, 115, 122, 135, 209, 284
Ethereum 2.0 55
European Banking Authority (EBA) 184, 197
European Carbon Border Adjustments Mechanism (EU CBAM) 198
European Emissions Trading Directive (EU ETSD) 180–181
European Securities and Markets Authority (ESMA) 184
Ex-ante certification 40–41

FCO_2 tokens 25–26
Financial Conduct Authority (FCA) 200–202
Financial Promotion Order (FPO) 2005 201–203, 213–216
Financial Services and Markets Act of 2000 200–203, 213–215, 217
Financial Times 11
Floodlight 21–22
Flowcarbon 11, 40, 109, 266
Fragmentation, market 7, 9, 37, 39, 51, 52, 62, 97–98, 109, 118, 119, 126, 266, 268, 270

Gambill, Paul 214
General Data Protection Regulation (GDPR) 124, 144
Geographic information systems (GIS) 23, 103
Global warming 2, 3, 35, 49–50, 262
Gold Standard (GS) 4, 7, 11, 18, 39, 48, 81, 118, 121, 137, 208, 210, 263
- carbon offset projects 264
- non-digital registries 153
- registry 153
- tokenisation 56–60
Gold Standard CO2 token (GCO2) 266
Goodcarbon 154–155
Green Claims Directive (GCD) 198
Greenhouse gas emissions (GHG) 2, 48, 75, 96, 261
- emissions 4, 228–229, 234
- environmental impact 227
- global warming 35–36

Hardware security modules (HSM) 140
Harmonised market standards 118, 121–122, 271
Howson, Peter 107

Information and communication technology (ICT) 189–190
Information asymmetries 14, 51, 75, 77, 79, 81–85, 185

Integrity Council for the Voluntary Carbon Market (ICVCM) 38, 81, 111, 122
Inter alia law 163, 171, 248, 250, 254
Intergovernmental Panel on Climate Change (IPCC) 2
International Emissions Trading Association (IETA) 58, 60
Internationally Transferred Mitigation Outcomes (ITMOs) 3
Internet-of-Things (IoT) 20, 23, 65, 103, 123
Interoperability, carbon markets 62, 98, 101, 113, 117, 118, 120, 122–124, 134, 230, 270, 271, 272, 280
InterPlanetary File System (IPFS) 274
Interpol 37

Joint Implementation (JI) 2
Jospe, Caitlin 7

Klima-DAO 11, 119, 121, 262
– regulatory and standardisation needs 119–122
Know-your-customer (KYC) process 58, 60, 110, 124, 144, 146, 279, 282
Kumo blockchain technology 97, 112–114, 124, 126, 155
Kyoto Protocol 2–3, 36

Legal nature
– agreement and delivery transfer 251–252
– Art. 70(1) MiCAR 245–246
– change of control, transfer 250
– claims 244–245
– crypto-assets regulation 241–244
– German civil law 246–249
– jurisdictions 240
– law of obligations 250–251
– Principle 3(1) UNIDROIT DAPL 246
– statutory obligations 253–255
Legal wrapper 112, 124
Lex rei sitae principle 164–165, 170
Lifecycle phases, voluntary carbon credits (VCCs) 8, 9, 110, 152, 229–230, 282–283
– additional requirements 143–145
– blockchain 135–136, 139–142
– climate mitigation 134
– design objectives (DO) 271–272
– German use cases 154–155
– international use cases 153–154
– mere marketplace tokens 155
– operational approach 137–138
– post-VCC-issuance phase 271
– pre-VCC-issuance phase 268–270
– stages 136–137
– tokenisation 135–136
– transactions 134
– transparency 269
– value propositions 138–139, 142–143
Liquidity 14, 26, 65, 67, 99, 113–114, 145, 187, 269
– accessibility and 275
– and coordination 109
– crypto-asset 196
– market 13, 123
– and volatility risks 108
Lummis-Gillibrand Responsible Financial Innovation Act of 2023 200

MakerDAO 112
Market abuse regime for crypto-assets (MARC) 202–203, 218
Market Abuse Regulation (MAR) 181
Market-based mechanism 228–229, 261
Market design 15, 66–68
Market failure 76, 90
Markets in Crypto-assets Regulation (MiCAR) 179–180, 241
– Art. 3(1)(5) 243
– Art. 70(1) 245–246
– classification of tokens 181–183
– crypto-assets and portfolios management 195–196
– European legislation on VCC tokens 197–198
– exemptions 183–184
– marketing communications 188
– offeror of 186–188
– persons and 184–186
– regulatory approaches 202–203
– service providers 189–195
– transfer services for crypto-assets 196–197
– in United Kingdom 200–202
– in USA 199–200
Markets in Financial Instruments Directives (MiFID and MiFID II) 37, 157, 180–181, 196, 204
– Art. 4(1)(15) 242–243
– classification of tokens 181–183

- crypto-assets and VCC tokens 184–186
- exemptions 183–184
Microeconomics of voluntary carbon markets 73–74. *See also* voluntary carbon credits (VCCs)
- asymmetric information 79–83
- carbon border adjustment mechanism (CBAM) 88–89
- economic effects 83–87
- standard structure 74–79
Miltenberger, Oliver 7
Monitoring, reporting, and verification (MRV) 7, 20, 37, 62, 64, 103, 123–124, 137, 263–264, 269, 275, 281
- robustness 108
- thematic analysis 42
Moss 8, 11, 56, 57, 97, 114–115, 125, 142
- Amazon NFT 116
- blockchain technology 115–116
- case studies 122
- challenges and limitations 116–117
- regulatory and standardisation needs 119–122
Moss CO_2 token (MCO_2) 97, 114–117, 121, 142, 266
Multilateral trading facility (MTF) 192

Nakamoto, Satoshi 54
Nasdaq 14, 20, 51
Nationally determined contributions (NDCs) 3, 38, 41, 111
Native tokenisation 11, 17, 21, 49, 60, 61, 63–65
Nature-Based Offset (NBO) token 210, 215
Nature-based solutions (NBS) 39, 41–42
Net-zero commitments 3, 23, 24, 198, 203–204, 218
NFTrees 21–22, 211, 216–217
Non-fungible tokens (NFTs) 9, 18, 55, 65, 114, 116, 183–184, 207, 211, 274
Nori Inc. 209–210
Nori Regenerative Tonne (NRT) 209

On- and off-chain registries 60, 98, 118
Oracles 55, 64, 140, 145, 274, 276, 280–281, 284
Orgen, Papa 26
Over-the-counter (OTC) trading 39, 57, 101, 193, 264, 273–274, 278–279, 282

Paris Agreement of 2015 3, 7, 24, 36, 41, 48, 56, 120, 133
Pittman, James 7
Plan Vivo Standard 210, 264
Polygon blockchain 20, 22, 98, 106, 122, 210, 266
Portfolio management 12–13, 16, 26, 110, 195–196, 264
Proof of Carbon Compensation (PoCC) 22, 211, 216–217
Proof-of-stake protocols 16, 65, 84, 103
Proprietary rights 156, 164, 172, 206, 240, 246, 249, 250, 255
Pseudonymity 146, 279, 282
Puro Earth 18–19, 79, 98, 100, 208, 209
Puro Registry 18–19, 153, 212

Qualitative thematic analysis, VCM
- global governance, lack of 40–41
- opaque market structure 39–40
- project supply, lack of 41–42
- restricted accessibility 43

REDD+ (Reducing Emissions from Deforestation and Forest Degradation) projects 7, 114
Regenerative finance 105
Regen network 11, 97–98, 122, 123, 153–154
- blockchain technology 103–106
- data integrity and verification 107–108
- decentralised governance (DAO) 102–103, 105
- ecological contracts 104
- ecological state protocols (ESPs) 103–104
- economic security risks 108
- end-to-end approach 130
- equitable participation 107
- governance imbalances 107
- interoperability 101
- registry 106
- role and utility of the Regen token ($REGEN) 105–106
- supply protocols (SPs) 104–105
- token valuation 108
Reputation-by-endorsement mechanism 86
Ripple Labs, Inc. 83, 200
Rome I regulation 164, 170, 172
- Art. 1(1) 156
- Art. 1(2)(d) 156–157
- Art. 3 159–160
- Art. 4(1)(a) 160–161
- Art. 4(1)(b) 161–162

- Art. 4(2) 162–163
- Art. 4(4) 163–164
- Art. 7(1)(b) 161
- negotiable instruments 157–159
Rome II regulation 156, 165

Securities Deposit Act (DepotG) of 1996 165–166
Securities Exchange Commission (SEC) 27, 199, 200, 212, 213, 217
- *v.* W. J. Howey Co. 199
Security Token Offering (STO) 16
Senken 11, 25–26, 95, 97, 108–109, 117, 124, 155
- Art. 4(1)(b) Rome I 162
- blockchain technology 109–111
- challenges and limitations 110–111
- five-stage framework 111
Service providers, crypto-assets
- authorisation 189–190
- European legislation 196–197
- execution of orders 193–194
- obligations 190–192
- operator 192–193
- placing 194–195
- portfolio management 195–196
- reception and transmission of orders 195
- transfer services 196–197
Smart contracts 9, 13, 16–19, 22–23, 66
- blockchain innovations 54–56, 83
Solana blockchain 19–20, 55
Solid World 25
Stablecoins 112, 182
Stakeholders 16, 17, 23–24, 107, 110, 118–120, 123, 126, 189, 228, 230
- biodiversity preservation 122
- carbon credits 64
- and components 273–275
- integrity 269
- policies and templates 191
- smart contract 104, 105
- supply chain 231
- trust 15
Statutory obligations, VCC tokens
- compensation for damages 254
- interference removal, absolute right 253
- possession, physical 253
- unjust enrichment 254–255
Suitability assessment 195–196
Sustainability 22, 24, 69, 96, 134, 146–147, 196–197, 228–229, 232–234, 263
Sustainable Development Goals (SDGs) 2–3, 133

Taskforce on Scaling Voluntary Carbon Markets (TSVCM) 41
Tether 83, 243
Thallo 109
Tokenisation 7–8, 135–136, 262, 265–266. *See also* carbon tokenisation; voluntary carbon credits (VCCs)
- blockchain 14–15
- carbon credits 17, 61–63, 85–87
- description 48
- double-counting 17
- Gold Standard (GS) 58–60
- information asymmetries reduction 83–85
- initiatives 49
- integrity 100–101
- market reputation 63
- native 63–64
- on-chain representations 62
- process of 8–9
- securities 203
- smart contracts 55
- standardised methodologies 120–121
- Toucan, Moss, and C3 56–60
- Verra 58–60
Tonnes of CO_2e (tCO_2e) 4, 50
Toucan's CO_2 token (TCO_2) 25, 98–99, 208–209, 211–212, 266
Toucan/Toucan Protocol Association 48, 103, 107, 117, 122, 125, 142, 153, 159, 171, 208–209, 265
- blockchain technology 98–99
- C3 and Moss 11–13
- global regulatory frameworks 101–102
- integrity 100–101
- international use cases 153
- protocol 18–19
- regulatory and standardisation needs 119–122
- retired carbon credits 121
- technical, interoperability, and volatility challenges 101
- tokenisation 56–60, 99–100
- traceability and transparency 98
Traceability, carbon offset 16, 19, 24, 27, 85, 96, 98–101, 103, 109, 116, 120, 126, 140, 144, 233, 265, 281–283

Transparency 7, 21, 27, 56, 60, 96–100, 109–110, 120, 142–144, 229
- blockchain technology 67, 113, 124
- circular economy 228
- and immutability 8, 38
- pre–VCC-issuance phase 268–269
- purchasers and asset-holders 185
- sustainability 192
- thematic analysis 40
- of trading 141
- and trust 15–19, 52, 117
Treaty on the Functioning of the European Union (TFEU) 204, 241, 245
24/7 trading 21, 136, 266

UN Environment Programme (UNEP) 2
Unfair Commercial Practices Directive (UCPD) 198
UNIDROIT DAPL (UNIDROIT Principles on Digital Assets and Private Law) 152, 169–171, 179, 205–208, 250, 255
- Art. 70(1) MiCAR and ownership rights 245–246
- Principle 2(2) 166–167
- Principle 3(1) and proprietary rights 246
- Principle 5, proprietary issues 167–168
- Principle 8(1)(a) 250
Unification of Private Law (UNIDROIT) principles
- digital assets and private law 206–207
- Legal Nature of Verified Carbon Credits 207–208
Unified regulatory framework 37, 43, 118–120
United Nations (UN) Conference 2
United Nations Framework Convention on Climate Change (UNFCCC) 2, 24, 35–36
Universal Basic Offset (UBO) token 210, 215
Upstream Emission Reductions (UER) 134
US Uniform Commercial Code (UCC) 169

Validation and Verification Bodies (VVBs) 66, 76–80, 82, 229, 230
Value proposition 50, 62, 134–135, 138–139, 142–143
Verified Carbon Standard (VCS) 4, 8, 115, 229
Verified Carbon Units (VCUs) 18, 24, 48, 56–60
Verified emission reduction purchase agreement (VERPA) 115–116
Verified emissions reductions (VERs) 48
Verra 4, 5, 7–8, 12, 39, 48, 50, 142, 210, 263, 277. *See also* Gold Standard (GS); voluntary carbon credits (VCCs)
- comparison of 13
- registry 11–12, 153
- regulatory and standardisation needs 119–122
- sub-accounts 115
- suspension 116
- tokenisation 56–60, 100
- Verified Carbon Units (VCUs) 18, 24, 25
- Verified Carbon Standard (VCS) 229–230
Vlinder 25–26
Voluntary carbon credits (VCCs) 4, 40, 42, 48–49, 51, 74–75, 261–265. *See also* digital product passports (DPPs); lifecycle phases, voluntary carbon credits (VCCs)
- asymmetric-information 74, 76, 79–83
- buyers and sellers 14
- cap-and-trade systems 4–5
- carbon emissions/removal 5–6, 75–76
- country-level income group 6–7
- economic effects 83–87
- European Union (EU) Emission Trading System (ETS) scheme 4–5
- global supply and demand 25
- lifecycle 8, 9, 110
- off-chain data 145
- over-the-counter (OTC) markets 14
- Principle 2(2) UNIDROIT DAPL 166–167
- private international law 155–156
- registries 18
- reputation 82
- standard structure 74–79
- tokenising and trading 145
- transfer 250–252
- value chain 16
Voluntary carbon markets (VCMs) 36–37, 48, 50–53, 79, 96–97, 118–119
- application patterns 96
- blockchain technology 13
- carbon credit lifecycle 20
- carbon offsets 15
- cumulative carbon emissions 5–7
- double-counting 7
- initiatives, tokenisation 49
- licenses 43
- lifecycle 102
- mitigations 117
- NASDAQ survey 14
- native tokenisation 63–65
- no action, traditional registries 61

- Paris Agreement 3
- qualitative thematic analysis 38–43
- representation 24
- tokenisation of traditional carbon credits 61–63
- transparency 37–38

Wall Street Journal 11
Web3 technology 20–23, 64

World Bank 18, 123, 264–265
World Economic Forum 18
World Meteorological Organization (WMO) 2
World Trade Organization 88

Yavaprabhas, Kongmanas 16

Zero-Knowledge Proofs 119, 124, 146

www.ingramcontent.com/pod-product-compliance
Lightning Source LLC
Chambersburg PA
CBHW080937240926
51849CB00004BA/476
9783111706603